W9-AEJ-930

Poets, Patrons, and Printers

Also by Cynthia J. Brown:

Critical edition of André de la Vigne's
La Ressource de la Chrestienté (1494)

The Shaping of History and Poetry in Late Medieval France:
Propaganda and Artistic Expression in the Works of the Rhétoriqueurs

POETS, PATRONS, AND PRINTERS

CRISIS OF AUTHORITY IN LATE MEDIEVAL FRANCE

CYNTHIA J. BROWN

CORNELL UNIVERSITY PRESS

Ithaca and London

Cornell University Press gratefully acknowledges a subvention
from the University of California, Santa Barbara, that aided
in bringing this book to publication.

First published 1995 by Cornell University Press.

Printed in the United States of America

Library of Congress Cataloging-in-Publication Data

Brown, Cynthia Jane.
    Poets, patrons, and printers: crisis of authority in late medieval France /
Cynthia J. Brown
        p.   cm.
    Includes bibliographical references and index.
    ISBN 0-8014-3071-2
    1. Authorship—History—16th century.   2. Copyright—France—History—16th
century.   3. Authors and publishers—France—History—16th century.   4. French
poetry—Publishing—France—Paris—History—16th century.   I. Title.
PN144.B76   1995
070.5'2—dc20   94-45472

To the memory of my father
W. Stimpson Brown, Jr.
(1916–1992)

CONTENTS

List of Illustrations
ix

Acknowledgments
xi

Introduction
1

Chapter 1
Late Medieval Writers as Owners and Protectors of Their Texts
17

Chapter 2
Paratextual Interaction between Poets and Book Producers
61

Chapter 3
The Changing Image of the Poet
99

Chapter 4
Changing Authorial Signatures in Late Medieval Books
153

Chapter 5
Authorial and Narrative Voices in Late Medieval Vernacular Texts
197

Contents

Afterword
247

Appendix 1
Documentation of André de la Vigne's 1504 Lawsuit and
Bibliographical Data
255

Appendix 2
Bibliographical Data for Jean Lemaire de Belges
258

Appendix 3
Bibliographical Data for Jean Bouchet
259

Appendix 4
Bibliographical Data for Jean Molinet
261

Appendix 5
Bibliographical Data for Pierre Gringore
264

Bibliography
269

Index
285

ILLUSTRATIONS

1.1. False authorship attribution of Sebastian Brant instead of Jean Bouchet, from *Les regnars traversant*, 1st ed.

1.2. Jean Bouchet's acrostic signature, from *Les regnars traversant*, 1st ed.

1.3. Pierre Gringore's first privilege, from *Les folles entreprises*, 1st ed.

1.4. Omission of publisher's name (Gringore) from printing announcement, from *Les folles entreprises*, 1st ed.

1.5. Jean Marot offering his work to Queen Anne of Brittany, from *Le voyage de Gênes*.

1.6. Jean Lemaire's first privilege, from *La légende des Vénitiens*, 1st ed.

1.7. Jean Lemaire's coat of arms, from *La légende des Vénitiens*.

2.1. Title without identification of author, from *Le temple de Mars*.

2.2. Title without identification of author, from *Le temple de Mars*, 1st ed.

2.3. A prince, representing Mars, enthroned and surrounded by courtiers, from *Le temple de Mars*, 2d ed.

2.4. A prince, representing Mars, observes a tournament, from *Le temple de Mars*, 3d ed.

2.5. Mars as a violent god, from *Le temple de Mars*, 4th ed.

2.6. Title with identification of author, from *Le temple de Mars*.

2.7. Title with identification of author, from *Les faictz et dictz*, 1531 ed.

2.8. Pigouchet's printer's mark, from *Le chasteau de labour*, 1st ed.

2.9. Michel Le Noir's printer's mark, from *Le chasteau d'amours*, 2d ed.

2.10. Title page, from *Le vergier d'honneur*, 1st ed.

2.11. Title pages, from *Les ballades de Bruyt Commun* and *Le libelle des cinq villes d'Ytallye*.

3.1. Poet offering his work to King Charles VIII, from *La ressource de la Chrestienté*.

3.2. Author-woodcut, from *Le vergier d'honneur*, 1st ed.

3.3. Author-woodcut, from *Le vergier d'honneur*, 5th ed.

3.4. Poet composing his work with his created characters, Lady Christianity, Lady Nobility, and Good Counsel, before him, from *Le vergier d'honneur*, 2d ed.

3.5. Dedication woodcut, from *L'art de rhétorique*, 1st ed.

3.6. Dedication miniature, from *L'art de rhétorique*, 1st ed.

3.7. Dedication miniature, from *L'art de rhétorique*, 1st ed.

3.8. Dedication miniature, from *Le roman de la rose moralisé*.

3.9. Dedication miniature, from *Le roman de la rose moralisé*.

3.10. Dedication miniature, from *Le roman de la rose moralisé*.

3.11. Author's publication mark, from *La naissance de Charles d'Autriche*, 1st ed.

3.12. Author-woodcut, from *La naissance de Charles d'Autriche*, 2d ed.

3.13. Dedication miniature, from *Les folles entreprises*, 1st ed.

3.14. Author's bookseller mark, from *Les folles entreprises*, 1st ed.

3.15. The Mère Sotte illustration, three author's marks, from *Les folles entreprises*.

3.16. Dedication woodcut, from *Les folles entreprises*.

3.17. Author-woodcut, from *Les fantasies de Mère Sotte*.

3.18. Gringore's coat of arms, from *Les fantasies de Mère Sotte*.

4.1. Charles VIII acrostics, from *La ressource de la Chrestienté*.

4.2. Author's name at the end of final verse (emphasized), from *La ressource de la Chrestienté*.

4.3. Author's name at the end of final verse (unemphasized), from *La ressource de la Chrestienté*, 1st ed.

4.4. Second acrostic pertaining to Charles VIII, from *Le vergier d'honneur*, 1st ed.

4.5. Madame Catherine de Tieullière's acrostic (emphasized) and De La Vigne's acrostic (unemphasized), from *Le vergier d'honneur*, 1st ed.

4.6. La Vigne's acrostic (emphasized), from *Le vergier d'honneur*, 1st ed.

4.7. La Vigne's illuminated acrostic, from *Le couronnement d'Anne de Bretagne*.

4.8. Pigouchet's, Simon Vostre's, and Gringore's acrostics, from *Le chasteau d'amours*, 1st ed.

4.9. Michel Le Noir's acrostic, from *Le chasteau d'amours*, 2d ed.

ACKNOWLEDGMENTS

This book has taken shape over a period of several years during which I have profited enormously from the exchanges I have had with many colleagues and friends. Their advice and suggestions have been invaluable to me as I reworked and fine-tuned my ideas. Discussions with Marian Rothstein at an early phase of this project and Jody Enders's incisive comments at a more advanced stage proved to be formative in the conceptualization of this book. I am also very grateful for the insightful remarks of those who generously took time to read one or more chapters of my manuscript in its various forms: Emmanuèle Baumgartner, Renate Blumenfeld-Kosinski, Zelda Bronstein, Dominique Coq, Jody Enders, Robert Freeman, Leonard Johnson, Myra Orth, Mark Rose, Marian Rothstein, Susie Sutch, and Mary Beth Winn. The challenging questions and helpful comments of Julie Carlson, Theresa Coletti, Sharon Farmer, and Carol Pasternack, and many others who read or heard papers related to this project, were likewise instrumental in my continued reevaluation of ideas. I am also indebted to Cynthia Skenazi and Leonard Johnson for helpful suggestions in my translations from Middle French to English and to Ernest Sturm for his stylistic comments in the book's final stages. Besides much appreciated support, Art Ludwig offered me the expert advice of a general reader, as he carefully combed through several versions of my manuscript. For this I am extremely appreciative. To Zelda Bronstein, who has closely watched this project develop from its inception to its completion and whose friendship has meant a great deal to me, I express my deep gratitude.

At numerous libraries in Europe and the United States, I have benefited from the assistance of specialists who have generously helped me during my long hours of research. I am most appreciative of their support and wish to offer a special thanks to the *conservateurs* in the Réserve of the Bibliothèque Nationale. I am also grateful to Marianne Grivel for her important role in expediting transactions with the Service Photographique of the B.N., from which I obtained most of this book's illustrations.

It is a pleasure to acknowledge the National Endowment for the Humanities, which awarded me a grant to attend Henri-Jean Martin's Summer Seminar on the Early Printed Book, held at the Newberry Library in 1986, and the American Council of Learned Societies, which supported research during an early phase of my project (1987–88). The Research Committee of the Academic Senate at the University of California, Santa Barbara, has repeatedly offered support for my work through all stages of this project, and the Interdisciplinary Humanities Center at UCSB has likewise funded my project with grants in 1990 and 1993. UCSB's Office of Research and College of Letters and Science have generously contributed to the costly production of this volume as well. For this intramural support, I am extremely grateful.

In contrast to the strained relationship between late medieval authors and publishers that figures at the center of my argument in this book, I have enjoyed a most productive association with Cornell University Press. I am especially grateful to Bernhard Kendler for his continued interest in this project, Charles Purrenhage for his scrupulous editing of my manuscript, and Kristina Kelsey for her careful attention to the many details of the final stages of production. I also wish to thank Cornell University Press for permission to use material in parts of Chapters 2, 3, and 4 that originally appeared, in an earlier version, in my "Text, Image, and Authorial Self-Consciousness in Late Medieval Paris," a chapter in Sandra L. Hindman, ed., *Printing the Written Word: The Social History of Books, circa 1450–1520*, copyright © 1991 by Cornell University.

Finally, I wish to acknowledge the work carried out by my graduate assistant, Deborah McGrady, on the bibliography; I also thank Gabriella Schooley, who, as administrative assistant during my tenure as chair, could not have been more accommodating and cheerful. To my family, friends, and departmental colleagues, I extend my deep gratitude for their continued support.

C. J. B.

Poets, Patrons, and Printers

INTRODUCTION

n April 30, 1504, André de la Vigne, former secretary-historian of the French king Charles VIII, filed a lawsuit against Michel Le Noir with the Parlement of Paris. La Vigne requested that one of the most prominent printers of the French capital be prohibited from publishing the *Vergier d'honneur*, a lengthy poetic anthology containing several of his own works. In order to obtain relevant information and to find witnesses for his case, the writer sought a two-week delay. Le Noir, however, challenged La Vigne by requesting authorization to continue his work. On May 11, 1504, La Vigne obtained the two-week delay he had requested, and Le Noir was allowed to finish printing those copies of the *Vergier d'honneur* already in press; he was not authorized, however, to sell those books, according to court records.[1] Some three weeks later, on June 3, 1504, the Parlement recorded the final ruling on the matter: Michel Le Noir and all other Parisian printers—with the exception of La Vigne—were prohibited from printing or selling the *Vergier d'honneur* and the *Regnars traversant* until April 1, 1505:

It is hereby declared that the said court has refused and refuses to approve the said petitioner's [Le Noir's] request and prohibits the said petitioner and all other booksellers and printers in this city of Paris, except for the said defendant [La Vigne], from printing or selling the books entitled the *Vergier d'honneur* and the *Regnars traversant*, until next April 1st, and this under penalty of an undetermined fine and confiscation of the said books; and the court

1. Archives Nationales, Conseil 1509 (12 novembre 1503–7 novembre 1504), fol. 154^v, le 11 mai [1504]. See Appendix 1 below for documentation regarding this trial.

condemns the said petitioner to pay the expenses of these proceedings, the determination of these expenses being reserved for the court.[2]

Thus, by means of a very early version of a French privilege, André de la Vigne acquired legal control over the printing and selling of the *Vergier d'honneur* for the following ten months. Le Noir had to pay the fees incurred as a result of the suit.

This legal decision is momentous in the history of French authorship. In the first known lawsuit in France initiated by a vernacular writer, an author legally assumes the duties of a publisher by challenging a printer's unsanctioned use of his texts.[3] Implicitly the case raises the issue of proprietorship and related questions: Who in fact owned the *Vergier d'honneur*? What rights did La Vigne have to his own writings? What rights did an unauthorized printer have to its profits?

This lawsuit and related aggressive actions by other late medieval writers, none of whom confronted legal authorities as dramatically as La Vigne, had a vital impact on textual production during the early years of print. The writer's entry into commercial domains, as evidenced by La Vigne's victory, comes with a changing perception of his role in the literary enterprise.[4] The perception of one's own text as a profitable end in itself on the open market, rather than merely as a source of economic gain through a court appointment, necessarily modified a writer's relationship to his work. In comparison with manuscript culture, the dynamics of the literary enterprise after the advent of print are clearly different. Authors' writings had become a marketable commodity outside the courtly circle of wealthy benefactors, and new participants in book production—the printer, the publisher, and eventually a different, more expanded reading public—came to play a role and affect authors' involvement in determining the physical and literary makeup of their books. Indeed, the hierarchical triad of patron, poet, and scribe that characterized the manuscript culture evolved into a more balanced sharing of authority in the association of patron, poet, and publisher in the

2. Ibid., fol. 171, le iii juin [1504]. See Appendix 1 below for the French version. This and all subsequent passages cited in English are my translations unless otherwise noted. Le Noir is referred to in this record as the "petitioner" and La Vigne as the "defendant," presumably because this decision was made in response to Le Noir's request of May 2, 1504, to continue printing his books.

3. See Armstrong, 35–36, who mentions both La Vigne's challenge and Guillaume Cop's March 1504 legal victory over Jean Boissier. (The decision prohibited Boissier from selling Cop's unsigned almanacs.) Given the date, it is possible that this legal challenge influenced both La Vigne's decision to sue as well as the outcome of his lawsuit.

4. Because of the ubiquitous male presence in the literary and legal matters discussed here, I have consistently used the masculine possessive.

print culture. In some cases, such as that of Jean Lemaire de Belges, the author went so far as to assume, legally and metaphorically, the function of sovereign in and of his text, thereby challenging the patron's traditional involvement in the bookmaking process and the publisher's newly developing governance of it. This reordering of roles was accompanied by a redefinition of roles, in particular that of the author.

In this book I propose answers to the following questions that arise from La Vigne's lawsuit against Le Noir and from the Parlement's subsequent decision: Why, as early as 1504, did French vernacular authors seek to control the publication of their works? What characterizes the interaction among writers, printers, and booksellers in the literary enterprise at this time, and how had that changed with the advent of print? How did the author's writings express this shift? How did the publisher and public acknowledge it? What impact did these developments have on the concept of literary ownership and authorship?

While scholars generally agree that the systematic use of copyrights, or signs of authorial ownership, in France and England dates from the eighteenth and nineteenth centuries (Febvre and Martin, Viala, Rose), a nascent consciousness about literary ownership in the sixteenth century has been noted, albeit in rather vague terms (Eisenstein, 1:120; Ong, *Orality and Literacy*, 130–31). I present here evidence of a sustained effort on the part of vernacular writers to protect their works through lawsuit, the use of privileges, an early form of copyright, and the supervision of their publication and distribution as early as the first decade of the sixteenth century. As a conscious and concerted move to control the destiny and public inauguration of their works, these forms of protection implicitly questioned existing patterns of publication behavior that often ignored authors' relationship to their writings after those writings left their hands. They also expressed writers' recognition of their inherent rights to their own words, at least during the first stages of publication, and their attempt to impose this consciousness on other participants in textual production. La Vigne's challenge to Le Noir's unwarranted actions dramatically marked this nascent consciousness by placing it squarely in the legal arena. Although La Vigne apparently did not seek a privilege for the first printing of the *Vergier d'honneur*, the terms of the Parlement decision resemble so closely what were to become stipulations of privileges that his actions appear to have paved the way for their regularized use by authors some fifteen months later.

Similar reactions at around the same time by La Vigne's contemporaries suggest that other vernacular literary figures were likewise concerned about issues of literary ownership. The early sixteenth-century confrontations discussed in this book do not involve authors attacking other authors over the rights to their words and their works, as was apparently the case among the troubadours;[5] in fact, there seems to have been a complicitous solidarity among them. It was rather a matter of authors challenging certain aggressive publishers, finding acceptable grounds for collaboration with others, or assuming many publishing functions themselves.

In late 1503 or early 1504, sometime before La Vigne's lawsuit, Antoine Vérard published an edition of a work by Jean Bouchet, having devised a title for it himself: the *Regnars traversant les perilleuses voyes des folles fiances du monde*. To enhance name recognition, he attributed authorship of the work to Sebastian Brant, the German who had written the tremendously popular *Narrenschiff*, instead of to Bouchet. Following in Vérard's footsteps, Le Noir printed a second edition of the *Regnars traversant* on May 21, 1504, without authorial consent (Britnell, 81–82, 304–6). Le Noir's publication appeared at the very time La Vigne was seeking witnesses against that same printer because of the unauthorized publication of the *Vergier d'honneur*. In fact, the designation of the *Regnars traversant* in the Parlement's response to La Vigne's protest against Le Noir furnishes evidence that Bouchet must have served as one of La Vigne's witnesses against the printer. As with the publication of the *Vergier d'honneur*, La Vigne obtained rights to supervise the printing and distribution of the *Regnars traversant* for ten months, thereby pre-empting any further publication of the work by Vérard, Le Noir, or other booksellers or printers until April 1505. One can probably assume that La Vigne obtained this right with the consent of Bouchet, who must already have returned—or was about to return—to his native Poitiers (Britnell, 1) and consequently could not have overseen the printing and distribution of the work in Paris. Bouchet, however, did not succeed in stopping the publication of his writing, as La Vigne had done, because by the time he became involved in La Vigne's legal challenge, the *Regnars traversant* had already appeared in two different editions. Nevertheless, as a result of a subsequent lawsuit that Bouchet brought against Vérard, the publisher had to compensate the writer for his unauthorized action. Bouchet's next work, *La déploration de l'Eglise*, did not come out in print until May 1512, but it bore a privilege granted to the printer by the Paris Parlement for two years (Britnell, 306–7).

Lemaire's publication strategy changed even more dramatically, as a comparison of his books printed in 1504 and 1509 suggests. Just a few weeks before La Vigne's lawsuit, on April 6, 1504, the second edition of

5. While Chaytor, 119–29, describes early medieval jongleurs' concern for controlling poetic production, their association with an oral tradition made it difficult to protect their works from rivals. For on recitation, a poet's words essentially became public property. McLuhan, citing Moses Hadas, 85, discusses how literature heard in public was not like property, because it was not easy to grasp in such an intangible form.

Lemaire's *Temple d'honneur et de vertus*, first printed by Antoine Vérard in the early months of 1504, appeared without authorization under Michel Le Noir's name (Hornik ed., 14). But Lemaire's next printed work in France, the *Légende des Vénitiens*, published in Lyons by Jean de Vingle in 1509, bore a royal privilege, which the author himself had procured from Louis XII and which accorded Lemaire control over the subsequent publication of his book for three years. In December 1505, Pierre Gringore had become the first vernacular writer to obtain a privilege for the publication of his *Folles entreprises*;[6] he continued to adopt the same strategy of protection for nearly all his subsequent works.

These legal actions initiated by French vernacular authors in the early sixteenth century came in the wake of technological advances related to the advent of print in late medieval Europe and the resulting economic pressures that precipitated changes in the ontology of the book. My investigation of print's impact on the late medieval author gives rise to the following hypothesis: as the increasing use of the printing press led to the objectification, commercialization, and commodification of the book (Ong, *Orality and Literacy*, 118, 126; McLuhan, 104, 174–75; Foucault, "Author," 148), that is, as the work acquired a monetary value of its own such that the book could bring personal gain to writers as well as book-makers, the relationship between authors and their texts changed along with the association between authors and book producers. As part of a fundamental socioeconomic shift in Western Europe during the Middle Ages, the commodification of the book, a result of technological advances made through new instruments of production, contributed to a growing distance between individuals and things in the external world. This development of an increasingly estranged form of subject–object relationships gave rise in turn to distinctions between private and public property (Gurevich, 7–15). In part because typography provided physical means for a writer to extend dimensionally in space and time (McLuhan, 131), a greater concern about authors in the print culture gradually replaced the earlier literary anonymity and general sharing of ideas. Furthermore, as books came to play an increasing role in the developing capitalistic system, authors sought more control of their writings, participating more actively in their publication and seeking greater identification with their own words. At issue, then, are the changing figures and forces of bookmaking and their influence on the creators of literary texts.

The increasing manifestation of the writer's proprietary relationship

6. Armstrong, 7, also provides details about one earlier, isolated example of a privilege for Jacques Despars's commentary on the canon of Avicenna (Lyons: Trechsel, December 1498).

to his works through legal decisions and through participation in their production, together with the increasing acknowledgment by producers, patrons, and readers of this concrete and financial connection, helped establish the author's role and prestige more definitely and publicly. That is to say, the author's consciousness of a need to adopt a protective posture vis-à-vis book producers and his audience and the public's awareness and recognition of increasing authorial concern for literary property and propriety led to a greater focus on the writer's individuality. Jean Molinet's replacement of his metaphoric signature (which purposely confused his name with a poetic *moulinet*, or mill) with a more straightforward signature, referring only to the author behind the name, provides one small example of this change in consciousness. He in fact resorted to print shortly thereafter, assuming the role of publisher at a time when his court position was increasingly insecure in financial terms. Such a movement toward increased emphasis on the individual characterizes the printed book much more than it characterizes the manuscript (Hindman and Farquhar, 201). Foucault's contention that the beginnings of the individualization of an author coincide closely with the point in time when discourse became product, or property, because only then did the possibility of transgression exist, is suggestive indeed ("Author," 148–49). But where Foucault implies that authors had become transgressors, I argue that in the early years of print it was the publishers themselves who acted like transgressors, because in some cases they assumed functions traditionally associated with the writer. And yet, instead of limiting literary creativity, these transgressions seem to have stimulated it through authors' defensive reactions.

In short, as authors grew more conscious of their changing relationship to their works, their presence became more manifest both inside and outside their texts. These developments were closely tied to a growing consciousness on the part of the public and the writer of the author's more prominent role in the literary enterprise and in society itself.

Although scholars such as Henri-Jean Martin, Elizabeth Eisenstein, and Roger Chartier have extensively investigated the technological, economic, and social impact of printing on society and the changes in the appearance of texts that print fostered, and although classic and still compelling studies by Walter Ong and Marshall McLuhan have explored the relationship between printing and epistemology, surprisingly few researchers have devoted attention to the profound impact of print on literary creators themselves during the early decades of printing history. In my investigation into the ways an author's consciousness of his craft was changed by the advent of print, I found evidence of an increasing use of self-promotional strategies—such as more author-centered images, more prominently publicized names, more directly accessible signatures, and a more author-identified narrative voice—which under-score the author's development from a conventionally medieval secondary stance to a growing authoritative presence. Furthermore, al-though it is a common assumption that the advent of print defined the modern authorial figure, few scholars have furnished evidence to dem-onstrate this contention convincingly, especially at such an early date. Mark Rose's extremely suggestive research about the author as propri-etor and Roger Chartier's provocative theorizing about Foucault's "author-function" concept (see Chartier's *Ordre des livres*, 35–67) are among the rare exceptions. The former, however, focuses on seventeenth-century England, and the latter does not address the changes during the five or six decades following the introduction of print into France. It is this crucial, late medieval period that constitutes my point of departure, and my refocus of current interest about issues of literary property and propriety on these early years necessitates a re-thinking of some traditional assumptions about authorship.

A paucity of archival documentation before the 1530s (Parent, 53) in-creases the difficulty of the researcher who seeks to untangle the com-plex web of relationships involved in the book trade and the mecha-nisms at work in the literary enterprise during the transition from manuscript to print. Nevertheless, a wealth of evidence of a different sort is extant. The so-called paratext of books themselves,[7] in both manu-script and printed form, offers precious information about textual pub-lication at this historical juncture, when printers' involvement in the lit-erary enterprise was emerging, authors' roles were expanding, and booksellers' functions were being redefined. No one, however, has yet demonstrated systematically how to glean such details from the para-text. Although Gérard Genette, for instance, may provide a useful defi-nition of the paratext as a privileged strategic zone of transition and transaction between the text and *hors-texte* (*Seuils*, 8), his modernist bias allows little light to be shed on the culture of manuscripts and early im-prints. I provide detailed analyses of the paratext from a period when many of its features were being developed or altered in response to the new print technology. Through an examination of a book's title pages and colophons, author-images in miniatures and woodcuts, privilege advertisements and prefatory material, authorial signatures and de-vices, particularly in relationship to the text itself, I uncover the inner workings of literary creation and production in late medieval Europe. My focus on the changing concept of authorship brings to light writers' assumption of a new protective posture, which prefigures the literary

7. Genette first uses this term in *Palimpsestes*, 7, and develops the concept further in his more recent *Seuils* (published 1987).

self-consciousness and self-confidence traditionally associated with Renaissance writers. For example, even the most cursory comparison of the frontispieces and title pages of the various manuscript and printed versions of La Vigne's *Ressource de la Chrestienté* provocatively demonstrates the growing presence of the author's identity, image, and voice in the transition from manuscript to print. Thus, the enthroned French king in the miniature that opens a 1494 manuscript of the *Ressource* is replaced by the illustration of the enthroned writer that decorates the second edition of the *Vergier d'honneur*, whose publication La Vigne oversaw as a result of the 1504 Parlement decision. Such a development exemplifies the link between the relationship of the physical presentation of a work and its writer's self-image and the change in literary authority that was occurring on a wider scale in the shift from manuscript to print.

This insistence on the book as a material object, dependent on the forces of production, providing insight into socioliterary patterns at a given historical moment, situates my argument somewhere between the so-called Old and New Philologies. Although it is not my purpose to redefine philology in modern theoretical terms or to seek precedents for contemporary notions of authorship in medieval works, the acknowledged interdependence of textual and codicological practices in the production of meaning warrants a more careful consideration of medieval texts as cultural artifacts. Recent views on how a study of manuscripts might lead to an understanding of the social dynamics of the medieval literary enterprise—for example, the suggestions advanced by Stephen Nichols and Bernard Cerquiglini—can help modern scholars assess the changing place and role of the poet in the developing technological and social climate of print. Through a sustained analysis of representative texts and such paratextual features as title pages, colophons, dedicatory material, and illustrations, I propose ways in which the literary work interacts with "the social context and networks [it] inscribe[s]" (Nichols, "Introduction," 9) as well as ways in which textual and paratextual discourses interact.

Whereas philologists of the nineteenth and early twentieth centuries, Lachmannians and Bédierists alike, showed little if any interest in the physical context of a work, and whereas their apparent followers give priority to the experience of text editing over its theorization, they nevertheless share common ground with the views expressed by Nichols and others in their concern for the medieval text's materiality. I would hope that a kind of "New Codicology," the artifact-oriented approach presented here—emphasizing the importance of a text's codicological signs as well as a work's philological development through its many changing versions as a means to expose the social and cultural dynamics at work in the literary enterprise—might serve to show how New and Old Philologists can interact.[8] In fact, the argument presented in the following chapters grew out of a text-editing project in which textual and paratextual comparisons of the various manuscript and printed versions of La Vigne's *Ressource de la Chrestienté* (Montreal: CERES, 1989; hereafter *Ressource*) led to the discovery of surprising changes. Appendixes 1–5 below, by providing legal documentation and bibliographical data for the main corpus of texts analyzed here, offer evidence of the need to ground any discussion of authorship theories, material artifacts, literary texts, and sociocultural practice in careful philological and bibliographical investigations.

I speak of a New Codicology, for I privilege not manuscript culture but the transition from script to print, that is, the intersection of the two ages of writing to which Walter Ong refers—the age of scribes and the age of "true" authors—and its impact on textual production. In this endeavor my work draws from both the recent research of French Chartistes, working under Henri-Jean Martin on the early printed book, and the related investigations of the research group of the Centre National de Recherche Scientifique (CNRS) known as "La Culture Ecrite du Moyen Age Tardif,"[9] who rely heavily on extensive bibliographical and archival research for their sociohistorical examinations. It also draws from the subfield of cultural history known as "l'histoire du livre," dominated by such figures as Roger Chartier and Robert Darnton, who seek to relate books to the political, economic, and intellectual context of their period.[10] The multivolume *Histoire de l'édition française*, coedited by Martin and Chartier, brings together these areas of investigation, bibliography, history, and cultural practice, providing a wide-ranging yet detailed overview of the book from the Middle Ages to modern times.[11]

8. For a discussion of this contemporary debate, see, for example, Hult, "Reading It Right," "Lancelot's Two Steps," "Steps Forward"; Uitti and Foulet, "On Editing Chrétien de Troyes"; Uitti, ed., "Poetics of Textual Criticism"; and *Romance Philology*, August 1991, especially Speer's "Editing Old French in the Eighties." See also Martin and Vezin, eds., *Mise en page*; and Dagenais, who shows how the careful study of manuscripts can shed light on cultural and interpretive issues in his work on the *Libro de buen amor*. I acknowledge my colleague, Jody Enders, for suggesting the term "New Codicology."

9. See M. Ornato and N. Pons, eds., *Pratiques de la culture écrite*, the *Actes* of the May 1992 colloquium sponsored by the CNRS research team.

10. See, for example, R. Chartier, ed., *Pratiques de la lecture*. In "Du livre au lire," 63, Chartier calls for an investigation of the uses, manipulations, and forms of appropriation and reading of imprints, in what he calls the history of "une pratique culturelle." For an excellent review and assessment of this research area, see Kaestle.

11. Hindman's recently edited volume, *Printing the Written Word*, a series of microhistories that contribute to a more comprehensive sociocultural history of the book, represents another rare example of this kind of research. For a discussion of the book in earlier medieval culture from a modern theoretical perspective, see Gellrich.

Chartier's discussion of the *mise-en-livre* (the layout and arrangement of a book's typographical features) and its powerful impact on the *mise-en-texte* (the implicit or explicit instructions inscribed by a writer in his work to elicit a reading) is among the few exciting scholarly works that address the changing relationship between the book as cultural artifact and the text it contains ("Du livre au lire," 79–80). However, he, like Genette in his work on the paratext, analyzes material forms and signs in an effort to define and interpret the various modes of reception.[12] Equally compelling, I believe, is the idea that the paratext can also shed light on the various producers of the text, by offering evidence of the simultaneous collaborative and competitive tensions involved in book production. Moreover, in questioning the assumption made by both Chartier and Genette, who deal with later literary imprints, that the author controls the text, or *mise-en-texte*, while the publisher oversees the presentation of the paratext, or *mise-en-livre*, I argue that in the years following the advent of print such distinctions were not always so clear-cut. Indeed, it is precisely the "blurred" examples of control that provide access to changing sociocultural patterns of book production. When printers and publishers like Le Noir and Vérard assumed certain authorial postures, writers such as La Vigne, Gringore, and Lemaire sought to acquire control over nearly all phases of the literary enterprise, at least during the initial period of publication, and succeeded in doing so.

But this expansion of authors' roles beyond literary creation into areas of book production, as writers undertook even more extensive publishing responsibilities than Guillaume de Machaut or Christine de Pizan had attempted earlier, accompanied the clearer segregation and compartmentalization of bookmaking duties. The functions of the early printer, who oversaw all aspects of book production, gave rise to at least three different roles: those taken over by the publisher, the printer, and the bookseller.[13] This simultaneous distinction and merging of roles in the bookmaking process further complicates an understanding of the social dynamics of textual production.

The intense efforts by authors to protect their works, once penned, by direct involvement in their publication points to another central issue

12. While Genette sees the paratext as ultimately subordinate to the text (*Seuils*, 16), Chartier feels that typographical devices and mechanisms are as important if not more important than textual signals ("Du livre au lire," 82). As early as 1945, Chaytor saw the significance of page layout for the learner or reader, deeming it as important as the book's content (7). See also Martin and Vezin.

13. McLuhan, 42–43, describes a separation and reduction of functions on a large scale as a result of the technological revolution brought about by print. He also discusses how printing split apart the role of producer and consumer and how, after print, one witnessed the separation of writer and reader, producer and consumer (95–96, 186, 209). See also Ong, *Orality and Literacy*, 122.

that comes to bear upon questions of authorship and ownership in the late Middle Ages: namely, the changing role of patronage. Richard Green has convincingly shown that by the fourteenth century, when the amateur household poet replaced the independent professional minstrel, the function of the author figure depended on court attitudes. The writer's shaky claim to professional status within "that elusive system of informal patronage" (11), where the literary enterprise fell somewhere between a job and a pastime, gained recognition only when the author assumed the role of court adviser and propagandist, making himself indispensable to his master's fame, yet dependent on it. Drawing on Green's work, which restricts itself to the manuscript culture, I suggest that the impact of print on the relationship between literary protectors and poets encouraged authors who were acting as court apologists into the domain of self-advertisement. While writing in order to shape how others would perceive their (potential) patrons, these authors learned, by collaborating with publicists who helped or provoked them, to promote their identity and authority in print for the sake of protecting their writings.

Indeed, La Vigne and many of his contemporaries spent a good deal of effort seeking a literary protector. They also demonstrated an unusual amount of independence regarding the publication of their works, sometimes going so far as to subsidize much of the initial publication cost of printing such volumes. How then was a writer's reliance on patrons for financial security under the manuscript system altered with the advent of another form of book publication? While an earlier writer such as Christine de Pizan might have dedicated various copies of one and the same work to several different patrons, authors in the early sixteenth century, knowing that their works would be printed, could write with both a prospective patron and a wider general public in mind. Thus, because printing fostered access to an audience that was wider, albeit less clearly defined, than the earlier court public that had commonly commissioned their works, and because writers sought to reach both the more limited court audience and the growing public, the absent reader was becoming more and more a part of their strategy of address.[14]

In a world in which writers had difficulty finding benefactors,[15] printing presented another option besides manuscript reproduction for the dissemination of their works, especially if they were interested in reaching a wider public. Printing also allowed writers to bypass, at least tem-

14. Ong, *Interfaces*, 282, discusses how the writer's transaction with paper gradually became part of the writing process with the advent of print. He sees the medieval and Renaissance periods, however, as "residually oral cultures" (105; see also Nelson).

15. For example, Bouchet, among others, was unable to appeal successfully to Charles VIII for support. Nor was Louis XII's court particularly generous in this regard.

porarily, the more traditional patronage quest, for now they could make independent financial agreements with a printer or bookseller. But since such arrangements were extremely precarious and hardly substantial enough to furnish long-term support, patronage still provided the writer with a more reliable means of livelihood (Parent, 119–20). Total reliance on printing would not have been a sound financial venture for writers at this time; still, it offered them a different kind of "freedom of expression," since they did not have to serve the commands of a patron. With the advent of print, although it may not have been until the eighteenth and nineteenth centuries that authors could live from their writings alone, writers were at least able to avail themselves of two options for the reproduction of their works.

It was no longer the wishes of the "commanditaire" that came to dictate book production after the advent of print. An author now had to contend with another force in the hierarchy of production, one who was potentially more powerful: the publisher (E. Ornato, 75).[16] Owing to competition and numerous crises, this new figure had to adopt a politics of editorializing that often affected the writer (E. Ornato, 81–82). In the end, then, because it was the buying public who shaped that politics, audience needs still determined writers' literary production and livelihood.

Because the printer became much more of an entrepreneur in the bookmaking process than the scribe, who was often a laborer working in a production-line system, and because the *libraire* had already found ways by the early fourteenth century (in Paris at least) to profit from the commercial market, this despite close governance of book copying by the University of Paris (Rouse and Rouse, "Book Trade," "Commercial Production"), the interaction among all those involved in bookmaking inevitably changed. Tensions developed between authors and publishers over the control of literary works, tensions either nonexistent in the manuscript culture or at least less publicly manifest or unknown to us. H. J. Chaytor's suggestion that the presentation of a manuscript copy to an audience was the equivalent of publishing the work, because the author abandoned to the recipient or patron control over subsequent copying of the text (133), contrasts with the thinking of the early sixteenth century, this period of lawsuits, which implicitly questioned that earlier system. Obviously publication no longer meant complete relinquishing

---

16. I use the term "publisher" to refer to the person overseeing book production, although the word could be used interchangeably with "printer" in the sense that E. Ornato defines it (67–68, n. 15). For him the term "imprimeur" designates someone with direct access to printing presses: professional printers who either obtained outside capital or had their own capital, or booksellers and editors who had professional printers working for them.

of control by the author to a patron, but rather a working out, a sharing of this control with the printer or publisher and sometimes with the patron of his works. The coexistence of the French royal insignia and the announcement of an author-procured privilège on the title page of Lemaire's *Légende des Vénitiens* in 1509 offers one paratextual example of this new kind of collaboration.

The additional possibilities that the advent of print offered a writer, then, did not lead to the replacement of one system by another. As in most transitions, old and new systems coexisted for some time.[17] In fact, because it presented more options and involved more individuals, printing seems to have complicated even more the author's attempts to find financial backing and to see his writings appear in print.

In its focus on paratextual evidence as an important means of access to the author's changing role in the literary enterprise, and in its textual analyses aimed at uncovering the writer's artistic consciousness, especially through an examination of how the "I" in late-medieval French works manifests itself, my discussion sets itself apart from most research on late medieval literature, which does not generally deal with the interaction between text and paratext. The few exceptions include Sarah Jane Williams's study of Machaut, David Hult's discussion of authorship in the context of author-images in the *Roman de la rose* manuscripts (*Self-Fulfilling Prophecies*), and Sylvia Huot's discovery of important associations between the appearance of single-author anthology codices in thirteenth- and fourteenth-century France and a new self-consciousness in "writerly" lyric and lyrical narrative modes (*From Song to Book*).[18] Nancy Regalado's fascinating study of literary *œuvres*, her insightful conclusions about François Villon's relationship to the court of Blois, arrived at through an original examination of the famous Charles d'Orléans manuscript, and her contribution to the Roesner edition of the *Roman de Fauvel* place her at the forefront of such research as well.[19] Taking off from these studies, centered on the manuscript culture, I argue that beginning with Jean Molinet—who wrote with manuscript reproduction in mind for the most part but, toward the end of his life, participated in the print culture in a way his predecessors could not—

---

17. Ong, McLuhan, and Stock all take care to point out the coexistence of manuscript and print culture. See also the articles of Goody and Watt, Havelock, Clanchy, and Olson, as well as Hindman and Farquhar's *From Pen to Press*.

18. For important discussions about the relationship between poet and narrator in late medieval texts, see Brownlee, *Poetic Identity*; J. Cerquiglini, *Un engin si soutil*; and Johnson. Zink analyzes earlier works from a similar perspective.

19. See "Gathering the Works"; "'En ce saint livre'"; and *Roman de Fauvel*, ed. Roesner. I am grateful to the author for furnishing me with copies of her articles before publication.

authors' needs to protect, defend, and identify with their works accelerated and reshaped their attitude toward themselves, their roles, and the creation of their texts.

The work of Molinet and his contemporaries, the poet-historians known as *rhétoriqueurs*, constitutes the only consequential body of French vernacular literature that spans the period of the transition from manuscript to print, dating approximately from 1460 to 1530.[20] The transitional place in history shared by these vernacular writers—at the crossroads of the medieval and modern periods, between two different systems of book production, one of which revolutionized communication for centuries to come—privileges their particular literary activity and anticipates the self-conscious stance of Renaissance writers more than has been previously thought. Even more influenced by printing than the first-generation *rhétoriqueurs*, such as Jean Molinet or Georges Chastellain, the second generation, comprising writers such as La Vigne, Lemaire, Bouchet, and Gringore, had much less support from patrons. Bringing together the issues of the changing role of protectors and the intensification of authorial self-consciousness at this time, the *rhétoriqueurs'* writings, tied as they were to polemical goals, reflect the reshaping of propagandistic modes into self-advertisement. While an examination of print's influence on contemporary Latin authors and, for that matter, on writers of other vernacular literatures, likewise merits close attention, it is not possible here to undertake such an investigation.[21] It is hoped, however, that this discussion may give rise to work on these worthy topics.

An examination of documentary and semidocumentary evidence in Chapter 1 reveals how writers, as their role in the literary enterprise expanded, came to act as first-stage proprietors of their texts and as authorities of textual propagation. My analysis of the French publication of Lemaire's early works sets the stage with an overview of the changing paratextual and textual features that contribute to the reconstruction of the author's image.

The structure of Chapters 2 to 5 derives from the progression made in moving from the exterior to the interior of a book. An analysis of the paratext precedes an examination of the text, as focus shifts from the interaction of writer and publisher in the book's most obvious manifesta-

---

20. See Zumthor, *Masque;* Brown, *Shaping;* Rigolot, *Des rhétoriqueurs,* 23–121; and Sutch, "Allegory and Praise."

21. Important works by Elsky and Newton have addressed some of these issues in England, although the authors they examine, Bacon and Jonson, date from the late sixteenth and seventeenth centuries. Why did writers in England get involved with the implications of authors' rights and print so much later than French writers?

tion as a commodity, its *mise-en-livre*, to the expression of the author contained within, its *mise-en-texte*.

The significance of the author's presence or absence in the paratext constitutes the focus of Chapter 2, which deals with the relationship between title pages and colophons in manuscripts and imprints and which assesses the writer's transactions with the various participants in the system of book production. A comparative study of the newly developing title page in different versions of the same work and in various works by the same authors, together with an examination of its relationship to the colophon in manuscripts and imprints, reveals a varied experimentation with paratextual publicity. As writers came to control the publication of their own works and even assumed publishing functions, more prominently placed authorial signs appear both on the title page and in the colophon announcement. For example, the absence of Gringore's name in the paratext of his first works is dramatically reversed by 1505 with the colophon announcement that he is overseeing publication of his writings.

Chapter 3 shows how author-images complemented writers' increasing visibility on title pages and in colophons. I devote special attention to the relationship between elaborately painted, patron-centered dedication miniatures and various author-centered images featured in woodcuts. An examination of the use of *devises* (visual and verbal identification marks of the patron, printer, or poet) links Chapter 2's discussion of title pages and colophons, the sites where these signs most often appear, with Chapter 4, which treats the use within the text of a related form of identification, signatures.

As Chapter 4 demonstrates, the author's name figures prominently in these works. Not only does it provide the most obvious evidence of a writer's self-consciousness, but it also represents the connection between the literary text, in which the author's identity is often anchored, and its paratext, in which the author's name is more arbitrarily advertised. Situated at the threshold between paratext and text, the writer's name can represent a site both of tension—as when it is replaced on the title page with the name of a bogus author, in the case of Bouchet's *Regnars traversant*—and of cooperation—as when Gringore's acrostic signature accompanies the acrostic identification of his publisher and printer at the end of the *Chasteau d'amours*. From an often cryptically encoded part of the writer's own text, authorial naming appears to have developed into more of an external, nonfictional feature that, by the time of printing, became associated with the text from without.

Chapter 5 offers a link between the preceding analyses and the texts themselves, associating the various paratextual examples of authors' increasingly prominent images and protective posture vis-à-vis their texts with a deeper level of authorial self-consciousness manifest within the texts. The narrative voice, coinciding more and more closely with that of the author, distances itself from fictional, intratextual interactions and addresses the extratextual reader more directly. Finally, in the Afterword, I suggest that these authorial shifts persist in the works of Clément Marot, the Renaissance poet whose involvement in and criticism of the publication of his own and others' works make him the undisputed heir to the defense of the literary enterprise in late medieval France.

LATE MEDIEVAL WRITERS AS OWNERS AND PROTECTORS OF THEIR TEXTS

he implications of the lawsuits of André de la Vigne and Jean Bouchet described above provide a convenient historical framework for the questions about literary proprietorship that French vernacular authors began to ask in the early sixteenth century. Carrying on the "tradition" of some of their forebears, such as Guillaume de Machaut, Christine de Pizan, and Charles d'Orléans, who had participated in the manuscript reproduction of their works, late medieval writers moved beyond their predecessors by showing evidence of a growing legal consciousness concerning their own words. An increasing use of self-promotional strategies and a more publicized concern about textual control marked their shift toward a more protective posture vis-à-vis literary creations. In a move toward the modern concept of plagiarism that implicitly called into question the medieval phenomenon Paul Zumthor has identified as *mouvance*, writers succeeded in redefining themselves legally and publicly as protectors and first-stage proprietors of their texts. By the 1550s, this development had led to an acceptance of authors as the best overseers of the publication of their own works. Numerous signs of this authorial shift to a protective mode are to be found in Jean Lemaire's works, as we shall see.

Facts implicit in surviving books and documents explain why La Vigne might have sought to prohibit Michel Le Noir from printing the *Vergier d'honneur* collection in the spring of 1504. Title-page evidence dating the publication of the first edition to circa 1502–03 confirms that the volume had already appeared by April 1504.[1] Since La Vigne did not

---

1. See the B.N. *Catalogue des incunables*, 2, 1:159, for the dating of these various editions, and Appendix 1 below for a bibliographical list of all the versions, including details about the relationship between La Vigne's *Ressource de la Chrestienté* and the *Vergier d'honneur*.

challenge that publication but rather the version Le Noir was to print, it is probable that he authorized the first edition and participated in its publication as well.[2] Moreover, the fact that the second edition of the *Vergier d'honneur*, published under La Vigne's direction between June 3, 1504, and April 1, 1505, was printed by the same person as the first, Pierre Le Dru, and that a close textual relationship exists between these first two editions (*Ressource*, 83, 94) all but confirms that La Vigne's probable involvement with the publication of the first edition paved the way for his supervision of the printing of the second. It is important to note that La Vigne, not Le Dru, initiated the lawsuit against Michel Le Noir, that it was the author, not the printer, who obtained publication control of the anthology.

Whatever role La Vigne played in these first two printings, he must have had something to gain from them. Records dating from later years reveal that an author usually received some form of compensation from the publication of his work (Parent, 101–5); it is likely, then, that he acquired some kind of income from the *Vergier d'honneur* printings.

At the time of the lawsuit, La Vigne was described as a university student (see Appendix 1 below). Even though the title page of the first edition of the *Vergier d'honneur* designated him as the secretary of the duke of Savoy, it appears that in the spring of 1504, La Vigne was unemployed.[3] His former patron, Charles VIII, had died six years earlier, and the poet had apparently not yet obtained the position with the French queen, Anne of Brittany, that he would hold by the time he made a record of her *entrée royale* into Paris in November 1504 (Stein). One may surmise that economic necessity dictated, at least in part, La Vigne's involvement in the publication of the *Vergier d'honneur*. In his view, the printing of a volume that contained some of his own works written on behalf of King Charles VIII may have been both a way to attract another patron and a form of publicity and means to private gain from a wider public. Why else would he have had it printed instead of transcribed by hand?

2. La Vigne's description as the queen's secretary on the title page of the second edition of the *Vergier d'honneur* places its date of publication "post 1504." The expiration of his court-sanctioned control of the publication on April 1, 1505, provides the terminus ad quem of this edition.

3. The exact nature and length of La Vigne's role as secretary to the duke of Savoy, who had died in September 1504, remains unclear, especially since this same designation reappears on the title page of all other editions of the *Vergier d'honneur*. If La Vigne was still in the duke's employ in the spring of 1504, why did he not qualify himself as the duke's secretary at the time of the lawsuit? Can we conclude that he was no longer in the duke's service? Had this been merely a titular post? Or did he need a designation associated with Paris for the purposes of his lawsuit? Whether or not La Vigne subsequently became secretary to the duke's son is also unknown.

This is what probably occurred: Le Noir, having acquired a copy of the first edition of the *Vergier d'honneur*, was about to print another edition of the work without consulting its principal author, when La Vigne somehow discovered the venture and sought to halt Le Noir's actions through legal means. Economic concerns that an unauthorized printer was about to reap profits from his own work must have motivated La Vigne's lawsuit. It is likely that he challenged Le Noir for moral reasons as well, calling into question the printer's right to publish his writings without his consent.

By deciding in favor of La Vigne in June 1504, the Parlement of Paris ostensibly supported the author's claims to his work over those of the printer. La Vigne doubtless considered it a victory. To grant the writer control over publication of the *Vergier d'honneur* for just one year, however, represented a rather timid endorsement. In fact, it was a compromise decision, implicitly recognizing that the author "owned" his work and could oversee its publication for a limited time subsequent to its completion. Afterward, it appears, the author's work was to become part of the public domain, a distinct advantage for printers. Indeed, four other editions of the *Vergier d'honneur* appeared in print between 1506 and 1525, apparently without the sanction of La Vigne, who lived at least until 1515. If he had in fact authorized Le Dru's publication of the first edition, as evidence suggests, then, in the end, La Vigne succeeded in controlling the printing and distribution of the volume for some two to three years.

Of course, the decision handed down did not spell out these ideas. Despite the lukewarm support given the writer by Parlement and the absence of any explicit legal explanation of the terms of the final decree, it is nonetheless momentous that an author prevailed in a law court over a printer and that the latter's actions were considered illicit. This outcome implicitly raised the issue of literary property to a level never before known. La Vigne's legal suit reveals an awareness of his literary rights and of his need to challenge those printers and booksellers who were appropriating his works without his consent. Authors were beginning to ask who owned a literary text.

In his work on modern authorship and copyright in seventeenth-century England, Rose outlines the necessary conditions for the development of what he calls the "modern proprietary author." These include the possibility of profit, the endowment of a "work" with legal reality (usually copyright), which in turn affirms the author's identity and role as a writer, a market for books that sustains cultural production, the understanding of an author as the originator of literature rather than as a perpetuator of certain basic truths, and a theory of property ("Author as Proprietor," 54–56). While all these conditions did not surface explicitly in early sixteenth-century France, actions like La Vigne's at this time tac-itly implicated several of them. The decision handed down as a result of his lawsuit suggests, for example, that although jurists had not yet for-malized a theory of property, the author was for all intents and purposes the first owner of his book.[4] The fact that he, not the bookseller or the printer, legally acquired the equivalent of a privilege, the form that an-ticipated copyright, confirms this important association between the au-thor and his writings. While the "privilege" endowed the *Vergier d'hon-neur* with "legal reality," the announcement on the title pages of these editions affirmed the very identification of La Vigne as author (see Chap-ter 2 below). Moreover, the institution of privileges, which developed in a regularized fashion shortly after La Vigne's trial, implied that there ex-isted in Paris at the time a viable market for such books. These events co-incide, moreover, with the first occurrences of the French word *œuvres* as a collective title for the works of a single author, marking an important shift in the significance of single-author anthologies and in the status of vernacular literature.[5]

This issue of literary property relates in important ways to that of pa-tronage, for late medieval authors involved in the publication of their works did not typically receive a literary subsidy in any regular fashion. La Vigne, Lemaire, Bouchet, Gringore, and others were all in search of patronage at the time they chose to oversee the printing and selling of their works. Even Jean Molinet, whose ties with the houses of Burgundy and Austria characterize him as one of the most well supported writers of his generation, turned to the printing press toward the end of his ca-reer, when he could no longer count on a consistent salary as court his-toriographer. An important correlation existed, then, between the un-stable state of authors seeking patronage at the end of the fifteenth and the beginning of the sixteenth centuries in France, their growing partic-ipation in the reproduction of their works, their concerted efforts to pro-tect their publications through privileges, and a new legal affirmation of their identities as authors. At this time, the precarious economic status of authors clashed with the aggressive behavior of Parisian publishers, and this conflict of interest gave impulse to a new realization by authors

4. Rose acknowledges the difficulty of distinguishing between matters of "propriety" and matters of "property" because of the economic implications attached to the right to control publication (*Authors and Owners*, 18).

5. Regalado points out in "Gathering the Works" that *œuvres* first appeared on the title page of Laurens de Premierfait's translation of Seneca's *Les euuvres* (Paris: Vérard, ca. 1500) and Robert Gaguin's translation of Caesar's *Euuvres et brefues expositions* (Paris: Michel Le Noir, 1502). The term first appeared in a title for the collected lyrics of one author in Galliot Du Pré's 1529 republication of *Les Oevvres feu Maistre Alain Chartier*. I am indebted to the au-thor for providing me with a copy of this article prior to publication.

about their texts and their relationship to them. For if a prospective patron did not commission, and therefore come to own, an author's text, as was often the case in the manuscript culture, then who ultimately did? Rose, who sees early printing privileges as versions of patronage, touches on this point when he concludes that "the concept of owning a work did not fit the circumstances of a traditional status society that functioned largely through patronage" ("Author as Proprietor," 55). Already in early sixteenth-century France, though, the concept of owning a work existed in outline, because the patronage and privilege systems did not always work in tandem. Writers clearly acted on their own behalf through publication channels, even while they continued to seek literary protectors. That is to say, authors such as La Vigne, Gringore, and Lemaire, who obtained their own privileges or versions thereof, did not necessarily seek or obtain patronage. On the other hand, many writers who possessed court positions, such as Jean Marot, never sought to have their works printed, a probable reflection of the security of their royal appointments.

This association of elements—the unsupported writer, the author's direct involvement in publication, and the development of the idea of the author as originator of his work—surfaces even more clearly with Jean Bouchet, whose unsuccessful attempt to obtain the patronage of Charles VIII at the end of the fifteenth century resulted in his return to Poitiers sometime between 1503 and 1507. There Bouchet eventually obtained support from the La Trémoille family.

The title pages from Vérard's late 1503 or early 1504 edition of the *Regnars traversant les perilleuses voyes des folles fiances du monde* (Figure 1.1) and Le Noir's May 1504 edition of the same text erroneously attribute the work to Sebastian Brant instead of to Bouchet, thereby confirming that the motivating force behind the publisher's involvement in the *Regnars traversant* editions had nothing to do with authorial integrity.[6] Information on these title pages does explain that the book contains compositions by writers besides Brant, presumably including Bouchet: "Et autres plusieurs choses composees par autres facteurs" (And several other items composed by other writers). But Vérard had clearly resorted to underhanded tactics in printing Bouchet's composition, and Le Noir had followed suit.

In fact, these two unauthorized editions preserve vestiges of both the false attribution and the actual identity of the author. While the title page of both versions advertises Sebastian Brant's name, we discover an acrostic of Bouchet's name in the middle of the volume (fol. 32, sig. fiiⱽ), where it would have been less accessible to someone leafing casually

---

6. See Appendix 3 below for a list of the various editions of this work.

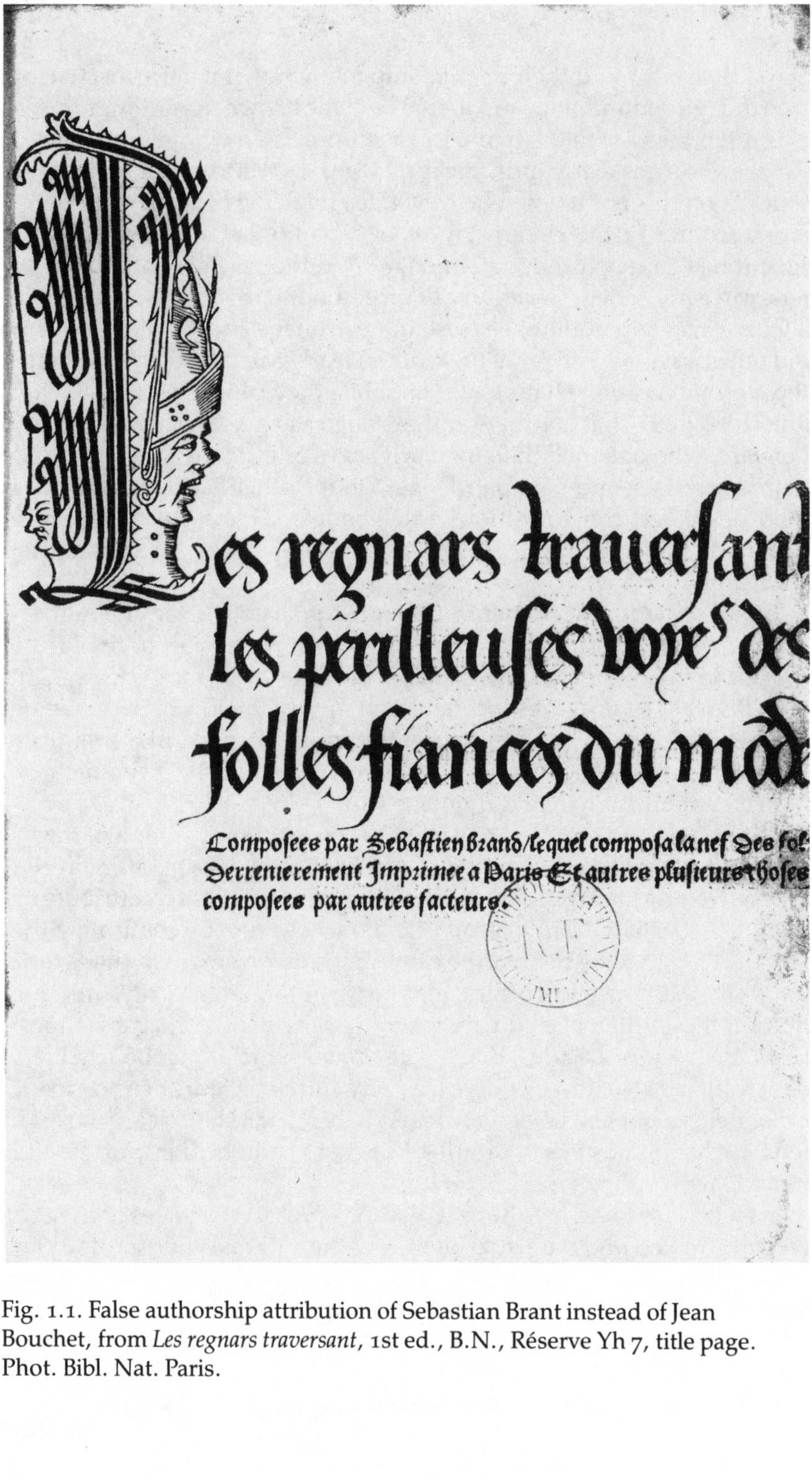

Fig. 1.1. False authorship attribution of Sebastian Brant instead of Jean Bouchet, from *Les regnars traversant*, 1st ed., B.N., Réserve Yh 7, title page. Phot. Bibl. Nat. Paris.

through the book than at the front or in the colophon. These verses, which appear to be the final lines of Bouchet's work, spell out in acrostic form IEHAN BOVCHET NATJF DE POICTIERS (Figure 1.2). Directions to the reader to reconstruct the author's name at this point provide evidence that Vérard was aware of his misleading title-page advertisement (see Appendix 3 below). Compounding the aggressive behavior of the publishers who omitted Bouchet's name on the title page of the *Regnars* are Vérard's and Le Noir's self-advertisements at the end of their respective editions (see Tchémerzine, 3:1, 4).

Several times in his writings, Bouchet condemned the materialistic ends of those Parisian printers and booksellers who wrongfully appropriated his *Regnars traversant*. In one passage, he refers to the unfinished state of his work when it somehow disappeared and mentions its false title and printing errors. These obviously constitute attacks against Le Noir and other printers who may have profited in the same way:

Certain temps après (qui fut l'an mil cinq cens ung),[7] avant qu'avoir prins fin et conclusion en ces petiz labeurs [*L'amoureux transi sans espoir*], ne es Regnars traversans et Loups ravissans, aulcuns imprimeurs de Paris, où lors faisois demourance, plus desireux du remplissement de leurs bourses que de leur honneur ne du mien, avoient trouvé moien de retirer partie de mes compositions petites, et les avoient incorrectement imprimées: et à icelles baillé nom et tiltre à leur plaisir, dont depuis y eut procès en la court de Parlement diffini à la confusion d'aulcuns desdictz Imprimeurs.[8]

A short time afterward (which was 1501), before I had concluded these little works [*L'amoureux transi sans espoir*] or the *Regnars traversant et loups ravissans*, certain printers of Paris, where I then lived, more interested in filling up their purses than in their honor or mine, found a way to take some of my short compositions. They

7. Britnell, 304, shows that although Bouchet ascribes the composition of the *Regnars traversant* to the years 1500–1501 here, passages in the work refer to dates as late as August 25, 1503.

8. Quoted by Britnell, 302, from the preface to the *Angoisses et remedes d'amours* of 1536. This passage is somewhat ambiguous since, as Britnell explains, the printing of the *Amoureux transi sans espoir*, parts of which later appeared in the *Angoisses et remedes*, was associated with the printing of the *Regnars*. What writings disappeared? That is, what constituted "mes compositions petites"? Was it the *Amoureux transi* alone, as Winn implies? Or did it include the *Regnars traversant* as well? I believe that these details refer to the publication of the latter, especially since the reference to the Parlement court trial does not bear any known relevance to the *Amoureux transi*.

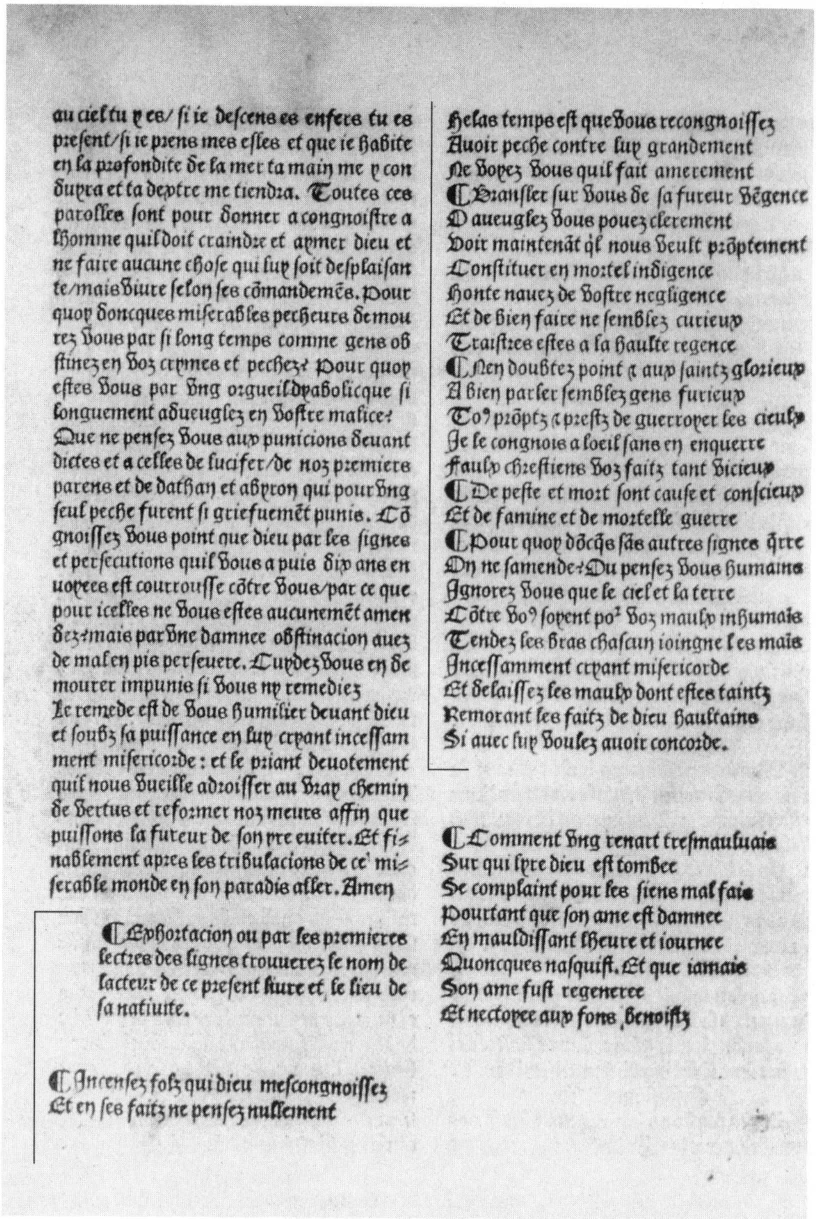

au ciel tu y es/ si ie descens es enfers tu es
present/si ie prens mes esles et que ie habite
en la profondite de la mer ta main me y con
duyra et ta dextre me tiendra. Toutes ces
parolles sont pour donner a congnoistre a
lhomme quil doit craindre et aymer dieu et
ne faire aucune chose qui luy soit desplaisant
te/mais viure selon ses commandemes. Pour
quoy doncques miserables pecheurs demou
rez vous par si long temps comme gens ob
stinez en voz crymes et pechez? Pour quoy
estes vous par vng orgueil dyabolicque si
longuement adueuglez en voftre malice?
Que ne pensez vous aux punicions deuant
dictes et a celles de lucifer/de noz premiers
parens et de dathan et abyron qui pour vng
seul peche furent si grieuemet punis. Con
gnoissez vous point que dieu par ses signes
et persecutions quil vous a puis dix ans en
uoyees est courrousse cotre vous/par ce que
pour icelles ne vous estes aucunemet amen
dez/mais par vne damnee obstinacion auez
de malen pis perseuere. Cuydez vous en de
mourer impunis si vous ny remediez
Le remede est de vous humilier deuant dieu
et soubz sa puissance en luy crpant incessam
ment misericorde : et le pziant deuotement
quil nous vueille adroisser au vray chemin
de vertus et refomer noz meurs affin que
puissons la fureur de son pre euiter. Et fi-
nablement apres ses tribulacions de ce' mi-
serable monde en son paradis aller. Amen

Exhortacion ou par les premieres
lectres des signes trouuerez le nom de
lacteur de ce present liure et le lieu de
sa natiuite.

Insensez folz qui dieu mescongnoissez
Et en ses faitz ne pensez nullement

Helas temps est que vous recongnoissez
Auoir peche contre luy grandement
Ne voyez vous quil fait amerement
Brancler sur vous de sa fureur vegence
D aueuglez vous pouez clerement
Doit maintenat ql nous veult promptement
Constituer en mortel indigence
Honte nauez de voftre negligence
Et de bien faire ne semblez curieux
Traistres estes a la haulte regence
Nen doubtez point q aux saintz glorieux
A bien parler semblez gens furieux
Tous prompts q prests de guerroyer les cieulx
Ie le congnois a loeil sans en enquerre
Faulx chreftiens voz faitz tant vicieux
De peste et mort sont cause et conscieux
Et de famine et de mortelle guerre
Pour quoy doncqs fans autres signes qrte
On ne samende?Du pensez vous humains
Ignorez vous que le ciel et la terre
Cotre vos soyent po voz maulx inhumais
Tendez ses bras chascun ioingne les mais
Incessamment crpant misericorde
Et delaissez ses maulx dont estes taintz
Remorant ses faitz de dieu haultains
Si auec luy voulez auoir concorde.

Comment vng renart tresmaluais
Sur qui lyre dieu est tombee
Se complaint pour les siens mal fais
Pourtant que son ame est damnee
En mauldissant lheure et iournee
Quoncques nasquift. Et que iamais
Son ame fuft regeneree
Et nectoyee aux fons benoiftz

Fig. 1.2. Jean Bouchet's acrostic signature, from *Les regnars traversant*, 1st ed.,
B.N., Réserve Yh 7, fol. f ii[v]. © cliché Bibliothèque Nationale Paris.

printed them incorrectly and devised their own title for them. Since then, there was a trial in the court of Parlement resulting in a decision against some of those printers.[9]

Thus, in the same passage in which he refers to La Vigne's trial, where the *Regnars traversant* played a role, Bouchet attacks the unscrupulous behavior of Parisian printers, implicitly defining their actions as dishonorable. His statements reflect the predominant financial concerns of Parisian printers and lend support to my earlier suggestion that economic considerations explain in part La Vigne's motives for filing a lawsuit.

Given Bouchet's comments, we can better understand why the judgment rendered in La Vigne's favor in June 1504 mentioned the *Regnars traversant*. Bouchet must have served as one of the witnesses La Vigne was seeking, when he asked for a delay in the court proceedings, against Le Noir. In the decision handed down, La Vigne obtained the legal right to supervise the subsequent printing and selling of Bouchet's book as well as his own, because the latter had returned (or was about to return) to his native Poitiers and was unable to oversee such an enterprise.[10] Bouchet thereby challenged Le Noir's unauthorized publication of his work by proxy and probably in absentia.

Moreover, Bouchet confronted the ever more culpable Vérard on the same issue and, according to the writer himself, received some kind of compensation for the so-called injury, when he filed a suit against him at the Châtelet:

> Le premier [livre] fut les Regnards traversans
> L'an mil cinq cens, qu'avois vingt cinq ans,
> Ou feu Verard pour ma simple jeunesse
> Changea le nom, ce fut a luy finesse,
> L'intitulant au nom de monsieur Brand
> Un Alemant en tout scavoir tresgrand,
> Qui ne sceut onc parler langue francoyse,
> Dont je me teu, sans pource prendre noise,

9. In an attack on booksellers in his circa 1531 manuscript revision of the *Regnars traversant*, Bouchet doubtless had Vérard's unauthorized publication of that same work in mind when he complained that seven or eight quires of his completed writing had somehow landed in the hands of certain booksellers, who had printed them with a title and author of their own choosing (see Britnell, 304; see also n. 11 below). Vérard was not himself a printer; as a bookseller, though, he owned his own printing material and often hired printers to do his work, thereby controlling much of the publication process. See E. Ornato, 67–68, n. 15, and Claudin, 2:507 for information on early printers' and publishers' functions.

10. This evaluation answers the question raised long ago by Picot and Piaget, 253, n. 1, who wondered how Bouchet's *Regnars traversant* came to be included in the court decision concerning the *Vergier d'honneur*.

> Fors que marri je fuz, dont ce Verard
> Y adjousta des choses d'un aultre art,
> Et qu'il laissa tresgrant part de ma prose,
> Qui m'est injure, et a ce je m'oppose
> Au chastellet, ou il me paciffia
> Pour un present lequel me dedia.
> (2 Epistre morale, xi, fol. 47^v)

My first [work] was the *Regnars traversant*, dating from 1500, when I was twenty-five years old [see n. 7 above]. The late Vérard, because I was so young and naive, changed its title—this was deceptive on his part—attributing it to Mister Brant, a German very knowledge-able in all things, who never knew how to speak French. I kept quiet about this, not raising any objection, but I was unhappy that this Vérard had added things from another work and that he had omit-ted a large part of my prose: in that he wronged me, and I opposed this action by taking my complaint to the Châtelet, where he paci-fied me with a gift.

Bouchet's comments provide some interesting facts. First, he specifi-cally accuses Vérard here in writing, an openness that probably reflects the fact that Vérard was no longer alive. Second, he explains that Vérard adopted another author's name, rather than using Bouchet's, because the actual author was too young and inexperienced. In other words, Bouchet's name did not appear on the title page because it was not fa-mous enough to attract the eye of a potential book purchaser. An impor-tant criterion publishers used in the choice of title-page features was thereby revealed.

More significant, Bouchet's words indicate that the author was less upset about the theft and false attribution of his work than about the lib-erties taken with his text by Vérard. It is possible that in the Châtelet suit Bouchet chose not to contest the association of Brant's name with his own work because the German author had in fact provided him with the framework of his composition (see Britnell, 82–83); by citing Brant at the outset, he acknowledged this debt.[11]

11. Bouchet explains in his revised manuscript of circa 1531 that Brant has inspired him (Poitiers ms. 440, fol. 1^r–1^v): "Je, Jehan Bouchet de Poictiers. . . . aprés la premiere tra-duction de latin en françois de la Nef des Folz, ou pour ouvrer je occupay mon petit en-tendement . . . deliberay en esjouir ma fantasie. Et considerant que a ce me pourroient grandement servir vingt et huit vers et metres elegamment composez par ce notable doc-teur messir Sebastian Brand, qui premierement avoit composé en langue theutonique la-dite Nef des Foulz. Sur iceulx vers et metres, pour contenter et satisfaire a mon entreprise . . . je commençay soubz la conduicte et inspiracion divine rediger par escript mes fanta-

Bouchet apparently won his case against Vérard based on the argument that a publisher did not have the right to tamper with an author's words. Nevertheless, Vérard's editorial alterations remained unchanged, even in the 1522 edition of the *Regnars traversant*, which, though printed during Bouchet's lifetime (by Le Noir's son Philippe no less), still announced Brant's authorship on the title page. Inspired perhaps by La Vigne's example, Bouchet challenged Vérard's pirating of his *Regnars traversant*; but, because he had lacked La Vigne's foresight, he was unable to prevent its unauthorized printing. Although Bouchet did profit in some way from his lawsuit, he never forgot Vérard's inappropriate action. It was likely that his position as *procureur* in the Poitiers law courts sensitized him to legal issues involving authorship and inspired these objections to the abuses he observed and experienced.

Bouchet's concern about textual tampering resurfaced in a later attack on printers who added other works to an author's writings out of context, corrupting both his verse and prose through great carelessness and going so far as to corrupt his very ideas:

> [V]ous Imprimeurs
> Estes souvent des facteurs reprimeurs,
> Et . . . adjoustez a vostre fantasie
> Chose maulvaise au propos mal choisie,
> En corrompant la rime bien souvent,
> La prose aussi, la mettant trop au vent,
> Et qui pis est corrompant la sentence
> De l'escripvant, c'est injure et offense.
> (2 *Epistre morale*, xi, fol. 48^r)

You printers are often repressers of poets, and according to your whim you add an inappropriate expression, poorly chosen for the passage, and you often corrupt the rhyme as well as the prose, with which you are careless. And what's worse, you corrupt the ideas of the writer, which is injurious and offensive.

---

sies par ung petit traictié entitullé le livre des Renars. . . . Et pource que je trouvay les loups povoir servir a ma matiere, voulu les y emploier et du tout redigeay par escript sept ou huit cayers" (I, Jean Bouchet of Poitiers, after the first translation from Latin into French of the *Ship of Fools*, at which I occupied my small mind, decided to activate my imagination. And I figured I could make great use of twenty-eight verses and meters elegantly composed by the notable doctor Mister Sebastian Brant, who had first composed in German the so-called *Ship of Fools*. Relying on these verses and meters to satisfy my enterprise, I began, under divine guidance and inspiration, to write down my vision in a small treatise entitled the *Book of Foxes*. And because I found that the wolves could serve my subject, I wanted to use them in it and in all wrote seven or eight quires).

In still another passage, Bouchet justified his revision of the *Regnars* because of the many errors and omissions of the earlier published versions, decrying the facility with which alterations could be made and the profit others could reap from them:

> [T]out homme de science speculative ou autre peut, sans doubte de reprehension muer et changer par oppinion et conseil de bien en mieulx, voire selon la mutacion des choses, non seulement pour corriger son euvre mais pour plus charitablement et proffitablement y ouvrer. (Poitiers ms. 440, fol. 1ᵛ)

> Any man of speculative or other science can, without fear of reprimand, alter and change according to [his own] opinion and counsel from good to better, in truth according to fortune, not only in order to correct his work but to use it more charitably and profitably.

Such concerns bring to light another issue, clearly associated with the advent of print. Bouchet's remarks reflect the consciousness of a writer who saw himself as the originator of a literary text. In other words, he complains of actions that we as modern readers would define as plagiarism. Specifically, he objected to the improper appropriation of his words; further, he contested their alteration. Bouchet's complaint, then, explicitly represents a turning point in the relationship between an author and his literary creation, for it concretely establishes the beginning of the end of the medieval phenomenon known as *mouvance*.[12]

As Zumthor and others have demonstrated, vernacular medieval texts were by nature alive and "moving"; that is, they were constantly and continuously being altered in conscious and unconscious ways. This was because of the oral nature of early literary composition, such as the *chansons de geste*, and of literary transmission throughout the Middle Ages. The method of medieval literary transcription—namely, manuscript reproduction—also played an important role in the workings of *mouvance*.[13] For every time a copyist transcribed a work, he inevitably

12. Already in 1461 François Villon had voiced concern about those who wanted to alter the title of his first work from *Lais* to *Testament* without his consent (*Testament*, vv. 753–60). But the fifteenth-century poet resigned himself to the fact that no one was the master of his own. See my "Author, Editor." Roger Chartier, in *L'ordre des livres*, 63–65, points out that Petrarch's concern about textual corruption led him to find ways to ensure the author's domination over textual production and transmission. As in many other areas, however, Petrarch was decidedly ahead of his time. Such ideas were to become more widely espoused in the world of print.

13. See Zumthor, *Essai*, 70–75, 507. His original use of this term had strong associations with orality, although he and other critics have extended its meaning to the written word as well. See also B. Cerquiglini and Sturges.

changed it through unintentional scribal errors or through intentional reworkings in the form of linguistic modernization, dialectic conformity, and minor to extensive additions and deletions. Medieval works were subject to *mouvance* in other ways, as well, for they often gave rise to prose adaptations or to lengthy continuations, similar perhaps to our modern obsession with film sequels. Translations, or vernacularizations, figure in this process as well, for translation in the early Middle Ages essentially consisted of the free use and adaptation of unavowed Latin sources (Dembowski, "Latin Treatises," 257). Moreover, compilers invariably combined texts with those of other writers in anthologies. Such collections could alter the original focus of a work by the nature of its new context. Medieval texts, then, were fluid and dynamic.

At the same time, medieval writers participated in an extensive network of intertextual relations, resulting in a more or less free exchange and appropriation of literary ideas, which anyone could adapt and rework.[14] These authors did not strive to be "original" in the modern sense of the term: originality consisted of adapting, imitating, or re-presenting well. Since invention was not dependent on a single author's originality, medieval writers and readers did not consider the re-creation of a text to be a deformation of an original; rather, it was an attempt to expand the volume and meaning of an earlier work (Burns, 26–29). Thus, interest lay less in the author and his identity than in his work and the intertextual web of which it was a part (Spitzer, 415–16). In other words, plagiarism, or the unlawful appropriation of another's words and ideas, could not have existed in medieval times. What eventually became illegal was what originally constituted to a great extent the very nature and substance of medieval literary creation.

A concrete example of this phenomenon, one that relates to the present discussion, can be found in the manuscript history of the first poem in the *Vergier d'honneur*: La Vigne's *Ressource de la Chrestienté*. Apart from the family of texts to which this work belongs, beginning with a 1494 royal manuscript and ranging up to the *Vergier d'honneur* editions (Brown, "Evolution," 115–25), two other related but textually divergent manuscripts have come down to us today (*Ressource*, 81–82, 95, 172–200). These versions did not rely solely on La Vigne's work, but involved adaptations of parts of it to another similar but different text. Dating from the end of the fifteenth century, these derivative manuscripts represent *mouvance* at work. In one case (Paris, B.N., ms. f.fr. 20055), an anonymous writer directly appropriated significant sections of La Vigne's words and interwove them with his own text. This process resembles in fact Vérard's adaptation of Bouchet's *Regnars traversant* just a

---

14. See, for example, Zumthor, "Intertextualité," and Dembowski, "Intertextualité."

few years later, although the bookseller was merely to juxtapose two works, instead of enmeshing them as the author or scribe of manuscript 20055 apparently did. The principal difference was that the manuscript appeared in one version, reproduced by hand, whereas the published edition came out in many printed copies.

The second derivative manuscript of the *Ressource de la Chrestienté* (Paris, B.N., ms. f.fr. 15215) contains several stanzas that are identical to those of the first derivative manuscript. Although its narrative line stems indirectly from La Vigne's work, none of its passages coincides exactly with it.

No trace of a complaint on La Vigne's part has come down to us regarding these manuscripts. It is quite probable that he did not know of their existence. It is also possible that if he was aware of them, he did not find their existence problematic. For unlike Le Noir's imminent publication of the *Vergier d'honneur*, these manuscripts did not likely represent a profitable venture for author or scribe. Just a few years later, however, La Vigne was legally challenging a printer for seeking to appropriate the *Ressource* and other works in the *Vergier d'honneur* collection.

With the advent of print, which, among other things, stabilized the text in a way never before possible, the status and nature of literary creation underwent a redefinition. We have seen, for example, that what motivated Bouchet's court action against Vérard as well as his circa 1531 revision of the *Regnars traversant* was an implicit desire to control the reproduction of his own words, to prohibit others—printers, booksellers, and publishers in particular—from changing them; that is, to limit or at least call into question the workings of *mouvance*.[15]

And yet, from the perspective of Bouchet's own participation in an intertextual system, a different set of rules seems to have been at work. It is true, for example, that the poet acknowledged his indebtedness to Brant for the framework of his *Regnars traversant*. However, Bouchet also relied on Alain Chartier in writing the *Regnars*, without ever citing his *Curial* and *Livre d'Espérance* (Britnell, 84–85). A general reference to borrowings doubtless includes Chartier, when Bouchet speaks of "plusieurs livres approuvez desquelz je me suis aydé" (several authorized books of which I made use) (Britnell, 84). But these remarks resemble Vérard's veiled allusion to Bouchet on the title page of his edition of the *Regnars traversant* ("And several other items composed by other writers"). Of course, Vérard's advertisement made it appear as if Bouchet's

---

15. Some characteristics of *mouvance* continued to exist after printing, but they took on a different form, becoming either marginalized (see my "Author, Editor") or of a cumulative nature, as in the case of additions to Montaigne's *Essais* (see Hoffman, "Montaigne's *Essais*" and "Montaigne's Book").

work was secondary, when in fact it represented a central text of his volume. And yet, the manner in which Bouchet adapted Chartier's writings to his composition shows that the sixteenth-century author was still participating in the system of *mouvance* that he himself implicitly criticized.

In principle, it is true, Bouchet's actions did not differ so much from Vérard's manipulation and alteration of Bouchet's work(s). Were it not for the detail that Vérard consciously used Brant's instead of Bouchet's name on the title page of the *Regnars traversant*, thereby adding an unscrupulous dimension to the publication, one could almost defend Vérard's actions with the explanation that he was merely imitating the standard behavior of medieval manuscript editors or compilers, who more or less at will created composite books from various sources, often omitting or wrongly identifying the authors (Goldschmidt, 46–47). A contradiction thus existed between Bouchet's own means of composition, which involved avowed and unavowed borrowings, and his disapproval of Vérard's similar behavior.

Nonetheless, several important differences do in fact distinguish Bouchet's and Vérard's actions and may well have figured in the writer's reasoning on this matter. First, having died some seventy years earlier, Chartier was not in Bouchet's position of powerlessly witnessing the rearrangement of his own work for profit. Second, two different traditions, manuscript and print, were at work here. An important dimension must have been the fact that the advent of print greatly facilitated the discovery of unauthorized textual appropriation by one's contemporaries. Manuscript reproduction, because it was a slower process, deferred such discovery, and by the time a manuscript had moved beyond an author's purview, that author was less likely to be aware of the fact that it was being recopied. Moreover, manuscript workshops did not make profits from bookmaking to the extent that printers and booksellers did, so authors, had they been concerned about control over their own words, might have not objected as vociferously.[16] Finally, Vérard and Le Noir were not professional writers like Bouchet. Perhaps the *rhétoriqueur* felt that a printer's or a publisher's training did not authorize him to assume the functions of an editor or to pass off works as another writer's. While Bouchet's and Vérard's roles as compilers coincided to a certain degree, each bringing together the ideas of different authors, living and deceased, Bouchet went much further than his nemesis by incorporating those ideas into his own words—not adopting the words of one writer, making arbitrary alterations, wrongfully attributing them to another, and juxta-

---

16. Febvre and Martin, 350, explain that from the beginning printers and booksellers worked with lucrative goals in mind.

posing them with still another text. Bouchet was obviously seeking to keep separate and distinct authors' and printers' roles, including the function of compilation.[17] Although he implicitly considered publishers ill-suited to the writer's task, Bouchet obviously felt that the direct involvement of authors in publication was appropriate. Bouchet's—and La Vigne's—attitude anticipates by several years the period when humanist scholars came to manage much of the French printing industry.

Thus, Jean Bouchet's desire to stem the tide of *mouvance* centered explicitly on the integrity of the text itself. Implicitly, though, he was also calling into question the bookmaker's function in the publication process. In other words, Bouchet's explicit challenge to Vérard's and Le Noir's actions in the printing of his *Regnars traversant* implied that the author's role should be redefined in such a way that authors would maintain greater control over textual reproduction and alterations. At the same time, La Vigne's attempt to halt the unauthorized publication of the *Vergier d'honneur* was an aggressive legal move that implicitly sought to privilege an author's rights over those of the publisher. In different yet complementary ways, each writer's actions reflected a new level of concern regarding authorship, bearing upon economic as well as moral issues. While La Vigne's involvement resulted in a decision that adumbrated the idea of authors as first owners of their writings, Bouchet's numerous criticisms about publishers tampering with texts signaled a rejection of the idea that anyone could freely appropriate others' ideas and combine and reproduce another's words. La Vigne and Bouchet also advanced the concept of authors as originators of their works. Bouchet underscores this point in a complaint to printers where he refers to his *original* copies:

> Je vous supply s'ilz [mes livres] viennent en voz mains,
> Mes chers amys, et mes freres humains
> Que vous gardez d'y faire tant de fautes
> Qu'aux precedans,
> [A]iez voz mains plus caultes
> Voz yeulx aussi, sur mes originaulx,
> Lors n'y ferez mensonges ne deffaulx.
>
> (2 *Epistre morale*, fol. 48)

I beg you if they [my books] come into your hands, my dear friends, my human brothers, that you take care not to make as many errors as in the preceding ones; be more prudent, with your hands as well as your eyes, with my originals: then you will not deceive or err.

17. See Minnis, "Discussions," who describes *compilatio* as a literary form by the fourteenth century.

If writers themselves did not consider literary material to be as mobile as before, then by implication authorial intention and design had gained in stature and significance. Moreover, because each copy of a work was now "an exact replica of every other," in contrast to manuscript books, which differed from one another in both their external and internal presentation (Ong, "Orality, Literacy and Medieval Textualization," 2), one can see that a printed work's "uniqueness" came to be associated more and more with a particular person. That person, however, was not the patron or the bookowner, whose name became increasingly anonymous with print and the circulation of many copies of a work. The individual associated with the book was someone whose name appeared on the title page of the publication: the author, printer, or bookseller.[18] These developments relate to the numerous paratextual and textual examples of the author's and publisher's presence that abound in late fifteenth-century and early sixteenth-century books, features that we shall examine in detail in the following chapters.

Bouchet's comments, some of which appeared in print during the later years of his career, the 1530s and 1540s, may have influenced his contemporary Clément Marot, who belonged to a later literary generation. Time and again, in the prologues and prefaces of his editions, Marot voiced complaints similar to those of Bouchet. As a member of a generation that received better patronage and depended less on seeking independent means of support, Marot, at the forefront of publication in his time, owed much to his predecessors' actions.

The tension over who controlled the reproduction of an author's words, brought to a head by La Vigne in 1504 and commented on at length by Bouchet, played itself out in the early years of sixteenth-century France in the halls of justice. The decisions in favor of these authors, however, remained more or less hidden in legal and personal records of the day, some of which were not published until years after the events in question. Yet their victories were significant. An author's rights to the publication and dissemination of his work gained legal

---

18. The substitution of a writer's name for his work is evident, for example, in a 1526 manuscript containing several of Jean Molinet's compositions (Paris, B.N., Cat. Rothschild 471), which reads (my emphasis): "Les nombres en ciffres designent les feuillés de *mon grand Molinet*, escript a la main; ou il n'y a pas de cifre, les vers ne sont pas en *mon dit grand Molinet*" (quoted in Dupire, *Edition critique*, 37) (The numbers designate the folios of my large Molinet, written by hand; where there are no numbers, the verses do not appear in my so-called large Molinet). The reference alludes to a major sixteenth-century manuscript of Molinet's works, Tournai, Bibl. Communale, 105 (now lost), which served as the scribe's source. See also Hoffman, "Montaigne's *Essais*," chap. 2, 15–16, who points out how prefaces and printers' notices "helped promote the idea that certain writing depended upon a specific writer" and how "the writer's name came to serve as a virtual trademark."

priority over those of a printer for the period of one year, a time limit that would gradually increase. The questioning by authors of their traditional relationship to their texts forced publishers and the legal system to face these issues. Consequently, writers had by the early sixteenth century come to act not only as literary creators, but as organizers of their publications and protectors and first-stage proprietors of them. These changes in status provided stepping-stones for other writers, such as La Vigne's and Bouchet's contemporary Pierre Gringore, who succeeded in extending the gains they had made with his promotion of privilege use.

Like La Vigne and Bouchet, Pierre Gringore was a poet without a patron and had grown increasingly sensitized to the relationship between writers and their texts, their publishers, their potential benefactors, and their public.[19] He plays an important part in this discussion of the first "voiced" concerns in favor of authors' rights to their works and the related issue of plagiarism in the early sixteenth century. Gringore, too, sought legal protection against aggressive publishers in order to gain control of and profit from his works. In Gringore's case, however, the scholar must glean much information from the paratext of the author's publications, since no other records of his thoughts on these matters survive.

In writing the *Chasteau de labour* (1499), his first known work, Gringore paraphrased an unacknowledged source, the late fourteenth-century composition of Jacques Bruyant entitled *La voie de povreté et de richesse* (Långfors; *Labour*, ed. Pollard, xxx–xxxiv). Like Bouchet when he penned his *Regnars traversant*, Gringore omitted reference to the earlier work, signing his poem as its unique author. While he too may have felt less obliged to identify a deceased author or may have expected his contemporaries to recognize the source, it is possible that Gringore never knew the author's name.[20]

Perhaps for that very reason, Gringore took steps to ensure that the reproduction of his own words in their first-edition state remained associated with his name: he composed a final acrostic-signature stanza for the *Chasteau de labour* and for nearly all of his many subsequent writings (see Chapter 4 below). Furthermore, from 1505 on, not only did he be-

19. There is no evidence that the house of France officially commissioned or subsidized Gringore's literary works, despite the fact that many of those works espoused royal policy. Archival records show that, along with a certain carpenter named Jean Marchant, Gringore received payment for the construction of sets, composition of "mystères," stage decoration, costumes, and so forth on the occasion of several royal entries into Paris between 1502 and 1515 (see *La vie de Monseigneur Saint Louis*, ed. Montaiglon, xx–xxiii).

20. Given the strong association between Gringore's edition of the *Labour* and the fifteenth-century Thomas manuscript of the *Voie de povreté* (see Chapter 5, nn. 58 and 60 below), which does not identify the author, it is quite likely he never knew Bruyant's name.

come directly involved in the publication and sale of his volumes, but he also sought legal validation of his control. The same rights that La Vigne had obtained through a lawsuit in June 1504 became a visible, authorized part of the paratext of Gringore's publications just eighteen months later. Following the last verses of the first edition of his *Folles entreprises*, published in December 1505, a printed summary of an "ordonnance de justice" obtained by the author details his legal right as "acteur" to control the publication and distribution of his work for one year (Figure 1.3):[21]

> Il est dit par l'ordonnance de justice que l'acteur de cedict livre nommé Pierre Gringore, a privileige de le vendre et distribuer du jourd'uy jusques a ung an, sans ce que autre le puisse faire imprimer ne vendre, fors ceulx a qui il en baillera et distribuera, et ce sur peine de confiscacion des livres et d'amende arbitraire.

> It is declared by a legal order that the author of this said book named Pierre Gringore has the right ["privilege"] to sell and distribute it from today for one year without anyone else being able to have it printed or sold, except those to whom he will give and distribute it, and this is decreed under penalty of confiscation of the books and an undetermined fine.

The similarity between the terms outlined here and those spelled out in the June 1504 judgment handed down for La Vigne's lawsuit against Le Noir is remarkable. This legal order gives Gringore the authority to select the printer and bookseller of his work for one year.[22] Gringore went even further than La Vigne's dramatic challenge, for he had his privilege publicly incorporated, in summary form, into the paratext of this first edition of the *Folles entreprises*. Such an advertisement of the privilege publicly authenticated the author's title to his own words and announced to all book producers and purchasers, in a more visible manner than La Vigne's and Bouchet's lawsuits, Gringore's consciousness concerning issues of literary property and propriety. This constitutes the first French privilege for a vernacular work, obtained and prominently publicized thanks to Gringore's initiative.[23]

21. For bibliographical details about the various editions of the *Folles entreprises*, see Appendix 5 below.

22. The formula "par l'ordonnance de justice" indicates that this was a privilege granted by the Prévôt de Paris, whose court was at the Châtelet (see Armstrong, 49).

23. It is also the first one granted by the Prévôt de Paris (Armstrong, 49, 141). For information about privileges granted to authors in other countries at an earlier date (Venice, 1486; Milan, 1492; etc.), see Armstrong, 1–20.

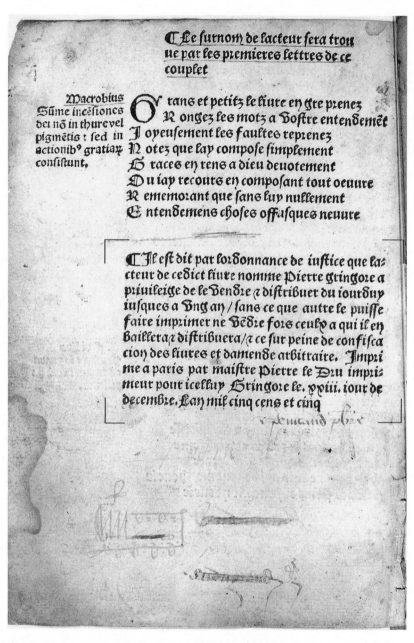

❡ Le furnom de lacteur fera trou
ue par les premieres lettres de ce
couplet

Macrobius
Sũme incẽstiones
dei nõ in thure vel
pigmẽtis: fed in
actionib⁹ gratiaȝ
confiſtunt.

G rans et petitz le liure en gre prenez
R ongez les motz a Voſtre entendemẽt
J oyeufement les faultes teprenez
N otez que lay compofe fimplement
G races en tens a dieu deuotement
O u iay recours en compofant tout oeuure
R ememorant que fans luy nullement
E ntendemens chofes offufques neuure

❡ Il eſt dit par lordonnance de iuſtice que la
cteur de cedict fiure nomme Pierre gringore a
priuileige de le Vendre ȝ diſtribuer du iourduy
iufques a Vnȝ an / fans ce que autre le puiſſe
faire imprimer ne Vedre fors ceulȝ a qui il en
Bailleraȝ diſtribuera/ȝ ce fur peine de confifca
cion des liures et damende arbittaire. Impri
me a paris par maiſtre Pierre le Dru impri
meur pour icelluy Gringore le. xxviii. iour de
decembre. Lan mil cinq cens et cinq

It is not exactly clear what motivated Gringore to obtain a privilege for the *Folles entreprises*. While the discovery of Michel Le Noir's December 1500 alteration of his *Chasteau d'amours* five years earlier may have awakened the writer to the need for such protection (Brown, "Confrontation"), Gringore apparently did not seek privileges for the works he had published since that time. These include the *Lettres nouvelles de Milan* (after April 15, 1500), *La piteuse complainte . . . de la Terre Sainte* (ca. 1500), and *La complainte de Trop Tard Marié* (October 1505). The abbreviated form and polemical dimension of the first two may not have warranted such protection in the author's eyes. It is more likely that the possibility of obtaining a privilege simply did not surface until La Vigne's victorious lawsuit in June 1504. Why, then, did Gringore not acquire a privilege for his *Complainte de Trop Tard Marié*? Did he deem it a less important work than the lengthier, moralistic *Folles entreprises*? Could it be that he had not yet learned of La Vigne's legal victory sixteen months before?

As one might expect, the privilege does not appear in any of the *Folles entreprises* editions that were printed after the one-year limit had expired. Still, several anomalies characterize certain copies of the first edition. For example, the privilege announcement was erased in a specially made vellum copy,[24] although the colophon naming the printer (Pierre Le Dru), publisher (Gringore), and place and date of publication remained in this version (Paris, B.N., Vélins 2245). The wealthy bookowner to whom this hybrid edition was likely destined probably deemed the privilege inappropriate; the intended recipient may not have wanted a reminder of the commercial monopoly that it represented.[25] This special version thus rendered visible—or, rather, invisible—an apparent contradiction between the two systems of book reproduction, manuscript and print. The proprietorship of the book by the presumably noble bookowner conflicted with that of the author during the period covered by his privilege. Although reference to Gringore's authorized one-year supervision of the publication and distribution of the *Folles entreprises* disappeared from this version, the preserved details about its publication suggest that the bookowner was not concerned about the fact that it had been printed. Despite these underlying contradictions, the coexistence of manuscript and print culture is manifest in this version of the *Folles entreprises*.

In another vellum copy of this first edition of the *Folles entreprises* (Chantilly, Musée Condé, XVII.B.7), the last lines of the colophon an-

24. The printing of works on vellum and the replacement of woodcuts with miniatures was a popular form of reproduction for those who could afford the higher cost of an imitation manuscript. Vérard often directed the publication of these hybrid editions.

25. Armstrong, 160–64, explains that for this reason privileges often did not appear in special copies.

nouncing that Gringore had had the work printed are missing, but the printer's name and the privilege announcement remain (Figure 1.4). Does this omission signify that the bookowner, not Gringore, subsidized the use of vellum and decoration in the particular volume? Do the missing details of publication in these two vellum copies even have such a specific explanation? Although it is impossible to answer these questions definitively, the colophon alterations in this version do suggest an inherent contradiction between the author's legalized control of his own publications and the purchase and ownership of specially made manuscript-like versions of them. Ownership rights were still vaguely defined. In fact, the manipulation of this privilege announcement may have involved Gringore himself. As the bookseller of certain copies of this edition and a seeker of patronage, as the dedication woodcuts in some of these versions suggest, he could have sanctioned these special printings.[26]

The appearance of Gringore's privilege in the 1505 edition of the *Folles entreprises* marks a critical stage in the evolution of authors' textual rights. His procurement of the privilege for this work as well as his reproduction of its stipulations in the volume represent a revolutionary gesture on behalf of all writers. Gringore's continued effort to obtain privileges for the first editions of nearly all his works, even after he had obtained patronage in 1518 and no longer resided in Paris, underscores his fundamental commitment to the legal protection of his writings. For Gringore, the author privilege had become an integral part of the literary enterprise. While certain printers and booksellers had already obtained privileges in their own names and would continue to do so (Armstrong, 208–95), Gringore blazed the new trail of action on behalf of writers. This move increased awareness by public and publishers alike of the authority of literary creators in early sixteenth-century France: the author had acquired a new, publicized legal status.

The self-conscious concerns of La Vigne, Bouchet, and Gringore may have played a role in Jean Lemaire's involvement in the French publication process, beginning with the 1503 printing of his *Temple d'honneur et de vertus*. A comparison of this work with the *Légende des Vénitiens* (1509), Lemaire's second work printed in France, provides traces of this influence. These volumes, which offer early examples of paratextual use by and for a living vernacular writer, mark the commercialization of the patronage process through the use of print in their focus on the author's "sovereign" rights to his works and in their explicit association with

---

26. For further details on Gringore's role as a bookseller and on the dedication woodcuts, see Chapters 2 and 3 below, respectively.

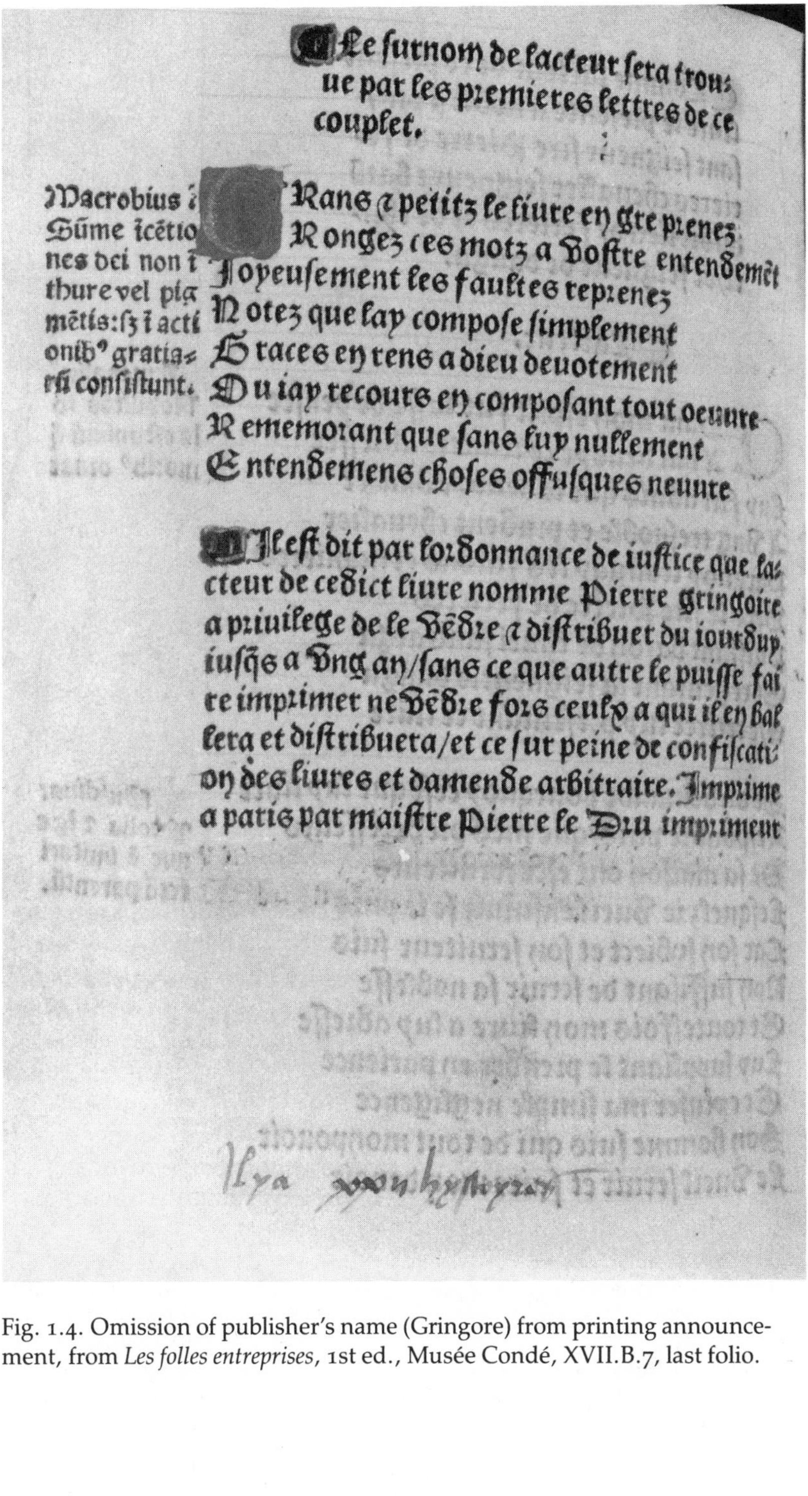

¶ Le surnom de lacteur sera trou-
ue par les premieres lettres de ce
couplet.

Macrobius ȷ
Sume icētio
nes dei non ī
thure vel pia
mētis:sz ī actī
onib' gratia=
rū confistunt.

Rans ȷ petitz le liure eȷ gre prenes
Rongez ces motz a Voftre entendemēt
Joyeufement les faulkes reprenez
Notez que lay compofe fimplement
Graces eȷ rens a dieu deuotement
Ou lay recours eȷ compofant tout oeuure-
Rememorant que fans luy nullement
Entendemens chofes offufques neuure

¶ Il eft dit par lordonnance de iuftice que lacteur de cedict liure nomme pierre gringoire
a priuilege de le Vedre ȷ diftribuet du iourdup
iufqs a Vnȷ an/fans ce que autre le puiffe faire imprimet ne Vedre fors ceulp a qui il eȷ bal-
lera et diftribueta/et ce fur peine de confifcati-
oȷ des liures et damende arbitraire. Jmprime
a paris par maiftre pierre le Dru imprimeur

Il y a xxxiȷ hyfteyres

Fig. 1.4. Omission of publisher's name (Gringore) from printing announcement, from *Les folles entreprises*, 1st ed., Musée Condé, XVII.B.7, last folio.

French royalty. More than with any of his contemporaries, the strategies Lemaire employed for his *mise-en-livre* and *mise-en-texte* became inextricably interconnected, as a growing, self-conscious control of his literary text from without accompanied his increasingly self-assertive mastery of it from within.

Published in Paris in early 1504 by Antoine Vérard, Lemaire's *Temple d'honneur et de vertus* glorified his former patron, Pierre, the duke of Bourbon, who had recently died.[27] There was nothing at all unusual about the content of this *poème de circonstance*; it constituted the common literary fare of a *rhétoriqueur* such as Lemaire. But its appearance in print through the author's initiative and the prominent advertisement of his involvement in its publication confirm the poet's increasingly authoritative status in late medieval France. One of the earliest French epideictic poems printed during the lifetime of its author,[28] Lemaire's first publication served as propaganda as much for himself as for his deceased patron. Since the *Temple d'honneur* was an uncommissioned work composed about and for someone who had already died, the author probably had more freedom in its manner of reproduction. But Michel Le Noir's unauthorized version of the *Temple d'honneur*, which appeared shortly after the first edition, reflects the tensions that could develop between authors and printers at this time.

The prominent advertisement of Lemaire's authorship on the title page of Vérard's edition of the *Temple d'honneur* did not necessarily constitute a customary feature at a time when title pages, essentially absent from manuscripts, were still in development (Hirsch, 63–66). Bouchet's comments about Vérard's misattribution of his *Regnars traversant* confirm that the names of contemporary authors, especially those who were unknown and at the beginning of their careers, did not always appear on title pages: "Le Temple d'honneur et de vertus. Composé par Jehan Le Maire disciple de Molinet a l'honneur de feu monseigneur de Bourbon" (*The Temple of Honor and Virtues*, composed by Jean Lemaire, disciple of Molinet, in honor of the late lord of Bourbon). Lemaire's name is thus linked here to that of his mentor, Jean Molinet, whose work inspired much of this composition (Hornik ed., 35–36), and to his former patron, Pierre of Bourbon, subject of the writing: one figure advertises a prestigious poetic connection, the other an important political association.

---

27. Pierre II, duke of Bourbon, whom Lemaire had served as "clerc de finances" since 1498, died on October 10, 1503. See Appendix 2 below for a listing of the various editions of this work. Unless otherwise indicated, all citations will be from the Hornik edition.

28. Jean Meschinot's *Lunettes des princes* was first printed in 1493 (Nantes: Larcher), two years after his death. See Chapters 3–5 below, regarding Molinet's *Naissance de Charles d'Autriche,* printed after March 1500, and André de la Vigne's *Ressource de la Chrestienté,* which was published as part of the *Vergier d'honneur* anthology circa 1502–3.

With author, mentor, and former patron sharing paratextual space, this arrangement of names reflects the interplay of authorities involved in the creation of the *Temple*. On one hand, the title page announces the subject of the text: the great honor and virtue of the duke of Bourbon and his family. Classically inspired pastoral characters and allegorical figures set in a dream landscape laud the deceased noble before and after his death. On the other hand, the advertisement of the author's literary qualifications here anticipates other features of the paratext, such as his device ("De peu assez") placed at the end of the text.[29] As a form of signature or an added sign of the author's presence, this expression punctuated Lemaire's first publication.

The colophon space, where one commonly discovers publication information, contains no other identification. While Lemaire makes reference in a dedicatory letter reproduced in the volume to "having given [his text] to Antoine Vérard, Parisian bookseller, who agreed to print it and publish it everywhere,"[30] no allusion to the bookseller, or to the printer he hired, appears elsewhere. This is rather unusual since, from 1503 on, Vérard, one of the most successful bookseller-publishers of his time, regularly signed his editions; they sometimes even bore a dedication miniature with his portrait as well.[31] Lemaire's affiliation with Vérard confirms that there were cases in which author and publisher successfully collaborated in textual production. An enterprising merchant himself, Vérard doubtless played an important role in determining the advertising strategies of the paratext of the *Temple d'honneur*.

Three letters placed before the text inform the prospective reader of the *Temple d'honneur* about the changing life of the work; they also take into account Lemaire's literary experience. One, a letter of dedication, presumably had accompanied a manuscript copy that the poet had presented to the count of Ligny several weeks earlier.[32] Anticipating the final verses of the text, in which the author dedicates the work to the count in traditionally modest fashion (vv. 1410–17), this dedicatory letter resulted in Lemaire's securement of Ligny's patronage. Unfortunately, the author's *mécène* died a few days after Lemaire had presented him with the *Temple d'honneur et de vertus*.

29. This device replaced "Penser, penser, penser, dire," which had appeared in a manuscript collection of Lemaire dating from 1498 (see Paris, B.N., ms. nouv. acq. f.fr. 4061).

30. ". . . après l'avoir communicqué à Anthoine Verard, libraire de Paris, lequel l'a bien voulu mettre sur ses formes impressoires et le publier par tout" (45).

31. I am grateful to Mary Beth Winn for this information, which will appear in her forthcoming work on Vérard. See also Macfarlane, 1–126, who shows that many other editions without Vérard's name do bear his bookseller's mark.

32. Lemaire's mention of the fact that he had asked Vérard to print the work postdates the death of Ligny, to whom he must have offered a manuscript version of the text, although to my knowledge no trace of it remains.

Why was this communication included in the first edition of the *Temple d'honneur*, which was published after the original dedicatee's death? The presence of the first letter in the volume, a dedication of the same work to Anne de Beaujeu, the wife of the deceased duke of Bourbon, provides an explanation. For the implicit message of this epistle was the following: if Anne's husband (the duke of Bourbon) and cousin (Ligny) had seen in Lemaire a talent worth supporting, then why wouldn't she? In other words, Lemaire hoped to secure the patronage of the wife of his former patron. As tradition dictated, this letter, like the previous one, explicitly flatters the dedicatee, with the homage accorded Anne de Beaujeu anticipating her equally glorified alter ego, Aurora, in the text.[33]

But the writer takes care to extol himself as well in these dedications. In his letter to Anne de Beaujeu, half of which details his own history with Ligny as his very devoted servant, Lemaire emphasizes the fact that Anne's late cousin had hired him after reading one of his poems (44–45). Assuming responsibility for the anticipated but unfulfilled desire of his deceased protector, Lemaire forwards to Anne a copy of the work about her husband. In his letter to Ligny, Lemaire is at once self-deprecating and self-aggrandizing, as he devotes half of the discussion to himself. Lemaire's modest self-description as the least important of Ligny's servants and the reference to his own work as humbly written are belied by the association he establishes between himself and other highly esteemed writers, including Molinet. While carefully characterizing his position as their "trespetit et incongneu disciple et loingtain imitateur" (very small and unknown disciple and distant imitator), Lemaire advertises his entry into this pantheon of noble writers and highly commended modern historians (48–49). As further proof of the author's literary authority, a laudatory verse epistle sent by his admiring mentor Guillaume Cretin accompanies the dedicatory letter in this paratextual space (45–47).

With both of Lemaire's letters published in the volume alongside Cretin's glowing words, the function of this traditional dedicatory space simultaneously takes on a self-promotional character. Of course, self-promotion was often an explicit or implicit feature of dedications; but the assemblage here of numerous reminders of Lemaire's literary prowess and past royal associations, especially of two *different* letters of dedication, is unusual. Such an unlikely combination would not have appeared in a manuscript version of the work, which typically addressed one bookowner or patron. The paratext thus reveals that Anne de Beaujeu was not the only intended reader of this edition. Such a publicity ges-

---

33. Lemaire was more effusive in the text than in the dedication, as a comparison of the letter of dedication (43–45) with his own verses (ll. 817–25) confirms.

ture suggests that author and publisher were attempting to reach an ever-expanding public. As anticipated on the title page and developed in the remaining paratextual space, mentors and patrons were "used" to promote Lemaire's talents and political associations in the first edition of the *Temple d'honneur*. Indeed, a kind of competition emerges, because the message proffered by the text differs from the one promoted in the paratext. The praise of a patron in the conventional text is recast in the paratext, which emphasizes less the subject of the work, Pierre of Bourbon, than it draws attention to the poet and his appeal for support. This shift of focus from the past benefactors to the possible beneficiary coincides with a new awareness on the part of author and publisher about the advertising potential that print offered.

Nevertheless, Lemaire's presence in the traditional, medieval-like text of the *Temple d'honneur*, or rather the presence of the narrator with whom he is identified, remains subordinate to that of the work's protagonists: the speaker merely introduces them and relates their actions.[34] Eventually, though, the author's paratextual prominence managed to infiltrate his later texts.

The example of Jean Marot provides a useful point of comparison with Lemaire. Marot's secure position as the French queen's secretary differed dramatically from Lemaire's precarious status as author of the *Temple d'honneur*, and this security distinctively marks his works.[35] For example, Marot remains excessively subservient in the letter to Anne of Brittany, in which he dedicates to her his *Voyage de Gênes*. He describes "my poor simple-mindedness . . . [my] heavy and extremely unsophisticated form as well as the crudeness of my feeble understanding" (ma povre simplicité . . . en lourde et par trop basse forme ainsi que la grosseur de mon petit entendement), while stating that he is unworthy and incapable of carrying out the queen's commission. Marot signs off as "your poor writer, most humble of your very humble and very obedient servants" (vostre povre escripvain, serviteur treshumble des vostres treshumbles et tresobeyssans serviteurs) (Trisolini ed., 83–84). Even though such formulaic modesty constituted part of the conventional rhetoric of address at the time, as Lemaire's letters of dedication show, the extreme tone of Marot's words reveals how his position as court spokesman encouraged this conventionally hierarchical discourse of humility. The dedication miniature adorning the manuscript of the *Voyage de Gênes* that Marot offered the queen reinforces this association vi-

34. The narrator does make one reference that seemingly coincides with the author's own experience (65, vv. 406–7).

35. Queen Anne had a history of supporting *rhétoriqueur* writers, beginning with her hire of Jean Meschinot, the Breton poet, in 1488 and continuing with André de la Vigne (ca. November 1504–12), Jean Lemaire de Belges (1511–12), and Marot (1507–12).

sually (Figure 1.5), an association that probably accounts for why none of Jean Marot's works was printed during his lifetime.[36]

The scenario is quite different in the case of Lemaire's first work, which came out in print a short time after he had written it. The exploitation of the various paratextual elements examined above aimed to draw public attention not only to Lemaire's talents, but to his economic plight in particular and to the problem of patronage in general. While trying to get his foot into the noble entryway of the house of France, he was also attempting to gain more widespread public recognition, a strategy that appears to have succeeded.[37] By having this work printed, Lemaire was, consciously or unconsciously, contributing to a dramatic change in the dynamics of the patronage system. No doubt the author was coming to understand the advantages print offered, as some of his later personal letters confirm.

Lemaire's awareness of the important link between a writer's renown and the more widespread distribution of his works through print is manifest in his letter of encouragement to Cretin in 1513: "Et quant il plaira à ta benignité faire ouuerture des tiennes nobles oeuures, et icelles publier par impression, on congnoitra facilement que tout ce peu que iay de grace et de felicité en ce langage, vient de ta discipline: à laquelle ie suis tenu, toute ma vie" (And when it pleases your grace to expose your noble works and have them published in print, everyone will easily recognize that my little linguistic grace and felicity come from your instruction, to which I am beholden for the rest of my life).[38]

Lemaire shows even earlier signs of understanding the import of print for his career. In a letter written in early 1509 to his patroness, Margaret of Austria, he mentions that he would soon have the three volumes of the *Singularitez de Troye* printed in Lyons because everyone was asking for them (Stecher ed., 4:395). In 1511 he proudly associates his increas-

36. Jean Marot's son Clément apparently supervised the posthumous edition of *Voyages de Gênes et de Venise* (dated January 22, 1532) and made significant editorial changes in his father's works. Several other editions of the *Voyage de Gênes* appeared at the end of Clêment Marot's works throughout the sixteenth century (Trisolini ed., 61–64). The letter of dedication to the French queen, however, did not appear in the posthumous editions; it was replaced by another.

37. Although Lemaire was unsuccessful in securing the patronage of Anne de Beaujeu or the French queen, to whom he dedicated a manuscript copy of his next work, the *Plainte du Désiré*, sometime between 1504 and 1506, Margaret of Austria did respond favorably to a similar dedication. Lemaire also became Anne of Brittany's court historiographer around the beginning of 1512. See my *Shaping*, 136–37, n. 54, and Jodogne, *Jean Lemaire*, 113–15, 127–31.

38. *Œuvres*, ed. Stecher, 2:257. According to Chesney, in her edition of Cretin's *Œuvres poétiques* (ci), only six of Cretin's poems were printed during his lifetime, probably without his supervision. One of them, *Plainte sur le trespas du sage et vertueus . . . Byssipat*, was in fact published by Lemaire with his own *Epistre du roy a Hector* in 1513.

Fig. 1.5. Jean Marot offering his work to Queen Anne of Brittany, from *Le voyage de Gênes*, B.N., ms. f.fr. 5091, fol. 1ʳ, frontispiece. © cliché Bibliothèque Nationale Paris.

ing international success as a writer with the advantages of print, explaining that his works had been so favorably received by the noble and humble alike that some three hundred volumes had already been issued in France, Italy, Burgundy, and Brittany (Munn, 70, n. 64). These statements confirm that the print industry politically empowered Lemaire in his search for a post at the court of France.

Lemaire's involvement in the publication industry appears to have had an irreversible, lasting effect on his literary behavior and attitude toward his works, which his securement of patronage never altered. For although he had obtained a literary position with Margaret of Austria by June 1504, Lemaire continued to promote his own interests, sometimes at the expense of Margaret's.[39] It is unclear, moreover, whether Lemaire's complaint at having to put aside his current literary project to fulfill his obligations in his prologue to the *Couronne Margaritique* (1504–5) (Stecher ed., 4:15–16) was a rhetorical strategy designed to emphasize the sadness of the recent death of Margaret's husband or a thinly veiled critique of the patronage system. Unlike nearly all of his other works, this lengthy allegorical poem of praise written in homage to his patroness never appeared in print during the author's lifetime, reflecting perhaps already at this relatively early stage in their relationship the differences between poet and patroness that would become increasingly strained over time.[40] In fact, Lemaire attributed his growing fame in the areas of Lyons and Bourbon to the printing press, as a 1509 letter to Margaret reveals, adding that such esteem and the public's desire to acquire copies of his works inspired him to write better (Stecher ed., 4:393–94). Although intent upon obtaining economic security through patronage, especially in France, Lemaire seems above all to have desired creative independence, a concern that coincided with, or perhaps grew out of, his increasing involvement in publication.

As the self-promotional tactics associated with the *Temple d'honneur* and the remarks made in his personal letters suggest, Lemaire was becoming aware of the crucial association between print and a writer's potential to reach a wide public and attain fame when he initiated the print-

39. In a letter to Louis Barangier, secretary and counselor to Margaret of Austria, dated March 28, 1512, Lemaire tries to justify the apparent contradiction between the popularity of his works in France and his service to Margaret. He explains that although he had followed the request of several French and Picardian nobles in having his *Illustrations de Gaule et Singularitez de Troye* printed in Lyons, the work had appeared in association with Margaret's name, title, and arms. The six thousand printed volumes of his *Conciles* and *Légende des Vénitiens* had also been published in her honor (*Œuvres*, ed. Stecher, 4:419–23).

40. See Jodogne, *Jean Lemaire*, 70–141, for details regarding Lemaire's relationship with Margaret of Austria and the fact that he would eventually seek a position at the French court.

ing of his very first work.[41] To my knowledge, no earlier vernacular author demonstrated such an explicit interest in book production or exploited the paratextual space of early imprints in such an insistent, consistent, self-conscious fashion.

Lemaire's contribution to the commercialization of the patronage process through the medium of print was indeed a decisive gesture, especially since such literary support had long been associated with the manuscript culture and continued to be so, even after printing had become well-established. He and others, such as La Vigne, Gringore, and Bouchet, clearly did not hold the condescending attitude toward print adopted by their English contemporaries.[42] This difference may be partly explained by the association with print of humanist scholars, such as Josse Badius and Symphorien Champier, in Lyons during the late fifteenth and early sixteenth centuries. It is true, moreover, that the house of France made a conscious use of printed tracts to promote its political policies at the time, and that propagandists such as the *rhétoriqueurs* were often active in the composition of such works, especially during the controversial Italian Wars (see Seguin). At the same time, the less polemical circumstantial poetry generated by court writers often remained in manuscript form, like most of the writings of Jean Marot, Octavien de Saint-Gelais, and Guillaume Cretin. One wonders whether court officials consciously sought to keep this sort of work in the less widely circulating manuscript form, considering it to be "documentation" worthy of posterity, in contrast to short-lived, topical propaganda which they had printed. In any case, by choosing to have his *Temple d'honneur* printed, Lemaire consciously adopted for his personal needs the propagandistic strategy the king had employed for his own political ends, a strategy that aimed for broader and more immediate validation. Like the king's, Lemaire's gesture was political, as he too saw the means and advantage of appealing to a wider readership. Indeed, like the French monarch, Lemaire needed the support of a broader public.

41. See also the remarks Lemaire makes in a June 1506 letter, written two years following the publication of the *Temple d'honneur*. This letter reveals his long-standing curiosity about printing presses, which he directly relates to Symphorien Champier, the humanist-physician of Lyons (Becker, *Jean Lemaire*, 88–89). Lemaire may have been influenced by Latin scholars such as Champier, whose early editions included self-promotional dedicatory letters. The volumes Lemaire saw in the Lyons printing shops in 1506 and earlier must have included some of Champier's Latin works printed up to that time, such as his *De medecine claris scriptoribus* (1506), *Dialogus in magicarum artium destructionem* (ca. 1500), and *Janua logice et phisice* (1498); or some of his French publications, including the *Nef des princes* (1501–2), *Nef des dames vertueuses* (1502–3), and *Le guidon en françoys* (1503). For details, see Wadsworth, 73–171. Jacques Lefèvre d'Etaples was another early humanist whose use of prefatory letters might have influenced Lemaire as well (see Rice ed., *Prefatory Epistles*).

42. See Rose, "Author as Proprietor" and Chartier, *L'ordre des livres*, 48.

Although Antoine Vérard played a central role in promoting Lemaire's publication strategy with the first edition of the *Temple d'honneur et de vertus*, the publisher was not always an ally of the author, as we learned in our examination of the cases of La Vigne and Bouchet. On April 6, 1504, Michel Le Noir printed the *Temple d'honneur et de vertus*, apparently having pirated Vérard's version of the work without Lemaire's authorization (Hornik ed., 14). Even though Le Noir virtually copied the title page of the Vérard edition of the work, his carelessness, or that of his compositor, resulted in several misspellings, including the name of the author himself, who is identified as "Jehan le Maistre."[43] Such inaccuracies annoyed Lemaire, ever conscious of the bad impression they might make on his readers, as he intimated in a letter to Cretin that was published with the third book of his *Illustrations de Gaule* in 1513:

> Toutes lesquelles euvres [two books of the *Illustrations*, the *Légende des Venitiens*, and the *Différence des schismes et conciles*] sont eschappees des bouticques des imprimeurs, tant à Lyon comme à Paris, assez mal corrigees. Car à peines sçauroit on garder les compositeurs de leurs incorrections, quelque diligence qu'on y face, mais les faultes soient imputees à eulx, et pensent les lecteurs et auditeurs que ce ne vient point du vice de l'acteur qui leur donne bons et vrayz exemplaires (Abelard, 114–15).

> All these works hastily left printers' shops in both Lyons and Paris rather poorly corrected. For one is hardly able to prevent compositors from making mistakes, whatever care one takes. Despite the errors ascribed to them, readers and auditors believe that this does not come from the vice of the author, who in fact gives them [readers and auditors] good and true copies.

Not only was Le Noir inattentive to such errors some nine years earlier when he published Lemaire's *Temple d'honneur*, but he took conscious steps to stamp his own identity on the versions he printed, replacing Vérard's name with his own in one of the dedication passages, thereby making it appear as if Lemaire had approached not Vérard but Michel Le Noir (see Hornik ed., 45, variants). He also added his name and address

43. Other typographical errors on the title page alone include "discipse" instead of "disciple" (1504 edition), "Melinet" instead of "Molinet," and "boubon" instead of "bourbon" (ca. 1520 edition). Hornik believes that Lemaire may have reviewed the Vérard edition of the *Temple* (14), but that the number of rhythmic and typographical errors by Le Noir suggests the author did not review his version (16).

at the end of the pirated edition.[44] While this action constituted standard practice at the time—printers seemingly published whatever they wished and often identified themselves in the colophon of such editions—Le Noir's behavior contrasts with that of the first publisher, Vérard, to whom Lemaire had freely given his work and who did not advertise his own name, as he usually did, at the time. Le Noir's unsanctioned appropriation of the work of a living writer, who had apparently initiated publication of his first edition, alerts us to the developing tension between authors and certain printers in early sixteenth-century Paris, a tension that was ultimately translated into La Vigne's and Bouchet's lawsuits a short time later. Whereas details in the paratext of Vérard's edition of the *Temple d'honneur* had focused on the writer and downplayed the role of the book producer, those of Le Noir's unauthorized edition inserted the printer more boldly into the volume's advertising space. The implicit challenge of such an act, both to Lemaire and Vérard, was all the more aggravated by Le Noir's carelessness in printing the work itself: it compromised both the quality of the author's composition and the author's advertising strategy.

A comparison of Lemaire's 1504 *Temple d'honneur* with the 1509 edition of his *Légende des Vénitiens*,[45] his next work printed in France, reveals that the author's approach to the composition and publication of his writings had changed dramatically in the intervening five-year period.[46] Encouraged perhaps by La Vigne's and Bouchet's legal challenges and by his association with humanist printing endeavors in Lyons, Lemaire called attention to his "sovereign" rights as author by emphasizing his control over his publications and over his subject and essentially by aligning himself with the king in the text and paratext of his volumes.

Dominating the title page of the 1509 edition of the *Légende*, printed with two other works by Lemaire, are the announcement of a three-year privilege on the first line—"Avec privilege de trois ans"—and a fleur-de-lis woodcut immediately below (Figure 1.6). The salient feature of this ti-

44. "Cy fine le temple d'honneur imprimé a Paris le vi. jour d'avril mil. cinq cens & quatre par Michel le noir demourant sur le pont saint michel a l'ymaige saint Jehan l'evangeliste" (Here ends the *Temple of Honor*, printed in Paris the sixth day of April 1504 by Michel Le Noir, residing on the Pont Saint-Michel at the sign of Saint John the Evangelist) (fol. d iv^v). Another printing of Le Noir's edition of April 6, 1504 bears the same information without the date (see Appendix 2 below).

45. See Appendix 2 below for a list of the various editions of the *Légende des Vénitiens*.

46. Some of Lemaire's works were printed during these intermediary years, when he was in the service of Margaret of Austria, but they appeared outside France. These include *Les chansons de Namur* (Antwerp: Henri Heckert, October 1507), *La pompe funeralle* and *L'épitaphe de Chastellain et Molinet* (Antwerp: Guillaume Vosterman, 1508 N.S.), and *La concorde du genre humain* (Brussels: Thomas de la Noot, January 1509 N.S.). There is no evidence that Lemaire played a role in their publication.

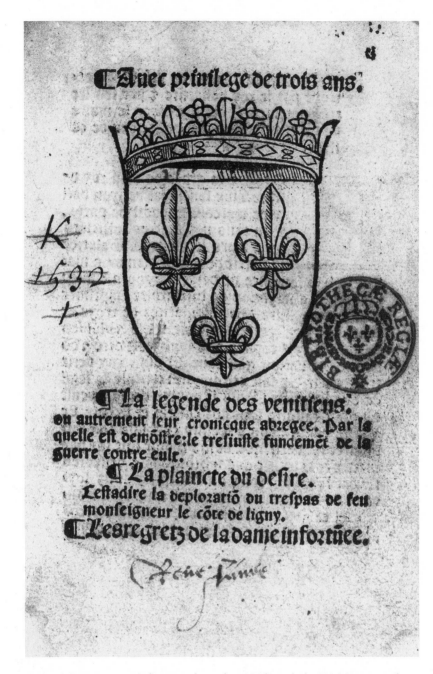

Fig. 1.6. Jean Lemaire's first privilege, from *La légende des Vénitiens*, 1st ed., B.N., Réserve Lb[29] 27, title page. Phot. Bibl. Nat. Paris.

tle page is the book's protection by a three-year privilege—not the author's name, which is deferred until the verso side, where he is announced as "Maistre Jehan Le Maire de Belges, hystoriographe, Acteur de ce livre" (fol. A i˅) (Master Jean Lemaire de Belges, historiographer, author of this book).[47] The displacement of the titles of the volume, usually located in the first line, by the privilege announcement marks Lemaire's strong defiance of other printers, not only in obtaining protection for his work but in advertising it so blatantly. Authorial naming had taken a backseat to publicized protection of the poet's work.

Moreover, the entire text of the privilege Lemaire obtained in July 1509 appears on the verso side of the title page and on the facing folio, where it outlines how he acquired complete control for three years over the printing of his *Légende*.[48] Compared with Gringore's privilege announcement in the *Folles entreprises* of 1505, Lemaire's has been placed in greater prominence. Not only did it move to the front of the volume, but it represents one of the first privileges printed in full in an edition.[49] Did this more evident and expanded advertisement of the privilege reflect a greater need to warn printers of the author's rights as original owner to his work? It would appear so.

The text of the privilege further points out that the author had approached the printer, Jean de Vingle, for the publication of the *Légende* (fol. A ii˄). Lemaire, in fact, exhibited even more initiative than he had for the printing of his *Temple d'honneur* five years earlier. For the privilege details how he had already invested a great amount of time and money in the publication enterprise before his volume was printed:

> . . . que inhibitions et deffenses soyent faictes a tous autres, quelz qu'ilz soyent, de ne les povoir imprimer jusques a trois ans, a ce que ledit exposant puisse estre recompensé de ses paines, sallaires, labeurs, coustz et mises qu'il a faictes a compiler iceulx livres. Et sur ce lui ottroyer noz lettres à ce convenables. (A i˅–A ii)[50]

47. Lemaire's name reappears at the end of the dedicatory letter to Louis de Gorrevod (fol. A iii), in the rubric announcing the *Plainte du Désiré* (fol. E ii˅), and at the end of the same work (fol. G iii). His device ("De peu assez") appears at the end of the *Légende* on fol. E ii.

48. He also acquired control over the publication of his *Illustrations de Gaule et Singularitez de Troye*, but the first of its three volumes did not appear until 1511. For the complete text of the privilege, see Abelard, 70–71. Although included in this edition, the *Plainte du Désiré* and the *Regretz de la dame infortunee* were not named in the July 1509 privilege.

49. One year before publication of Lemaire's *Légende*, Eloi d'Amerval's *Liure de la deablerie* (Paris: Michel Le Noir, 1508) bore on the title page a versified summary of a privilege, the first royal privilege granted by Louis XII (Armstrong, 142). A full text of the privilege appears after the table of contents. See Ward's facsimile edition of the work.

50. Compare with Amerval's privilege, which reveals a similar effort on the part of the author.

. . . that all others [besides Lemaire], whoever they might be, be prohibited from printing [these works] for up to three years, so that the stated requester can be compensated for the pains, salaries, efforts, costs, and services that he has incurred in compiling these works. And upon this, grant him our letters fitting this action.

Lemaire went even further to ensure his control over publication by having the Letters Patent he received from Louis XII registered with the lieutenant general of Lyons, thereby apprising the latter's court of his rights as author. The lieutenant general subsequently issued his own "lettres d'atache," dated August 20, 1509, to accompany the royal privilege (Abelard, 70–71). Lemaire, then, not only sought to control reproduction of his works by initiating their publication in the first place; he also took legal steps to prevent another unauthorized appropriation of his writing, such as Le Noir's, by obtaining a royal privilege and registering his Letters Patent. Influenced perhaps by the actions of his contemporaries a few years earlier, Lemaire adopted Gringore's privilege strategy with this publication.[51] Lemaire, however, ensured an even longer term of control and even more prestige for himself by procuring the king's sanction with a *three-year* rather than just a one-year protection.

By spelling out the effort Lemaire had already made in setting out to print his works, the 1509 privilege reveals the author's increasing commitment to the publication process. The fact that he had sought out a specific printer and that he was seeking to be paid back for the "pains, salaries, efforts, [and] costs" already incurred, presumably through the sale of his books, implies that he had come to serve as his own publisher. In this capacity he doubtless made many decisions regarding the paratext of his edition.

Besides the challenge to other printers that the privilege announcement represents, the title page of the *Légende* also promotes the French king's presence by means of the fleur-de-lis woodcut. The illustration presumably underscores the fact that Lemaire obtained the privilege from Louis XII, who had entered Lyons in late July 1509 on his return to France, following a military campaign against Venice.[52] The monarch's action was not entirely selfless, since the polemic presented by Lemaire in the *Légende des Vénitiens* was fully endorsed by the royal house. Acting

51. Abelard, 60, n. 18, suggests that Lemaire may have been influenced by the use of privileges in Venice during his visits there in 1506 and 1508. Still, it is likely that he was aware of related developments in France itself.

52. In a letter dated July 15, 1509, Lemaire explains to Louis Barangier that he had been hired to organize a festival in honor of the king's *entrée* into Lyons at the time (*Œuvres*, ed. Stecher, 4:375, n. 3).

more as a historian than a poet, the author distances himself from the traditional allegorical dream scenario that had informed much of his earlier work and writes an anti-chronicle in which he attacks past Venetian political activities, particularly from a moralistic stance.[53] It is likely that Lemaire knew he had a better chance of procuring a privilege from the king—not to mention the financial support he also sought—if the work itself promoted a controversial aspect of Louis XII's foreign policy (see Brown, *Shaping*, 51–63). The text's implicit message was that Lemaire would support the king in visible, far-reaching ways through print, if the latter supported him financially.

The fact that the *Légende* functioned at once as a polemical tract that favored the king's foreign policy and as an attempt by the author to obtain French royal support reveals how cleverly Lemaire interwove his needs with those of the monarch. Although the privilege informs the reader that the author had acquired rights to the work from the king, it is impossible to determine whether the monarch actually subsidized this publication in any way.[54] Perhaps the royal privilege represented a compromise form of patronage on the monarch's part. That is, by granting it, the king allowed the author to control publication of his work, at least for a defined period of time, and to profit from its sales. In so doing, however, the king did not have to guarantee the author direct financial support on either a short-term or a long-term basis. As Armstrong points out, "Book-privileges cost the Crown nothing to give" (27). Indeed, Louis XII himself never became Lemaire's official patron, and while the French queen eventually hired him, it was not until several years later.

Although the fleur-de-lis woodcut on the title page of the *Légende* reminds the reader of the king's authorization and anticipates Lemaire's sanctioning of royal policies in the text, it probably does not signify that the author dedicated this edition to the king—however, he might have offered him a copy of it. In fact, a June 1509 letter that precedes the *Légende* in the first edition reveals that it was dedicated to Louis de Gorrevod, bishop of Maurienne, in Savoy, the territory of Margaret of Austria. Ever conscious of maintaining ties with his patroness's domain, Lemaire

53. In his prologue to the *Légende*, discussed below, Lemaire makes the following statement regarding this change: "iay plus eu de regard à ce que la narration historiale soit garnie de verité, que coulouree de fleurs de rhetorique" (I was more concerned that the historical narration be filled with truth than embellished with flowers of rhetoric) (Stecher ed., 3:364).

54. Book specialists would probably disagree with Abelard's assessment (64, n. 32) that the fleur-de-lis woodcut offers proof that the work was edited at the expense of the French king. Many editions published at this time bore the same woodcut, and certainly the house of France did not subsidize them all.

nonetheless invokes a French connection at the end of the *Légende* by thanking Claude Thomassin, King Louis XII's adviser, for interceding on his behalf to obtain the privilege of August 12, 1509 (Stecher ed., 3:402). Lemaire often adopted this bipartisan form of dedication, as evidenced by the complicated publication history of his later works, including the *Illustrations* and the *Epistre du roy a Hector*. That is to say, the author's focus on his search for patronage, which had punctuated the paratext of his *Temple d'honneur et de vertus* in 1504, became a more complex, expanded motivation that dominated the paratext of his subsequent writings.

Thus, Lemaire's explanation of how Gorrevod's name would elicit favor from his readers marks his own double aim: "La decoration de vostre nom tres venerable mise en front de ceste mienne petite euvre, Monseigneur reverend, à qui elle est par droit intitulee, luy donra faveur et autorité entre les lisans, selon la coustume ancienne" (Becker, *Lemaire*, 358–59) (The decoration of your very venerable name, my reverend lord, placed at the head of this little work of mine, for whom it is by right entitled, will give to it favor and authority among its readers, according to ancient custom). The readers mentioned in this dedication are directly addressed as "lecteurs" in Lemaire's prologue to the *Légende*, where he outlines for them the motivation and reasoning behind his writing. There he confirms his own authorial voice as an eyewitness of Venetian events in 1506, as a chronicler, and as an interpreter of events relating to French policy, while relying on classical authorities for each chapter of the work (Brown, *Shaping*, 59–63). Absent from the earlier *Temple d'honneur*, this explicit interaction with a new, vaguely defined group of book purchasers reflects Lemaire's developing consciousness concerning the importance of different reader strategies, a consciousness that informs the composition of his text as well.

This new sensibility is visually borne out in later versions of the *Légende* in which the dedication to Gorrevod is absent and a different woodcut is displayed on the title page. Printed in Paris by Geoffroy de Marnef during the term of Lemaire's control—the 1509 privilege is again incorporated into the paratext—the title page of these editions bears the arms not of the king but of the author (Figure 1.7). Indeed, the initial folio is dominated by the first appearance of Lemaire's elaborate coat of arms, bearing his device "De peu assez," which had earlier found its place at the end of the *Temple d'honneur et de vertus*. In an appropriation of royal attributes that assumes a dramatic form of self-aggrandizement, Lemaire had the insignia of the house of France, which decorated the title page of the first edition of the *Légende*, replaced by his own on the title page of the later editions. In some versions, the reader discovers an announcement that Lemaire was in the queen's employ as well as the joint

Fig. 1.7. Jean Lemaire's coat of arms, from *La légende des Vénitiens*, B.N., Réserve La² 3 (1), title page. Phot. Bibl. Nat. Paris.

arms of King Louis XII and Queen Anne of Brittany.[55] But these are placed on the second folio, after the arms of the author.[56] In an affirmation of Lemaire's new image, his arms later appeared on the title pages of editions of a variety of his works, even those over which he no longer had publication control.[57]

A growing self-conscious control of the text itself accompanied Lemaire's increasing involvement in the publication of his work, and a comparison of the paratext of the *Temple d'honneur* and the *Légende des Vénitiens* reveals that progression. The earlier *Temple d'honneur*, a more traditional epideictic work, had focused exclusively on praising the deceased duke of Bourbon within a mythologic-allegorical framework that embraced both the classical and the *rhétoriqueur* tradition (Hornik ed., 17–39). The author's indirect presence in the text through the voice of the *acteur*-narrator is minimal. Although the letters appended to the poem to promote the author's own literary talents represent a form of self-advertisement unusual for its time among vernacular writings, this publicity remained outside the confines of the text. Beginning, however, with his tribute to the Cambray Peace Treaty of December 1508, the *Concorde du genre humain*, published in Brussels in January 1509, Lemaire succeeded in weaving these paratextual features into the very fabric of his writings, providing a self-reflexive discourse underlying and often entangling with the threads of the principal political discourse of his text. In this intricately woven religious metaphor and allegorized dream vision, Lemaire explicitly and repeatedly presents himself as a self-conscious writer. From the outset, he encourages the reader to identify the *acteur*-narrator with himself through numerous rubrics that announce his manipulation of the text. Moreover, Lemaire's direct references to the creative process often surface from within the political narrative, subtly undermining while at the same time ostensibly promoting it (Brown, "Rise," 64–71).

In one revealing textual passage, Lemaire wittily asks his own work to greet two of his well-placed French associations in Lyons should the volume, published in Brussels, ever end up in that part of the world. The

55. A line added to the rubric introducing the prologue on fol. [aa ii^v], absent from the first edition of the *Légende*, confirms this: "Composee par Jan Lemaire de Belges a present Indiciaire et Historiographe de la Royne" (Composed by Jean Lemaire de Belges, at present chronicler and historiographer of the queen). This version, we may conclude, was published between the time Lemaire was hired by the queen, sometime in late 1511 or early 1512, and the expiration date of the privilege in July 1512.

56. Compare the Paris, B.N., editions Rés. La²3 and Rés. La²3A with the other editions.

57. See, for example, in Tchémerzine, 7:130–71, later editions of the *Légende*, the first, second, and third books of the *Illustrations*, and various editions of the *Epistre du roy a Hector*, many of which were printed after Lemaire's death but followed the title-page strategy of the first editions of these works, whose publication he had supervised.

author refers to the book's unbridled desire to expand to a thousand copies and expose itself to the danger of critics. At the same time, he assures it of a positive reception at the French court by Claude Thomassin and Jean de Perréal, whose names he will immortalize.[58] Here, then, Lemaire integrates his own consciousness of the usefulness of print to attract distant patrons—or their contacts—into his very text, written ostensibly to promote Margaret of Austria's role in the Treaty of Cambray. Indeed, tensions related to Lemaire's experience with Margaret's patronage are evident in this contradiction between subject matter and self-advertisement within his very text. Here the poet thematizes and plays on the distancing that print effected between author and text in such a personal, amusing, and endearing fashion that although the printed volume had become a commodity, Lemaire succeeded in highlighting its engendering process in strong self-conscious terms.

Similar dynamics are at work in the *Légende des Vénitiens*. Published one year after the *Concorde du genre humain*, it supported the French monarch's policies against Venice through a negative presentation of Venetian history. As anticipated in the prologue, Lemaire's remarks about his own qualifications and his actual creation of the work interrupt this so-called *chronique* time and again; special attention is placed on the establishment of his credibility, the veracity of his facts, and the ordering of his material. Through a tightly controlled structure punctuated by extensive use of the first-person plural and underpinned by a contrived naïveté, the author manifests an inordinate preoccupation with providing numerous signposts to help keep his readers on track.[59]

Thus, having gained temporary control over publication of the *Légende*, as the privilege details spell out, Lemaire, demonstrating a verbal independence, had entered the center of his text. That is to say, the author's title-page appropriation of royal signs accompanied the insertion of his voice and credentials into the text not only in the name of the king, but in his own name as well. The implication that the author understood he had to sell "himself"—his genius or his vision—as a way of selling his work, that he had to satisfy a public (and not simply a patron) by guiding its reading, illustrates how Lemaire's new awareness of the text as commodity had been translated into his self-presentation in the narrative. In the evolution from the printing of the *Temple d'honneur* to the *Légende*, strategies regarding the *mise-en-texte* and *mise-en-livre* had become inter-

58. See Jodogne's edition of the *Concorde du genre humain*, fol. C VIIIʳ, for this passage. As pointed out above, Thomassin played a crucial role one year later by helping Lemaire obtain his first royal privilege for the publication of the *Légende des Vénitiens* and the *Illustrations de Gaule et Singularitez de Troye*.

59. For more details on this work and others by Lemaire that demonstrate this aggressive kind of self-consciousness, see my *Shaping*, 52–55, 59–63, 93–107.

connected. Stated another way, Lemaire's experience as publisher directly influenced his writing process. His subsequent works provide equally revealing signs of the author's dual role as a publishing and poetic-historical authority.[60]

Comparison of the paratext and text of the editions of Jean Lemaire's *Temple d'honneur et de vertus* of 1504 and the *Légende des Vénitiens* of 1509 thus offers evidence of the more aggressive, legalized function of the author and the related shift in relationships among bookmakers in late medieval France. We witness a tension arising from writers' dependence on printers for the publication of their works and on patrons for their livelihood, compounded by authors' consciousness of the limitations such involvement imposed on their control over their own words. This tension is at times rendered visible in the paratexts and texts of their literary editions. With the new awareness that his own words had become more commercial and public, that they represented a profitable commodity that others might govern, the author came to see the need to fashion his own image in order to maintain some kind of sovereignty over his literary domain. He no longer simply had to please the king; he, like the king, was now trying to please another public.

It can be maintained, then, that thanks both to the supportive and to the rather unscrupulous activities of early book producers such as Antoine Vérard and Michel Le Noir, French writers chose to stand up for their authorial rights. By implicitly calling attention to their role as owners and originators of their texts and explicitly making advertised use of privileges they had obtained for the protection of their words, La Vigne, Lemaire, Bouchet, and Gringore laid the foundation for the future legislation of copyright laws. They also called more attention to themselves as authors, becoming more self-conscious writers. We discover, for example, how a shift in literary strategies regarding the first-person voice, such as the one that informs Lemaire's *Légende des Vénitiens*, coincided with an alteration in paratextual strategies that brought more prominence to the author's name, function, and image. My discussion in subsequent chapters, concentrating on distinct features that characterize the text and paratext of other late medieval writings, aims to bring to light further details concerning these parallel shifts.

It is true that printers and booksellers came to be protected by privileges more often than authors in the later years of the sixteenth century

60. For details about Lemaire's involvement in the publication of his three-volume *Illustrations de Gaule* in later years, see Abelard. The history of Lemaire's participation in the printing of his other works, such as his *Epistre du roy a Hector*, is equally complex and merits a separate study.

(see details in Armstrong, 208–95). But this evolution can be attributed to the better protection many writers received from literary patrons during the reign of Francis I, as well as to the fact that printers themselves came to form something of an elite, their publication projects becoming an integral part of the humanist enterprise (Renaudet). Surely, signs of an authorial legal consciousness are already visible with Lemaire and several of his contemporaries and would inspire other writers such as Clément Marot. By the 1550s, in fact, not only did the poet Pierre de Ronsard obtain a perpetual privilege from King Henry II, but royal grants stated that authors best oversaw the publication of their own works. While Armstrong maintains that such ideas, although perhaps "in the mind of some authors and of some officials," were not expressed in privileges before 1526 (83–84), the evidence presented here strongly suggests that well before that date vernacular authors used official means aggressively to publicize these attitudes. Indeed, recognition of the crucial role played by late medieval poets in the institutionalization of their rights as writers is long overdue.

2

PARATEXTUAL
INTERACTION BETWEEN POETS
AND BOOK PRODUCERS

he use of title pages, a development that gradually emerged after the invention of the printing press and took hold in France more than elsewhere at the end of the fifteenth century, initially had the practical function of protecting the first page of the text (Hirsch, Labarre). Since the title page constituted readers' or potential bookowners' first contact with a work, however, it also came to play an important role in establishing their relationship with the book and with those engaged in textual production. A crucial component of the paratext, which organizes the book's relationship with its public, the title page embodies one of the most socialized dimensions of literary practice.[1] Because it ultimately served as a tool for different forms of advertisement, moreover, the title page came to symbolize the capitalistic nature of printing. Many people stood to profit from the publicity it potentially provided and from the distortions that could and did occur.

But the title page as well as the colophon also shed light on the relationship between the author and the book producer. For as Genette implies, the publisher constitutes part of the book's public, which encompasses not just the sum of its readers but also those who participate in the diffusion of books (*Seuils*, 72). Moreover, just as authors are guarantors (*auctors*) of their texts, so are publishers the potential guarantors of the authors they present (46). Although Genette, who focuses on modern works for the most part, portrays the relationship between author

---

1. See Genette, *Seuils*, 18, who elsewhere claims that the title page and colophon are the ancestors of what he calls the modern peritext (34, 62–63). While Genette makes the distinction between the *peritexte*, information surrounding the text, and the *épitexte*, information outside the book, both of which make up the paratext (10–11), I am using the term "paratext" to refer to book-related material physically surrounding the literary text, and "extratext" to refer to relevant information beyond the limits of the book.

and publisher as positive and generally unproblematic, in that they share the same goals in the production of the paratext, this was not necessarily so during the early years of print. The paratext was not only a site of transaction between author and reader, as Genette says (8), but also a space that offered insight into the dynamics between author and publisher.

I will argue in the following pages that innovations involving the title page and colophon during the transition from manuscript to print were related to key transactions between writers and publishers. In particular, I suggest that the association between book producers and authors of works reproduced in manuscript form gave rise not only to new kinds of extratextual interaction between these agents with the advent of print but also to modifications in paratextual features. Coinciding with the increasingly defensive posture of French writers by the early sixteenth century, these developments resulted in the enhancement and cultivation of the author's image. Examining the title pages and colophons of writings by Jean Molinet, André de la Vigne, and Pierre Gringore in light of Jean Lemaire's early paratexts, I will probe the changing relationship between vernacular poets and publishers. In some cases, such as Molinet's *Temple de Mars*, the text acquired an importance and identity apart from the writer, as publishers who appropriated it essentially altered the poet's original intent through false title-page publicity. Molinet's later works and those of his contemporaries confirm, however, that as authors participated directly in the publication process, the advertisement of their identity became a more integral part of title pages and colophons. Focus on the author also emerged as a major component of other paratextual features, such as illustrations (Chapter 3 below), and of the text itself (Chapters 4–5). In other words, the *image* of the contemporary vernacular writer, in both its literal and metaphoric sense, gained prominence and visibility with the advent of print, a development that coincided with authors' increasing collaboration with or challenge to book producers and with their growing authority over their audience.

The publication history of Molinet's *Temple de Mars*, his most reproduced work, illustrates these book-production developments in francophone Europe after the introduction of the printing press. A study of the eight manuscripts and twelve printed editions of the *Temple de Mars* shows that the most striking aspect of this transitional period is the coexistence and mutual influence of both systems of reproduction, manuscript and print. Neither fifteenth-century manuscript anthologies nor printed editions of the *Temple de Mars* identify the author paratextually, in contrast to surviving sixteenth-century manuscripts, which promote Molinet in various ways. Moreover, a study of the imprints of the *Temple de Mars* reinforces my claim that Jean Lemaire's paratextual presence in the first edition of his *Temple d'honneur et de vertus* (published 1504) was not necessarily a common development for vernacular authors during the early decades of printing. It appears that new, vernacular authors had little chance of seeing their names appear on the title pages of the first editions of their works, unless they had already established another kind of reputation, such as a religious affiliation. The names of such authors, however, were likely to be featured on title pages of later editions, presumably after their earlier volumes had proved to be good profitmakers.[2]

As with the works of his contemporaries, most of Molinet's writings were originally destined for manuscript reproduction. This relates to the novelty of printed vernacular texts during his lifetime—Molinet began to write poetry before printing even reached France or Burgundy, where he lived—and to the relative financial stability he enjoyed as the official historiographer for the Burgundian court.[3] In fact, Molinet probably offered the *Temple de Mars* to his patron, Charles the Bold, sometime after September 13, 1475. The work, a call for peace presented allegorically as a visit by the wounded narrator to the Temple of Mars, may have celebrated the Truce of Soleuvre, signed by the Burgundian duke and King Louis XI on that date.[4] In Molinet's poetic tour de force the narrator praises Truce and Peace, decries the horrors and evils of War, and calls for a renunciation of Mars. Subsequently, the *Temple de Mars* appeared in

2. An examination of Tchémerzine's work corroborates the observation that the authorship of books written by living vernacular writers did not appear on the title page in many cases. See, for example, the first three known editions (1486–90) of Guillaume Alexis's *Blason de faulses amours* (the title page of the fourth edition [Paris: Lambert, 1493] is missing), his *Déclamation . . . sur l'Evangile* (Paris: Levet & Alisset, 1485), and his *Débat de l'homme et de la femme* (Lyons: Mareschal & Chaussard, ca. 1490; Paris: Trepperel, 1493), as well as Vérard's 1499–1505 edition and subsequent versions of Alexis's *Passetemps des deux Alecis freres* (Rouen: Le Forestier, n.d.). The title page of Jean Bouchet's works written up to 1512 does not advertise his name. See also the many editions of Olivier de la Marche's *Chevalier délibéré* and *Parement et triumphe des dames* as well as Martial d'Auvergne's *L'amant rendu cordelier* (1490), *Louenges* (1492), *Matines* (ca. 1492), and *Arrêts d'Amour* (1508). The name of Olivier Maillard always appeared on the title page of his works, in part because it was always featured in the title (e.g., *La confession de Frere Olivier Maillard* [Paris, 1481]; *Sermons de adventuris Oliveri Maillard* [Paris, 1497]). The fact that he was a well-known religious figure may well explain his greater prominence on title pages. For similar reasons, the name of Octavien de Saint-Gelais, archbishop of Angoulême, likewise appeared on the title pages of his works, most of which were printed after his death in 1502.

3. See Chapters 3 and 5 below for evidence that Molinet's need of financial backing toward the end of his career probably led to his decision to supervise the printing of his works.

4. Without suggesting that the work commemorated this event, as I believe, Picot and Stein, 13, uncover a veiled reference to this event in the text. See Cornilliat, *Couleurs*, 660–75, for an excellent analysis of this work.

numerous anthologies and single editions, attesting to its popularity. Probably it was the poem's lack of historical specifics that facilitated its widespread adaptation.

In three fifteenth-century manuscript anthologies in which it exists, the *Temple de Mars* appears with poems by Molinet's most celebrated predecessors and contemporaries, such as Alain Chartier and Georges Chastellain.[5] Whereas the presence of Molinet's poems in these collections reveals that his works were popular, these manuscript anthologies fostered at the same time a certain anonymity, for the author of the *Temple de Mars* is not advertised anywhere. The lack of title pages, where one might expect to find the author's name, in manuscripts (Vezin, 41) explains in part Molinet's absence. Yet, even on the folio on which the poem appears in the different anthologies, the reader discovers only its title (Figure 2.1).[6] Thus, the *Temple de Mars* figures in these surviving fifteenth-century manuscripts as an anonymous work, at least until the very last words of the poem, which contain Molinet's metaphoric signature (my emphasis): "Pour Dieu, excusés ma simplesse, / S'il est obscur, trouble ou brunet: / Chascun n'a pas son *molin net*" (For God, excuse my simplemindedness, if it is dark, obscure, or somber: everyone does not have his mill clean).[7] Perhaps the author and his poems were so well known in the milieus in which they circulated that it was not necessary to announce or publicize his name. Since metaphoric signatures had been popular in court circles for some time, the audience of this poem would have readily understood the double entendre resulting from the author's name. It is also probable that the compiler of these manuscript anthologies was less interested in focusing on specific authors than on the subject matter that ostensibly unified the different compositions.[8]

Besides its presence in these fifteenth-century manuscript collections, and in a number of sixteenth-century manuscript anthologies that I will discuss below, the *Temple de Mars* appeared in at least eight single edi-

---

5. See Appendix 4 below for bibliographical information on the *Temple de Mars*. For specific details about these anthologies (Paris, B.N., ms. f.fr. 1642, fols. 456^r–460^v; Brussels, Bibl. Royale, ms. II 2545, fols. 275^r–280^v; and Paris, Bibl. de l'Arsenal, ms. 3521, fols. 288^r–292^v), see Dupire, *Etude critique*, 51, 77, 80. Some of these remarks appeared in a different form in my "Du manuscrit à l'imprimé," 104–12.

6. In Paris, B.N., ms. f.fr. 1642, and Brussels, Bibl. Royale, ms. II 2545, the title appears simply as "Le temple de Mars." In the Arsenal ms. 3521 the title reads: "S'ensuit l'istoire du temple de Mars" (Here follows the story of the Temple of Mars).

7. *Les faictz et dictz*, ed. Dupire, 1:76. All subsequent citations of Molinet's works will be from this edition unless otherwise noted. For a discussion of Molinet's signature, see Chapter 4 below.

8. For a discussion of late medieval poetic anthologies, see J. Cerquiligni, "Quand la voix s'est tue."

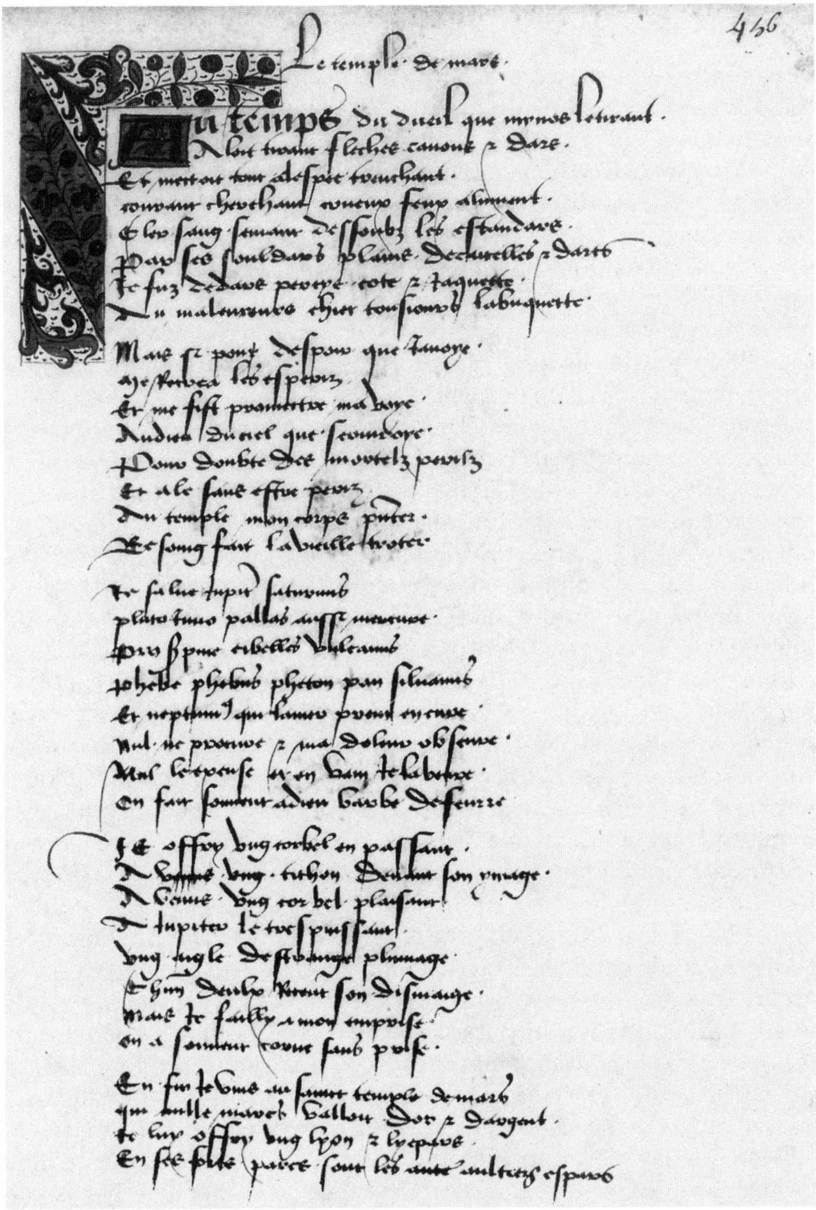

Fig. 2.1. Title without identification of author, from *Le temple de Mars*, B.N., ms. f.fr. 1642, fol 456ʳ. © cliché Bibliothèque Nationale Paris.

tions printed before 1520 and in four anthologies printed during the second quarter of the sixteenth century. Whereas most of Molinet's works were published only after his death in 1507, at least five printed editions of the *Temple de Mars* came out during his lifetime. The fact that publishers reproduced this particular poem more than any other text written by Molinet suggests that the work had acquired an importance and identity of its own, apart from his other works—and, indeed, apart from his identity and jurisdiction. For Molinet's authorship was never advertised in the paratext of these early imprints of the *Temple de Mars*. Moreover, their title-page details reveal that many publishers ignored the author's original intent in writing this work.

Published around 1476 in Flanders or the Netherlands shortly after Molinet had composed it (Picot and Stein, 31–33), the *Temple de Mars* represents a very early printed French text.[9] Yet because it bears no title page and consequently offers no information about its author, readers did not obviously link this edition to Molinet. The first folio merely presents the title, "S'ensieut le temple de mars" (Here follows the *Temple of Mars*), followed immediately by the text (Figure 2.2), while the explicit reads, "Cy fine le temple de mars" (Here ends the *Temple of Mars*). The absence of authorial publicity in the fifteenth-century manuscript versions of Molinet's *Temple de Mars* probably served as a model for this first-known printed edition, as evidenced by a comparison of the title with that of the Arsenal ms. 3521 (see n. 6 above). It is not possible to determine if Molinet, who was living in Valenciennes at the time, knew of or played a role in this first publication of the *Temple de Mars*.

The Parisian printing of the *Temple de Mars* some fifteen years later by Le Petit Laurens (ca. 1491) and by at least three other French printer-booksellers (Jean Trepperel, Jean de Vingle, and Michel Le Noir) over the next decade or so confirms that French publishers had appropriated Molinet's work. I use the word "appropriated," because manipulated title-page information in these imprints suggests that these versions were not published to support the cause of peace and, therefore, did not reflect the author's original critique of warfare actions. Rather, they appear to promote war. Since the use of the word *temple* in a title traditionally implied the glorification of its accompanying name, as exemplified by Lemaire's *Temple d'honneur et de vertus*, publishers apparently misread or used in a consciously misleading manner Molinet's pacifist message, which in fact criticized Mars. The title-page woodcuts bear this out.

Two contemporary versions of the *Temple de Mars* present warrior-positive illustrations in a prominent position (title page verso), as the

9. Coq, 72, claims that the first book printed in French was a translation of Donatus, *Des VIII parties d'oraison* [Pays-Bas, ca. 1471–73].

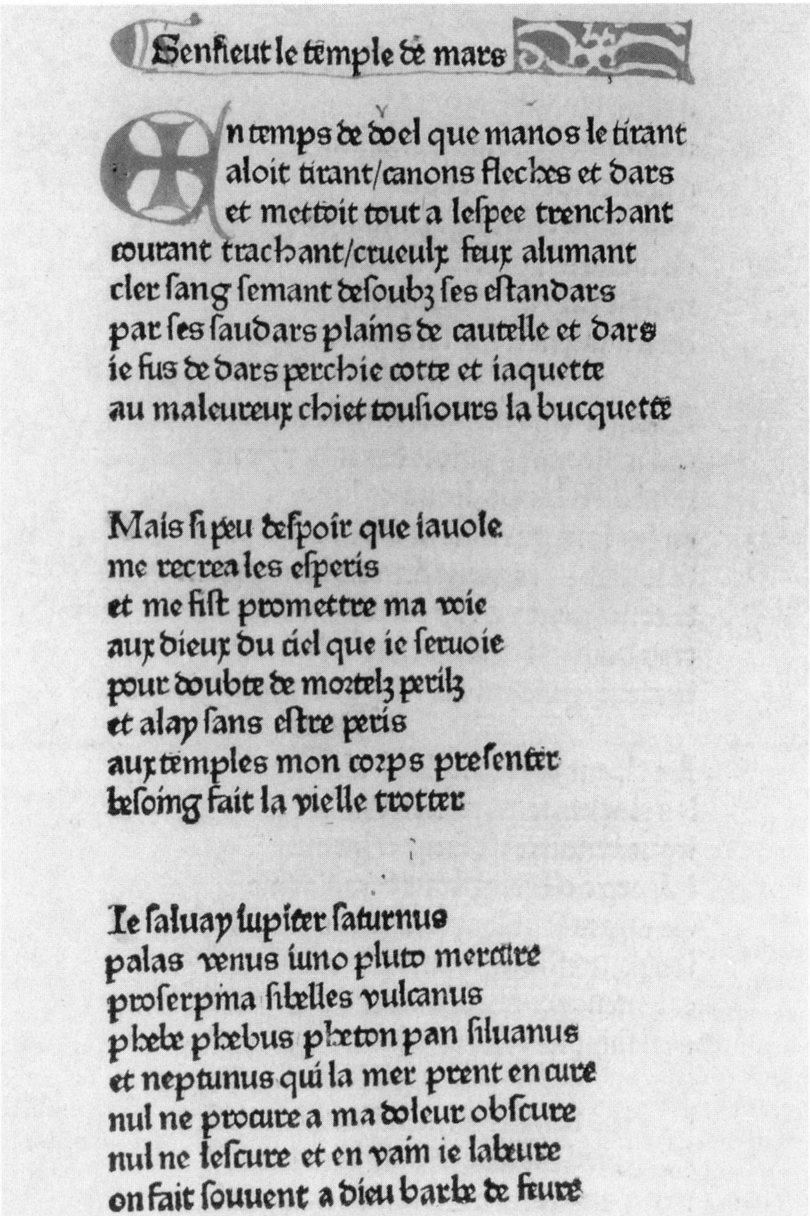

Senfieut le temple de mars

En temps de doel que manos le tirant
aloit tirant/canons fleches et dars
et mettoit tout a lespee trenchant
courant trachant/crueulx feux alumant
cler sang semant desoubz ses estandars
par ses saudars plains de cautelle et dars
ie fus de dars perchie cotte et iaquette
au maleureux chiet tousiours la bucquette

Mais si peu despoir que iauole
me recrea les esperis
et me fist promettre ma voie
aux dieux du ciel que ie seruoie
pour doubte de mortelz perilz
et alay sans estre peris
aux temples mon corps presenter
besoing fait la vielle trotter

Ie saluay lupiter saturnus
palas venus iuno pluto mercure
proserpina sibelles vulcanus
phebe phebus pheton pan siluanus
et neptunus qui la mer prent en cure
nul ne procure a ma doleur obscure
nul ne lescure et en vain ie labeure
on fait souuent a dieu barbe de feurre

Fig. 2.2. Title without identification of author, from *Le temple de Mars*, 1st ed., Musée Condé, IV.G.15, fol. 1.

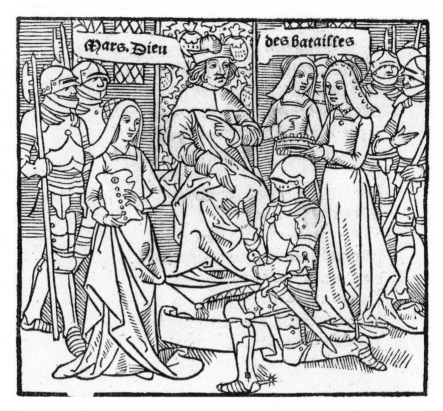

Fig. 2.3. A prince, representing Mars, enthroned and surrounded by courtiers, from *Le temple de Mars*, 2d ed., title page verso. The Pierpont Morgan Library, New York. PML 75124.

reader views a prince surrounded by his knights and courtiers (Figures 2.3 and 2.4).[10] A striking contrast exists in these imprints between the images appearing in the paratext and the author's critique of war, for these illustrations glorify the Temple of Mars, representing the court of a prince (presumably that of the French king). In a gesture that anticipated Vérard's false attribution of Bouchet's *Regnars traversant* in 1504, publishers of these volumes apparently reprinted the *Temple de Mars* in order to reap benefits from their support of the French king in his bellicose confrontations. The dates of publication of all these Parisian editions (ca. 1491, 1497–98, 1501–5, 1506–9) suggest such political motives, for they coincide with periods of conflict between the house of France and its ad-

10. Three posthumous Parisian editions printed around 1520 likewise contain woodcuts depicting court scenes (see the copies in Paris, B.N., Rés. Ye 1282, Rés. Y² 2579, and Paris, Bibl. de l'Ecole Nationale Supérieure des Beaux-Arts, Rés. Masson 469). For reproductions of two of these title pages, see Tchérmerzine, 8:365, 367.

Fig. 2.4. A prince, representing Mars, observes a tournament, from *Le temple de Mars*, 3d ed., B.N., Réserve Ye 1127, title page verso. Phot. Bibl. Nat. Paris.

versaries: the war waged by King Charles VIII against Brittany, ending in October 1491; Charles's descent into Italy in 1494, capture of Naples in 1495, and continuing struggles to maintain a stronghold there until his death in 1498; the confrontation between the Milanese and Louis XII in 1499 and 1500, between the French monarch and the king of Aragon in Naples from 1501 to 1504, and between the French king again and the Genoans from 1499 to 1507 (Bridge, vols. 2–3). The Parisian editions of the *Temple de Mars* likely reflect the intersection of the French king's need to obtain public support for his controversial military actions and the publisher's desire to attract a wide book-purchasing readership, irrespective of the author's original intent.

Thus, the Parisian imprints of the *Temple de Mars*, virtually ignoring authorship identification, focused paratextually on a distorted version of Molinet's text. These visual exaltations of the prince and a corresponding manipulation of the author's original message demonstrate that a definite correlation existed between the title-page advertisement and the publication objective of the work. They confirm as well that years before the lawsuits of La Vigne and Bouchet, Parisian book producers were printing spurious versions of authors' works, very likely without their knowledge. Royal propagandistic desires may have influenced, if not sanctioned, such action.

This misrepresentation of Molinet's *Temple de Mars*, a revised, early print version of *mouvance*,[11] coupled with the absence of any acknowledgment by publishers of his authorship, suggests that living vernacular authors lacked a widespread, public authority in the late fifteenth and early sixteenth centuries. Although the last verse of the text always contained Molinet's metaphoric signature, the noncourtly reader must less readily have understood the reference to both a mill and the poet's name, as the printed versions of the *Temple de Mars* multiplied and spread to areas distant from Molinet's home in Valenciennes. Nevertheless, the poet did lay claim to a certain renown at the time, and it is difficult to believe that the French publishers themselves did not recognize his signature at the end of the work. Perhaps Molinet's authorship went consciously unadvertised for political reasons. His earlier association with the Burgundians and his continuing role as official court chronicler for Maximilian of Austria and then his son Philip the Handsome, with whom the French monarch had rather strained relations, may explain the absence of the author's name in the paratext of the French editions. In any case, from the moment it made its way into France, and perhaps even beforehand, the printed version of this work apparently had an independent and near-anonymous existence.

In contrast, printers' names and marks appeared in many of these editions. For example, the Le Petit Laurens edition of circa 1491, which bears the first surviving title page of the *Temple de Mars* series, portrays the printer's mark squarely on the first folio, below the title (see Tchémerzine, 8:362), superseding in importance the woodcut of the prince and his court that is displayed on the verso side of the title page. If the potential book purchaser did not recognize the title-page mark of Le Petit Laurens, the colophon provided additional information: "Cy finist le temple de Mars, Dieu des batailles. Imprimé a Paris. Par Le Petit Laurens en la rue Saint Jasquez pres saint Yvez" (Here ends the *Temple of Mars*, god of all battles. Printed in Paris by Le Petit Laurens on the rue Saint-Jacques near Saint-Yves). Clearly the printer's use of paratextual space aimed at advertising his name and function as well as his implicit association with the French court, rather than promoting the literary significance and authorship of the work itself. Furthermore, the epithet "Dieu

11. See my "Author, Editor," in which I argue that *mouvance* had moved to the margins, or paratext, of works by the late fifteenth century.

des batailles," appended to the title here and elsewhere, heightens the misleadingly positive characterization of the *Temple de Mars* depicted in the woodcuts. Its glorification of the god of war—that is, of the French prince at war—again contradicts the author's original message. This distorting epithet eventually worked its way from the colophon of the Petit Laurens edition to the title page of nearly all single published versions, beginning with the 1501–5 edition attributed to Michel Le Noir (see Tchémerzine, 8:366).[12]

Even more predominant is Jean Trepperel's mark on the title page of his first edition of the *Temple de Mars*, dating from circa 1497–98 (see Tchémerzine, 8:363), with the colophon adopting the misleading epithet and providing the printer-bookseller's address as well: "Cy finist le temple de Mars Dieu des batailles. Imprimé a Paris. Par Jehan Treperel demourant sur le pont Nostre Dame A l'ymaige Saint Laurent" (Here ends the *Temple of Mars*, god of all battles, printed in Paris by Jean Trepperel, residing on the Notre Dame bridge at the sign of Saint Lawrence). Whereas the very first edition of the *Temple de Mars*, dating from circa 1476 and printed outside France, lacked a title page, epithet, and related publication information, we can see that by the 1490s Parisian publishers had consistently seized the advertisement potential offered by the title page. This doubtless reflects the competitive spirit of those involved in the Parisian book trade at the time.

By contrast, the title page of the Lyons edition of 1502 bears not a printer's mark but a woodcut depicting the horrors of war on the recto and verso sides of the title page (Figure 2.5). Although the colophon of this edition presents the date and place of publication for the first time in the history of the *Temple de Mars*—"Sy finist le temple de Mars imprimé a Lyon. L'an.Mil.cccc.&.ii. Le xviii. jour de desembre" (Here ends the *Temple of Mars*, printed in Lyons in 1502, the 18th day of December)—the printer, subsequently identified as Jean de Vingle, remains unnamed (Picot and Stein, 39–41). This more modest advertising style seems to reflect the less intense competition of Lyons. As the only known single imprint of the *Temple de Mars* in which the title-page illustration faithfully translates the text's message, the Lyons edition avoids as well the added textual distortion of the ambiguous epithet "Dieu des batailles." In the end, none of the editions printed during Molinet's lifetime announced his authorship in the paratext, thus following the pattern set by the

12. The title page of the Le Noir edition reads (my emphasis) "Le Temple de Mars, Dieu *de bataille*" (The Temple of Mars, God of Battle). The same title reappears in Trepperel's second edition (1506–9), which, like his first (1497–98), bears the printer's mark on the title page. The similarity between the Le Noir and Trepperel versions can probably be attributed to the familial ties of these two men (Renouard, 354), who may have collaborated in these publications.

Fig. 2.5. Mars as a violent god, from *Le temple de Mars*, 4th ed., B.N., Cat. Roth-schild 2580, title page. © cliché Bibliothèque Nationale Paris.

fifteenth-century manuscript anthologies as well as the first edition of the work. Yet, diverging from the first edition, some printed versions did display the sign of the printer on the title page and announced his name in the colophon, indicating that the printer controlled paratextual space in a self-promotional way during the early years of print and that his identity, rather than the writer's, carried greater authority in the book market. But, as happened in the case of La Vigne and Lemaire, Molinet's subsequent involvement in the reproduction of his texts would change this.

While one might have expected the printing of a single work to give rise to a higher profile for the writer who created it, as it would a decade later with the publication of Lemaire's first literary narrative, in fact the imprints of Molinet's *Temple de Mars* downplayed his identity. Several sixteenth-century manuscript copies of the text promoted Molinet's authorship, however. In the first-known manuscript anthology of 129 of Molinet's own poems, apparently transcribed during his lifetime at the beginning of the sixteenth century, the author's role receives singular prominence.[13] Despite the absence of a title page, the scribe draws attention to the author at the outset of the manuscript, through a series of verses written on the verso of the first folio. These reflect his admiration for the talents of Molinet, whom he reveres like a noble ("o gentil Molinet") as he focuses on his name, strategically located at the rhyme of the first verse and recalled through a *rime équivoquée* in the third line (my emphasis):

> Pour collauder, o gentil *Molinet*,
> Ton nom, ton art, ton sens, ta theoricque,
> J'ay reduict en ce beau *mol lit net*,
> Qui bien escript ne orthographié n'est,
> Plusseurs tes fais en prose ou rethoricque,
> Priant a ceux qui cest livre liront
> Et qui pour toy de profundis diront
> Que avec Fenin qui aincoires ne fine
> . . . soient sine fine.[14]

In order to praise, O noble Molinet, your name, your art, your meaning, your theory, I have put in this beautiful, soft, clean bed, which is neither well written nor well spelled, many of your works in prose or verse, beseeching those who will read this book and who will say "de profundis" for you that with Fenin, who still does not finish . . . may they be without end.

13. See Dupire, *Etude critique*, 9, who describes and dates the Tournai, Bibl. Communale, ms. 105 (destroyed by a fire in 1940). The passage quoted below seems to confirm that Molinet was still living at the time of transcription, unless the seventh verse, which is written in the future tense, refers to his recent death.

14. Quoted in Dupire, *Etude critique*, 9. Philippe de Fenin was a contemporary poet and friend of Molinet, but because of the fragmentary nature of these lines, it is difficult to understand the allusion to him.

This dedication to Molinet suggests that the poet himself may have ordered the manuscript book to be copied. If he in fact did serve as the compiler-editor of his own anthology, Molinet would have been following in the footsteps of his illustrious predecessors Guillaume de Machaut, Christine de Pizan, and Charles d'Orléans. In any case, the decision to create an anthology of Molinet's works contributed to a heightened awareness of the writer. Even though the reader finds only the title *Le temple de Mars* on folio 119ᵛ, it is obvious that Molinet is its author, since the anthology contains his writings alone.

Thus, the copyist's verses draw the reader's attention first to Molinet's identity and talent—and then, in imitation or anticipation of the writer's conventional self-deprecating tendencies, to his own function in the book-producton process, as he emphasizes his concern for a careful transcription of Molinet's works.[15] Given that the author supervised the print publication of several single editions of other works of his around the same period,[16] it is noteworthy that a collection of his poetry appeared in manuscript form. Perhaps the anthology was destined to be the private, single issue of the author alone, or the collection was to circulate within a restricted literary circle, or manuscript reproduction of such an anthology was considered to be more desirable than print reproduction at the time. What is clear is that this collection served as a source for subsequent versions that also carefully identified the author.

This version of the *Temple de Mars*, then, reflects a change of authorial presence—from the fifteenth-century manuscript anthologies and imprints, which contained in more or less anonymous form one to several works of Molinet, to a sixteenth-century manuscript collection of his poems alone, which advertised from the outset the author's name and talents. In each of the three surviving manuscript anthologies dating from the sixteenth century, Molinet's name follows the title of his work. Despite the fact that these collections included works by other authors and that the title page announces no names whatsoever, a rubric preceding the *Temple de Mars* publicizes Molinet's authorship (Figure 2.6).[17]

15. Compare verse 4 of this liminal poem—"Qui bien escript ne orthographié n'est"—with Molinet's own words in the last verses of the *Temple de Mars*: "J'ay paint son temple ou j'ai ouvré / Rudement, selon ma faiblesse" (I painted his temple where I worked / In simple form, due to my weakness).

16. *La ressource du petit peuple* (Valenciennes: [Jean de Liège], n.d. [ca. 1500]; *La robe de l'archiduc, nouvellement composee par Maistre Jehan Molinet* (Valenciennes: Jean de Liège, n.d. [ca. 1500]); and *La naissance de Charles d'Autriche* (Valenciennes: Jean de Liège, n.d. [ca. 1500]). For details, see Giard and Lemaître.

17. For specific details on these manuscripts (Paris, B.N., ms. f.fr. 1717 [entitled *Vers du temps du dernier duc de Bourgogne*], fols. 70ᵛ–76ᵛ; Paris, B.N., ms. f.fr. 12490, fols. 148ʳ–154ᵛ; and Paris, B.N., ms., nouv. acq., f.fr. 10262, fols. 194ʳ–201ᵛ), see Dupire, *Etude critique*, 52–54, 66–67, 73–75.

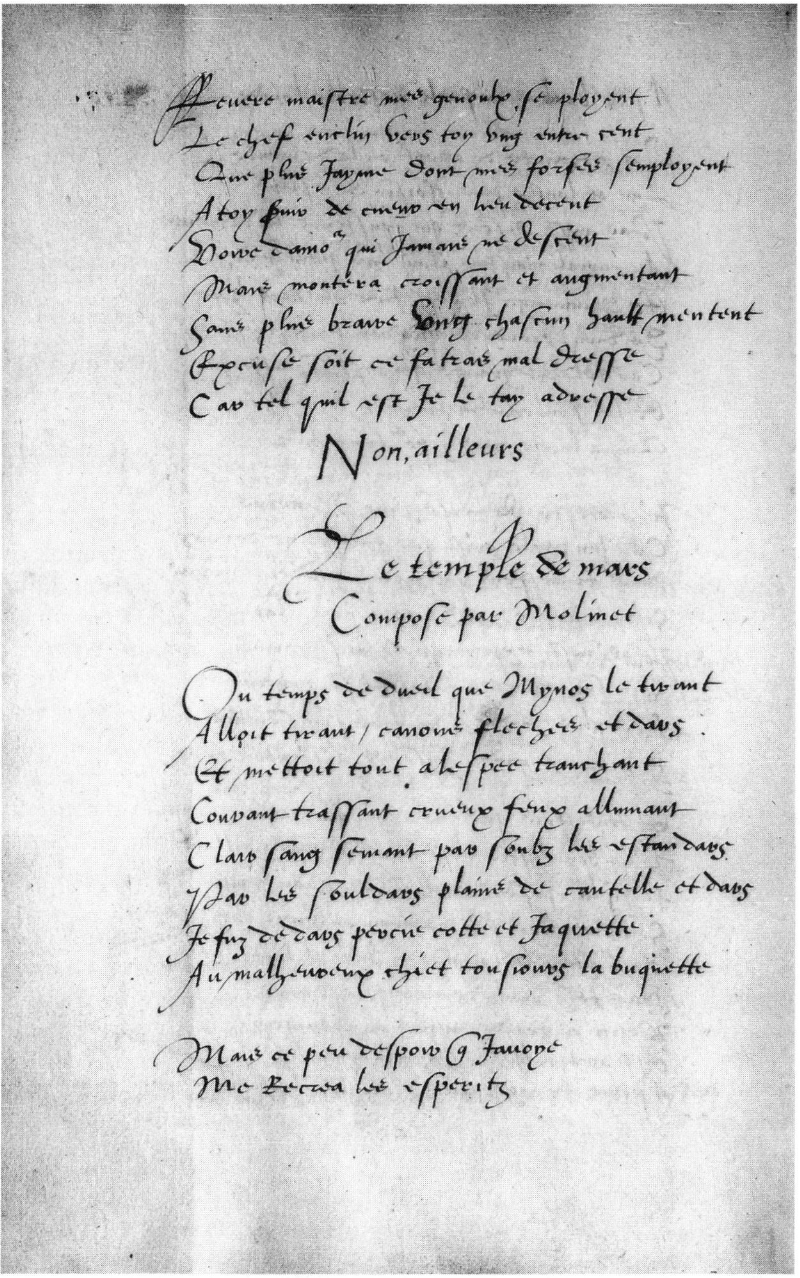

Heurese maistre mes genoulx se ployent
Le chef enclin vers toy ung enter rent
Que plus Jayme dont mes forces semployent
A toy suis de cueur en hurterent
Dowe amo qui Jamais ne sofrent
Mars montera croissant et augmentant
Sans plus braue Songs chascun hault mentent
Excuse soit ce fatras mal dresse
Car tel quil est Je le tay adresse

Non, ailleurs

Le temple de mars
Compose par Molinet

Ou temps de dueil que Mynos le tirant
Alloit tirant / canons flecches et dards
Et mettoit tout a lespee tranchant
Couvant traissant crueulx feux allumans
Clair sang semant par soubz les estandars
Par les souldars plains de cautelle et dars
Je fuz de dars perce cotte et Jaquette
Au malheureux chiet tousiours la buquette

Mais ce peu despoir G Janoye
Me recrea les espritz

Fig. 2.6. Title with identification of author, from *Le temple de Mars*, B.N., ms. f.fr. 1717, fol. 70^v. Phot. Bibl. Nat. Paris.

Whereas three posthumous single editions of the *Temple de Mars* dating from circa 1520 seem to derive from the anonymous Parisian imprints of the work, since publicity of Molinet's name is absent from the paratext and the distorting epithet accompanies the title, the prominent advertisement of Molinet's authorship in several other posthumous Parisian editions indicates an affinity with the sixteenth-century manuscript anthologies. These include a collection of multiauthored poems printed in February 1526 and three principal editions of his collected works, the *Faictz et dictz*, published in 1531, 1537, and 1540, whose title page and colophon focus on the author.[18] Despite Molinet's death some twenty-five years earlier, his renown obviously lived on, thanks in part to his own editorial initiatives at the end of his career.

It is not just the author's name, however, that figures on the first folio of these editions. In all these later versions, Molinet shares title-page space with the *librairie* (Figure 2.7). That is to say, the title page displays the bookseller's name more prominently than it does the printer's.[19] Thus, the paratext of the later editions of the *Temple de Mars* and other works of Molinet suggests that both author and bookseller had come to play increasingly decisive roles in the book-production process during the first quarter of the sixteenth century.

The fascinating publication history of the *Temple de Mars* represents an exceptional case in Molinet's literary repertoire, for most of his other compositions remained more or less anonymous in manuscript collections, at least until his death, and so reflect a more medieval concept of book reproduction. Because it was such an early imprint and was re-edited so many times, the *Temple de Mars* provides access to important changes precipitated by the advent of print in Europe, changes that inevitably influenced the creative enterprise of vernacular writers: (1) the existence of manuscript and printed versions of the same text at the same time; (2) the simultaneous reproduction of anthologized and single versions of the same work; (3) the adoption and evolution of title pages,

18. The title page of the 1526 *receuil* announces "Le Temple de Mars fait et composé par J. Molinet" (The *Temple of Mars* written and composed by J. Molinet), and the author's name appears both at the point the poem was inserted in the collection (fol. F ii) and again in the colophon. The title page of the other editions reads: "Les Faictz et Dictz de feu de bonne memoire Maistre Jehan Molinet" (The *Events and Words* of the deceased Master Jean Molinet). For other details, see Dupire, *Etude critique*, 105, and Picot and Stein, 44–64.

19. Although Molinet and five other authors are carefully listed on the first folio of the 1526 edition—each name stands out in contrasting red letters—they share title-page space with the bookseller-publisher Jean Longis, whose name and address appear at the bottom of the page as well as in the colophon. The title page of the *Faictz et dictz* editions publicizes this sharing of privileged paratextual space by providing the work's title, author, bookseller-publisher's address and sometimes (1531 ed.) his mark as well, date of publication, and privilege. See Dupire, *Etude critique*, 105, and Picot and Stein, 44–64.

Fig. 2.7. Title with identification of author, from *Les faictz et dictz*, 1531 ed., B.N., Réserve Ye 41, title page. Phot. Bibl. Nat. Paris.

which reflected the shifting relationship between the author and other book producers; and (4) the contradiction between an author's intended message and the publisher's paratextual advertisement of it.

An examination of other works by Molinet, such as his *Art de rhéto-rique*, provides evidence of other forms of paratextual manipulation by publishers. Elsewhere, for example, I have shown how Vérard's 1493 publication of the *Art de rhétorique* eliminated mention of Molinet's name, which had figured in the incipit and dedicatory prologue of a fifteenth-century and a sixteenth-century manuscript of the work ("Eveil"). In fact, several luxury copies of that edition identified a bogus author, Henry de Croy. All subsequent editions, moreover, continued to omit reference to the author, although publishers like Vérard and Trep-perel advertised their own names and marks in the paratext. Even though Molinet's name disappeared in the transition from manuscript to print in this case, it was restored to title-page prominence in 1500 with the publication of his *Roman de la rose moralisé*:

> C'est le romant de la rose
> Moralisié cler et net
> Translaté de rime en prose
> Par vostre humble molinet.

This is the *Romance of the Rose*, morally expounded in clear and pol-ished fashion, translated from verse into prose by your humble Mo-linet/little mill.

This trend culminated in the 1503 Lyons edition of Molinet's *Naissance de Charles d'Autriche*, in which the printer Guillaume Balsarin arranged the print on the title page in such a fashion that the author's name stood out, because it alone occupied the last line:

> Cy comence la tresdesiree et prouffitable naissance
> du tresillustre enfant Charles d'Autriche filz de trespuis
> sant prince monseigneur l'archeduc tresredoubté prince
> Laquelle nativité a esté composee par ung fatiste appellé
> Molinet.

Here begins the very desired and profitable birth of the very illus-trious child Charles of Austria, son of the very powerful prince, lord the archduke, very revered prince, whose nativity was composed by a writer named Molinet.

The juxtaposition of Molinet's prominently placed name with an author-woodcut (see Figure 3.12 below) reinforces his newly acquired visibility on the title page of his works and reflects his enhanced literary status by the end of his career. The author's decision around 1500 to direct the publication of three of his works in single editions (see n. 16 above) and his apparent engineering of the manuscript collection of much of his life's work at about the same time are in my opinion more than coincidental occurrences. These very likely constituted defensive gestures on the part of Molinet in response to the inequities he and other living authors had endured at the hands of publishers.

In the following chapters, we shall see how modifications to illustrations and signatures in the manuscripts and imprints of some of Molinet's other works accompanied an increase in the publicity of his image. The title pages and colophons of the writings of his contemporaries tell a similar story.

While Molinet's initial compositions appeared in manuscript form, Gringore's works, beginning with the appearance of his *Chasteau de labour* in October 1499, almost uniformly reached their audience in printed form.[20] Perhaps the author's lack of official literary status at the time led him to seek his fortune through print, much like Lemaire five years later. A reading of the paratext of Gringore's first two printed works, the *Chasteau de labour* and the *Chasteau d'amours*, reveals that publishers' authority dominated textual production and marketing more than the author's. Signs of Gringore's growing presence and involvement in book production, however, began to emerge at this early date.

Just as the early Parisian imprints of Molinet's *Temple de Mars* emphasized the printer's presence on the first folio, so too the printer Philippe Pigouchet dominated the title page of the four early editions of Gringore's first work, the *Chasteau de labour* (Figure 2.8).[21] His initials and name are prominently displayed in large letters inside his mark, which itself occupies three-fourths of the folio. Below, letters one-third the size of those used for the printer's name present the title and date of the work: "Ce present livre appellé le Chasteau de labour a esté achevé le .xxii. iour de octobre. Mil. CCCC. iiii xx. & dix-neuf pour Symon Vostre:

20. The few works of Gringore that remained in manuscript form tended to commemorate royal figures, who probably preferred individualized manuscript books: *La vie de Saint Louis* (Paris, B.N., ms. f.fr. 17511); *L'entrée de Marie d'Angleterre à Paris le 6 novembre 1514* (London, B.L., Cot. ms. Vespasian B.II); *Le couronnement, sacre et entrée de la royne à Paris, le 9 mai 1517* (Nantes, Bibl. Mun., ms. 1337). Manuscript copies of works that appeared in print exist as well: *L'entreprise de Venise* (Soissons, Bibl. Mun., ms. 204, fol. 85); *Les abus du monde* (New York, Pierpont Morgan Library, ms. 42); *L'obstination des Suysses* (Paris, B.N., ms. f.fr. 1690, fols. 5^r–7^r); part of the *Menus propos* (Paris, B.N., ms. f.fr. 2274); and parts of the *Heures de Nostre Dame* (Paris, B.N., ms. f.fr. 2336).

21. For bibliographical details about this work, see Appendix 5 below. Some of the following ideas appear in different form in my "Interaction," 33–50.

Fig. 2.8. Pigouchet's printer's mark, from *Le chasteau de labour*, 1st ed., Bibliothèque Mazarine, Inc., 1055, title page.

libraire demourant a Paris en la rue Neufve Nostre Dame a l'enseigne sainct Jehan l'evangeliste" (This present book entitled the *Castle of Labor* was finished the 22nd day of October 1499 for Simon Vostre, bookseller-publisher residing in Paris on the rue Neuve Notre Dame at the sign of Saint John the Evangelist). The name and address of the *libraire*, features absent from the early imprints of Molinet's *Temple de Mars*, alert the reader to the increasingly important role played by booksellers in Parisian book production by the end of the fifteenth century. Again, the author's name is absent from this privileged advertising space. Gringore's identity remains unmentioned until the end of the text, where the final stanza is generated by his acrostic signature.[22]

While it is impossible to ascertain who determined the particular arrangement of names on the title page of the *Chasteau de labour*, the fact that Gringore's paratextual presence became more obvious in his subsequent works, whose publication he controlled, suggests that only later did the author become actively involved in such decision making. Nonetheless, evidence associated with a second publication, as we shall see, implies that the team of Pigouchet and Vostre had the author's sanction to print his first book.

The two series of verses immediately following the text of the *Chasteau de labour* offer further evidence that marketing purposes dictated the use of paratextual space. The first directly solicits potential book purchasers by informing them of the work's moralistic subject matter:

> Prenez en gré ce simple livre
> Lequel vous monstrera l'adresse
> De povreté ou de richesse:
> Mais que vous le veuillez ensuyvre.

Take willingly this simple book, which will show you the residence of poverty and richness, provided you wish to find it.

It is not clear whether these words were "borrowed" from the text by the publisher, or whether the author collaborated with the book producers in rewriting the verses that end his prologue.[23] The voice of Gringore's authoritative narrator has nonetheless found an important place in the paratext, as it unites the author's moralistic textual concerns with the bookseller's extratextual capitalistic desires.

The second series of verses functions more like a colophon, reminding book producers of the momentous date of the collapse of the Notre Dame bridge, the location of many booksellers' shops:

22. See Chapter 4 below for a discussion of Gringore's signatures.
23. Compare them with the lines of the prologue itself, quoted in Chapter 5 below.

Le vendredi de devant la Toussainctz
Vingt et cinquiesme octobre du matin
Mil. CCCC. nonante neuf rien mains
Le noble pont Nostre Dame print fin.

The Friday before All Saints' Day, October 26th, 1499, in the morning, nothing less, the noble Notre Dame bridge met its end.

Did Gringore himself compose these verses, which presumably marked the day on which printing of his *Chasteau de labour* ended? It is likely that he did.

Thus, prominent advertisement of both printer and bookseller in the paratext of the four Pigouchet editions of the *Chasteau de labour* suggests that these figures wielded great authority in their aggressive marketing strategy, while the author, whose name did not merit a place on the title page or in the colophon, perhaps because he was not known well enough at the time, played a secondary role in book production. Moreover, even those editions of the *Chasteau de labour* that were printed later, when Gringore had established a literary reputation, never bore his name in the paratext. The pattern set with the first edition of Gringore's work—namely, omitting the author's identity—was simply repeated in all its subsequent editions.[24] Control of the initial phase of reproduction clearly had important ramifications for an author's identity and image.

With Gringore's second publication, a year after his first, the author had an even more disconcerting experience. Like the title page of the *Chasteau de labour*, that of the first edition of the *Chasteau d'amours* bears the mark of Philippe Pigouchet (see Tchémerzine, 6:40).[25] Noticeably absent from the title page, in comparison with Pigouchet's editions of the *Chasteau de labour*, are the date of publication and the publisher's identity. Again, the poet's name does not appear paratextually. Acrostics generating the final stanzas of the text, however, do identify Gringore; they also name the printer and bookseller (see Chapter 4 below). Some

24. Although later editions of the *Chasteau de labour* generally follow this initial pattern (see Jacques Le Forestier's 1500 Rouen edition and Gaspard Philippe's Parisian edition [1502–5]), Gilles Couteau's circa 1505 edition does not identify the printer on the title page; his name and address are relegated to the colophon, and his mark appears on the last folio. For details, see Tchémerzine, 6:30–33. Is it a coincidence that, at about the same time Couteau's edition of the *Chasteau de labour* reversed an established trend by downplaying the printer's presence, Gringore obtained the first-known vernacular author privilege in France for his *Folles entreprises*?

25. For bibliographical details about the *Chasteau d'amours*, see Appendix 5 below.

sort of collaboration between the author and the two book producers had led to this absorption of traditional colophon material into the text itself. Here is a concrete sign of Gringore's growing involvement in the publication and marketing of his own writings. Yet, subsequent editions of the *Chasteau d'amours* do not reflect such cooperation.

No name of an author, printer, or publisher is present on the title page of Michel Le Noir's December 1500 edition of the *Chasteau d'amours*; it bears only the title along with a rather strange, doubtless reused wood-cut, which does not have an obvious association with Gringore's narra-tive (see Tchémerzine, 6:38). Since, as I have shown elsewhere, this par-ticular edition constituted an unauthorized printing—Le Noir replaced the author's name with his own in the final acrostic stanza—it may well be that the printer chose not to advertise his identity too prominently by placing it on the title page or even in the colophon.[26] Le Noir acted more boldly, however, in placing one of his printer's marks, which repeats his entire name in prominent letters, on the last folio of his February 1501 edition of the *Chasteau d'amours* (Figure 2.9). Exhibiting in more extreme terms the behavior of other publishers, Le Noir took care to advertise his own name both within and outside the text of this edition, while sup-pressing the author's. Such actions, which further justified the legal challenge launched against him by La Vigne just three years later, reveal the potential abuse of power printers and publishers often displayed. For presumably a good number of copies of these editions of the *Chasteau d'amours* circulated and were sold without acknowledgment of Grin-gore's authorship. The only name associated with the work in the read-er's mind was Michel Le Noir's.

By printing only the first forty-one stanzas of the *Chasteau d'amours* in his circa 1500 edition, which probably derived from Le Noir's version, Jean Trepperel also omitted the final stanza containing Gringore's name.[27] Thus, in contrast to those editions whose text, and therefore au-thorial signature, Pigouchet and Vostre faithfully reproduced, even though prominent paratextual display of Gringore's identity was ab-sent, the editions published by Trepperel and Le Noir marked a serious stage in textual tampering, as all traces of Gringore's authorship disappeared.

While the publication of Gringore's earliest works confirms the grow-ing use of the printing press by vernacular writers, title-page and colo-

26. For details, see my "Confrontation," 105–18. See Chapter 4 below for a discussion of the English editions of the *Chasteau de labour*, which also eliminated Gringore's acrostic signature.

27. Trepperel's title, *Le casteau d'amours*, also appears to imitate that of Le Noir's edition of February 1501 (N.S.). No other versions spell *chasteau* in this way.

Fig. 2.9. Michel Le Noir's printer's mark, from *Le chasteau d'amours*, 2d ed., B.L., IA.40470, last folio. By permission of the British Library.

phon information reveals, nonetheless, the lack of attention accorded them, especially those at the beginning of their careers, and the relative unimportance of their role in the capitalistic world of book production some thirty years after the introduction of print into France. At the same time, the continuing influence and presence of the printer in book production is manifest, and the increasingly important role played by the bookseller-publisher emerges. Both contributed to the unfair advantage some book producers such as Le Noir could and did take of writers. Yet, even in these early publications, signs of Gringore's desire to participate in textual production accompany a subtle upgrading of his authorial image: his apparent collaboration with book producers in composing paratextual verses at the end of the *Chasteau de labour* and the incorporation into his text of colophon-like material at the end of his *Chasteau d'amours*. These developments paved the way for Gringore's dramatic emergence as the advertised author-publisher of the *Complainte de Trop Tard Marié* in October 1505.[28]

As in the case of Molinet's *Temple de Mars* and Gringore's first two publications, paratextual reference to the author is lacking in the fifteenth-century versions of André de la Vigne's *Ressource de la Chrestienté*, which appeared in two manuscripts and a single edition.[29] Yet La Vigne's visibility surfaces prominently in a series of early sixteenth-century editions of the *Vergier d'honneur*. The emphasis on authorial publicity in these later anthologies appears to be directly related to La Vigne's involvement in the publication of the first two editions of this *receuil*. The increase in paratextual advertisement of the printers and booksellers of those volumes published after the expiration of La Vigne's officially sanctioned supervision, furthermore, again argues for a strong connection between the writer's control of his publication and the enhancement of his image.

Owing to the conventional lack of title pages in manuscripts, neither the title nor La Vigne's name appears on the initial folios of the surviving manuscripts of the *Ressource de la Chrestienté* (Paris, B.N., mss. f.fr. 1687 and 1699). In each version the first words constitute the beginning of the

28. Between the publication of the *Chasteau d'amours* (1500) and the *Complainte de Trop Tard Marié* (1505), Gringore wrote several short, polemical pieces that circulated in print, including his *Lettres nouvelles de Milan* of circa 1500 (see the one known copy, housed in Paris, B.N., Rés. Lb[29] 21) and his *Piteuse complainte que faict la Terre Saincte aux princes, prelatz et seigneurs crestiens* of circa 1500 (see the copy housed in Paris, B.N., Cat. Rothschild 494). The Lyons printers Pierre Mareschal and Barnabé Chaussard prominently advertised their mark on the title page of the *Complainte*, but neither publication identified the author in the paratext.

29. See Appendix 1 below for bibliographical details.

text itself.[30] It is only in the very final verses that they are identified. Like Molinet, La Vigne ended his poem with a punning signature, which the scribe emphasized by capitalization or punctuation in the manuscript versions (see Figure 4.2 below). The expanded title announced at the end of manuscript 1699—"Explicit La Ressource / de la Crestienté Sur l'entreprise / De Naples" (fol. 45ʳ) (Here ends the *Resource of Christianity for the Naples Enterprise*)—is featured alone on the title page of the first extant imprint of the *Ressource*, published circa 1495 in Angoulême: "La resource de la crestienté / Sus l'emprise de Naples." Despite the use of a title page, however, the identities of author and book producers remain unknown. Even the author's punning signature, marked by a capital letter in the manuscripts, is in no way emphasized at the end of the Angoulême version (see Figure 4.3 below).[31] Thus, the absence of authorial identification that marks the manuscript verses is maintained in this first known edition of the *Ressource de la Chrestienté*.

The visibility of La Vigne and of the other book producers is enhanced, however, in the *Vergier d'honneur* editions of the *Ressource*, through title-page and colophon details that are lacking in the previous versions. This series of six surviving editions reflects the gradual evolution of paratextual publicity in early sixteenth-century France. Dating from circa 1502 to 1525, these anthologies contain a large number of poetic texts, many of which La Vigne composed himself, with his *Ressource de la Chrestienté* opening the collection and serving as a formal link to all its other works. Although this *recueil* marks a shift in focus from an individual composition to a collection of works, the title page signals a heretofore absent interest in authorial identification.

In all of the *Vergier d'honneur* editions, the title page provides many details, including the place of publication (Paris), a lengthy explanation of the contents of the collection, with a special announcement of La Vigne's two introductory works (*L'entreprise de Naples* [*La Ressource de la Chrestienté*] and *Le voyage de Naples*), and, for the first time in the known history of the *Ressource*, the name of La Vigne.[32] The author's involvement in the publication of the *Vergier d'honneur* likely influenced this new level of advertisement (Figure 2.10) (my emphasis):

30. In manuscript 1687 the text is preceded by a dedication miniature on the facing folio (see Figure 3.1 below), and a historiated initial of a dreaming poet marks the first word on folio 2ʳ. For more details, see my "Text," 104–7, in which some of the following remarks appear in different form.

31. According to Delisle, 322, the Angoulême printers were André Cauvin and Pierre Alain. For further discussion of this work, see my "Evolution," 115–25.

32. In order to link the initial poem of the *Vergier d'honneur*, the *Ressource de la Chrestienté*, with the following work, La Vigne's *Voyage de Naples*, the title of the *Ressource* was changed to read *L'entreprise de Naples*, a name that incorporated the second half of the title

Le vergier dbonneur nouellement imprime a paris.

De lentreprise et Voyage de Napples . Auquel est compris comãt le roy Charles huitiesme de ce nom a banyere desployee / passaet t apassa de iournee en iournee de puis Lyon iusques a napples g de napples iusques a lyon . ésemble plusieurs aultres choses faictes g composees Par reuerend pere en dieu monseigneur octouié de sainct Gelais euesque dangolesme et par Maistre Andry de la Vigne secretaire de monsieur le duc de sauoye Auec aultres

Fig. 2.10. Title page, from *Le vergier d'honneur*, 1st ed., B.N., Réserve 4° Lb[28] 15a. © cliché Bibliothèque Nationale Paris.

Le Vergier d'honneur nouvellement imprimé a Paris. De l'entreprise et voyage de Napples . . . ensemble plusieurs aultres choses faictes et composees par Reverend Pere en Dieu Monseigneur Octovien de Sainct Gelais, evesque d'Angolesme, et *par Maistre Andry de la Vigne secretaire de Monsieur le duc de Savoye* avec aultres.[33]

The *Orchard of Honor* newly printed in Paris, concerning the *Enterprise and Voyage of Naples* . . . together with several other works written and composed by the Reverend Father in God, Sir Octavien de Saint-Gelais, bishop of Angoulême, and by Master André de la Vigne, secretary of the duke of Savoy, with others.

In this first edition of the *Vergier d'honneur*, though, La Vigne's name appears after that of Octavien de Saint-Gelais, who receives first-place billing on the title page, even though he can be identified with certainty as the author of only one poem in the entire collection, whereas La Vigne had composed many of its works (*Ressource*, 1, n. 1). Saint-Gelais's better-established reputation at the time of publication doubtless warranted such prominence for marketing purposes.[34] Whether or not La Vigne's literary career had advanced enough at this stage to warrant title-page publicity of his name, this self-promotional feature may well have aided the author in obtaining the queen's attention and patronage a few years later.[35]

Just as La Vigne achieved greater paratextual status in the *Vergier d'honneur* editions of the *Ressource*, so too the other producers of the anthology gradually acquired more title-page and colophon visibility, particularly in those editions printed after La Vigne's authority over the

---

as it had appeared in the colophon of ms. 1699 and on the Angoulême title page. The author-woodcut decorating this and other editions calls more positive attention to the writer than the manuscripts of the *Ressource* (see Chapter 3 below).

33. The description of La Vigne in the five later editions of the *Vergier d'honneur* is expanded to include his position as secretary to the French queen, with the final words reading "Maistre Andry de la Vigne secretaire de la Royne et de Monsieur le duc de Savoye" (Master André de la Vigne, secretary to the queen and to the lord duke of Savoy). See *Ressource*, 83–89.

34. Octavien de Saint-Gelais was perhaps best known for his translation of Ovid's *Heroides* at the behest of Charles VIII in 1492 and for his *Séjour d'honneur* of 1489–94 (see Jacques Lemaire).

35. Most of the works La Vigne had written by the time the *Vergier d'honneur* editions appeared had a very limited circulation in manuscript form: the *Ressource de la Chrestienté* (1494); the *Voyage de Naples* (1495); *Le mystère de Saint Martin* (1496); *La moralité de l'aveugle et du boiteux* (1496); *La farce du meunier* (1496); and *Les louenges à Madame de Savoie par les sept planettes* (ca. 1500). La Vigne's *Complaintes et épitaphes du roy de la Bazoche* was apparently printed by Jean Trepperel after July 1501 without any paratextual advertisement of his name. For details, see *Ressource*, 13–15. See also n. 39 below.

work's publication had expired in 1505. While the first two *Vergier d'honneur* editions (ca. 1502–3 and post 1504) omitted all information about their printer (Pierre Le Dru), the announcement of the printer-bookseller's address in the colophon of the third surviving edition, published by Trepperel between 1506 and 1509, and the appearance of his mark on the following folio signaled that another was overseeing the volume's publication (see Tchémerzine, 7:121). Indeed, this edition of the *Vergier d'honneur* appeared after La Vigne had to relinquish legal control of the work: "Cy fine le Vergier d'honneur nouvellement imprimé a Paris par Jehan Trepperel, libraire demourant a Paris en la rue Neufve Nostre Dame a l'enseigne de l'escu de France" (Here ends the *Orchard of Honor* recently printed in Paris by Jean Trepperel, bookseller living in Paris on the rue Neuve Notre Dame at the sign of the shield of France).[36] Instead of being relegated to the colophon like Trepperel's name some three to six years earlier, the identity of the bookseller Jean Petit appears in the center of the title page of the fourth edition (ca. 1512) in letters three times the size of those used for La Vigne's name (see my "Text," 128). With the absence of authorial control over the *Vergier d'honneur* editions after 1505, those who made editorial decisions regarding the later versions gained in paratextual visibility. As in the case of Molinet and Gringore, the dominance of the bookseller's identity on the title page of the *Vergier d'honneur* editions appearing in the second decade of the sixteenth century coincides with his increasing involvement as manager of its production. And yet, unlike the *Temple de Mars*, *Chasteau de labour*, or *Chasteau d'amours* publications, all of the *Vergier d'honneur* editions featured the author's name prominently on the title page. La Vigne's crucial role in the first two editions of the *Vergier d'honneur* was therefore decisive in the maintenance of his identity in the later versions of the work.

The fifth and sixth editions of the *Vergier d'honneur*, versions that derived textually from the Trepperel edition and were printed and sold by Michel Le Noir's son Philippe in 1522 and 1525 (literally keeping it all in the family), advertised the printer-bookseller's presence on the title page and in the colophon. Combining the functions and strategies of Trepperel and Petit, Philippe Le Noir made extended use of both forms of paratextual advertisement. His experimentation with title-page usage, including red and black contrasting inks and an elaborate Renaissance-like border, doubtless served to impress the potential book purchaser by calling attention to his publishing talents as well as his

---

36. Since Trepperel was related to the Le Noir family through marriage (see n. 12 above), it is possible that his edition was based on or was the very one Le Noir had been allowed to finish printing in May 1504 but could not legally sell before April 1505.

name (see my "Text," 129). The separate disposition of the two roles Le Noir played in these editions—the bookseller's, advertised on the title page, and the printer's, featured in the colophon—coincides with the developing pattern described above: the printer's identity was relegated to the final paratextual space of the edition, while that of the bookseller adorned the first folio, his address providing an interested book purchaser with easy access to the place of purchase. In contrast with the first imprints of the *Vergier d'honneur*, greater emphasis was now placed on the identity and function of the printer and bookseller.

The shifting placement of the author's and book producers' names in the paratext of this series of La Vigne's printed works relates directly to the crisis of authority—the struggle between poet and publisher for control of the text—that characterized the early decades of the sixteenth century in France. The strong association between the author's control of publication and the advertisement of his name more prominently than the names of the book producers typifies the later publications of La Vigne, as well as of Gringore and Lemaire.

Presumably because of his earlier direct experience with book production, La Vigne did not appear in a self-effacing, Marot-like posture once he obtained the post as secretary to the French queen in late 1504. Instead, his new position ensured an advertised presence all the more, a presence that always related to but was never dominated by that of his patroness, a presence that, moreover, overshadowed that of printer and bookseller. For La Vigne's later works, short polemical tracts published in 1507 and 1509, bore prominent advertisements of his name and court affiliation as "secretaire de la Royne" (secretary of the queen) on the title page and, sometimes, after the composition as well (see Brown, *Shaping*, 163–86). Royal publicity reflecting either the subject of the works, Louis XII, or the supporter of them, Anne of Brittany, is evidenced through coats of arms that share paratextual advertising space with the name of the author (Figure 2.11, *a* and *b*).[37] The absence of subservient dedications prefacing these texts seems to reflect the development of a more equal relationship between patron and poet several years before the first (1509) and second (1512) editions of Lemaire's *Légende des Vénitiens*, which marked the replacement of the potential patron's arms by the author's, as we saw in Chapter 1 above. Indeed, one can speak of a reordering of these particular relationships at the time, for, as I have suggested elsewhere (*Shaping*), the controversial foreign policies of the French kings at the end of the fifteenth and beginning of the sixteenth

37. See the title page of the *Atollite, Bruyt Commun*, and *Libelle* and the last leaf of *Atollite* (Brown, *Shaping*, 163, 168, 173, 179). A fleur-de-lis image adorns the *Atollite*, whereas joint coats of arms signifying the union of Louis XII and Anne of Brittany decorate the *Bruyt Commun* and the *Libelle*.

centuries led monarchs and princes to depend more than ever on court polemicists to elicit public backing. Patronage, then, was becoming a more even exchange of support, power, and authority.

The fact that La Vigne never shared title-page or colophon space with the publishers of his later works argues for a connection between royal protection and the prominence of his identity at the expense of the publishers.[38] Once La Vigne became the queen's secretary, the appearance of his name alone on the title pages of his publications seems to have been more or less assured.[39] The author may well have played some controlling role in their printing—whether indirectly, by virtue of his court position, or directly, by his participation in their actual publication.

With La Vigne, then, we witness an evolution similar to, though more compressed than, that of Molinet concerning the enhancement and cultivation of authorial identity on the title page and in the colophon of works written and produced during the transition from manuscript to print. In both cases, the author's participation in the reproduction of his works coincided with increased authorial visibility in the paratext. With Gringore, too, we witness an evolution toward more prominently placed authorial signs. Although Gringore's authorship was not publicized paratextually in his two early works, the *Chasteau de labour* and the *Chasteau d'amours*, his presence increased dramatically in 1505, precisely at the time he began adopting privileges.

It was not until the October 1505 printing of his *Complainte de Trop Tard Marié* that Pierre Gringore's name appeared paratextually for the first time in a colophon. This moment coincided with the author's direct involvement in the publication of his book. Even though none of Gringore's works actually bore his name on the title page until the 1509 publication of the *Chasse des cerfs*, by that date the use of personalized author-woodcuts on the title page had firmly established his visual presence in this privileged space (see Chapter 3 below). From the beginning, moreover, Gringore's consciousness about authorial identification was

38. Two of the editions bear no mention at all of the publishers (*Atollite, Bruyt Commun*), while a third (*Patenostre*), published in an anthology called the *Louange des roys de France*, does place importance on the printer, Eustache de Brie. The single edition of the *Patenostre*, however, does not mention any printer or bookseller (see my *Shaping*, 163–78).

39. The last known example of a printed work by La Vigne, the *Epitaphes en rondeaux de la royne* dating from circa 1514 (see B.N., Rés. Ye 1371), again advertises his name on the title page. Some of La Vigne's later commissioned works never appeared in print: *Récit du sacre d'Anne de Bretagne et son entrée à Paris*, dated November 18–19, 1504 (Waddesdon Manor, Rothschild Collection, ms. 22); *Le blason de la guerre du pape, ses aliez prelatz, gens d'Eglise et les Veniciens ensemble, contre le roy tres chrétien*, dated 1509 (Paris: B.N., ms. f.fr. 2248); and *Croniques . . . du roy Françoys premier de ce nom*, ending in January 1515 (Paris, B.N., ms. nouv. acq., f.fr. 794).

Fig. 2.11a. Title page from *Les ballades de Bruyt Commun*, B.N., Réserve pYe 385.
© cliché Bibliothèque Nationale Paris.

Fig. 2.11*b*. Title page from *Le libelle des cinq villes d'Ytallye*, B.N., Réserve Ye 1039. © cliché Bibliothèque Nationale Paris.

always manifest through the consistent appearance of his acrostic signature at the end of his works.

First printed on October 1, 1505, according to surviving evidence, the eight-folio *Complainte de Trop Tard Marié* enjoyed a decided success until at least 1535, both in France and in England, to judge from the numerous extant editions.[40] Unlike the *Chasteau de labour* and the *Chasteau d'amours*, which highly publicize the names of the book producers but not the author in the paratext, Gringore's is the sole name associated with the *Complainte*. With only the title provided on the first folio, no information identifies the printer or bookseller. The colophon indicates that Gringore wrote the work and that the book was printed for him. That is to say, the author had become his own publisher (my emphasis): "*Fait et composé par Pierre Gringore. Et imprimé pour icelluy* a Paris Le premier jour d'octobre. L'an mil cinq cens et cinq" (Written and composed by Pierre Gringore and printed for him in Paris the first day of October 1505). As we discovered in the case of La Vigne, the absence of the other book producers' names in the paratext coincides with the prominent advertisement of the writer's name, both within and without the text of a work he himself published.

This advertisement of the poet's publication role further reveals that four years before Lemaire's involvement in the printing of his *Légende des Vénitiens*, Gringore had already made an investment in the reproduction of his text. Because the *Complainte* comprised only eight folios, it is conceivable that the poet subsidized its publication, for it would not have been as costly as the much longer *Chasteau de labour* and *Chasteau d'amours*, which contained sixty and forty-four folios respectively. In the end, the multiple printings of the *Complainte de Trop Tard Marié* show not only that the author had made a sound decision in choosing to publish this work, but also that he had directed its publication with considerable success.[41] Thus, by October 1505 Gringore had begun to play as decisive a role in the reproduction of his works as Molinet some five years earlier, when he had several of his writings published in Valenciennes, and La Vigne, who had controlled the printing of the first two editions of the *Vergier d'honneur* slightly before that time.

These developments led to Gringore's more significant involvement in the publication of his *Folles entreprises* just three months later. The presence in this volume of the first privilege obtained by a vernacular

40. For bibliographical details, see Appendix 5 below.

41. Only the latest editions, presumably printed after the author's death, identify the printers or publishers of the *Complainte*. The English edition, published by the famous printer Wynkyn de Worde, did not associate the author's name with the translation and was probably not sanctioned by Gringore, who may not even have known of its existence. See Chapter 4 and Appendix 5 below.

writer marks a turning point for authorial participation in French book production and for Gringore's own relationship to his works. This change accompanied the adoption of a more self-promotional strategy. As with the paratextual publicity of his earlier editions, printer and bookseller are advertised here; yet this first edition of the *Folles entreprises* prominently announces Gringore's identity as well.

On the title page of two different issues of the first edition of the *Folles entreprises*, the reader discovers the mark of Pierre Le Dru, the same man who had printed the two editions of the *Vergier d'honneur* supervised by La Vigne (see Tchémerzine, 6:48, 52). The printer's sign visually dominates the page—without, however, providing his name. Identification depended on the book purchaser's recognition of Le Dru's mark or consultation of the colophon information, which specifies the name. Le Dru, then, appears to have played a less dominant role in the publication of Gringore's work than Philippe Pigouchet had previously in the reproduction of the *Chasteau de labour* and *Chasteau d'amours*.

Verses at the bottom of the *Folles entreprises* title page provide the bookseller's address:

> Qui en veult avoir se transporte
> Sans deshonneur et sans diffame
> Pres du bout du Pont Nostre Dame
> A l'enseigne de Mere Sotte.

He who wishes to procure copies should go without dishonor or infamy to the sign of Mother Folly near the end of the Notre Dame bridge.

Most Parisians would probably have recognized this reference to Gringore, who acted the role of Mother Folly in the popular dramatic presentations of the theatrical troupe known as the Enfants sans Souci. He must have been earning money selling his own works, perhaps as part of a financial arrangement with Le Dru, and it is likely that the author-bookseller composed these verses, providing a poetic framework for his new publishing function. Thus, Gringore's new level of involvement in the publication of his work, that of bookseller, is prominently advertised on the title page of his *Folles entreprises*.

First presented on the title page as a bookseller, Gringore goes on to identify himself as author in an acrostic at the end of the work; not only that, but the colophon of the edition clarifies that he had engaged Pierre Le Dru to print the *Folles entreprises* for him (my emphasis): "Imprimé a Paris par maistre Pierre Le Dru imprimeur *pour iceluy Gringore* le XXIII jour de Decembre. L'an mil cinq cens et cinq" (Printed in Paris by Master

Pierre Le Dru, printer, for the above-named Gringore the 23rd day of December 1505). For the second time, then, Gringore had acted as publisher of the first edition of his work and had advertised the fact. In the first editions of almost all Gringore's subsequent writings, his name would appear in some similar paratextual form, confirming that he continued to play an important role in the production of his works.[42] His name was commonly placed on the second folio of an edition and, especially from 1516 on, he was regularly identified on the title page itself.[43] In those cases where the paratext featured the identities of both author and publisher, Gringore's name tended to dominate the title page, while that of the printer or bookseller was relegated to the colophon, as in the *Abus du monde*, the *Coqueluche*, and the *Espoir de paix*.

But with the publication of the *Fantasies de Mère Sotte*, the author came to share title-page or colophon publicity with the booksellers of his volumes, a modification that seemingly anticipated Gringore's departure from Paris for Lorraine in 1518.[44] While he continued to maintain control over the publication of his works, as the paratext confirms, Gringore's absence from France's printing capital meant that he could no longer sell his own volumes. He had to rely on Parisian *libraires* to carry out that function on his behalf, and this doubtless explains their reappearance on the title page. Moreover, once Gringore assumed his post as the duke of Lorraine's *héraut d'armes* (king of arms) in 1518, the elaborately publicized name of his patron also appeared in the colophon and then on the title page with the name of the author.[45] Gringore, following in the footsteps of Lemaire with his *Temple d'honneur et de vertus* of 1504 and La Vigne with his *Vergier d'honneur* publications, obviously felt that the presence of his patron's name would add prestige to his own. Despite

42. See, for example, the June 1509 edition of his *Abus du monde*; the circa 1509 edition of his *Entreprise de Venise* (Paris, B.N., Rés. Ye 4108); the *Union des princes* of circa 1509 (Paris, B.N., Cat. Rothschild 2824); and the 1512 N.S. edition of the *Jeu du Prince des Sotz* (Paris, B.N., Rés Ye 1317). For details, consult Oulmont, *Pierre Gringore*, 34–40, and Tchémerzine, 6:70–73. Gringore's *Obstination des Suysses* of circa 1513 (Paris, B.N., Rés. Ye 2954), his *Complainte de la Cité crestienne* of circa 1525 (Chantilly, Musée Condé, IV.D.106), and his *Quenoulle spirituelle* of circa 1525 (Paris, B.N., Cat. Rothschild 498) bear no paratextual reference to the writer, but his acrostic signature at the end of each text announces his authorship.

43. See, for example, *La coqueluche* of August 1510 (Paris, B.N., Rés Ye 1428); *L'espoir de paix* of February 1511 N.S. (Paris, B.N., Rés Ye 1324); and the *Fantasies de Mère Sotte* of circa 1518 (Paris, B.N., Rés. Ye 291).

44. See also the *Menus propos*, *Blazon des heretiques*, *Heures de Nostre Dame*, and the first edition of the *Notables enseignemens* (see n. 45 below).

45. See Gringore's *Menus propos* of December 1521 (Paris, B.N., Rés. Ye 293); the *Blazon des heretiques*, published after December 21, 1524 (Paris, B.N., Rés. Ye 4106); the *Heures de Nostre Dame* of circa 1527; the *Notables enseignemens* of February 1528 (Paris, B.N., Rés. Ye 1328); and the *Paraphrase . . . sur les sept . . . Pseaumes* of 1541 (Paris, B.N., Rés. A 6804).

the security of his position as protégé of the duke of Lorraine, Gringore nevertheless continued to have his texts printed in Paris and to obtain privileges for their publication.

Thus, in this first edition of the *Folles entreprises*, one whose publication the author himself explicitly supervised, new paratextual features include the presence of the writer's stage name and address on the title page, indicating his new function as bookseller, and the printing of an author-procured privilege at the end of the edition. These announcements reveal that Gringore had taken action even before publication to head off the sort of pirating that had previously been inflicted on Bouchet, La Vigne, and himself; no doubt they represented a warning to all Parisian publishers—and an advertisement to his readers—that the author had taken control of book production.

In conclusion, an examination of the title pages and colophons of Gringore's two works published in 1505 suggests that the poet's involvement as publisher and bookseller of his own writings had a direct influence on modifications in paratextual features and on the enhancement of his—and probably other writers'—authorial status. It shows, furthermore, how these changes announced in the paratext set the stage for the publication of all Gringore's subsequent books. Clearly he and his contemporaries had learned from printers and publishers—their collaborators but at times their competitors—to advertise their own role in the bookmaking process by placing their names in the colophon or on the title page and by calling attention to the terms of the privileges they obtained for their own protection. Prominent placement of this verbal information played a key role in promoting an author's literary status. But visual promotion of the writer likewise contributed to his greater presence and authority in book production. The development, function, and changing significance of the author-images that appeared in the paratexts of the works of Gringore and his contemporaries are the focus of the next chapter.

3

THE CHANGING IMAGE
OF THE POET

In the previous chapter, we examined the presence, absence, and arrangement of title page and colophon details in French manuscripts and imprints during the late medieval period. It is clear that a certain tension existed in the bookmaking process: between authors, whose growing involvement in the production of their works coincided with the increasing prominence of their name in the paratext, and book producers, whose identity likewise became more publicized as their participation in textual reproduction evolved.

We shall now see how author-images visually complemented the developing verbal publicity of writers and how the new context in which these illustrations appeared—namely, printed and hybrid books—altered the conventional meaning associated with these images. Although the generic quality of woodcut illustrations in imprints might seem to offer a more depersonalized author-image in comparison with manuscripts, the commonly absent paratextual advertisement of authors' names in the latter often made specific identification of the portrayed writer difficult. By contrast, the development of title pages providing authorial information in printed volumes encouraged readers to attach specific names to the general depictions of authors. In fact, more personalized forms of representation gradually appeared in these imprints, perhaps in reaction to their generic quality. In special editions produced on vellum, for example, miniatures were sometimes painted over printed illustrations, along with specific signs referring to their authors. An increase in the paratextual use of nonportraiture forms, such as personalized author symbols, arms, or devices, constitutes yet another way in which a writer's visual association with his text was enhanced.

Because this discussion of the changing author-image intersects with that of the literary *mécène,* or benefactor, I will direct special attention to the association between patron and poet and the modifications in that relationship effected by the increasing interaction between poet and publisher. For the commercial, money-oriented association that typified the author–publisher relationship contrasted with the gift-exchange association more characteristic of the relationship between writer and patron. While the patron commonly figured in personalized presentation miniatures, which often served as frontispieces to manuscript books made for him or her, the association between writer and publisher was rarely portrayed visually. Instead, generic woodcuts depicting the author-figure alone often appeared in the introductory positions of imprints, and printers' or booksellers' marks separately advertised their publishing functions.

Both of these images depicting writers—presentation scenes of poet and patron and generic woodcuts of the writer alone—find their source in conventional miniatures that had decorated manuscripts for centuries. In fact, author-images apparently gave rise to presentation illustrations. In the early Middle Ages, the seated author, the most widely used illustration in imperial scriptoria, especially in Carolingian art, was adapted to the representation of the evangelists. Placed at the head of the gospel in an architectural space borrowed from antique theater, the author-evangelist, often surrounded by secondary characters and related symbols, was typically depicted either as a scribe recording dictation from God or as an author dictating to a scribe, although by the thirteenth century evangelists and other authors were shown copying from an exemplar. By the end of the Middle Ages, many author-portraits of ancient as well as contemporary writers presented the writer at a desk bedecked with lecterns and surrounded with reference materials (Toubert, 100; Saenger, 388). Throughout the fifteenth and early sixteenth centuries, the image of Saint Jerome in his study writing the Vulgate informed many single-author scenes in Italy and the North (Rice, *Saint Jerome,* 104–13).

Although they were not perceived as true portraits, these later author-images seem to have represented more than a traditional imitation of the earlier theological iconographic motif (Hult, *Prophecies,* 75). In thirteenth- and fourteenth-century France, with a growing interest in the act of writing more than in the performance of literary texts, and with the evolution of the author from dictator of his works to writer of them, single-author portraits became increasingly prevalent. Appearing at a time when *écrire* had come to signify more than "to copy" and was acquiring its modern meaning, these illustrations, which showed writers composing, conferred an important individuality and authenticity on a work.[1] Sylvia Huot associates the appearance of single-author images in the French narrative tradition with a new authorial consciousness that was developing at this time. She interprets the vernacular author-portraits in the *trouvère* chansonniers as well as those in poetic anthologies of writers such as Adam de la Halle, Guillaume de Machaut, and Jean Froissart as an attempt to offer a sense of distinct poetic identity, although she never intimates that these were really individual, personalized portraits (*From Song to Book*, 53–64; see also Avril, Ferrand).

One derivative of this genre of author-portraits was the dedication scene, which brought together the writer and the dedicatee. Based on antique iconographic patterns such as the single-author image, these illustrations depicted the circumstances of the commission or final offering of a work. From the thirteenth century on, they typically portrayed the author, usually kneeling, before the seated dedicatee. Often intermediaries, such as the one who had commissioned the work or a patron saint, appeared alongside these main figures (Toubert, 100).

The use of single-author images and presentation scenes in imprints, then, derived from a well-established manuscript tradition, which had depicted authors presenting or authors authoring according to established patterns of ritual and ceremony in which gesture and symbolic objects often served an important hermeneutic function.[2] The new context in which these illustrations appeared, however, altered the conventional meaning associated with them. For example, as the print culture adapted manuscript presentation scenes into the form of generic dedication-woodcuts, the idea of the specific relationship between patron and poet traditionally associated with the manuscript tradition lost much of its personalized character. With the repeated use of such woodcuts in the editions of other works and the widespread dissemination of multiple copies of a volume illustrated in this fashion, a shift of focus emerged: the general idea of patronage, rather than a specific dedication ceremony, was being publicized.

For the same reason, the author-woodcuts that abounded in imprints were not as personalized as the manuscript miniatures of the writer. Repeatedly presenting a generic writer, these woodcut images tended to emphasize the idea of authorship. But, placed in a context that provided increasingly prominent advertisement of the author's name, these ge-

1. Chartier, *L'ordre des livres*, 60. See also Saenger, 388–90, for a list of manuscript author-images that marked the development from the author dictating to the author writing.
2. For a fascinating discussion of the influence of gesture and ritual on the early medieval narrative, see Pizarro. See also Buettner, 78ff., for a discussion of visual memory and visual narratives in illumination.

neric woodcuts played a greater role than manuscript miniatures in drawing attention to vernacular writers. This expanding visibility accorded authors—expanding because their image appeared in more books, reaching more readers—coupled with the growing advertisement of their names conferred greater prestige on the profession of authorship, just as the propagandistic use of print by royal leaders lent greater credibility to their political actions. This new means of authorial promotion was particularly attractive to those who found it difficult to obtain patronage in the late fifteenth and early sixteenth centuries, in particular Northern humanists who needed to draw the interest of aristocratic and bourgeois supporters alike (Panofsky, 218).

Generic author-woodcuts also served as transitional images between the single-author illustrations portrayed in manuscript miniatures, which were not yet portraits but did offer a sense of distinct poetic identity, and the tailor-made, engraved author-portraits that prefaced the texts of vernacular writers during the second half of the sixteenth century. While the development of personalized author-portraits was related to the general rise of portraits in the sixteenth century,[3] printed personalized author-images of French vernacular writers do not appear to have existed before that of Maurice Scève in the 1544 edition of his *Délie*.[4]

3. For a discussion of the enormous subject of Renaissance portraits, in particular artists' self-portraits, see Campbell. Laufer, 488, explains that the author-portrait was common during the second half of the sixteenth century, but he does not provide details concerning the earliest author-portraits in France. In "Portrait," Mortimer traces the use of author-portraits in sixteenth-century France from the appearance of several woodcuts in the circa 1505 edition of Robert Gobin's *Loups ravissans* (which were not, however, personalized images) to Pierre de Ronsard's portrait in his 1552 *Amours*. But Mortimer does not distinguish between the generic author-woodcuts and personalized author-portraits that appeared in some sixteenth-century imprints. Many earlier examples exist of vernacular generic author-portraits in French print, including those in Pierre Levet's 1489 edition of François Villon's works (see my "Author, Editor"). Rice, *Saint Jerome*, 106–8, points out that sometimes, in a flattering form of testimonial, the features of certain scholars, such as Nicolas of Cusa, Jacques Lefèvre d'Etaples, or Martin Luther, were adapted to Jerome's image as an author at work in his study. See also Jardine, 55–82.

4. An author-portrait copied from Hans Holbein's drawing appears on the verso of the last folio of Nicolas Bourbon's *Paidagogeion*, printed in 1535 at Lyons for Philippe Rhoman by Jean Barbou (see Mortimer, *Harvard Catalogue*, 1:148). I am indebted to my colleague Cynthia Skenazi for calling my attention to this image. In the second and third decades of the sixteenth century, Albrecht Dürer's drawing and etching as well as paintings by Quinten Massys and Hans Holbein directly portrayed Erasmus. Holbein decorated the margins of a copy of Johann Froben's 1515 edition of the *Praise of Folly* with pen-and-ink drawings (for a copy of these drawings, see the edition published by the Folio Society in London in 1974). Holbein's woodcuts of Erasmus front a 1533 edition of the author's *Adagia* and a 1540 edition of his *Opera*. For copies and a discussion of the portraits of Erasmus, see Jardine, 27–54.

As with the latter, the familiar engraved author-portraits of Pontus de Tyard, Pierre de Ronsard, and Michel de Montaigne marked an important change from earlier author-portraits that grew out of the medieval iconographical tradition, for the writer no longer appeared at work in his study in these illustrations. Such a modification ennobled his image by testifying to the fact that the writer, as an individual, had come to acquire a special social status. It was his particular physiognomy, rather than his function, that served to identify him. I am suggesting here that the increasingly personalized author-woodcuts of Molinet, La Vigne, Gringore, and Lemaire played an important role in this change, which affected all aspects of book production.

The intersection of the worlds of literary creation, patronage, bookmaking, and marketing is striking in the illustrations decorating the volumes of late medieval French writers. These do not reflect an evolution from a poet reliant on patronage to one independent of such sponsorship by dint of direct participation in the print industry. Such a development did not in fact arise at this time, for authors were apt to participate in both systems simultaneously. It is rather an overlapping of private and commercial associations that often characterizes the presentation scenes and author-illustrations in the manuscript and printed books studied here, particularly images decorating hybrid editions. In an attempt to imitate manuscript books, publishers had these volumes printed on vellum and their woodcuts erased and/or painted over with miniatures. Deriving both from the manuscript and the printed forms of reproduction, such illustrations provide the most interesting traces of the changing image of late medieval authors. Attracted at once by the pseudo-independence of their associations with the printing industry and the greater economic stability of the patronage system, writers sought to work out new compromises for their literary careers. Authors' increasing prominence through personalized representations, especially in those publications they themselves supervised, constitutes another gesture in defense of their new and changing role.

Two kinds of images decorating André de la Vigne's works provide models of the dedicatory motifs and author-illustrations that typically appeared in the manuscript and printed books of his contemporaries. Whereas the frontispiece miniature of a manuscript version of La Vigne's *Ressource de la Chrestienté* (Paris, B.N., ms. f.fr. 1687) depicts the poet on bended knee offering the book to his future patron, Charles VIII (Figure 3.1), the woodcut decorating the first printed edition of the *Vergier d'honneur* (Paris: Pierre Le Dru, 1502–4) offers a conventional image of the author alone in his study (Figure 3.2).

Fig. 3.1. Poet offering his work to King Charles VIII, from *La ressource de la Chrestienté*, B.N., ms. f.fr. 1687, frontispiece. © cliché Bibliothèque Nationale Paris.

Fig. 3.2. Author-woodcut, from *Le vergier d'honneur*, 1st ed., B.N., Réserve 4°
Lb²⁸ 15α, title page verso. © cliché Bibliothèque Nationale Paris.

Figure 3.1 portrays the author of the book and his targeted public (also
the book's subject) as La Vigne presents the *Ressource* to the French king
in 1494. By bestowing his work on the monarch, the poet essentially
gave a part of himself to the king—his creation, his words—for the book
incarnated the spirit of the writer.[5] His offering thereby formed a bond

5. These ideas form part of the gift-exchange economy described by Mauss. Although
he was studying archaic societies, many of his observations pertain to early Western cultures as well. See Macherel, 152, who summarizes Mauss's work in a useful way; Davis,
"Beyond the Market," 69–88, who first associated Mauss's ideas with sixteenth-century
France, discussing the dedicated book in terms of a gift; and Kettering's description of the
gift-giving relationship among sixteenth- and seventeenth-century French nobles (131–
32).

with the dedicatee that projected into the future; it was a gift that both sought and obliged a worthy return.[6] Even though the author depended upon his would-be patron for support and was essentially subordinate to him, as his position in Figure 3.1 suggests, the fact that La Vigne served the king by writing about him in a positive political light made it all the more incumbent upon the monarch to respond favorably to the poet. In fact, Charles VIII subsequently hired La Vigne as his secretary for the military campaign into Italy in 1494–95. Unfortunately, the king's death some three years later left the writer without a sponsor (*Ressource*, 3–4).

In the patronage system, then, the author's writing represented his personal rendition of the patron's desires, needs, or image, inspired either by some form of commission or by the hope of obtaining one. The presentation of the book itself, an image that was absent from the poet–publisher relationship,[7] symbolized visually this sharing of literary and politico-cultural concerns: the writer possessed an outlet for his talents; the patron, a vehicle for self-display. The dynamics of this association, with the author directing his energies to a specific reader and sponsor, explain the individualized nature of the accompanying visual renditions.[8]

The woodcut in Figure 3.2 belongs to a different system of book reproduction and mode of exchange, that of the marketplace, where books had a price. In its simplest form, the poet initially sold his manuscript to a printer, who then, having essentially become "owner" of the manuscript, reaped the financial benefits from the sale of that book in print form.[9] As the marketing of books came to involve booksellers and publishers who did not actually print the texts themselves and as writers questioned the profits gained by others from the writers' words, the system became more complicated.

In this capitalistic economy, in which a thing was taken objectively for a price, the book was a commodity whose role of bringing profit to both author and publisher (unequal though that might have been) did not

6. Kettering, 131–37, emphasizes the mutual obligation of client and patron in this system, where gift giving was a euphemism for patronage. Although Kettering studies patronage among nobles, her remarks relate to the poet–patron relationship depicted in the dedication miniatures I discuss. See also Davis, "Beyond the Market," 73–74, who provides details about the gift-giving ritual involving patron and author, and Green, 60–64, 98.

7. Green, 59–60, discusses how books themselves were often considered an important part of a prince's assets. See also Buettner, 75–76.

8. Compare the oft-cited passage from Jean Froissart's *Chroniques*, in which the author describes the 1395 presentation of one of his manuscripts to King Richard II (*Œuvres*, 15:167), with the miniature depicting that very scene (reproduced in Buettner, 77).

9. See Parent, for details of these transactions from a slightly later period.

promote a reciprocal sharing of its internal message so much as it encouraged an impersonal assessment of its external, pecuniary value. The fact that the author's text became an object that in and of itself could attract money suggests a detaching of the author's spirit from his written word, an association characteristic of the gift economy. Moreover, because the public was dispersed and anonymous, because the book was not a gift with direct reciprocity implied, there inevitably developed a greater distance between author and audience.

Thus, the relationship between a writer and a particular publisher was quite different from an author's association with those involved in manuscript production. The author dealt directly with the person(s) who would reproduce the book, which was sometimes the case in the manuscript culture, but not with the persons who would read it. Moreover, unlike the patron, who had more than an economic interest in the book's life, the publisher's stake in the enterprise was defined exclusively in financial terms. This purely commercial interaction may explain why the writer was often illustrated alone and why the publisher was usually identified separately by a special mark, not by means of a portrait.[10]

Oftentimes, though, a more ambiguous picture of relationships surfaces in the works reproduced during this transitional period from manuscript to print. In some cases, one of these two model illustrations appears. But both kinds of images commonly coexist as well, either in different copies of the same edition of a text, usually in the form of a miniature painted over a woodcut, or side by side in the same volume. This superimposition and juxtaposition of images reflects the intersection of the world of the gift and the world of the marketplace, with all the ambiguities associated with the changing role of poet, patron, and publisher.[11]

The intersection of these two mechanisms of exchange appears not only in the various images that I discuss below, but also in documents describing the terms of the relationship between Jean Molinet and his patrons at the end of the fifteenth and the beginning of the sixteenth cen-

10. An exception was Antoine Vérard (see Chapter 1, at n. 31 above).

11. Macherel, 151, speaks of the coexistence of the gift economy and the market form of exchange. See also Davis, "Gifts, Markets and Historical Change," 3–4, who supports Macherel's contention, thereby rejecting the evolutionary theory of Mauss and historians after him who considered that gift exchanges began to decrease with the development of commercial markets. Davis claims that the most important thing about interactions in the sixteenth century was "the possibility of moving back and forth between the gift mode and the sale mode, while always remembering the distinction between the two registers" (11). I am grateful to Zelda Bronstein for this reference, whose pages are cited from its English manuscript form, as it has been published in a Russian translation (see Bibliography).

turies. Georges Chastellain, Molinet's predecessor as Burgundian court historiographer, had refused direct reimbursement for his services, as the following document of circa 1465 shows:

> Une chose est de quoy ne me puis taire, c'est que m'avez tout esver- gondez de m'avoir envoié argent, dont je ne suis point costumier de le prendre, ne aussi qu'on m'en envoie, car je ne veul point vendre mon service fait as gens de bien, a pris d'argent. (Dupire, *Jean Molinet*, 13, n. 4)

> One thing about which I cannot be silent is that you have shamed me by sending me money, which I am not accustomed to taking or receiving, because I do not wish to sell my service to good men for a price.

Chastellain's aristocratic status undoubtedly allowed him to take such an idealistic position on the matter. But his experience differs from Moli- net's, whose more commercial association with the same court of Bur- gundy and house of Austria offers evidence of a changing relationship between the author, his patrons, and his text a short time later.

Archival records reveal, for example, that Molinet not only lived off his benefices but also received a pension of a hundred écus annually as court chronicler (Dupire, *Jean Molinet*, 17). This allowance was actually defined as a gift, or *don* (my emphasis):

> A maistre Jehan Molinet, chanosne de la Salle en Vallenchiennes, a present ordonné historiographe et chroniqueur du Roy [Maximi- lian], la somme de VI^xx livres de XL gros, monnaie de Flandre, la livre, apparant du *don* de ceste pention par mandement, en date du XVIIe d'octobre mil IIII^c IIII^xx chincq, declarant en oultre ledict maistre Jehan Molinet estre partant tenuz de servir audit estat et mettre et redigier par escript tous les fais, gestes, proesses et aultres vertus comendables de feuz les prédecesseurs du roy, que Dieu ab- soille, et de luy et au surplus faire bien, deuement et lealment, toutes et singulieres, les choses que bon et leal historiographe et chronicqueur dessys dit poelt et doit faire et qui audit estat compete et appertient.[12]

12. Dupire, *Jean Molinet*, 17, n. 1. The same text appeared in documents for the years 1487–90. In 1491 Maximilian was unable to pay Molinet, but through a reassignment the poet succeeded in recuperating lost back pay as well as his pension for the following three years. As official chronicler from 1494 to 1506 in the service of Philip the Handsome, Moli- net again encountered financial difficulties. His annual allowance was cut in half in 1496 and 1505, but it was repaid the following years; he apparently did not receive his pension in 1498 and 1499.

To Master Jean Molinet, canon of the Salle in Valenciennes, presently named historiographer and chronicler of the king [Maximilian], the sum of 120 pounds of 40 gros, Flemish currency, the pound, a sign of the gift of this ordered pension, on the 17th of October 1485, declaring moreover the said Master Jean Molinet to be on this condition held to serve the said state and to put and redact in writing all the deeds, actions, valorous acts, and other commendable virtues of the king's predecessors, may God absolve them, and of him as well and, moreover, to render well, dutifully and loyally, all the unique things that the good and loyal above-stated historiographer and chronicler, who belongs to the said state, can and must do.

The document makes it clear that the "gift" given to Molinet was to be reciprocated by his literary service, which, described in terms of duty and loyalty, recalls the feudal sources of the patron–client system. The words here form part of what Kettering calls the language of courtesy, "the polite fiction that service was freely given because gift-giving was more a courtesy than a compulsorily reciprocal act" (135). On the one hand, the use of the word "don" places the relationship between Molinet and Maximilian squarely in the gift-exchange system. The fact that Molinet received the allowance for his general literary talents before the actual composition of the required works corroborates this relationship by making it a true exchange of "dons-cadeaux" for "dons-talents" (Guery, 1255). In other words, the money Molinet received did not actually buy a specific object; it paid for his literary expertise. On the other hand, this document bespeaks a relationship that embodied commercial elements; for money, even when disguised as a gift, served as payment. This document strikingly defines the similarities between the system of patronage as gift giving and the world of the marketplace, making it unclear whether distinctions between the two registers were always maintained, as Davis contends (see n. 11 above).

We also know that sometime between March 1500 and September 1501 Molinet received fifty livres from his patron, Philip the Handsome, for a specific text, probably the *Naissance de Charles d'Autriche*, which was printed at about the same time (my emphasis): "et vous mandons . . . que vous faictes payer et delivrer a maistre Jehan Molinet la somme de cincquante livres . . . en consideration ce que presentement il nous a presenté en *don* ung livre qu'il a fait et composé a nostre louenge" (Dupire, *Jean Molinet*, 19–20, n. 4) (and we request . . . that you have paid and sent to Master Jean Molinet the sum of 50 pounds . . . in consideration of the gift of a book, which he made and wrote to our glory, that he has just given us). Unlike the situation described in the first document, the author received payment in this case for a specific work *after* having written it. This explicit attachment of a price to a literary work as object makes it a commodity in a way that Molinet's other compositions generally were not, bringing the relationship closer to the market-economy association that his predecessor, Chastellain, pointedly avoided. Because this money supplemented Molinet's annual pension, however, it more resembled a gift.[13] Furthermore, the term "don" reappears. This time it refers to Molinet's book, confirming that the word alluded to the action that precipitated the exchange.

These several documents show, then, the developing commercial relationship between writers and their sponsors that existed along with the service-oriented, gift-exchange association that characterized patronage. The relationship between patrons and their clients was thereby double-edged: the former could recompense their protectees either by the formal rules of a contract or by the more informal, spontaneous mode of gift giving. As a result, though, the latter acquired a "double self-image": one defined through quantified work, the other by a personal service rendered.[14] In fact, this double image was even more complex in the case of such writers as La Vigne, Molinet, and Gringore, who participated in the patronage as well as the book-production system. The interesting configurations in the illustrations decorating their books reflect this kind of "schizophrenia."

The author-images in the literary production of André de la Vigne provide us with signs of a more-or-less linear development from a patron-dependent status to one of more authorial independence. This movement can be traced through an examination of the three stages of reproduction of the poet's best-known work, his *Ressource de la Chrestienté*, which appeared in manuscript form, in a single edition, and as part of a printed poetic anthology entitled the *Vergier d'honneur*.[15] Our model illustration, the dedication miniature that opens the royal manuscript of the work (Paris, B.N., ms. f.fr. 1687), depicts a writer as he offers his closed, finished book to a seated royal figure (see Figure 3.1). The former is on bended knee, a characteristic posture for authors in a presentation miniature, whereas his patron is crowned and enthroned. The fleur-de-lis motif of the backdrop and the robe signals that the monarch hails from the house of France, and the three marginal shields portray a

13. See also Dupire, *Jean Molinet*, 19, who provides details of a "gratification" Molinet received in 1499, to cover the purchase of material for clothes, in return for his daily "good and pleasant services."

14. Davis speaks of this double self-image in "Gifts, Markets and Historical Change," 11–13, which evaluates a later period.

15. Some of the following remarks appear in a different form in my "Text."

French union with the ermine devices of Brittany (right) and those of a dauphin (left). These anticipate the decorative program of the entire manuscript: on each and every folio the text is surrounded by an alternating pattern of the same heraldic devices, constituting a visual tribute to King Charles VIII of France, his queen, Anne of Brittany, and their short-lived son, the dauphin Charles Orland. As an endorsement of this visual code and an insurance that the king's identity will be maintained throughout the text, two series of illuminated acrostics within the work specify the name of Charles de Valois. Although we do not know if Charles VIII actually commissioned the *Ressource de la Chrestienté*, this particular manuscript was specially decorated for his viewing. Securing the king's patronage was clearly La Vigne's goal in writing this work, for French royal-political aims—support for the anticipated Naples expedition of 1494—constitute the raison d'être of the volume.

By contrast, the other characters in the frontispiece are unidentified and unidentifiable. The author-figure represents one of a multitude of anonymous dedicators of works. It is only at the very end of the text that the reader discovers the identity of the author-figure in the frontispiece: the last words form La Vigne's punning signature.[16]

Thus, from the first to the last folio of ms. 1687 of the *Ressource*, the specific presence of Charles VIII dominates the poetic composition visually, as the illuminations show, and textually, since the work strongly encourages support of royal policy.[17] The author's image remains traditionally anonymous until the end, where even his metaphoric signature is undermined by the invading presence of the joint royal coats of arms below it (see my "Text," 110, fig. 4.3). Just as the political theme and subject dominate the action in the text itself, so too the patron's political stature visually overshadows the poet's creative function in the paratext. The dedication miniature, then, represents symbolically the very political relationship of the patron and poet: the *mécène*, the object of the dedication and the object of glorification in the work itself, dominates the literary enterprise of the author, who is beholden to his protector for support and for the subject of his work. Understood retroactively in association with the text, however, the kneeling figure of the frontispiece, despite the subservient pose, does call attention to the writer, whose specific identity surfaces at the end of the text.

This *Ressource* illustration thus played a crucial role in the transmission of the patron's and the author's image by providing a concrete visual translation of the very names contained in the text. While the print-

16. The acrostics of Charles VIII's name and La Vigne's signature are discussed below in Chapter 4.

17. For details on the other illustrations in this manuscript, see my "Text," 104–17.

ing of the *Ressource* resulted in a less ambitious decorative program, it nevertheless precipitated modifications that offered the writer, rather than the patron, more prominent forms of visibility.

Such changes appear in the *Vergier d'honneur* versions of the *Ressource de la Chrestienté*, printed in at least six different editions in Paris sometime after May 1498 up until 1525.[18] Each of these versions bears a woodcut relating to the writer and thereby emphasizes his role over Charles VIII's, even though the names of both are announced on the first folio.[19] The two different author-images that appear on the verso of the title page of five of the editions (Figures 3.2 and 3.3) mark a change from the dedication scene of Figure 3.1. Instead of appearing in a subordinate position, the author is depicted alone, contemplating or reading his book.[20] Moreover, in print, in contrast to manuscript, more readers would view the author-figure in his place of greater visual prominence. This configuration suggests an important link between the public and the illustrations decorating a book. When the reader was a special, wealthy bookowner such as Charles VIII, the miniaturist focused on the dedicatee's image in an introductory scene. Like the author's text itself, this portrait, the artist's token of respect and honor, served as a mirror for the viewer's self-reflection or self-aggrandizement. When the readership encompassed a vaster, more vaguely defined public, however, as would have been the case for the *Vergier d'honneur* editions of the *Ressource*, the generic author-woodcut that commonly appeared reflected the new distance between the poet, whose presence alone is publicized, and the absent audience. Thus, the image of the writer that most readers saw was that of an independent figure. On one hand, these representations offered an impersonal view of the author, because they were not linked specifically to the *Ressource* text and because the same woodcuts appeared in other printed volumes.[21] By means of these reusable illustrations, then, publishers advertised the idea of authorship more than they did the image of a particular author. On the other hand, the juxtaposition of this image with the title-page announcement of La Vigne and

18. The single printed edition of the *Ressource* (Angoulême, 1495) bears no illustrations or decoration. For details, see *Ressource*, 82–95, and my "Text," 118–19.

19. See above, pp. 86–88, for a discussion and transcription of the title page.

20. In Figure 3.3 the seated figure's religious attire and the angel, commonly associated with Saint Matthew, represent traces of the earlier evangelist illustrations from which author-images derived. Even though the dress, possibly inspired from the Saint Jerome imagery of literary clerics, would have more closely depicted Octavien de Saint-Gelais (archbishop of Angoulême and the other announced author of the anthology) than it would La Vigne, medieval readers were not disconcerted by such inconsistencies.

21. In 1502–3, for example, Michel Le Noir used the woodcut reproduced in Figure 3.2. I am indebted to Dominique Coq, former Curator of Rare Books in the Réserve of the Bibliothèque Nationale, Paris, for this information.

Fig. 3.3. Author-woodcut, from *Le vergier d'honneur*, 5th ed., B.N., Cat. Roth-schild 479, title page verso. © cliché Bibliothèque Nationale Paris.

Saint-Gelais as authors of the volume called attention to these particular writers in a more obvious manner than the manuscript versions, which did not identify the author paratextually.

Two images associated with the *Vergier d'honneur* editions provide other perspectives of authorship. The third extant edition of the work, published by Jean Trepperel between 1506 and 1509, differs from all the others, because its woodcut, placed at the end instead of at the beginning of the volume, portrays a large ecclesiastical author-figure dictating to a more diminutive scribe (see *Ressource*, 85, fig. 6). Why did Trepperel emphasize the hand-copied reproduction of the text rather than its presentation or dissemination, as in the manuscript miniature? It is likely that this was the only author-woodcut Trepperel had on hand. One wonders, though, whether the printer was consciously attempting to promote this work by relating it to the manuscript tradition and to the more intimate, interdependent culture of bookmaking depicted by the appearance together of scribe and author.

Another version of the *Vergier d'honneur* furnishes an unusually individualized visual staging of La Vigne himself. In an attempt to imitate the high quality of the decorated manuscript tradition, one particular copy of the second edition of the anthology, the one published under the author's direction, was printed on vellum instead of paper, and the numerous woodcuts throughout were painted over with miniatures (Paris, B.N., Rés. Vélins 2241). Unlike the generic author-woodcut that prefaces the paper copies, the opening miniature of this version, painted over that woodcut, relates specifically to La Vigne and his *Ressource de la Chrestienté*. Unique among all the illustrations associated with the work, because it personalizes and concretizes the fictional imaginative process of the author, this miniature presents not the king but the poet, enthroned as it were, pen in hand, with personified characters from his text, Lady Christianity, Lady Nobility, and Good Counsel before him (Figure 3.4).[22] Not only has the poet literally replaced the patron on his "throne," but the subject chosen for depiction is a more unusual dimension of author-image portrayal: namely, the poet's visualization of his allegorical creation, rather than a scene of dedication. It is in this hybrid illustration of the printed *Vergier d'honneur* that the author and his work receive the most attention. Visually, the image is more individualized, recalling the donor depicted in the presentation scene of the manuscript version of the *Ressource*.[23] Although this hybrid scene places the author-figure and not the patron on stage, the reader must still rely on features associated with the print tradition, such as the title page, to identify the writer.[24] These coexisting forms of book illustration and reproduction have powerfully merged here into the most individualized image of La Vigne as the creating writer. Placed in its printed context, this miniature simultaneously looks back to the manuscript tradition and forward to the individualized authorial engravings that would preface works of later Renaissance writers.

22. Although there is no specific reference to La Vigne's characters in the illustration, I am convinced that the figures depicted here represent the three protagonists of the *Ressource de la Chrestienté*. Its opening verses appear on the folio facing this miniature. Moreover, no other works in the *recueil* offer the same coincidence of characters.

23. Myra Orth, of the Getty Center for the History of Art and the Humanities, notes that miniatures in this same style appeared in Paris over a period of twenty to thirty years, up until about 1530, and were associated with royal commissions and Parisian publishing. I am indebted to her for this information.

24. Because of an alteration of the final lines of the *Ressource* text (see pp. 172–74 below), these editions also publicize La Vigne's name even more directly than in the manuscript and Angoulême versions.

Fig. 3.4. Poet composing his work with his created characters, Lady Christianity, Lady Nobility, and Good Counsel, before him, from *Le vergier d'honneur*, 2d ed., B.N., Réserve Vélins 2241, title page verso. © cliché Bibliothèque Nationale Paris.

This emphasis on the author authoring contrasts with the focus on the patron in the earlier manuscript illumination of the *Ressource* and coincides both with the growing prominence of La Vigne's advertised name in these versions and with his direct involvement in the printing of the first two editions of the *Vergier d'honneur*. Although it is impossible to determine whether the author personally ordered the use of the author-woodcut at the front of the first two printed editions, his supervision of their publication suggests some influence in the matter. Moreover, subsequent editions imitated the idea of the author-woodcuts.

But one wonders for whom this hybrid edition of the *Vergier d'honneur* was made. The fact that the opening miniature did not portray a dedication scene in honor of a specific bookowner who might have subsidized the decoration of this copy, but rather an individualized tribute to the author himself, sets this copy apart from all others in the series. Moreover, the miniaturist would have had to have received specific directions from someone familiar with the *Ressource* text. It is quite possible that this vellum copy, which contains no indication of its owner, was specially made for the author himself. Whether or not La Vigne was the bookowner, the fact that the artist visually highlighted his persona, instead of a wealthy proprietor's, brought prominence to the writer in particular and to the literary enterprise in general. Given the fact that this illustration decorates a copy of the edition published by La Vigne, its unique depiction of the author in his inventive mode may well have served notice that André de la Vigne himself "owned" the words he had created and the characters he had imagined into existence. The paratextual modifications made to the image of the writer in the different versions of the *Ressource de la Chrestienté*, ranging from a dedication miniature to generic single-author woodcuts to a personalized portrait of the individual writer in the act of creating, coincide with La Vigne's growing self-awareness as a writer, a development that was crystallized in his 1504 lawsuit victory.

No illustrations appeared in La Vigne's later publications, composed when he served as Anne of Brittany's secretary (see my *Shaping*, 163–85). While the advertisement of his name and position as the queen's secretary on the title pages of these editions offered verbal affirmation of the author's new literary role, the addition of an author-woodcut might have seemed too extravagant for these eight-folio, political pamphlets, whose relevance was short-lived. Since La Vigne had succeeded in obtaining patronage, presumably through the aggressive self-promotional strategies described above, he did not, perhaps, need to publicize his image in the same manner.

The author-images associated with La Vigne's *Ressource de la Chres-tienté* correspond to his own professional evolution from patron dependence to authorial independence to a more enlightened form of royal dependence with his 1504 appointment as secretary to Anne of Brittany. The illustrations in several works of Jean Molinet, however, offer an example of the more complicated kinds of ambiguity that characterize both the image and the role of the author in the late fifteenth and early sixteenth centuries. Although Molinet's career epitomized the manuscript tradition of book production in many ways, his association with print in the later years of his life reflected the path that his younger contemporaries would follow more closely. While the house of Austria subsidized Molinet's literary career through an annual pension and ecclesiastical revenues, signs that the poet could not completely rely on these means of support surfaced in the last fifteen years of his life. They likely explain why he resorted to print as a means of textual reproduction.

The illustration program of three of Molinet's works, the *Art de rhéto-rique* (1493), the *Roman de la rose moralisé* (ca. 1500), and the *Naissance de Charles d'Autriche* (1500–1501), all written and printed during this later period, marks the poet's increasing visual presence at a time when he seemed almost caught between the conventional manuscript culture and the new technological possibilities of the print culture. Whereas the dedicatory images in the different versions of Molinet's *Art de rhétorique* created ambiguities about the author's identity, the presentation scenes in the manuscripts and imprints of his *Roman de la rose moralisé* placed greater attention on the writer himself, often providing visual clues to his name. Woodcuts in the *Naissance* editions went still further toward promoting Molinet's role as author and publisher.

Although no miniatures appear in either manuscript version of the *Art de rhétorique*, the work is attributed to Molinet in two places (see p. 159 below). By contrast, each of the extant copies of the 1493 Vérard edition bears an introductory dedication woodcut, although Molinet's name is absent from the paratext.[25] But the role of the generic author in these versions is ambiguous. The paper copies present a seated cleric with halo, holding an open book with another male figure, while several other men look on from the right (Figure 3.5). Even though this scene shares certain features with our model dedication miniature (Figure 3.1), the differences make it difficult to interpret the associations depicted here, partly because the woodcut originally decorated another work.[26] It was the idea

25. Some of the following ideas appeared in different form in my "Eveil," 18–35. For bibliographical details about the *Art de rhétorique*, see Appendix 4 below.

26. This woodcut appeared, for example, in Vérard's 1492 edition of the *Art de bien mou-rir* (*Recueil d'Arts*, ed. Langlois, lvii, and Macfarlane, illust. 24).

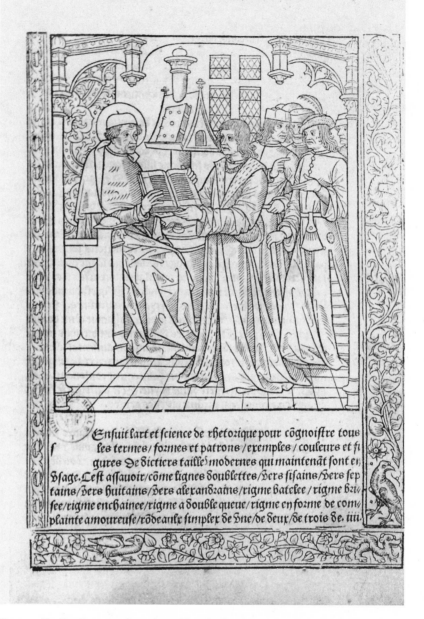

Fig. 3.5. Dedication woodcut, from *L'art de rhétorique*, 1st ed., B.N., Réserve Ye 10, fol. 2. © cliché Bibliothèque Nationale Paris.

of a presentation, rather than a real-life scenario like that typically depicted in a manuscript miniature, that was being portrayed here.[27]

However, the specially made vellum versions of this edition of the *Art de rhétorique*, those hybrid copies in which miniatures have been painted over the woodcut, represent more specific dedication scenes. As a result, some of the inherent ambiguities of the paper copy's illustration are resolved; but other uncertainties are introduced. In one illumination (Paris, B.N., Rés. Vélins 577) (Figure 3.6), an enthroned royal figure replaces the seated cleric of the woodcut, the lectern has been transformed into another onlooker, and the book is now closed. The fleur-de-lis on the noble's robe and throne, on the offered volume, and in the surrounding margins of the folio indicate that the seated figure represents a French king. The date of this printing (1493) and the appearance of the monarch's name in an acrostic at the end of the volume confirm that the protagonist in this scene of dedication, of gift giving, is Charles VIII.[28] One aspect of this illustration, then, recalls the model miniature decorating La Vigne's manuscript of the *Ressource de la Chrestienté* (Figure 3.1). But the addition of another central character to this scene, an action that implicitly acknowledges the ambiguity of the original woodcut which has been painted over, undermines the dedication, for it does not help to distinguish the other main figures in the miniature.

The uninformed reader might wonder who is presenting the book and who is the person standing between the figure and Charles VIII, although presumably the French monarch as targeted bookowner would have known.[29] It seems likely that one figure represents the writer, in this case the bogus Henry de Croy, whose name replaces that of the true author in the prologue of Vérard's printed editions of the *Art de rhétorique* (see p. 160 below). Is the other meant to represent the publisher? Given Vérard's associations with Charles VIII (Macfarlane, xii, 129–31) and his sometime self-portrayal in the opening miniature of vellum copies of the books he published, it is possible that Vérard is the figure presenting the book in this scene. Yet, with the dedicatory prologue in the voice of Henry de Croy and the strong association traditionally made in these visual renditions between author and book, one could just as easily

27. A modern reader might wonder whom the figure at the left represents. The dedicatee, because he is seated? The writer, because he is surrounded by books? A patron saint? Dupire (*Jean Molinet*, 62), and Langlois (*Recueil d'Arts*, lvii) suggest that the seated cleric is the dedicatee.

28. The B.N. *Catalogue des incunables*, 2, 1:289, corroborates that this volume belonged to Charles VIII.

29. Langlois, ed., *Recueil d'Arts*, lvii, claims that the part of the illustration that was changed from the original woodcut (i.e., the figure covering the lectern and Charles VIII) was painted by a different artist than the one who produced the rest of the miniature.

Fig. 3.6. Dedication miniature, from *L'art de rhétorique*, 1st ed., B.N., Réserve Vélins 577, fol. 2. © cliché Bibliothèque Nationale Paris.

interpret the image as that of Croy. In the end, one cannot determine whether what is seen is the dedication of the author to the patron, or of the publisher to the patron. Is this a literary or a commercial relationship that is depicted?

In another vellum copy of the *Art de rhétorique* (London, B.L., IB.41139) (Figure 3.7), which likewise presents a miniature painted over the woodcut, three central figures are again placed on stage, the original lectern having again been modified into one of these protagonists. This time, however, the latter is writing in a very small book and thus probably represents the author-figure.[30] Such an interpretation further suggests that the other, more prominently placed protagonist represents the bookseller-publisher Vérard.[31] Ironically, then, if this interpretation is valid, even though these images seek to imitate manuscript miniatures and the more traditional method of book reproduction, the presence of a publisher figure in them calls attention to the new commercialized form. Just as the publisher's arrival on the scene played a role in modifying the relationship between patron and poet in the world of book reproduction, so too his apparent portrayal in this illustration would have altered the traditional interpretation of a dedication scene.

Moreover, given the associations just made, it would appear that the seated person in the miniature is a dedicatee figure. The English royal arms in the lower margin point at this date to Henry VII.[32] Are we to understand that in this miniature the main figures depict the king of England and the publisher, while the author, standing as a witness in the background, plays a secondary role?[33]

Corroborating such an interpretation is another significant alteration

---

30. Unlike the author-figure portrayed in the hybrid version of the *Vergier d'honneur* (Figure 3.4), who, in a realistic rendition of poetic composition, writes on leaves of paper, the author-figure is here shown unrealistically, writing in a bound book. See Hult, *Prophecies*, 79–80, who observes the discrepancy between portraits of authors writing in already-bound books and the reality that medieval books were transcribed on leaves before being folded and bound.

31. The long robe hardly corresponds to the clothes of a publisher, but since it formed part of the original woodcut, the artist probably decided to retain it without change.

32. In a British Museum exhibition of the miniature in 1988, this figure was identified as such. Macfarlane, xiv, points out that the enterprising Vérard, who had several French editions translated into English, also had some copies of his editions printed on vellum and illuminated for Henry VII. But the supposed king's depiction as a robed, religious figure belies such an identification. Mary Beth Winn doubts the dedicatee is the English king, for in the copies of those editions made for him he is always depicted in royal garb; here he is not. It is possible that these arms were added at a later date.

33. Whoever the intended dedicatee was, it is nevertheless problematic that the acrostic bearing Charles VIII's name remained in this copy of Vérard's edition, thereby undermining the supposed meaning of the specially painted dedication scene depicted in the opening miniature.

Fig. 3.7. Dedication miniature, from *L'art de rhétorique*, 1st ed., B.L., IB.41139, fol. 2. By permission of the British Library.

to the woodcut illustration: hand gestures presumably indicating a conversation exchanged between the seated figure and the central standing figure have replaced the book, which drew the viewer's eye to the center of the scene in the original woodcut. Instead of the offering of a book, as depicted in the other hybrid illustrations, another kind of association is suggested here, one between noble and publisher, which overshadows the act of composition and presentation. Was this scene intended to portray their commercial interaction?

In comparison with the woodcut prefacing the paper versions of Vérard's edition of the *Art de rhétorique*—an illustration that, as a reused commodity, did not specifically relate to the historical context of its publication—the unique illustrations decorating the vellum copies of the same edition ostensibly depict specific relationships. Sometimes royal insignia, such as fleurs-de-lis, identify the dedicatee in these scenes. Although the addition of a second character makes it more probable that one is seeing both writer and publisher, it is not always easy to distinguish between them, because no signs reveal their respective identities. While the prologue and colophon do in some cases provide clues about the identity of these figures—indeed, the paratext always publicizes Vérard's name—Molinet's authorship is never acknowledged and is sometimes falsely attributed to Henry de Croy. The various versions of a slightly later work by Molinet, however, do furnish means to identify the author visually and verbally.

The first-known edition of Molinet's *Roman de la rose moralisé*, written in 1500 and presumably printed soon thereafter, provides the same dedication woodcut as that decorating the *Art de rhétorique*. This can be explained by the fact that it was again Vérard who published the volume, as his mark at the end of the edition indicates (see Tchémerzine, 7:251).

One illustration in a vellum copy of this edition closely resembles the original woodcut (see Paris, B.N., Rés. Vélins 1102, fol. 1). The miniaturist has simply colored the characters figuring in the woodcut scene, without making any changes, without painting a new scene over it. The relationship between this illustration and the particular publication in which it is found is difficult if not impossible to define since, with Molinet playing the role of translator-moralizer, as prominently announced on the title page (see p. 78 above), the main figures in the woodcut could represent one of the original authors (Guillaume de Lorris or Jean de Meun), the translator-moralizer (Molinet), the bookseller-publisher (Vérard), and/or a patron.[34] Once again, these visual ambiguities would

34. The coat of arms at the bottom of the folio is that of the d'Urfé family (Van Praet, 4:164, no. 229). The library of Claude d'Urfé (1501–58), containing some 4,400 imprints and 200 manuscripts, had quite extensive holdings for its time. For details, see *Claude d'Urfé*, ed. Conseil Général de la Loire, 183–89, 198–203. I am grateful to Myra Orth for this reference.

have disturbed a contemporary reader much less than they would a modern reader, because printers were known to use whatever illustrations they had at their disposal. The changes in the other hybrid copies of this image, however, coupled with more prominent advertisement of the author's name on the title page, suggest a conscious attempt to focus more insistently on the writer's identity.

The hybrid illustration in another copy of Vérard's edition of the *Roman de la rose moralisé* (London, B.L., C.22.C.2) depicts a more conventional manuscript dedication scene, with a diminutive poet on bended knee offering a closed book to a larger standing figure (Figure 3.8).[35] This presentation scenario resembles the miniature that decorates one of the two known manuscripts of the *Roman de la rose moralisé* (The Hague, Koninklijke Bibliotheek, ms. 128 C5) (Figure 3.9).[36] The Flemish manuscript, however, clearly depicts Molinet as donor. His ecclesiastical status and his name, echoed in the distant windmill (*moulinet*), provide very specific references.[37] The donor presents his work to an enthroned noble, Philippe de Clèves, who is identified by his coat of arms displayed on the tent above as well as through Molinet's mention of his name in the dedication of this manuscript to him.[38] Although the windmill, the image of Molinet's metaphorical signature that closes the text itself, symbolically identifies the author, recognition of this authorial allusion depended on the reader's understanding of Molinet's unique linguistic relationship with the windmill. Since this was a specially ordered volume, and since the prologue announces Molinet's name and the very last line of the work invokes it through metaphorical allusion (see Chapter 4 below), the dedicatee, Philippe de Clèves, would have made this important connection. The appearance of the windmill at a time when Molinet and those producing his books were placing increasing emphasis on the writer may explain the unexpected reference to the author.

35. The artist has switched the position of dedicatee and donor, who has replaced the seated cleric of the original woodcut. The character that replaced the donor in the earlier hybrid miniatures here depicts the dedicatee, who is standing.

36. Does the edition necessarily follow ms. 128 C5? For dating, see Dupire, *Jean Molinet*, 73, and Bourdillon, 160–62. The other extant manuscript of the work (Paris, B.N., ms. f.fr. 24393) contains no illustrations.

37. Dupire, *Jean Molinet*, 72, n. 1, sees the uncomely ("laide") figure in this miniature as a sign that authenticates the portrayal of Molinet.

38. Dupire, *Jean Molinet*, 72, quotes the dedication, which is absent from the Vérard editions. Molinet again makes reference to his *commanditaire* in chapter 76 of the *Roman de la rose moralisé*: "Il nous souviegne de monseigneur Philippe de Cleves, seigneur de Ravestain, au commandement duquel j'ay entreprins faire ceste labeur" (We remember my lord Philippe de Clèves, lord of Ravestain, under whose commission I undertook to write this work) (Ms. 128 C5, fol. 181ᵛ).

ꝏ Le prologue
IL suffist aûostre tref/
haulte seigneurie pro
sperât en fleur de ieu/
nesse militer soubz se
triüphant estâdart de
mars le grât dieu des
batailles dont ûo⁹ aues ûeu ses exploits
plus q̃ nul prince de ûostre aage Se auec

ques ce comme embrase dardant desir e
prins damoureuses estincelles ne desire
estre champion des dames ensuyuant si
tresplaisant guidon de ûenus deesse da
mours . Dont iasoit ce que ses arcz / ses
dartz/ses sances ꞇ ses harnoys de samou
reuse artisserie soient de plus tendre trê
peure que ceulx de guerre que son forge
a misan. Touteffois quant ilz sont sub=
                                                    ß i

Fig. 3.8. Dedication miniature, from *Le roman de la rose moralisé*, B.L., C.22.C.2, fol. 1. By permission of the British Library.

Fig. 3.9. Dedication miniature, from *Le roman de la rose moralisé*, The Hague, Koninklijke Bibliotheek, 128 C 5, fol. 6ʳ.

Let us return to the printed vellum edition of Molinet's *Roman de la rose moralisé*, which bears a similar dedication miniature (Figure 3.8). Since the title page that opens all of the printed versions of this work names Molinet as its author-translator, the reader can readily identify the kneeling figure in the dedication miniature on the following folio of this particular edition. The difference in the dress and the portraits of the donors in Figures 3.8 and 3.9, however, suggests that it was in fact Vérard, the one profiting from the different dedications of the same edition, who was being depicted in Figure 3.8. The placement of his name in the colophon of the editions and his publisher's mark on the following folio announce Vérard's involvement more obviously than that of any author. The absence of the dedicatee's name here reflects the fact that bookmakers were increasingly replacing bookowners as the prominent personalities associated with book production.

In the miniature of still another vellum copy of Vérard's printed edition of the same work (Paris, B.N., Rés. Vélins 1101), the use of a windmill in an even more overt fashion emphasizes the author's identity over that of the other characters (Figure 3.10). The windmill is so large and, in its unusual foreground position to the right of the person presenting the work, so out of place, that it is virtually impossible to overlook its reference to the author. To my knowledge, no other vernacular writer is visually portrayed at this early date in such a personal, punning, and obvious manner in a dedication miniature.[39] Although the enthroned figure is the one receiving the book being offered, the *moulinet* and centrally placed donor overshadow all other figures.[40]

What can explain this insistence on the author's specific identity in one manuscript and in two hybrid vellum copies of Vérard's edition of the *Roman de la rose moralisé*? The answer, I believe, relates to the fact that Molinet's name, which had been absent from the earlier editions of his *Art de rhétorique*, is prominently displayed on the title page of all the printed versions of the *Roman de la rose moralisé*. That is to say, a concerted effort seems to have been made to acknowledge—and perhaps profit from—the celebrity of Molinet's name. Whether or not Molinet participated in the decision to advertise his name on the title page of these works or to portray the windmill, or *moulinet*, in the two presentation scenes described above is impossible to determine. The visual prominence granted him in these instances nonetheless brought greater attention and distinction to his name and role as author than in his previous works, whether in manuscript or print. Moreover, it coincided with the increasingly accessible signature Molinet was adopting within his texts at this time, as I suggest below in Chapter 4.

Thus, during the period between Vérard's 1493 publication of Molinet's *Art de rhétorique* in near-anonymous fashion and the same publisher's 1500 edition of the *Roman de la rose moralisé*, which placed greater attention on the writer himself in both the manuscript and the printed dedication scene, the writer appeared more and more frequently in a prominent visual role. The readjustments being made by the principal

39. Myra Orth contends that the windmill wings ("ailes") in the margins of a manuscript made for Louise de Savoie in 1496 constitute a visual pun with the *L* of her name (see Lecoq, *François Ier imaginaire*, 471, fig. 228) but also refer to the author François Du Moulin (Desmoulins). Such an association between symbol and writer is quite a bit more subtle than that in our Figures 3.9 or 3.10. Moreover, one never finds the conjunction of this image in any other work by Du Moulin.

40. It has not been possible to determine to which family the coat of arms painted at the bottom of the folio refers or who the seated figure might be.

Fig. 3.10. Dedication miniature, from *Le roman de la rose moralisé*, B.N., Réserve Vélins 1101, fol. 1. © cliché Bibliothèque Nationale Paris.

players in the book-production process of the early sixteenth century—the patron, poet, and printer—are mirrored in the re-creation and resituation of figures painted over the original Vérard woodcut in these hybrid editions of the *Roman de la rose moralisé*.

This more manifest emphasis on the author continues in Molinet's *Naissance de Charles d'Autriche*, printed around the same time his *Roman de la rose moralisé* appeared. That no single manuscript of the *Naissance* remains extant suggests that this rather medieval author chose print as the optimal form of reproduction for this text. In fact, the first extant edition of Molinet's *Naissance*, written after March 7, 1500, and published before September 1501 in Valenciennes, verbally and visually displays Molinet's name by means of a *printed*, not a painted, illustration. What follows the colophon, which identifies the printer,[41] is not Jean de Liège's but Molinet's mark, bearing his name (Figure 3.11).[42] Thus, just as Vérard's mark at the end of his editions of Molinet's *Art de rhétorique* and *Roman de la rose moralisé* advertised his involvement in the publication of these works, so too the sign designating Molinet dramatically announces his direction of the publication of the *Naissance*.

To my knowledge, this is the first printed French mark advertising an author's participation in the publication of his work. Well before Lemaire's replacement of the king's coat of arms with his own on the title page of the second edition of the *Légende des Vénitiens* in 1512, Molinet, in his role as publisher, had already set the stage by having his publisher's sign printed at the end of the *Naissance*. Modeled in part on printers' marks and in part on royal insignia, this device probably provided the source of a related design that Molinet adopted for his official coat of arms when he was knighted in 1504.[43] This publisher's mark at the end of the Valenciennes edition of the *Naissance* announces a historic change in Molinet's relationship to his text and to the producers of it. The author was in control of the text's reproduction, choosing to put it in *printed* form and to publicize his new authority in the book industry in a personal fashion.

What would have moved Molinet to oversee the publication of the *Naissance* and to identify himself so directly? The motivation here, I believe, was related to Molinet's desire to avoid losing his authorial asso-

41. It reads: "Imprimez en Vallenchiennes de par Jehan de Liege demorant entre le pont des ronneaux et le toucquet de leu devant le soleil" (Printed in Valenciennes by Jean de Liège, living between the Ronneaux bridge and Le Toucquet at the place before the [sign of the] sun).

42. The association suggested in this image is not with a poetic windmill but with another kind of *moulinet* image, a toy, perhaps because a child was the subject of the work.

43. The design apparently met with disapproval by Burgundian court officials, because of its less-than-noble character (Roy, 21).

Fig. 3.11. Author's publication mark, from *La naissance de Charles d'Autriche*, 1st ed., B.N., Réserve Ye 1077, fol. 6ᵛ. Phot. Bibl. Nat. Paris.

ciation with his writings, a loss that had characterized the Paris editions of his *Temple de Mars* and *Art de rhétorique,* and to make a profit from his imprints so that he would not have to depend solely on his increasingly unreliable pension. Perhaps the money Molinet received for this work (see above, p. 109) helped defray the printing costs he must have incurred. The combination of direct payment for the *Naissance* and his reproduction of the work in printed form reflects Molinet's simultaneous interaction with patron and printer, with private and commercial book-reproduction systems. This suggests that even writers more or less guaranteed patronage may have resorted to commercial forms of book reproduction, exchange, and support. Molinet's decision at around the same time to have his entire works reproduced in manuscript form shows, nonetheless, a continued commitment to the older system.

Although Molinet's new involvement in book production is strategically publicized in the first edition of the *Naissance* so as not to eclipse the text's focus on the son of his patron, both of whom are announced via the title page and the woodcut of their arms on the title page verso (see Tchémerzine, 7:368),[44] Molinet's mark nonetheless balances and complements his *mécène*'s image. Just as the archduke's coat of arms reminds the reader of his political power, so too Molinet's publisher's mark, displaying similar political and quasi-aristocratic attributes, directs attention to his new literary and *livresque* power.

The second extant edition of the *Naissance*, printed in Lyons around 1503, does not reproduce Molinet's arms, since Molinet did not publish it; the title page, however, does place the writer in greater authorial prominence. As we learned above (Chapter 2), Molinet's name is announced in an emphasized fashion on the first folio. Moreover, it bears a prominently displayed author-woodcut below the title (Figure 3.12). Proper name and human image, verbal and visual identification, come together here to promote the author of the work. It is not the object of the *moulinet* that is associated with Molinet, but rather the human literary figure himself. Thus, the metaphorical mill image, which had been associated with Molinet's more subservient relationship to patronage and the manuscript culture, gave rise to the printed arms bearing his name, which in turn were replaced by the printed, albeit generic, image of the author on the title page itself.[45] Thus, Molinet attained the highest level of paratextual tribute in a publication neither endorsed by the house of Austria nor controlled by the author, an edition printed outside Paris

44. The title page reads: "La tersdesiree [*sic*] et proufitable naissance de tresillustre enfant Charles d'Austrice, filz de monseigneur l'archiduc nostre tresredoubté prince et seigneur naturel" (The very desired and profitable birth of the very illustrious child Charles of Austria, son of my lord the archduke, our very revered prince and natural lord).

45. Corroborating this increasingly visual emphasis on Molinet in the *Naissance* editions of circa 1500 and 1503 is the appearance of author-woodcuts, instead of dedication scenes, in the two later printed editions of the *Roman de la rose moralisé*. See the edition printed at Lyons by Balsarin in 1503 (fol. b) and the edition published by Michel Le Noir's widow in 1521 (title page verso). Because these particular publications have no hybrid traces and because they display a scene of the author alone, their portrayal of Molinet does not have the ambiguities of the various copies of the Vérard edition.

Fig. 3.12. Author-woodcut, from *La naissance de Charles d'Autriche*, 2d ed., B.N.,
Réserve Ye 221, title page. Phot. Bibl. Nat. Paris.

and presumably free of external political association. Although he may not have known about or received any proceeds from this Lyons publication, Molinet stands out prominently here as a writer whose role and presence, if not his rights, France had finally acknowledged.

With Pierre Gringore we witness a convergence and concentration of the visual signs of authorship that characterized La Vigne's literary output and Molinet's later career. The use of author-images in Gringore's works reflects the writer's participation in both the marketplace and the gift-giving economy. But such illustrations tended to be juxtaposed instead of superimposed in Gringore's editions, revealing more obviously to the reader the author's double self-image as independent author and dependent court protégé. As with every other paratextual detail related to the work in its first-edition form, Gringore's *Folles entreprises* marks a dramatic use of authorial images. Given the poet's involvement at nearly all levels of the literary enterprise, his visibility, which often represents a defensive gesture, signals more than ever the growing importance of authorial intention at both the paratextual and the textual level.

Just as Gringore's name never appeared in the paratext of his earliest works, including the *Chasteau de labour, Chasteau d'amours, Lettres nouvelles de Milan*, and *Complainte de la Terre Sainte*, visual signs of his identity are likewise absent in these works.[46] This was not the case, however, with his *Folles entreprises* of 1505, whose illustrations correspond to the sharing by printer and author of the verbal publicity on the first folio. In two issues of the first edition of this work, for example, the printer's mark, stamped on the title page (see Tchémerzine, 6:52), is followed on the verso by a generic author-woodcut similar to the one that appeared in three of the *Vergier d'honneur* editions (Figure 3.2).[47] It falls appropri-

46. Later versions of the *Chasteau de labour* did include author-images (see Appendix 5 below for bibliographical details). Strategically placed to echo Gringore's acrostic signature on the recto of the same folio, a generic author-illustration of a seated monk appears at the end of the Rouen edition of 1500, balancing Le Forestier's printer's mark on the title page (Tchémerzine, 6:30). An author-woodcut resembling Figure 3.2, instead of a printer's mark, is displayed on the title page of Trepperel's circa 1504 edition of the *Chasteau de labour*. The title page verso of Gilles Couteau's circa 1505 edition bears a woodcut of a cleric in the process of composing his text, while the printer's name and address are relegated to the colophon (see Tchémerzine, 6:32, fig. 1). Thus, even though Gringore did not participate in the publication of these later editions of his *Labour*, book producers chose to emphasize visually the idea of authorship. This development anticipated the intensification of Gringore's paratextual presence in the first edition of the *Folles entreprises* in December 1505.

47. The details in these illustrations, however, are different, as a comparison of the *Vergier d'honneur* editions with the two versions discussed here (Cat. Fairfax-Murray 206 [Tchémerzine, 6:48] and Paris, B.N., Rés. Ye 1323 [including Vélins 2244 and 2245]) indicates.

ately on the folio opposite the beginning of the text and the rubric that reads "L'acteur" (The Author). Thus, printer and author visually shared first-folio space, as they did publishing activities. Gringore's verbal depiction as bookseller on the first folio recto and his visual representation as author on its verso balanced the prominence accorded Le Dru, whose printer's mark appeared prominently on the title page itself.

In one vellum copy of the *Folles entreprises*, whose title page displays Le Dru's mark, woodcuts throughout have been covered with miniatures in an attempt to imitate a manuscript book (Paris, B.N., Rés. Vélins 2244). Instead of an author-illustration, however, one finds a miniature that depicts the Crucifixion, with two kneeling figures positioned in the foreground (Figure 3.13). This medieval-like manuscript artifact seems to honor potential patrons rather than emphasizing the idea of authorship, like the woodcuts in the paper copies of the same edition.[48] Ironically, the preservation of the printer's mark on the title page and the details about Gringore's privilege and role as author-publisher in the colophon contradict the ultimate aim of this hybrid edition, which was to serve as an imitation manuscript book.[49]

An even more dramatic change occurred on the title page of two other issues of the December 1505 edition of the *Folles entreprises* (Paris, B.N., Rés. Ye 1321, and Paris, Bibl. de l'Ecole Nationale Supérieure des Beaux-Arts, Rés. Masson 428[1]). The printer's mark has been replaced by a woodcut depicting Mère Sotte and two younger fools (Figure 3.14). This image suggests that in order to announce his address as bookseller, Gringore adopted a mark that represented his dramatic role as Mother Folly, because the character had gained greater recognition than he had as a comparatively new author. Like printers and other booksellers, the author had his image affixed to the title page of certain issues of this edition that he published; it thereby drew attention to his publicized address which, beneath the image, directly mentions "the sign of Mother Folly." But why do two different title-page arrangements exist, one bearing the printer's mark, the other a woodcut identifying the author-bookseller? It is likely that the two title pages corresponded to books al-

48. Since the first edition of the *Folles entreprises* contains a prominently placed dedication to the lord of Ferrières (see below), it is conceivable that the kneeling figures in this illustration represent Ferrières and his wife and even that this copy was the one offered by Gringore to Ferrières.

49. The first quire is missing in Paris, B.N., Vélins 2245, so it is impossible to ascertain if the author-woodcut (or printer's mark) was replaced. Unlike Vélins 2244, this version eliminated the privilege announcement at the end of the work, suggesting that a greater effort was made to dissociate the print and manuscript traditions in this case. For a discussion of this issue, see pp. 37–38 above.

Fig. 3.13. Dedication miniature, from *Les folles entreprises*, 1st ed., B.N., Réserve
Vélins 2244, title page verso. © cliché Bibliothèque Nationale Paris.

Fig. 3.14. Author's bookseller mark, from *Les folles entreprises*, 1st ed., B.N., Réserve Ye 1321, title page. © cliché Bibliothèque Nationale Paris.

lotted to Le Dru and Gringore, respectively, as part of a prepublication agreement.

For the first time in France, then, as far as can be determined, a writer was not only verbally advertised on the title page in his function as bookseller, but in two particular issues of this first edition of the *Folles entreprises*, the title page features his personal woodcut, effectively displacing the mark of the printer. This use of a personal woodcut *on the title page* postdates the placement of Molinet's personal publication mark *at the end* of the first-known *Naissance* edition by some five years, and it predates the appearance of Lemaire's coat of arms on the title page of his *Légende des Vénitiens* by some six years. This specific visual emphasis on Gringore's presence corresponds to his deeper involvement with the printing of this work, marked dramatically by his publication of the *Complainte de Trop Tard Marié* a few months earlier and by the display of the author-privilege he had obtained for the *Folles entreprises*. With the appearance of this title-page woodcut of Mother Folly, then, Gringore's paratextual presence in the *Folles entreprises* was significantly enhanced.

Of even greater importance than the presence of Gringore's bookseller sign on the title page of the *Folles entreprises* is the appearance of the Mère Sotte illustration in the later versions of the work, whose publication the author no longer supervised. What had originally served as a bookseller's mark on the title page of two issues of the Le Dru edition came to function as an author-woodcut in the later editions of the work, since Gringore's only association with these volumes was through his acrostic signature in the final stanza of the text. Despite the fact that others had replaced the poet as bookseller and publisher, as the changed address on the title page indicates, the same Mère Sotte illustration remained in its prominent position (Figure 3.15a–c). Moreover, identification of both printer and bookseller is absent from the volume.[50] Perhaps the publishers of these editions decided it was good advertising policy to continue using the Mother Folly woodcut, or a copy of it, figuring that the image of the three *sots* would promote interest in the book's subject.[51] Or its reuse might simply reveal that one of the two Le Dru issues that bore the Mère Sotte woodcut on the title page served as the source of these editions.

Thus, in spite of itself, this self-perpetuating image came to play a different role than that originally intended. It had become a writer's mark, a much more personalized sign of authorship than the generic author-woodcuts commonly found in these and other volumes. Gringore had essentially appropriated the idea of a book producer's mark in his role as bookseller (though other publishers' signs did not portray such a close representation of the person in question), but the retention of the mark

50. Only the title-page address indirectly provides information about the bookseller (see my "Text," 137, n. 45).

51. If this were the case, however, it would have been a misrepresentation of the book's very moralistic contents. In fact, the expanded title of the Trepperel and anonymous 1510 editions obviously sought to avert such a misunderstanding by explicitly providing details about the moralistic nature of the work (my emphasis): "Les Folles Entreprises *qui traictent de plusieurs choses morales*" (The *Folles entreprises*, which discusses several moral issues).

Fig. 3.15a–c. The Mère Sotte illustration: *a*, author's mark, from *Les folles entreprises*, B.L., 241.g.43, title page, by permission of the British Library; *b*, author's mark, from *Les folles entreprises*, B.N., Cat. Rothschild 495, title page, © cliché Bibliothèque Nationale Paris; *c*, author's mark, from *Les folles entreprises*, Bibliothèque Mazarine, Inc., 44251, title page.

by subsequent publishers transformed its function. In fact, this reappearance of what had become an author-illustration was repeated in many of Gringore's later works, and Mère Sotte woodcuts came to figure on the title page even when Gringore did not publish the volume.[52] In some cases a rubric, serving as a second title to mark the beginning of the text, directly linked Gringore and his alter ego, Mère Sotte, making certain the reader understood that bookseller and author were the same.[53] Again, although Gringore had employed his personalized woodcut at the outset to publicize his function as distributor of his books, that same image in other publishers' hands promoted instead his authorship. In this fashion, Gringore's role as bookseller ended up enhancing his image as a writer.

Although Gringore's Mère Sotte illustration was not exactly an author-portrait, its personalized nature and repeated appearance on title pages of his editions mark an important stage in the evolution of the author's image in France. This stage is defined by the coincidence of several factors: (1) the author's legally validated control over the publication of his work; (2) the growing use of paratextual verbal announcements of the author's varying functions; (3) an increasingly individualized visual representation of the writer in the paratext; and (4), as I argue in Chapter 5, a more marked presence of the authorial voice within the text itself. Steven Rendall's observations about how author-portraits accompanied a more personalized or individualized discourse at a later period pertain nonetheless to Gringore and other late medieval writers studied here:

> Such portraits [author-portraits] underline the connection between the text and an individual producer and thus contribute to the individualization of discourse that Foucault associated with the "author function." They differ from the portraits of the artist that often appear in Renaissance paintings . . . because they are not part of the "text" or "composition" itself but rather part of its "frame," and because they figure a subject that claims not only to have produced the work but also, through the immanence of an individual intention, to determine—that is, to limit—its *meaning*. (143–44)

52. Both known editions of *Le jeu du Prince des Sotz et Mère Sotte* (Paris, [after February 1512]; see Tchémerzine, 6:76), all the extant editions of *Les fantasies de Mère Sotte* (see Figure 3.17) and all the editions of *Les menus propos* (see Tchémerzine, 6:92–98) feature the Mère Sotte woodcut.

53. The following appears on folio 2 of the *Abus du monde* (1509) and the *Coqueluche* (1510): "composez [*Coqueluche*: composee] par Pierre Gringore dit Mere Sotte" (composed by Pierre Gringore, known as Mother Folly). Folio 2 of the *Fantasies de Mère Sotte* makes a reference to "Pierre Gringore dit Mere Sotte."

The expanding advertisement and visibility of authors through visual as well as verbal means can be seen to be directly related to the ending of medieval *mouvance*, for "individual intention" was becoming an integral part of literary creation.

The Mère Sotte woodcut's appearance in the various editions of the *Folles entreprises* and in later works, then, revealed Gringore's gradual overshadowing of printers by means of a conscious stamping of identity and intent in his publications. The association between poet and patron surfaced in these spaces as well, but in a more ambiguous, contradictory fashion, alerting readers to the fact that patronage was still an economic necessity, even though the "rules of the game" had changed.[54] For in the two issues of the 1505 *Folles entreprises* edition that bear a Mère Sotte woodcut on the title page, presumably those volumes Gringore himself sold, the reader also discovers a dedication woodcut on the verso side of that folio (Figure 3.16). Reminiscent of the relationship portrayed in the manuscript frontispieces of La Vigne's *Ressource de la Chrestienté* (Figure 3.1), though less personalized because of its generic quality and repeated use in other copies, this illustration depicts a poet on bended knee offering his book to a more highly positioned, seated figure. In contrast to the two issues of the *Folles entreprises* bearing Le Dru's mark and an author-woodcut, thereby focusing on printer and poet in their separate, more equal but interdependent roles, the two issues with this dedication-woodcut recall an earlier, pre-print association whereby a noble figure was given a place of greater importance than the poet. Its presence in a printed work indicates that the search for a benefactor had come to form an integral part of the new means of reproduction, that the gift-giving and marketplace modes existed side by side.

Still, there was an inherent contradiction in the juxtaposition of the Mère Sotte and dedication illustrations in these two issues of the *Folles entreprises*: the verbal and visual allusions on the title page to Gringore's enterprising role as bookseller essentially conflicted with the subservient relationship depicted in the presentation scene on the verso, where the generic author is offering, not selling, his volume. We have here a visual confrontation between—or merely a juxtaposition of—the money- and object-oriented market system, represented by the middle-class book trade, and the gift exchange and cultural sharing of the aristocratic patronage system.

The presence of this dedication woodcut apparently confirms that Gringore was in search of a long-term patron or perhaps simply that he needed some ad hoc support to help defray the cost of printing copies of

54. Mortimer, "Portrait," 14, uses this expression in a different context. See also Davis, "Beyond the Market," 74, who explains how the character of the dedicated gift changed.

Fig. 3.16. Dedication woodcut, from *Les folles entreprises*, Paris, Ecole Nationale Supérieure des Beaux-Arts, Masson 428, title page verso.

his work. In fact, in all editions of the *Folles entreprises* a verbal tribute sheds light on the identity of the seated figure in the generic dedication-woodcut and on the nature of the support sought by the author. Announced toward the end of the work by a rubric that recalls the poet–patron relationship portrayed in the presentation scene (see Chapter 5, n. 75, below), these self-conscious verses, incorporated into the text itself immediately before Gringore's final acrostic stanza, describe the poet's decision to offer his work to the lord of Ferrières:[55]

> L'acteur
> Quant mon esprit fut lassé de penser
> A qui devoye ce traicté adresser,
> Luy fut advis que le devoye bailler
> A ung tresnoble et prudent chevalier,
> Parquoy trouvay les façons et manières
> Vers le sire Pierre de Ferières,
> Puissant baron de Thuri sans argu,
> Et regentant la seigneurie Dangu,
> Me retirer, luy presentant ce livre.
> Se on demande pourquoy c'est que luy livre,
> Respondre puis que mes predecesseurs
> De sa maison ont esté serviteurs,
> Lesquelz je vueil ensuivir, se je puis,
> Car son subject et son serviteur suis,
> Non suffisant de servir sa noblesse,
> Et toutesfois mon livre à luy adresse,
> Luy suppliant le prendre en patience
> Et excuser ma simple negligence.
> Son homme suis qui de tout mon pouvoir
> Le vueil servir, et faire mon devoir.
>   (142–43)

When my mind was weary of thinking to whom this tract should be addressed, it decided that it should be given to a very noble and prudent knight. Therefore I found the means to go to Lord Pierre of Ferrières, powerful baron of Thury without displeasure, and over-

55. All citations are taken from Gringore's *Œuvres*, ed. Héricault and Montaiglon, 1:11–144. The identity of the noble portrayed in the dedication woodcut is thus deferred until these verses, but their placement within the text ensured that the author's dedication would not be dissociated from the work, as it was in Molinet's *Art de rhétorique*. It is conceivable that the hybrid vellum version that bears a miniature of the Crucifixion with kneeling figures (Figure 3.13) was the very copy Gringore presented to Ferrières. Gringore's attempt to obtain Ferrière's patronage was apparently unsuccessful.

seer of the lordship of Dangu, and presented him this book. If anyone asks why I offer it to him, I can reply that my predecessors were servants of his house, and I wish to follow in their footsteps if I can, because I am his subject and servant, not sufficient to serve his nobleness. But I dedicate my book to him, nonetheless, asking him to accept it with patience and to excuse my simple carelessness. I am his man, and with all my power I wish to serve him and do my duty.

The personalized dedication that marks all the copies of this edition alerts us to Gringore's new tactic. By adding verses that specified who the generic woodcut-character represented (at least in those versions in which the illustration appeared), by essentially flattering a potential patron in manuscript-like terms that would reach a wide public, the author may have felt that he had a better chance of obtaining patronage. For praise of a potential patron that extended well beyond his or her court circle, because of its printed form, increased the value of the dedicated book in the eyes of the recipient (Davis, "Beyond the Market," 75). At the same time, it provided the donor with the possibility of benefiting from public support through the sale of his volumes. Like Lemaire some eighteen months earlier with the publication of his *Temple d'honneur et de vertus*, Gringore exploited the potential that publication of his work offered him by seeking at once to attract the sponsorship of a wealthy, aristocratic patron, the baron of Ferrières, and to reach a wide bourgeois public. In a sense, the generic dedication-woodcut democratized the author's quest for support, allowing more openness and creativity, for the author could approach many different patrons simultaneously.[56]

Because the Mère Sotte image on the title page of several later editions of the *Folles entreprises* functioned as an author's mark, rather than a bookseller's mark, a more apparent contradiction existed between the writer's independent mark displayed on the title page and his more dependent status as a kneeling figure offering his book on the verso of the folio.[57] It is unclear, however, why dedication woodcuts appeared in editions whose publication Gringore did not control.[58] Were the images sim-

56. Whereas Erasmus was particularly successful in using specially prepared dedications for the same book, others simply changed the dedication with a new edition (see Davis, "Beyond the Market," 74–75, and Jardine).

57. The dedication woodcut appears, for example, in a Lyons edition of October 1507, after Gringore's one-year privilege of December 1505 had expired. Two Trepperel editions (Widow (?) Trepperel, ca. 1506 [B.N., Cat. Roth. 495], and Widow Trepperel (Lotrian?), ca. 1510 [B.N., Rés. Ye 292]) also bear the dedication woodcut on the title page verso. See Appendix 5 below for bibliographical details.

58. The Trepperel editions of the *Folles entreprises* feature the author more than the other later editions. While the circa 1506 edition (B.N., Cat. Rothschild, 495) bears a dedication woodcut on the verso side of the Mère Sotte title-page illustration, a generic author-

ply copied from earlier editions, or did these serve a specific dedicatory function? Is it possible that other publishers dedicated their editions of Gringore's work to several different dedicatees, à la Vérard?

The same presentation woodcut that decorated these editions of the *Folles entreprises* continued to appear on the title page of Gringore's later works, including *L'entreprise de Venise* (ca. 1509),[59] *L'union des princes* (ca. 1509),[60] *L'abus du monde* (October 1509),[61] and *La coqueluche* (1510).[62] Since two of these works, the *Entreprise de Venise* and the *Union des princes*, directly supported Louis XII's political policy, it is likely that the author, having failed to attract the support of the lord of Ferrières, attempted to find patronage at the house of France.[63]

To recapitulate, the continued use of generic presentation-woodcuts in some of the *Folles entreprises* issues of the 1505 edition, the presence of specific verses of dedication in all editions of the same work, and the appearance of the dedication woodcut in other works by Gringore dating around 1509–10 signal the author's continued search for a benefactor through the medium of print, like Lemaire before him. These features imply that Gringore's privileges for one year (or less) as bookseller-publisher of the *Folles entreprises*, *Abus du monde*, *Union des princes*, *Chasse du cerf des cerfs*, *Coqueluche*, and *Espoir de paix* and his role as Mother Folly in the Enfants sans Souci theatrical troupe were not as attractive or viable as the permanent position a patron could offer him. Further, they

---

woodcut follows the colophon. Two other Trepperel editions (ca. 1506 [Méjanes Rés. D. 107] and ca. 1510 [B.N., Rés. Ye 288]) employ an author-woodcut instead of the dedication woodcut on the title page verso.

59. See Paris, B.N., Cat. Rothschild, 2823. A different dedication scene appears in a woodcut at the end of a Lyons edition (P. Maréchal & B. Chaussard, ca. 1509).

60. A privilege featured on the verso side of the title page of this edition indicates that Gringore supervised its publication.

61. The dedication woodcut is on the verso of the title page, which bears the Mère Sotte woodcut on the recto. Two later editions dating from 1515 and 1525/27 (Paris: Lotrian) bear a dedication illustration on the title page. A manuscript version of the *Abus du monde* (New York, Pierpont Morgan Library, ms. 42) places focus on the noble bookowner. Written in a Roman script, it features the arms of James IV (king of Scotland, 1473–1513) on the title page and a conventional dedication miniature on the verso.

62. Two Le Dru printings of August 1510 bear the same dedication woodcut on the verso of the title page, which features the Mère Sotte woodcut.

63. Gringore's first known edition of the *Espoir de paix* (February 1511, N.S.), a political pamphlet in support of French policy whose publication he supervised, was probably intended for the king, as suggested by a woodcut of the joint arms of Anne of Brittany and Louis XII (see Tchémerzine, 6:73, fig. 2, which bears a remarkable similarity to Lemaire's *Légende des Vénitiens* title page of 1509) and by an announcement on folio 2 that the work was written by Gringore "a l'honneur du treschrestien Loys douziesme de ce nom Roy de France" (in honor of the very Christian Louis, the twelfth of this name, king of France). The second edition of the work, which was not published under Gringore's control, displays another illustration of the arms of Louis XII.

suggest that Gringore had particular trouble securing long-term patronage, for he had to wait until 1518 for such an opportunity.[64] His difficulty in this regard was no doubt related to the weakening spirit of the gift economy around this time, attributable both to the growing influence of the market economy and to increasing pressures of obligation (Davis, "Gifts, Markets and Historical Change" 14–15).

Whether functioning as the mark of a bookseller or of an author, Gringore's ubiquitous, personalized Mère Sotte woodcut served as his device, for it embodied not only an image but a motto as well, one that can be understood as an invitation to explore the text behind his own and his book's exterior: "Raison par tout, par tout raison, tout par raison" (Reason everywhere; everywhere reason; everything with reason). In his discussion of Ronsard, Montaigne, and Erasmus, Steven Rendall makes this important association between author, image, and text by contending that the juxtaposition of image and motto in a work's peripheral space represents the author's body and soul, "because both picture and text are considered simulacra, signs of signs: the picture represents the body, which in turn represents the soul, just as writing represents speech, which in turn represents the soul" (144–45). Let us explore briefly the significance of Gringore's device in this light.

Described as "a para-literary form which . . . participated in the poetic function of communication" (Russell, 32), the device was "a concise form of intellectual advertising" (Mortimer, "Portrait," 32); although similar to heraldic arms, in that it served as an identifying mark, it was much more personal in that it distinguished an individual by providing a figurative description through an idealized aspect of his or her character, status, or aims. If by the fourteenth century such devices were being used by the powerful and rich as a public relations strategy to create and promote an imposing image, then poets, in imitating these aristocratic signs to publicize their authorship, doubtless understood the power it gave them to advertise the image they wished to promote. Most adopted a form of rhetorical encoding, the device motto, such as Lemaire's "De peu assez," as a kind of signature. Others, like Molinet, adopted the metaphorical encoding of a device figure (or device object), with the message implicit in it, an experimental, short-lived creation that was more closely associated with the court.[65]

---

64. There may be a relationship between Gringore's lack of success in finding a patron, the absence of works written and/or published between 1511 and 1516 (except for the *Jeu du Prince des Sotz*), and the composition in *manuscript* form of his *Entrée de la reine Mary Tudor* in 1514 (London, B.L., Cot. ms. Vespasian B.II) and *Couronnement, sacre et entrée de la royne a Paris* in 1517 (Nantes, Bibliothèque Mun., ms. 1337).

65. Much of the foregoing summary about the general aspects of devices derives from Russell, esp. 24–25.

This semiological simulation, this imitation of what was essentially a commercial mode—advertisement—established a curious correspondence between poets and those they served, and it embodied the ambiguities of the patron–client relationship discussed above. Its most "successful" expression appears in Molinet's work through the evolution from the symbolic windmill to its reconstitution and incorporation in his publisher's mark around 1500 and finally into his official coat of arms, designed on the occasion of his promotion into the nobility in 1504. Indeed, Molinet's imitation and arrogation of aristocratic signs actually materialized into his appropriation of aristocratic social status as well. The appearance of Jean Lemaire's personalized coat of arms and motto on the title pages of his works from 1511 on, beginning with those editions of the *Légende des Vénitiens* which he himself published, does not only represent an appropriation of the royal attributes that had decorated the 1509 edition of the work (Figure 1.7).[66] It also coincides with the period of his advancement into the house of France in late 1511 or early 1512. Gringore's "rise" might not have been as dramatic, but his use of devices in association with the Mère Sotte woodcuts allows us to trace it visually as well.

In Gringore's Mère Sotte device, both motto and figure are present but in a contradictory and incongruous fashion, mirroring the patterns of the day (Russell, 32–33). For the expression that frames the Mère Sotte image, "Raison par tout, par tout raison, tout par raison," contrasts with the three fools depicted in the illustration. Yet, if Gringore's focus on reason and attack on folly in his previous works, especially in the *Chasteau de labour* and the *Chasteau d'amours*, are taken into account, the moralistic words of his device are merely a logical extension of his literary concerns. The *Folles entreprises* harshly criticized all kinds of foolish behavior, of "folz entrepreneurs," examples of which Gringore provides throughout the long volume. The *Fantasies de Mère Sotte* likewise presents a series of very moral attitudes on contemporary events (Frautschi ed., 14–15). Therefore, the figure and motto of Gringore's device merged two sides of his creative genius: the theatrical role he played as Mère Sotte, often involving a demonstration of rational behavior in an irrational world (Brown, "Political Misrule"), and the moralistic stance he always promoted in his writings. As bookseller, publisher, author, and ac-

66. The same coat of arms decorates the title page of the various editions of Lemaire's *Illustrations de Gaule et Singularitez de Troye*, published in separate volumes during the same period. See also the edition of Claude de Seyssel's *Victoire du roy contre les Veniciens*, published in Paris in 1510 by Vérard, which features both the king's and the author's arms on the title page and which bears an author-woodcut that incorporates the author's own arms on the title page verso. I am grateful to Ursula Baurmeister, Curator of Rare Books in the Réserve of the Bibliothèque Nationale, Paris, for calling my attention to this work.

tor,[67] Gringore exploited this device, disseminated in print form for personal publicity, just as aristocrats had done for centuries.

The publication of Gringore's *Fantasies de Mère Sotte* in 1516 altered to a degree the motto and image of his device. The "Raison par tout, par tout raison, tout par raison" expression framing the Mère Sotte woodcut, which again decorated the title page (Figure 3.17), reappears in abbreviated form ("Raison par tout") in the center of a new illustration, whose more serious design better corresponds to the moralistic message of his motto (Figure 3.18): a hooded falcon perched on a tree stump holds a scroll with the words "Post tenebras spero lucem (After darkness, I hope for light)."[68] This configuration recalls the more intricate image of Lemaire's coat of arms, with its combined images from the zoological and botanical worlds coupled with Latin quotations. In fact, the aristocratic spirit of this new device balances the woodcut on the opposite folio, which depicts the political powers of the day through animal symbols (see Frautschi ed., 41–43). Instead of using a dedication woodcut scene in this last of his works published before he became the *héraut d'armes* (king of arms) of the duke of Lorraine in April 1518, the publisher-author created a visual "dialogue" on facing folios that implies a more balanced relationship between author and aristocracy. Two personal illustration appear, then, in these editions of the *Fantasies*. The title-page image of Mother Folly signals Gringore's paratextual bookmaking role as publisher of the volume and directs attention to the textual character, Mère Sotte herself, who as Gringore's alter ego merges his dramatic position in theatrical contexts with the narrative role in this particular literary production. The Mère Sotte image thus draws the reader into the author's and the book's soul: the text. The hooded-falcon device, along the lines of Molinet's and Lemaire's coats of arms, serves as a personalized author-woodcut, representing the "acteur" announced in the text's opening rubric and lines and presenting a more aristocratic configuration.

The Mère Sotte woodcut would reappear on the title page of only one other work—Gringore's *Menus propos* of 1521, the first work published in the poet's position as the duke of Lorraine's king of arms—and the hooded-falcon device would never resurface in his publications.[69] In sub-

67. Gringore's talents embodied both the medieval and modern meaning of the term *acteur*, as I discuss in Chapter 5 below.

68. An apparent homage to Francis I's rise to power, this design constitutes a reference to the peace brought to France with the ascent of Francis I to the throne in 1515, according to Picot, *Les français italianisants*, 178.

69. The disappearance of the Mère Sotte device can perhaps be attributed to the king's opposition to *sots* in 1516. After the *Menus propos*, Gringore wrote more strictly religious texts, for which the woodcut would probably have been inappropriate. See details about the controversy surrounding the publication of the Passion woodcut, which apparently portrayed the author, in Gringore's *Heures de Nostre Dame* (Picot, *Pierre Gringore*, 13–27).

Fig. 3.17. Author-woodcut, from *Les fantasies de Mère Sotte*, B.N., Réserve Ye 290, title page. Phot. Bibl. Nat. Paris.

ꟼE qui ma fait en ma fantasie mettre
Plusieurs propos tant en prose que en mettre
Cest que en leglise ay veu scismes erreurs
Et sur les champs gens differens erreurs
Lors les lyens de iulius rompirent
Dont serfz de mars en plorent et souspirent
Durant ce temps lansquenetz et gascons
Duydoient tonneaulx/quartes/potz et flaccons
Laigle ie vis porteur de doubles testes
Voller par tout et sans faire conquestes
Les ours aussi rauissans et rapteurs
Se disoient lors des princes correcteurs

Fig. 3.18. Gringore's coat of arms, from *Les fantasies de Mère Sotte*, B.N., Réserve Ye 290, fol. 4ʳ. Phot. Bibl. Nat. Paris.

sequent works, Gringore refers to himself not as Mère Sotte but in terms that emphasize a more aristocratic position: "Pierre Gringore dit Vaudemont, l'herault d'armes de treshault et vertueux . . . duc de Lorraine" (Pierre Gringore, known as Vaudemont, king of arms of the very distinguished and virtuous . . . duke of Lorraine).[70] The only element of either of these devices that remained in Gringore's subsequent writings was the motto.

Appearing alone for the first time at the end of the *Fantasies de Mère Sotte*, following the acrostic stanzas of Gringore's entire name, the "Raison par tout" motto came to serve as a supplementary signature for the writer. In the *Menus propos*, the same shortened expression interrupts the text several times, often in tandem with Gringore's acrostic stanza, not only at the edition's end but throughout the volume as well.[71] Succinctly embodying the text's principal message, Gringore's motto, separated from its image and recoupled with his name in acrostic form, insistently and repeatedly reminds the reader of his authorial presence. The retention of the motto and the disappearance of an author-woodcut in the poet's subsequent works may well reflect the Renaissance idea that "a man can be known . . . better by what he says than by his external appearance" (Russell, 30). After his success in obtaining a permanent court position, Gringore, like La Vigne, no longer applied the same aggressive strategy of paratextual self-promotion. His new function and identity as the duke of Lorraine's king of arms doubtless enhanced his "image" vis-à-vis the average book purchaser. Perhaps the most obvious sign that his relationship with patronage had entered a new phase was the absence of a dedication woodcut in his remaining publications.

Gringore's motto, then, moved from its somewhat contradictory position in the Mère Sotte woodcut frame to the center of Gringore's pseudo-heraldic image in the *Fantasies de Mère Sotte*, where its message seemed more appropriately located, to a signature that not only punctuated the final paratextual space of the work but also surfaced unexpectedly throughout the narrative. The peregrinations of this motto from a visual to an exclusively verbal setting trace Gringore's own journey from a paratextually prominent bookselling, publishing, and authorial presence into the very text itself.

In conclusion, although late medieval writers continued to depend on various forms of patronage, the development of increasingly personal-

---

70. See Lepage, 1–41, for a discussion of the various designations used to refer to Gringore in contemporary documents.

71. See folios 4[r], 16[r] (both motto and acrostic), 31[r], 33[v], 40[r] (both motto and acrostic), 101[v] (acrostic only), 123[r] (both motto and acrostic) in the first edition (1521).

ized images coincided with crucial extratextual defensive gestures on the part of various writers. The placement of Molinet's printed arms, with its emblematic *moulinet*, at the end of the first edition of his *Naissance de Charles d'Autriche* (ca. 1500) resulted from the writer's decision to act as publisher of his works. The personalized image of La Vigne as the enthroned, creating author—depicted on the frontispiece of a vellum copy of the second-edition *Vergier d'honneur*—followed the legal decision granting him rights to supervise publication of that very anthology (1504). Gringore's securement and advertisement of an author-privilege and his new role as bookseller and publisher of the *Folles entreprises* coincided with the first appearance of his Mère-Sotte woodcut on the title page (1505). Finally, Lemaire's adoption of a new, personalized coat-of-arms on the title page of his *Légende des Vénitiens* in 1512 corresponded to the period during which he obtained a long sought after position as the French queen's secretary. In every case, these images replaced an earlier patron-related or printer-related illustration in an edition supervised by the author. Such a gesture reveals the author's struggle to redefine and publicize an increasingly independent status while continuing to utilize and depend on the patronage system. The ego-centering intent of these images marked a new level of paratextual self-promotion, which accompanied a different form of textual self-consciousness. Through a study of the changing use of authorial signatures and narrative voices, I shall follow the traces of this defensive self-consciousness in my final chapters.

{ 4 }

CHANGING
AUTHORIAL SIGNATURES IN
LATE MEDIEVAL WORKS

n the two preceding chapters, we have examined the paratextual presentation of authors: those cases in which their names appeared in an incipit and explicit, on the title page and in the colophon, and those cases in which their images figured in their books. In this chapter, I enter the confines of the literary work itself with a study of writers' signatures, those marks which represent one of the most obvious signs of textual appropriation and authorial self-consciousness, the visible and supposedly definitive "proof" of the origin and authenticity of a work (Sala, 118). In fact, in late medieval and early Renaissance Europe, a link can be drawn between the emergence of portraits, including self-portraits, and the vogue of signatures, as the visual translation of Molinet's name in the illustrations analyzed above exemplifies.[1]

I do not treat actual autograph signatures here, because, with the gradual privileging of print following the invention of movable type, they had more of an impact on the juridical and even the art world than on the literary world. Nevertheless, the history of autograph signatures underpins my following remarks in a crucial way, because it uncovers an important relationship between the displacement at this time of medieval symbolic imagery by representational realism and a changing, more personalized concept of identity (Fraenkel, 11). This association was translated most concretely perhaps into Henry II's Ordonnance of Fontainebleau in 1554, which invested not only the written word but the written name with a new legal power by requiring that all notarized acts, contracts, legal obligations, receipts, and private transactions be signed.

---

1. Fraenkel, 275, calls attention to the association between the first realist portrait of a French king, John the Good, and the fact that he was the first monarch to sign his own letters of patent. See also Chastel, 8–9, who speaks of this relationship in Northern Renaissance Europe, and Sala, 119–27.

I focus here on what one might call textual signatures, the incorporation of writers' names and identities into their texts in the late medieval period. By the nature of their very personalized formulations, textual signatures came close to functioning like autograph signatures. Moreover, unlike the advertisement of an author's name on title page and colophon—commonly subject to distortion by forces beyond the writer's jurisdiction—the textual encoding of authorial identities represented the surest means writers had to publicize and control their association with their works. If, at this time, a writer transformed a piece of paper into a juridical act by signing it, as Fraenkel argues (12), then it is equally true that the coupling of an author's textual signature with the advertisement of his legalized control over his publications both authorized and validated writings in a previously unknown way. What is important here is not the actual use of textual signatures, which dates back at least to the Latin Middle Ages, but the way they are reinforced by paratextual material and the fact that authors' changing signatures reflect a more defensive literary consciousness than that of their predecessors.[2]

Textual signatures took on a variety of forms, and medieval authors often presented them playfully.[3] Simple proper names that were directly accessible to the reader figured in the early medieval works of Chrétien de Troyes, Marie de France, Béroul, Thomas, and Jean de Meun, who identified both himself and his predecessor, Guillaume de Lorris, in the well-known passage near the midpoint of the two parts of the *Roman de la rose*.[4] But textual signatures could be ambiguous as well. Sometimes the reader had to rearrange, reconstruct, or re-view the letters of a name in order to decipher it properly, a phenomenon that had to do with the tastes of the court. Guillaume de Machaut, who named himself directly in his *Jugement dou roy de Navarre* and the *Prise d'Alexandrie*, more often followed the vogue set by Nicole de Margival in the *Dit de la panthère d'amours* (ca. 1300) and in nearly all his other *dits*: punctuation of the text with anagrammic signatures that were not always easy to decode. The signatures extensively adopted by Jean Froissart were equally difficult to

2. It is perhaps no coincidence that many vernacular authors of the fifteenth century, including Alain Chartier, André de la Vigne, and Jean Lemaire, were royal secretaries who often signed documents for their patrons. They may have developed a particularly acute sense of the relationship between the signature and one's identity, which by 1554 would be extended to French society as a whole.

3. For details on the different kinds of signatures, see Kooper, and the *Revue de l'Art* 26 (1974): 8–54. See also Kane, 53–57, who investigates the fourteenth-century convention in which authors of dream-vision poems signed their work by naming the dreamer-narrator after themselves.

4. For an excellent discussion of these and other earlier signatures see Huot, *From Song to Book*, and Dragonetti's "Noms," 13–40.

unravel.[5] In fact, many anagrams, such as the one that appears at the end of the *Bestiaire d'amour rimé*, remain unsolved because of their complicated nature.[6] Punning signatures, which worked simultaneously in two directions, could be ambiguous as well, though in a different sense. Referring outward and identifying the writer, the punning name served to mark the text as his creation. At the same time, its playful expression drew attention away from the extratextual, proper name of the text's creator to other, more common meanings of the name which were associated with the language of the text in such a way that the reader could overlook or misunderstand the author's proper name (Kamuf, 12–13).

Maintaining the ambiguity of both the name itself and its potential meanings was, however, the ultimate goal of many authors, who sought to delight their audience with onomastic games. Potentially irretrievable, these punning signatures, such as those which Rutebeuf incorporated into many of his poems (*Œuvres*, ed. Faral and Bastin, 1:34–35), were nevertheless more accessible than their cryptogrammic counterparts, because, like acrostic signatures, they retained the order of the letters in the proper name. But success in understanding these signatures depended upon the mode of transmission: the decoding of punning names often necessitated oral delivery, whereas acrostic signatures were retrievable only by a visual reception of the text.

These two forms of signatures, metaphorical and acrostic, appeared most commonly in the works of late medieval and early Renaissance French authors, who, more than any other literary generation, were preoccupied with names and name games (Rigolot, *Poétique*, 27). For it is not writers' signatures per se that are of interest here so much as the striking modifications late medieval authors made in their signatures over the course of their careers.[7] How do we explain why the acrostic device or the straightforward, capitalized name tended to replace the pun-

---

5. See Hoepffner, "Anagramme"; Looze, "Mon nom trouveras"; and Cartier.

6. Huot, *From Song to Book*, 164, associates the late thirteenth-century, early fourteenth-century delight in anagrams with the development of a more writerly mode of poetics, whereas Cartier, 100, suggests that anagrams reflected the discretion required by courtly love codes.

7. For examples of earlier punning signatures, see the works of Colin Muset and Rutebeuf, Jakemes's *Roman du castelain de Couci* (see Huot, *From Song to Book*, 117–34), Tibaut's *Roman de la poire* (see Marchello-Nizia ed., xxiv–xxxi), and the works of Eustache Deschamps (see Hoepffner ed., 3:381, 4:114). For earlier examples of acrostic signatures, see Guillaume de Deguileville's *Pèlerinage de la vie humaine* (see Kane, 54), Deschamps (Hoepffner ed., 4:222, 5:164), and François Villon's *Ballade pour prier Notre Dame, Ballade à s'amie, Ballade de la Grosse Margot, Ballade des contre-vérités, Débat du cueur et du corps,* and *Ballade de bon conseil* (see Uitti, "Villon's Poetics"). See also Gros, 49–61; Minnis, *Theory*, 170; Quilligan, *Language of Allegory*, 164; Smalley, 135; and Trapp.

name as the more favored form of textual signature at this time? I argue that these signatures represent another example of writers' changing perceptions of themselves and of their publics at a time when the economics of the print culture threatened their literary reputations. As vernacular authors became more concerned about the need to maintain control over their own words, they became attuned to the importance of affixing their names to their texts in a more immediately recognizable fashion. This shift to more easily decipherable names coincided with a general movement toward the literal and a privileging of the written word that came with the advent of print.[8] In several key cases, the aggressive behavior of Parisian publishers caught up in the book-trade competition precipitated this shift. Although they often appropriated works without writers' authorization, combined them with other texts in a manner unacceptable to the author, and failed to publicize authors' names in the paratext, publishers rarely tampered with authors' signatures once these were incorporated into the texts. For example, even though publishers never acknowledged Molinet's authorship in their editions of his *Temple de Mars*, they never altered his punning signature at the end of the text. Whereas Vérard had inappropriately taken and published Bouchet's *Regnars traversant*, wrongly attributed it to a more famous writer, and eliminated some words while appending another's to it, he did maintain Bouchet's acrostic signature. Thus, there appears to have been a reluctance on the part of publishers to change the author's textual signature.

Paratextual material placed between title pages and texts, however, such as the prologues in which writers often identified themselves, could be unreliable vehicles for authorial signatures, especially in manuscript form (although their incorporation into the printed book eventually provided a more stable space for self-identification). Translations represent another example of how authors' textual signatures could disappear through publishing changes. And evidence shows that at least one printer, the infamous Michel Le Noir, dared to alter an author's signature after the poet had integrated it into his text.

The changing poet–patron relationship relates directly to these modifications. Charles Sala, in speaking of artists, has recognized that the act of signing a work, as a claim of intellectual proprietorship, led to a sense of autonomy and to the establishment of new rules of social conduct between patron and author: the created work is linked definitively to a per-

---

8. See Zumthor, *Masque*, 81–82, who describes the movement of allegory toward the literal, and Foucault, *Order of Things*, 38, who, among others, speaks of the privileging of writing with the advent of print. Wilson, 54–59, argues that the movement from Rutebeuf's punning signatures to Villon's acrostic signatures reflects the change from a hearing to a reading public. See also Gros, 51.

sonality, or at least a name, and to the talent of an author, who thereby stands outside the protective shadow of tradition (121). I argue that the growing effort of late medieval vernacular writers to spell out their own names unambiguously when incorporating them into their texts reflects their gradual refusal to hide behind the names of their patrons and parallels their search for more self-promotional opportunities and for greater validation as literary creators. This move is all the more evident in the context of increasing paratextual advertisement of the author. For there was an inherent contradiction between the manifest way in which authors had come to integrate their patrons' names into their texts and the more modest fashion in which they identified themselves. One can see the fundamental ambiguity of a work written for the sake of an "idealized Other" by a poet increasingly conscious of his own identity and artistic role.[9] If, as Laurence de Looze has so convincingly argued, the use of anagrammic signatures presupposed that an initiated audience already knew the author's name ("Mon nom trouveras," 550–52), then the gradual adoption of more straightforward signatures suggests that authors knew they could no longer assume such complicity between poet and public. The nature of their audience was changing with the advent of print. Vernacular writers' more publicly conscious appropriation of their works in this late medieval period through the adoption of more accessible textual signatures represents yet another sign of their increasingly defensive posture as authors and their more attuned sense of self-importance and proprietorship in the face of growing market pressures. These developments accompanied their growing control of book reproduction and their greater paratextual visibility, as I have discussed above, as well as the gradual separation of their own voices from their protagonists', as I argue in the final chapter.

With Jean Molinet, the reader witnesses this transition from a playful signature, which typified a court poet's attempt to please the ludic instincts of his patron and associates, to the adoption of a more straightforward name, whose increasing appearance in texts written after the advent of print suggests the existence of a new impulse to lay claim to one's words and to ensure a less elite readership more immediate access to the author. In many of Molinet's works, especially his earlier, more traditional writings, the reader discovers one of several versions of his punning signature.[10] The similarity in pronunciation at the time between

9. See Starobinski, 17, who adopts this term, and Le Coq, "Cadre et rebord," 20, who offers a similar reflection about painters.

10. Of the forty-five "circumstantial" poems edited by Dupire in volume 1 of Molinet's *Faictz et dictz*, fifteen bear his signature, including his *Complainte de Grèce* (1464), *Trosne d'honneur* (after June 1467), *Temple de Mars* (after 1475), *Chapellet des dames* (after 1478), *Res-*

his name and a small "moulin" or "moulinet," led the *rhétoriqueur* to create an extended metaphorical comparison between the workings of a mill in producing flour and those of the poet Molinet making verse.[11] Instead of incorporating into his text his capitalized proper name, limiting its significance to the identification of his person, Molinet reified his name and verbally metamorphosed himself into a mill, whose workings resembled the poetic process itself. The process of creating verse was thereby recalled each time the writer signed his text, in a gesture that recalls Rutebeuf's name games (see Wilson, 53). While other contemporary poets, such as André de La Vigne and Guillaume Cretin, adopted a punning signature to identify their works, it was Molinet who most successfully exploited his metaphorical name.

Toward the end of his career, though, Molinet replaced this punning signature with his more straightforward name. The underlying explanation of this remarkable change may possibly be connected with the publication history of his *Art de rhétorique*, which offers a striking example of the potential dangers of authorial self-naming in a prefatory rather than a textual manuscript space. Although Molinet punningly refers to himself when addressing his patron in the manuscript versions of the work, the dedication was manipulated in its later printed forms in such a way that his authorship disappeared. This development coincides with the adoption of more accessible and more reliably placed signatures by the writer, suggesting that Molinet had come to realize the importance of maintaining control over the reproduction of his name and his works, especially those which might circulate beyond the confines of the court for which they were originally composed.

Written between 1482 and 1492, the poetic treatise contained in the *Art de rhétorique* provides the very rules for creating verse that form part of the image to which Molinet's punning signature gives rise: namely, the rules that make the *rhétoriqueur*'s poetic mill function.[12] The reader finds the symbol of his name, the poetry mill, literally and fully decoded in the body of the *Art de rhétorique*. The relationship Molinet so masterfully develops between his proper name and the text in which he inscribes it not

---

source du petit peuple (after May 1481), *L'arbre de Bourgogne* (after April 1486), and *Voyage de Naples* (after September 1496). After 1496, Molinet tended to compose briefer works, perhaps because his eyesight was failing; his signature is found in several short poems (36–184 vv.) written between 1497 and 1502. In volume 2, which contains religious, parodic, and personal poems as well as some prose works, six poems bear Molinet's signature; in addition, there are a good many letters, exchanged with his contemporaries, in which his name is played upon at length.

11. Some of the following remarks appear in different form in my "Eveil," 15–35.
12. Appendix 4 below provides a list of the various versions of this work.

only reinforces the text's meaning but also plays a major role in generating it.[13]

The incipit announcement of the author's name in the fifteenth-century manuscript of the *Art de rhétorique* (B.N., ms. f.fr. 2159) is reinforced by the appearance of Molinet's punning signature in its dedicatory prologue (my emphasis): "De laquele rethorique, mon tres honnorés sire, se c'est chose qui gaires vaille: vous prenderez en gré s'il vous plaist tant la fleur comme la farine tele que vostre tres humble et petit *molinet* a sceut tourner entre ses meules" (Please accept willingly this rhetoric, my very honorable lord, if it is worthy, both the wheat and the flour, such as your very humble and little mill [Molinet] was able to turn between its millstones) (fol. ii[v]).[14] Yet, just as Vérard in 1493 and other publishers after him failed to announce the author's name on the title page of their editions of the *Art de rhétorique*, so too the punning signature that Molinet had incorporated into the dedication of his work is missing in those versions. Molinet's name had disappeared because of its association with a patron in a manuscript dedicatory prologue, which had been removed in those editions printed for a more general public. Like the signature that artists might originally place on the frames of their paintings, a signature that could be lost through replacement of the frame, Molinet's identity was eliminated when his work was "packaged" in a different way.[15] As a result, the copies that the largest number of readers (those who were not very familiar with the poet) would have purchased were copies that furnished no details about the author of the *Art de rhétorique*.

Two vellum copies of this edition, however, do feature a dedication, which is partially derived from Molinet's manuscript prologue (Paris, B.N., Vélins 577; London, B.L., IB.41139).[16] The following passage replaces the one containing Molinet's punning signature (my emphasis):

13. Rigolot, *Poétique*, 12ff., discusses the relationship between the phonics, graphics, and ideology of the name. See also Gros, who discusses the graphics of the name in late medieval Marial poetry.

14. The same dedicatory prologue appears in the sixteenth-century manuscript of the work (B.N., ms. f.fr. 2375 [5]).

15. The signature in art, examined by Chastel and others in a series of articles on "L'art de la signature" in the *Revue de l'Art* 26 (1974): 8–54, offers a number of interesting points of comparison with signatures in literature. If the canvas finds its counterpart in the literary text, the picture frame can be equated with the paratext: the prologue, title page, and colophon. Le Coq, "Cadre et rebord," 16, makes a comparison between the picture frame and the manuscript margin. See also Fraenkel, 168–74, and Adams, who draws a fascinating parallel to the issues raised here in her discussion of signatures in the seventeenth-century world of Dutch artists.

16. For a comparison of the printed and manuscript prologues, see Langlois's edition of Molinet's *Art de rhétorique* in *Recueil d'Arts*, 214–15.

"vostre treshumble et tresobeissant subject et serviteur *Henry de Croy*" (fol. ai^v) (your very humble and very obedient subject and servant Henry de Croy).[17] Because none of the other surviving printed editions of the *Art de rhétorique* bears Molinet's name, scholars mistakenly attributed the treatise to Henry de Croy until the late nineteenth century (Byvanck, 80, n. 2).

Molinet's authorship of his text is manipulated in yet another way in the transition from manuscript to print. At one point in Vérard's edition of the *Art de rhétorique*, there appears a reference to the poet, absent in the manuscript. In furnishing examples of the "rime batelée" from his own works without identifying himself as author, Molinet obviously assumed that his dedicatee would know he had written them: "De ceste nouvelle mode sont coulourez la Complainte de Gresse, le Trosne d'honneur, le Temple de Mars, les ouvrages de la pucelle et la Resource du petit peuple" (With this new mode are embellished the *Complainte de Grèce*, the *Trosne d'honneur*, the *Temple de Mars*, the *[Naufrage] de la pucelle*, and the *Ressource du petit peuple*) (fol. b ii^v). In Vérard's printed edition, however, the following sentence is added at this point: "Et en a esté inventeur maistre Jehan Molinet de Valenciennes" (And Master Jean Molinet of Valenciennes was the inventor of this) (fol. b ii^v). This edition indicates that the publisher knew his readers would not automatically associate Molinet with the listed works. Although Vérard explicitly named Molinet as inventor of the "rimes batelées," the author did not receive credit for composing the entire treatise of which these references form a small part.

One cannot know for sure if Vérard was aware that Molinet was the author of the *Art de rhétorique* or if Henry de Croy was solely responsible for replacing Molinet's name in the dedication with his own. But Vérard's unauthorized publication of Jean Bouchet's *Regnars traversant* just ten years later suggests he was involved in these earlier modifications, which may have been considered "legitimate" in the early stages of printing by publishers (see also Langlois, ed., *Recueil d'Arts*, lxiv, n. 2). Nevertheless, the fact that the edition designated Molinet as the inventor of "rimes batelées" reveals that both Croy and Vérard knew at the very least that the poet had an established reputation.

By the time Jean Trepperel printed the second known edition of the

17. Langlois, ed., *Recueil d'Arts*, lxi–lxiii, pointing out the careless mistakes in the Vérard edition, suggests that Molinet might have originally dedicated the manuscript treatise to Philippe de Croy, or even to his son Henry de Croy, who then appropriated it as his own in the printed edition and dedicated it to the French king. The Croys, known as supporters of the arts, were then an important family in the Burgundian region through the marriage in 1455 of the seigneur de Croy with Jacqueline de Luxembourg.

Art de rhétorique, six years later in May 1499, neither Molinet's nor Henry de Croy's name was associated with the work. Like the paper copies of Vérard's edition, which probably served as Trepperel's source, no dedication and therefore no authorial identification whatsoever figured in this or subsequent editions.

Thus, the identity of the writer of the *Art de rhétorique* disappeared in the transition from manuscript to print, having been replaced in the prologue of Vérard's vellum copies by the bogus authorship of Henry de Croy or eliminated altogether in the paper copies. This eradication of the true author's identity occurred because Molinet had not integrated his name into the text of the *Art de rhétorique* and because his writing had become a marketable imprint outside the manuscript community for which he had originally produced it.

Another feature that contributes to the deformation of the *Art de rhétorique* text is a passage, added in the later printed versions, that identifies the French king. Whereas the original dedicatee of the *Art de rhétorique* remained unnamed in the manuscript prologue, Charles VIII, who had had no connection with Molinet's commission to write a guide to poetic writing, is named in all the printed editions of the work in a rondeau-acrostic that spells out CHARLES DE VALOIS on the final folio. So that readers would not fail to recognize his name, verses following the passage direct them to reconstruct it:

> Comme tresor florissant par nature,
> Hault triumphant par eternelle fabrique,
> A vous honneur, trescrestien roy puissant,
> Resplendissant soubz science auctentique,
> Louer on doit tel sens tant magnifique
> En rethorique quant on y prent pasture;
> Sens est parfaict adjoustant sa musique,
> Dont fault venir aulx termes contestant
> Equivoquant, congnoissant la droicture
>> Comme tresor, etc.

> Vault il pas mieulx adjouster la replique
> A composer quant l'engin s'y procure
> L'euvre parfaicte? Le cas est congnoissant.
> O quel renom quant sens a bien s'applique!
> Yeulx regardez, fuyez la chose inique
> Sans repugner les termes de droicture
>> Comme tresor, etc.

Visez, musez, de hault en bas lisez
Nom et surnom du Roy vous trouverrez,
Charles huitiesme que Dieu doint bonne vie
Et en la fin la grant joie parfournie. (fol. b v^v)

Examine, study, read from top to bottom, and you will find the name and surname of the king, Charles VIII. May God grant him good life and in the end great, fulfilling joy.

The adoption of the acrostic form here allows for a two-dimensional homage to the French king. For the vertical staging of Charles VIII's name gives rise to a horizontal celebration of his virtues. Described as a perfect work, a resplendent treasure of nature, the king is lauded for his magnificent power, knowledge, justice, and understanding. This onomastic strategy, which many of Molinet's contemporaries would eventually adopt to publicize their own identities, graphically associates the name and fame of the person glorified.[18]

Absent from both manuscript versions of the *Art de rhétorique*, because the work was not originally dedicated to the French monarch, these verses, presumably added by Vérard (or Croy?), doubtless served as thanks for (or anticipation of) Charles VIII's patronage. The CHARLES DE VALOIS acrostic thereby functioned as a self-reflecting mirror for Vérard's or Croy's, but not Molinet's, potential benefactor. Moreover, because it appeared in all subsequent publications of the work, the acrostic and the horizontal message generated by it presented the king's name and image as a model for each book purchaser. In replacing the names of both author and patron of the original work with others that more appropriately met his personal capitalistic needs, the publisher Vérard had in essence reappropriated Molinet's work and reformulated the dynamics of the text. What had originally served to teach a noble about the art of writing love poetry had become an excuse to praise another noble.

Molinet had often faithfully accorded textual publicity to his aristocratic sponsors through the use of acrostic-like forms, such as his homage to Philip the Good in the *Trosne d'honneur* (1467) or to Mary of Burgundy in the *Chappellet des dames* (1478) (Scheidegger, 214–25). But he had balanced this focus on his patrons with self-references, albeit less imperious ones, through the incorporation of his name into these verses (my emphasis):[19]

---

18. Rigolot, *Poétique*, 31–32, discusses this association in another context.

19. See Machaut's earlier use of anagrams for both his own and his patron's name in works such as the *Fontaine amoureuse* (Jean de Berry) and *Confort d'ami* (Charles de Navarre) (see Hoepffner, "Anagramme," 404–7) or Froissart's *Espinette amoureuse* (Fourrier ed.),

Du vent tel que Dieu donna
Au limeur de gros limage,
Mon gros *molinet* tourna
Et rima ce gros rimage.
(*Trosne*, 1:58, vv. 40–43)

D'ung verd champ ou le *mol lin n'est*
En soufflant tant de vent widasmes
Qu'en tournant nostre *molinet*
Molut le Chappellet des dames.
(*Chappellet*, 1:126, vv. 21–24)

The appropriation of Molinet's *Art de rhétorique* by someone other than the true author and the addition to it of verses paying homage to a different patron represent one more example of why vernacular writers resorted to self-defense in the early years of the sixteenth century. Like the altered illustrations decorating the *Art de rhétorique* editions, the presence or absence of Molinet's textual signature in these versions reflects the ambiguous status of authorship at the end of the fifteenth century. The text and its subject, which was often an aristocratic figure, were more valued and publicized than the originator.

But this situation was to change. The growing advertisement of Molinet's authorship on the title page and in the images associated with a later work, the *Roman de la rose moralisé*, published by the very same Vérard around 1500, is reinforced by the author's textual self-inscription, which reappeared in all editions of the work.[20] The final verses, which remained firmly anchored to the text, furnish evidence of how Molinet artfully wove the multiple meanings of his proper name into the metaphorical texture of his poetic creation (my emphasis):

L'an quinze cent tournay molin au vent,
Et le couvent d'amours ouvri ma baille,
Chargiet de grain [l]'engranay telement
Que rudement, a mon entendement
Prins du fourment la fleur que je vous baille,

---

where both his and his lady's name (Marguerite) are integrated together into verses 3385–89. These combinations are, however, much more difficult to decipher than those found in the poets examined here.

20. Appendix 4 below provides a bibliographical listing for this work.

Rués la paille, aprez qui maint sot baille
A la happaille, et loing du jardinet
Le monnoier doibt avoir son *molin net*.[21]

In the year 1500 I turned the windmill and the convent of love initiated my servitude. Laden with grain I filled it with so much seed that crudely, according to my understanding, I took from the wheat the flour that I give to you, having discarded the chaff, whereas most fools offer the chaff. And far from the little garden, the miller must keep his mill clean.

Even though the designation of Philippe de Clèves as dedicatee of the manuscript version of the *Roman de la rose moralisé* is absent from the printed editions of the work, Molinet's name figures prominently in both, for he had originally integrated it into the last lines of his text. While it is not possible to ascertain whether Molinet was actually reacting to the omission of his authorship in the Parisian publications of the *Art de rhétorique* seven years earlier, evidence suggests that his self-perception and attitude toward printed works had undergone a dramatic change by 1500. Molinet's decision to publish some of his works accompanies a growing tendency to sign his writings straightforwardly.

An examination of Molinet's other signed texts reveals an interesting pattern. The metaphorical signatures of those works written before 1493 focus on the object of the "moulin" itself, as the poem is "mollu d'un gros mollinet" (ground by a large mill) (*Complainte de Grèce* [1464], 1:26, v. 24). Sometimes the "moulinet" is possessed by the author, instead of representing the author, as it lacks or receives wind from God.[22] Or it can potentially be owned by others: "Chascun n'a pas son molin net" (Everyone does not keep his mill spotless) (*Temple de Mars* [after September 1475], 1:76, v. 320; *Complainte sur la mort Madame d'Ostrisse* [after

21. The Hague, Koninklijke Bibliotheek, ms. 128 C5, fol. 239. The prologue also contains allusions to Molinet's metaphorical Other: "Et affin que je ne perde le fourment de ma labeur et que la farine qui en sera molute puist avoir fleur salutaire, j'ay intencion, se Dieu me donne la grace, de tourner et convertir soubz mes rudes meules le vicieux au virtueux, le corporel a l'espirituel, la mondainté en divinité et souverainement de le moraliser" (And so that I do not lose the wheat of my labor and that the meal which will be ground by it can yield wholesome flour, I intend, if God gives me grace, to turn and convert beneath my plain millstones the corrupt into the virtuous, the corporal into the spiritual, the worldly into the divine, and to moralize about it in so excellent a manner) (fols. 3ᵛ–4).

22. See the final verses of the *Chappellet des dames* (after July 1478, vv. 21–24) and the *Arbre de Bourgogne* (after April 1486, vv. 47–48). Molinet's references to the lack of wind to turn the mill's arms often allude to his lack of financial support, as the opening lines of the *Ressource du petit peuple* (after May 1481, (11. 1–4) and the final lines of the *Trosne d'honneur* (after June 1467, vv. 40–43) confirm.

March 1482], 1:180, v. 496). This signatory gesture omitting the capitalized letter *M* essentially eliminates the author's individuality (Scheidegger, 209). Yet, in a poem dedicated to Margaret of Austria in 1493, the same year the Vérard edition of the *Art de rhétorique* appeared, the author adopted his proper name instead of his punning signature when he announced, "Molinet vous salue" (Molinet greets you) (*Collaudation a Madame Marguerite*, 1:265, v. 98). In a circa 1494 poem, the metaphor is reduced to a simile, which equates author and object—"Je suis un molinet sans vent" (I am a little mill without wind)—but immediately thereafter, the image disappears and the narrator directly complains about his financial situation, in a conscious separation of name and image (*Le revid a ung nommé Maitre Pol*, 2:826, vv. 1–13). When Molinet again adopted the poetry-mill metaphor in two works written in 1496, he qualified the *moulin* with a human adjective, *povre* (poor). In one case, it modifies the object, but in the other the poet himself is thus portrayed: he describes "les vollans d'ung povre molinet" (the flywheels of a poor little mill) in the *Voyage de Naples* (1:277, l. 7), whereas in *Gaiges retrenchiés* the final verses allude to the poet, not to the object, by referring to "le retour du povre Molinet / Qui n'a deja plus d'encre en son cornet" (2:771, vv. 79–80) (The return of the poor little mill/Molinet who no longer has any ink in its horn).[23] Coexisting with textual allusions to the poetic windmill, the signatures of two poems dating from around 1497 depict only a human figure, the second one all the more clearly since the author's name appears without the definite article: "Le Molinet qui ne void que d'ung oeul" (The little mill/Molinet who sees with only one eye) ("A Madame Marguerite," 1:342, v. 42) and "Molinet . . . vous escripra" (Molinet will write to you) (*Ballade*, 1:346, v. 43). And in later examples: "Molinet prie a Dieu" (Molinet prays to God) (*Nativité Madame Lienor* [ca. 1498], 1:351, v. 113) and "Molinet . . . se prend au rimer" (Molinet begins to rhyme) (*Lettre a monseigneur l'archiduc quand il alla en Espaine* [after November 1501], 1:372, v. 28).

What accounts for this post-1493 shift from the plurality of meanings associated with the author's name to the one-dimensionality of the proper name? What explains Molinet's interest at the very end of his career in overseeing the publication of some of his own works, one of which, the *Naissance de Charles d'Autriche*, portrays a mark prominently bearing his name? Molinet's efforts to ensure that his identification with his texts be maintained were seemingly related to the aggressive actions of Parisian publishers who had deformed his works in the various ways

23. Since Molinet's economic difficulties constituted the subject of this piece, he exploited the metaphor of the *moulinet* here more than in any other poem. The poet alternates between references to the poetry mill's difficulties in functioning and the writer's own financial problems (see Chapter 5 below for an analysis).

noted above. At first, like a painter's name that constituted an integral feature of the *tableau*, Molinet's signature was incorporated into the fabric of his texts because of that signature's capacity to function as a depersonalized object; these were texts that placed greater emphasis on the name and fame of his protectors. Eventually, though, Molinet's signature came to resemble that of the artist of his time which, painted on the canvas without being integrated with the subject matter, stood out from the work itself and, in certain cases, from the images of patrons portrayed therein.[24] In such a form, the signature of the poet—or painter—more boldly proclaimed one's authorship.

André de la Vigne's association with the world of print accompanied important modifications in his signature. Whereas Molinet authorized his texts more and more often with his proper name instead of his punning signature toward the end of his career, La Vigne had replaced his metaphorical signature with a more straightforward form of his name by mid-career. This modification coincided with changes in how he expressed his relationship with his patrons.

Two series of acrostics naming the French king generate the speeches of Magesté Royalle, the monarch's alter ego, in La Vigne's *Ressource de la Chrestienté* of 1494. Like Vérard's (or Croy's) adoption of CHARLES DE VALOIS at the end of his edition of Molinet's *Art de rhétorique*, the appearance of this same acrostic in the *Ressource* derived from the author's hope of obtaining Charles VIII's patronage by this and other forms of flattery. Unlike Vérard's publication, however, which bore no sign of Molinet's authorship, La Vigne inscribed his name into the last verses of the *Ressource*, thereby seeking for himself the same kind of immortality provided by the incorporation of his prospective patron's name into the work.

As a verbal mirroring of the presentation scene depicted on the frontispiece of B.N. ms. f.fr. 1687 of the *Ressource* (see Figure 3.1), the first acrostic, CHARLES DE VALOIS, generates the text, sometimes in reverse order and sometimes along two vertical axes, at the beginning and at the hemistich of the verse. The patron's name thereby determined the pseudo-ballad's structure, giving rise to the list of virtues associated with him and essentially leading the reader "du nom porte-lettres au renom porte-vertus" (from the letter-bearing name to virtue-bearing fame) (Figure 4.1).[25] In Magesté Royalle's second speech, an acrostic spells out

24. For details on parallel developments of artists' signatures, see *Revue de l'Art* 26 (1974): 24–26, 29–43, 46–54.

25. This expression is adopted from Rigolot, *Poétique*, 31. See *Ressource*, 124–25, for a transcription of these verses; all citations are taken from this edition, unless otherwise noted.

an entire idea (*Ressource*, 139–41): CHARLES HUITIESME ET DERNIER DE
CE NOM PAR LA GRACE DE DIEU ROY DE FRANCE A QUI DIEU DOINT
BONNE VIE ET LONGUE ET PARADIS A LA FIN (Charles VIII and last of this
name, king of France by the grace of God, may He grant him a good,
long life and Paradise in the end). Wishing to pay homage to the king,
the author not only generated horizontally an entire speech from the
monarch's name but, as a kind of intercessor, he himself voiced a prayer
on Charles VIII's behalf on the vertical plane. In both manuscript versions of the *Ressource de la Chrestienté* (B.N. mss. f.fr. 1687 and 1699) an
artist highlighted these acrostics referring to the French monarch by the
use of different colors and spaces between the first and second letters,
thereby stimulating the reader's eye to take account of the French king's
name in its repeated and reversed vertical forms, even before recon-
structing the horizontal text. Since Charles VIII was both the subject and
the dedicatee of the manuscript version—Magesté Royalle, his literary
counterpart, plays a decisive role in the debate that takes place, and
manuscript 1687 was offered to the king—and since his presence dominates the work in both its literary and its ornamental conception, it is obvious that the goal of these versions was above all to praise and to please
Charles VIII.[26]

In contrast, the author's association with the text, marked by his signature, takes on a more sober character. It is not until the end of the work
that he identifies himself. As in Molinet's earlier compositions, La Vigne
accomplishes this indirectly by means of a pun on his name and his poetic art, when he makes reference to the "fruyt De la vigne" (fruit of the
vine) (my emphasis):

> Et pour conclure, je vous pry, treschier sire
> Que le traicté vous plaise avoir en grace,
> Quoy que n'y soit la scïence Porphire,
> Ne la prudence de Virgille ou Bocace.
> Se mon engin eust plus grant efficace,
> J'eusse trop mieulx labouré et enté
> La Ressource de la Chrestïenté,
> Qui a vous, sire, de presenter n'est digne,
> Ne plus ne mains que le fruyt *De la vigne*.
> (vv. 1461–69)

And in conclusion, I pray, my beloved lord, that it please you to hold
this treatise in favor, even though Porphyry's wisdom cannot be
found in it, nor the prudence of Virgil or Boccaccio. If my abilities

26. Some of these ideas appear in different form in my "Text."

Fig. 4.1*a*. First 22 lines of Charles VIII acrostics, from *La ressource de la Chrestienté*, B.N., ms. f.fr. 1687, fol. 24[r]. © clichés Bibliothèque Nationale Paris.

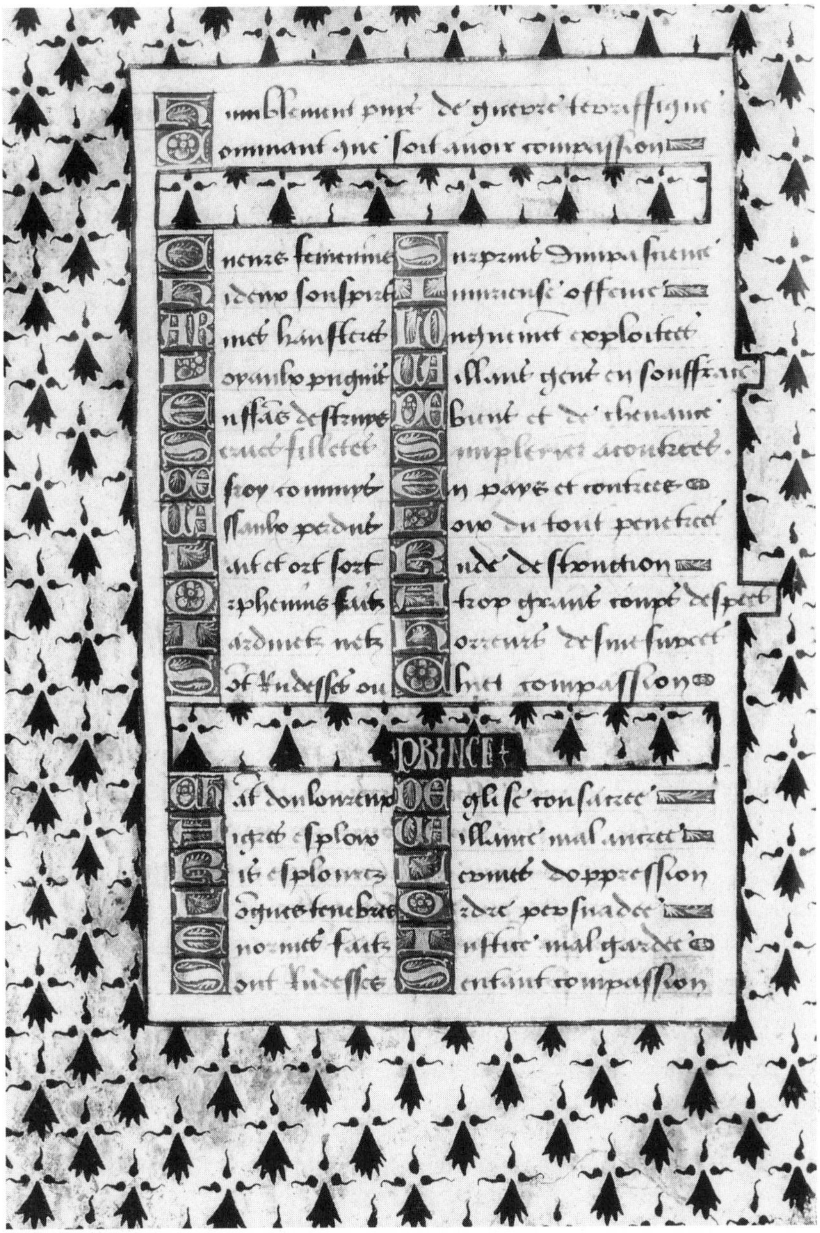

Fig. 4.1*b*. Last 20 lines of Charles VIII acrostics, fol. 24[v].

were more effective, I would have labored on and grafted much more the *Ressource de la Chrestienté*, which is not worthy of being presented to you, sire, any more or less than the fruit of the vine/La Vigne.

Exploiting the traditional parallels made between poetic production and the fruits of a gardener's labors, La Vigne's verses, his "fruit of the vine," develop after much labor and grafting. These words, the last of the poem, serve as the author's signature. At the same time, however, the author's identity risks being lost, because "De la vigne" plays a critical semantic role in the text, its concrete meaning bringing the horticultural discussion to a conclusion.[27] Moreover, because no artist illuminated La Vigne's name like his patron's, it does not stand out so much visually. Nevertheless, in both manuscript versions, "De la Vigne" is set off from the rest of the verse with a capital *D*, as in manuscript 1687 (see my "Text," 110, fig. 4.3), or with a slash, period, and capital letter, as in manuscript 1699 (Figure 4.2).

Thus, the arrangement of names in the manuscript versions of the *Ressource de la Chrestienté* reflects a greater focus on the person in whose honor the text was written than on the author of the text. This self-aggrandizement was, of course, what the patron was paying for.[28] The decoration and placement of names in manuscript 1687, then, complement the presentation miniature depicting the poet on bended knee before his future patron: in both instances, the writer is deferential to the patron; but he is not completely absent.

The 1495 Angoulême edition of the *Ressource*, the first known printed version of the text, emphasizes neither the acrostics that focus on the identity of Charles VIII nor La Vigne's signature. Because this version completely lacked decoration, the two series of acrostics in it were not emphasized. Rubrics or other instructions to reconstruct the monarch's name are absent; nothing stimulates the reader to identify Charles de Valois as the focus of the work (see folio cii). For reasons of time perhaps, or cost, or lack of sophistication, the printers did not accentuate the acrostics. It is also possible that they simply were unaware of their existence, in which case they may have obtained the text through oral transmission. The Angoulême edition is the only extant version of the *Res-*

27. La Vigne signed his *Complaintes et epitaphes du roy de la Bazoche* with an even less accessible metaphorical signature (my emphasis): "Cy j'estandré de la vigne ung vert jus" (Here I will squeeze from the vine a green juice). See *Recueil de poésies*, ed. Montaiglon and Rothschild, 13:412.

28. Manuscript 1699, made for Duke Charles d'Angoulême, would have served as a model for its owner, although the glorification of his relative Charles VIII certainly reflected back on the duke as well.

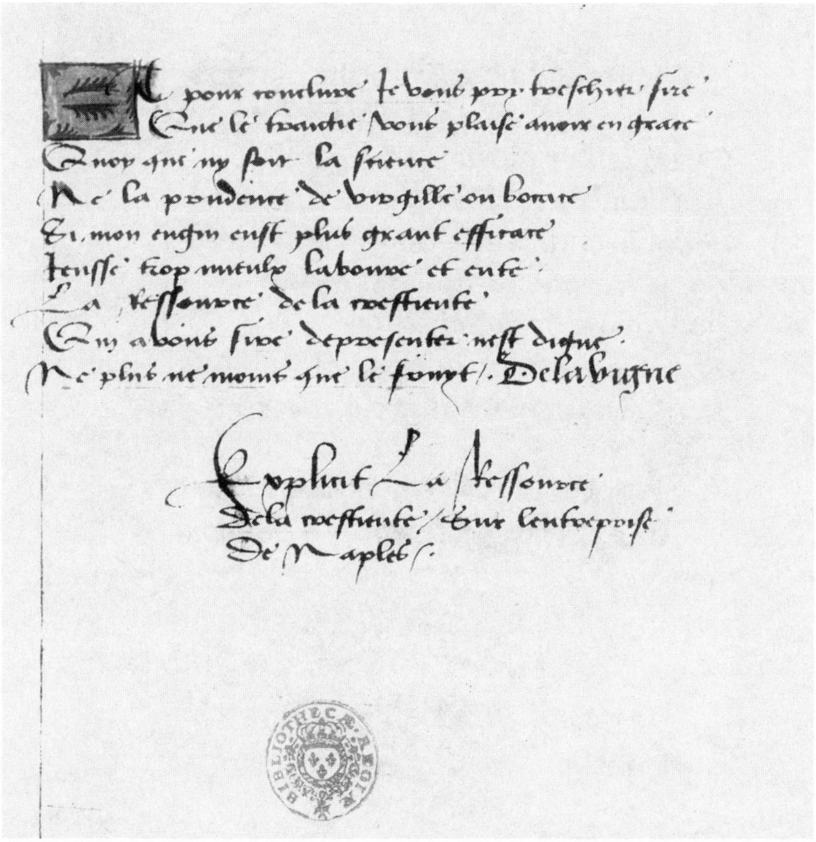

Fig. 4.2. Author's name at the end of final verse (emphasized), from *La ressource de la Chrestienté*, B.N., ms. f.fr. 1699, fol. 45ᵛ. © cliché Bibliothèque Nationale Paris.

source de la Chrestienté in which the acrostics remain unhighlighted. Moreover, the work's final words, which had functioned at once as a signature and as an integral part of the metaphorical conclusion in the manuscripts, are not emphasized at the end of the Angoulême edition (Figure 4.3). Just as readers would have been likely to overlook Charles VIII's presence in this version, because of a lack of ornamentation and an absence of highlighted acrostics, so too they probably would not have noticed the author's signature.

The editors of the *Vergier d'honneur* editions, however, do underscore the acrostics and La Vigne's signature in the *Ressource de la Chrestienté*, albeit in a different way than in the manuscripts. To call attention to the king's name, they have left a space between the acrostics on the vertical

Et pour conclure ie Vous prie cher sire
Que le traicte Vous plaise auoir en grace
Quoy que ny soit la science porphire
Ne la prudence de Virgile ou Bocace
Se mon engin eust plus grant efficace
Jeusse trop mieulx laboure (z ente
La resourse de la crestiente
Qui a Vous sire de presenter nest digne
Ne plus ne moins que le fruict de la Vigne

Cy fine ce petit traicte appelle la resourse
de crestiente sur lemprise de naples.

Fig. 4.3. Author's name at the end of final verse (unemphasized), from *La ressource de la Chrestienté*, 1st ed., Bibliothèque Méjanes, D.14–15, fol. 35ᵛ.

plane and the horizontal verse (Figure 4.4).[29] The author, too, is given a place of greater importance in these versions of the *Ressource*. As I pointed out above, these editions call attention to André de la Vigne from the outset with the placement of his name on the title page, a development that the change from patron-oriented to author-oriented illustrations decorating these versions reinforces. Corroborating this new paratextual emphasis on authorship, the final verses of the *Ressource* draw our attention to the poet's identity by naming him directly instead of through the pun on his name that had appeared earlier in the manu-

29. In the fifth and sixth *Vergier d'honneur* editions, however, the acrostic generating the second speech of Magesté Royalle is not visually emphasized. Was this another example of a publisher's carelessness?

audeuant.En teboutant et defprifant fes pas
toffee dudict Ie ne fcay qui Ainfi que cellequi
du diuin redempteur efperoit et attendoit con=
feil confort ayde et fecours de cueur gay ç defi
bere commança a parler,et dire ainfi

Maiefte roy alle

C har ite mife en pitoyable office
L omme coutonne de diuin benefice
Es dignes cieulx ou repofēt fes faincts
H aulte louenge lup tend fon facrifice
D zay brupt donneur lentretiēt en police
I nnumerable entre tous fes humains
T ous gentilz cueurs tendēt ad ce fes mais
I opeufemēt et de biens de foy plains
E n font douez tant a lame quaucorps
S e ie Boy donc fur creftiente mains
M aulx perpetrer En doyge pas du mains
E ftre apres dieu fur tous mifericors

Et pource donc moy q telz faitz contemple
De dens le chief nay ceruelle ne temple
R is cieup/efbas/en fenfualite
N e aultre chofe qui de pitie ne femple
I e qui congnois deftruite noftre temple
E t molefter dame creftiente
R aifon commande y pourruoit dequite
De fir ardant ne ma le faict quitte
C onfeil ordonne y mettre refiftance
E fpoir de mieulx et confanguinite
No blefſe auſſi par fingularite
M ont mps au train den piendie la Bēgeance

Par quoy de bzief fans plus rien en debatre
La men ptay me deduyre et efbatre
H oztierement quoy qu on parle ou quñ diſſe
R uer par terre fes maftins et combatre
A force darmes pour du tout les abatre
Ce cy faifant dieu me fera propice
D e tebouter tel cruel malefice
E ft enuers lup ma finguliere office
D ont pour bacquict et falut de mon ame
I e Beulx aller fans nul mal et fans Bice
E n ma pfonne faite ce facrifice
D euffent ou nő plufieurs de mon royaulme

Royne des anges emperiere des cieulx
Didze diuine. Lix treffubftancieux

y mage doulce paffe rofe eternelle
D amant nect rubis folacieux
E fcharboucle du hault dieu precieux
F ille Bitgine et mere fupernelle
R uiffeau de ioye dame perpetuelle
A ffin que mieulx ma perfonne fe garde
N emoubliez durant cefte querelle
C onfeillez moy gardez moy de cautelle
E t me tenez en Boftre fauluegarde

A nges celeftes du trofne deifique
D ui auez noms deffence feraphique
D eillez priet le treſhault confiftoire
I ufques adce que damour magnifique
D onner me puiſſe fur cecy paciffique
I oye auctentique et entiere Bictoire
E t Bous auffi de confore repertoire
D rais faicts et fainctes en cōmun auditoite
Do ulces patolles deuant dieu prefentez
I nceſſamment affin que de fa gloire
N ous enlumine et defpee et Bulglaire
T ous mes ennemps foyent mal contez

Bon s champions et finguliers foubdars
N obles francoys qui de fcience et dars
E ftes au monde plus Bertueux nommez
Di fte et de brief Boz efpees et dars
E ſtandez to⁹ deſſoubz mes eftandars
Et Bous ferez mieulx quonicques renõmez
L euez Bous fus comme gens bien famez
D u ie Bo⁹ tiens pour iamais diffumez
N udz et defpris de plus honneur acquerre
G entilz ruftres et Baillans gens clames
D eillez monftrer prefent fi Bous maymez
E t me fupuez tant par mer que par terre

Et pour conclure Benez tous hardyment
P our Boit fanez en Boz corps hardemēt
A ceſte emprife ou dieu nous conduyra
Ra liez Bous car Beritablement
Di eu a donne a celuy fauluement
S i toft que lame defon corps partita
A uffi le pape nous fauorifera
L e commun peuple biē ioyeux en fera
A infi doncques fans faire autre examen
Fi lz de iefus on nous deffaitera
N oz corps es cieulx il glouifiera

In fecula feculozum. Amen
Lacteur

scripts and the Angoulême edition. Consequently, there no longer exists any ambiguity about the author's name or his function in the *Vergier d'honneur* editions. While changing the original title of the *Ressource* to an announcement about the subsequent work in the anthology, his *Entreprise de Naples*, La Vigne identifies himself in a straightforward manner as the king's orator:

> J'eusse trop mieulx *e(s)t sans nulle reprise*
> *Mis en avant de Napples l'ent[r]eprise*
> *Que vous presente en vers, coupletz et ligne,*
> *Vostre treshumble orateur*, De la vigne.

I would have put forward in better fashion and without any reprimand, the *Naples Enterprise*, which is presented to you in verse, stanza, and line by your very humble orator, De la Vigne.[30]

Even though he ended up signing in the more distanced third-person voice, La Vigne's name, by participating in the first-person discourse of this last stanza, becomes more personalized in comparison with its metaphorical rendition in the manuscript and Angoulême versions. While this is impossible to confirm, there is very likely a relationship between La Vigne's change of signature and his involvement in the publication of the *Vergier d'honneur* collection.

Surely the evolution of signatures in the different versions of the *Ressource de la Chrestienté*, the author's increasing paratextual visibility in the *Vergier d'honneur* editions, and his historical control of them must be more than coincidental. Like the shift from the multiple meanings of the proper name to the one-dimensional form that characterized Molinet's signature in his later works, the change from La Vigne's punning signature to its direct expression reflects the author's redirection from a more sophisticated court audience, which enjoyed decoding name games, to a more literal-minded bourgeois public, which was sure to recognize the more straightforward signature. Occurring at the same time that La Vigne took control of the publication of the *Ressource*, the latter change can also be read as an affirmation of the author's desire to control from within and from without not only his creation, but also the dissemination of his work, name, and image.

Other examples of playful signatures and name games figure in the same *Vergier d'honneur* anthology, making it a virtual repository of ono-

---

30. [Paris: Pierre Le Dru, ca. 1502–3], fol. 12[r]. The emphasized words represent the textual alterations made to the earlier versions. All citations from the *Vergier d'honneur* versions will be taken from this edition unless otherwise noted.

mastic devices. In several compositions, La Vigne and his cohorts render homage to different French nobles by structuring poems around their names through the use of acrostics.[31] In every case, a space between the first letter and the remainder of each verse highlights the vertical name created by the acrostic. One even finds poems in which La Vigne's admirers pay him tribute by using his name metaphorically and in acrostics.[32] Unlike the acrostics constructed around the names of nobles in many poems in this collection, however, the acrostics of La Vigne's name in these works do not stand out. In one poem, an acrostic contains both La Vigne's name and that of Madame Catherine de Tieullière, in whose honor the author presumably penned the verses (fols. L iii–L iii^v). But only Catherine's identity is highlighted here (Figure 4.5). Why did the poet's name not figure prominently like that of his aristocratic dedicatee? Was La Vigne, who participated in the publication of the first two editions of the *Vergier d'honneur*, conscious of this differentiation? Perhaps the fact that this was a love poem had something to do with the greater discretion used by the poet in signing his name acrostically, especially since the voice of the poetic "I" plays such a critical role in these verses. The configuration of names nonetheless recalls the manuscript version of the *Ressource*, which accorded prominence to the patron's identity over that of the author.

La Vigne's acrostic signature is accentuated, however, in several other writings in the *Vergier d'honneur* collection. He signs his *Voyage de Naples* in the following manner (Figure 4.6):

> D edens Lÿon en trespuissant seig(n)eur
> E t en triumphe de bruit chevaleureux,
> L e per sans per, de vertus enseigneur,
> A lors se tint comme victorïeux,
> V ray pocesseur de renom glorïeux,
> I ncomparable en decoration,

31. See the ballades and rondeaux that are constructed around the following names: François de Vendôme (fol. o iv^v), Charles (fol. v ii^v), Philippe de Savoye (fol. v iv^v), George d'Amboise (fol. v v^v), Charles de Bourbon (fols. A iv, A vi–A vi^v), Charles d'Angoulême (fol. A vi^v), le duc et la duchesse de Lorraine (fols. B ii and F v^v), etc. It is not possible to determine whether La Vigne wrote all these poems himself, although the rubric on fol. v iii^v, "faictes et composees tant par les devant ditz acteurs [La Vigne and Octavien de Saint-Gelais] que plusieurs autres fatistes, orateurs et habilles compositeurs" (written and composed as much by the aforementioned authors as by several other poets, orators, and talented composers), suggests that these poems were composed by many different poets.

32. See fols. B v^v, B vi, and C i. Since these verses praise the poet, it is very unlikely that he composed them on his own behalf. Nevertheless, they were presumably incorporated into the anthology by La Vigne himself, thereby offering another example of his growing sense of self-importance.

He ne parlez denuie ou dire
Nul ne Vous osera desdire
De cela ie Vous en auise

Ymaginez quelque deuise
Laissant aller deul et soucy
Mais que la matiere soit mise
Entrain auant que soit desinise
Je dire quelque chose aussi

Nul ne dit mot / dea quesse cy
Veult on point matiere entamer
Madame qui estes icy
Puis que chascun en fait ainsi
Deuisons du deduyt daimer

ComBien que le doulx en amer
Aussi souuant que le Vent Vente
Tourne dessus terre et sus mer
Jen Veulx pour mon Vueil consumer
Parler par raison apparente

Amour deul et soucy presente
A plusieurs petiz niueletz
Comme moy qui mis mon entente
De me mettre en la dure sente
Dont iay Ben mains maulx nonueletz

Ballade

M A tresHonoure et excellante dame
A qui ie doys honneur et reuerâce
De tous mes biens du corps aussi de lame
A Vous seruir metz mon obeyssance
Miroir donnent remply de grat plaisâce
Estoille clere plus que rose Vermeille
De tout mon sens et toute ma puissance
En tout honneur Vous seruit ma peille

Honneur haultain chef de toute Beaulté
Amour notaBle corps de magnifficence
Royne des belles plaine dumilite
Droicte et haulte comBle de loyaulte
En tous Voz faitz Voit on lexperience
Marbre poly ymaige de plaisance
Onques au monde ne fut Veu la peille
~~Ne ne sera parquoy sans difference~~
Touiours sans fi Vous seruit ma peille

Mais quoy quil soit se ie me trenue indigne
Tresdoulce dame de haultayne Valeur
Atout le moins mon amour qui Vous guigne
NouBliez pas car Vous auez sa fleur
De Vous seruir sans cesser de Bon cueur
Raison commande quad ce ie me traueille
Et qui plus est de dire par honneur
Vous bien serair toutsiours ie mapateille

De toutes dames de femmes ne de filles
Lesquelles Veisse oncques iour de ma Vie
Amour nauoit tant fussent elle habilles
Haincu mon cueur fors Vous ie Vous affye
Je Vous promectz que Vous serez seruie
Gallart de moy qui que parler en Vueille
Ne dautre dame iamaismauray ennie
En cestup monde Vous estes nompateille

Prince

Et se Vne foys Vostre amour eslargie
Trenue en droit moy croyez se ne sommeille
Que haultement ditay sans Villenpez
Oncques sur terre nen fut Veu la pareille

Ballade

M On bien mamour et ma seulle espance
A qui ie doys houneur et reuerance
D umBle Vouloir toutsiours attribuer
A Vous louer de toute ma puissance
Me Veulx mettre sans nulle difference
C omme celuy qui Vous Veult hault louer
A toutsiours mais sans point y Variet
T iendra son cueur liberal et entier
H onnestement endroit Vous sans fallace
E t quoy quil doiue pour Vous Belle endutee
R ien ne luy est / car pour tout deul passet
Ne quiert auoir que Vostre bonne grace

D oulce maistresse remplye de beaulte
E t de bonte parfaicte humilite
T ient en Vous seulle son siege tribunal
I eune ioyense franchise loyaulte
E n Vous saffient doulceur / benignite
V oit on sur Vous dun geste triumphal
Humble des humbles estes amont a Val
L a plus doulcette qui fut onc sans nul mal
Jesuis transy quant ie Voy Vostre face

L iii

Fig. 4.5*a*. First 21 lines of Madame Catherine de Tieullière's acrostic (emphasized), from *Le vergier d'honneur*, 1st ed., B.N., Réserve, 4° Lb²⁸ 15*a*, fol. L iii. © clichés Bibliothèque Nationale Paris.

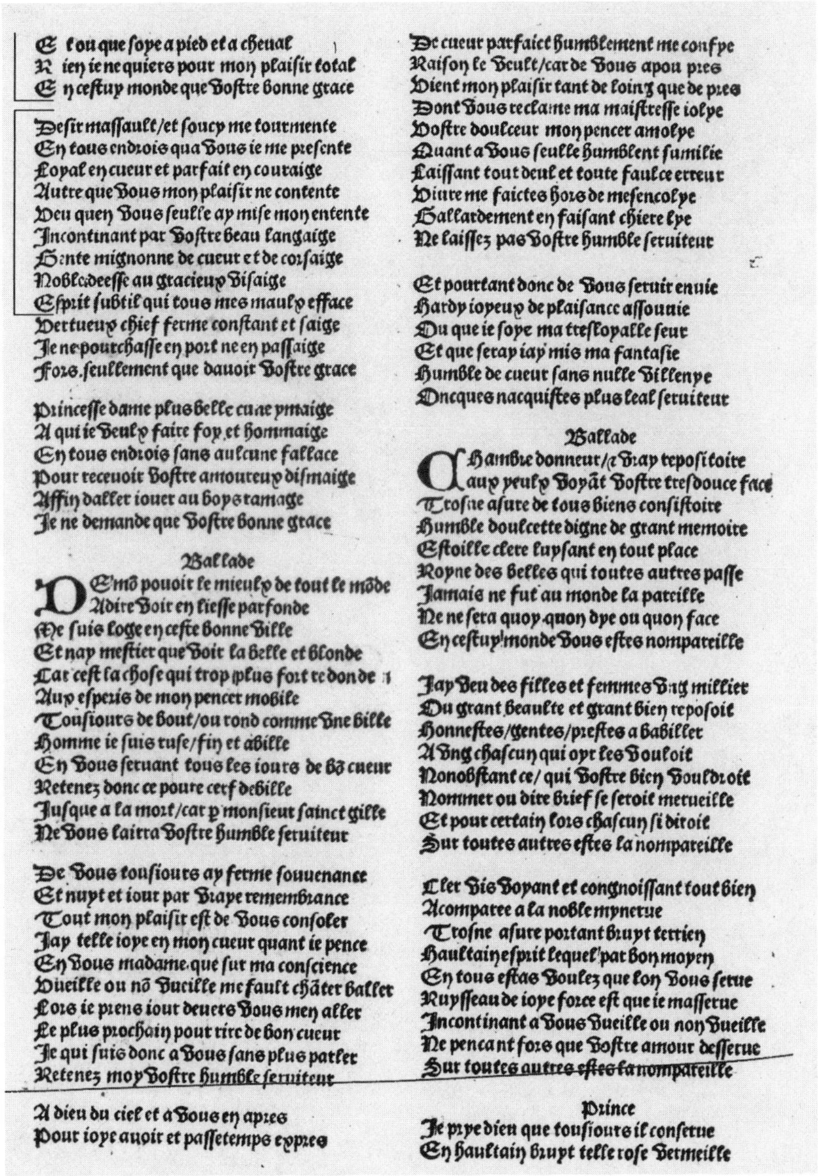

<table>
<tr><td>

E l'ou que soye a pied et a cheual
Rien ie ne quiers pour mon plaisir total
E n cestuy monde que Vostre bonne grace

Desir m'assault/et soucy me tourmente
En tous endrois qua Vous ie me presente
Loyal en cueur et parfait en couraige
Autre que Vous mon plaisir ne contente
Veu quen Vous seulle ay mise mon entente
Incontinant par Vostre beau langaige
Gente mignonne de cueur et de corsaige
Noblecdeesse au gracieux Visaige
Esprit subtil qui tous mes maulx efface
Vertueux chief ferme constant et saige
Je ne pourchasse en port ne en passaige
Fors seullement que dauoir Vostre grace

Princesse dame plus belle cuae ymaige
A qui ie Veulx faire foy et hommaige
En tous endrois sans aulcune fallace
Pour receuoir Vostre amoureux dismaige
Affin daller iouer au boys ramaige
Je ne demande que Vostre bonne grace

Ballade
DE mo pouoit le mieulx de tout le mode
A dire Voir en liesse parfonde
Me suis loge en ceste bonne Ville
Et nay mestier que Voir la belle et blonde
Car cest la chose qui trop plus fort re don de
Aux esperis de mon pencer mobile
Tousiours de bout/ou rond comme vne bille
Homme ie suis ruse/fin et abille
En Vous seruant tous les iours de bo cueur
Retenez donc ce poure cerf debille
Iusque a la mort/car p monsieur sainct gille
Ne Vous lairra Vostre humble seruiteur

De Vous tousiours ay ferme souuenance
Et nupt et iour par Vraye remembrance
Tout mon plaisir est de Vous consoler
Jay telle ioye en mon cueur quant ie pence
En Vous madame que sur ma conscience
Vieille ou no Vueille me fault chanter baller
Lors ie prens iout deuers Vous men aller
Le plus prochain pour rire de bon cueur
Je qui suis donc a Vous sans plus parler
Retenez moy Vostre humble seruiteur

</td><td>

De cueur parfaict humblement me confye
Raison le Veult/car ie Vous apou pres
Vient mon plaisir tant de loing que de pres
Dont Vous reclame ma maistresse iolye
Vostre doulceur mon pencer amolye
Quant a Vous seulle humblent sumilie
Laissant tout deul et toute faulce erreur
Viure me faictes hors de mesencolye
Gaillardement en faisant chiere lye
Ne laissez pas Vostre humble seruiteur

Et pourtant donc de Vous seruir enuie
Hardy ioyeux de plaisance assourie
Du que ie soye ma treslopalle seur
Et que seray iay mis ma fantasie
Humble de cueur sans nulle Villenye
Onques nacquistes plus leal seruiteur

Ballade
CHambre donneur/et Vray repositoire
Aux yeulx Voyat Vostre tresdouce face
Trosne asure de tous biens consistoire
Humble doulcette digne de grant memoire
Estoille clere lupsant en tout place
Royne des belles qui toutes autres passe
Jamais ne fut au monde la pareille
Ne ne sera quoy quon dye ou quon face
En cestuy monde Vous estes nompareille

Jay Veu des filles et femmes vng millier
Du grant beaulte et grant bien reposoit
Honnestes/gentes/prestes a babiller
A vng chascun qui oyr les Vouloit
Nonobstant ce/qui Vostre bien Vouldroit
Nommer ou dire brief se seroit merueille
Et pour certain lors chascun si diroit
Sur toutes autres estes la nompareille

Cler Vis Voyant et congnoissant tout bien
Acompate a la noble mynetue
Trosne asure portant brupt settrien
Haultain esprit lequel par bon moyen
En tous estas Voulez que lon Vous serue
Ruysseau de ioye force est que ie masserue
Incontinant a Vous Vueille ou non Vueille
Ne pencant fors que Vostre amour desserue
Sur toutes autres estes la nompareille

</td></tr>
</table>

A dieu du ciel et a Vous en apres
Pour ioye auoir et passetemps expres

Prince
Je prye dieu que tousiours il consserue
En haultain brupt telle rose Vermeille

Fig. 4.5b. Last 3 lines of Madame Catherine de Tieullière's acrostic (emphasized), and De La Vigne's acrostic (unemphasized), fol. L iii[v].

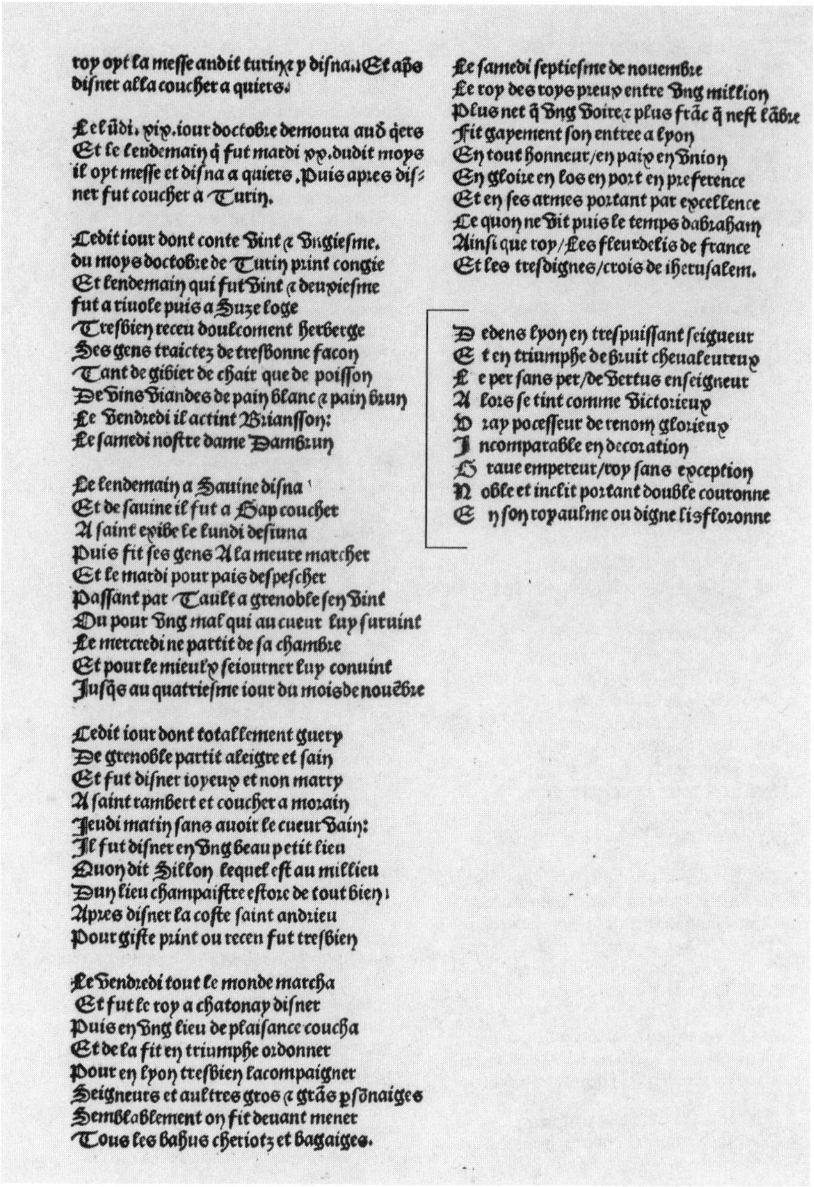

roy opt la messe audit tutine y disna.Et aps
disner alla coucher a quietz.

Le lüdi. xix.iour doctobre demoura aud gers
Et le lendemain q̃ fut mardi xx.dudit moys
il opt messe et disna a quietz. Puis apres disner fut coucher a Tutin.

Ledit iour dont conte Vint e Vngiesme.
du moys doctobre de Tutin print congie
Et lendemain qui fut Vint e deuxiesme
fut a riuole puis a Suze loge
Tresbien receu doulcement herberge
Ses gens traictez de tresbonne facon
Tant de gibier de chair que de poisson
De Vins Viandes de pain blanc e pain brun
Le Vendredi il actint Briansson:
Le samedi nostre dame Dambrun

Le lendemain a Sauine disna
Et de sauine il fut a Gap coucher
A saint exibe le lundi desiuna
Puis fit ses gens A la meute marcher
Et le mardi pour pais despescher
Passant par Tault a grenoble sen Vint
Ou pour Vng mal qui au cueur luy suruint
Le mercredi ne partit de sa chambre
Et pour le mieulx seiourner luy conuint
Iusqz au quattriesme iour du moisde nouẽbre

Ledit iour dont totallement guery
De grenoble partit aleigre et sain
Et fut disner ioyeux et non matry
A saint tambert et coucher a morain
Ieudi matin sans auoir le cueur Vain:
Il fut disner en Vng beau petit lieu
Quon dit Sillon lequel est au millieu
Dun lieu champaistre estore de tout bien:
Apres disner la coste saint andrieu
Pour giste print ou recen fut tresbien

Le Vendredi tout le monde marcha
Et fut le roy a chatonay disner
Puis en Vng lieu de plaisance coucha
Et de la fit en triumphe ordonner
Pour en lyon tresbien lacompaigner
Seigneurs et aulltres gros e grãs psõnaiges
Semblablement on fit deuant mener
Tous les bahus cheriotz et bagaiges.

Le samedi septiesme de nouembre
Le roy des roys pieux entre Vng million
Plus net q̃ Vng Voire,e plus frãc q̃ nest l'ãbre
Fit gayement son entree a lyon
En tout honneur/en paix en Vnion
En gloire en los en port en preferrence
Et en ses armes portant par excellence
Ce quon ne Vit puis le temps dabraham
Ainsi que roy/Les fleurdelis de france
Et les tresdignes/croix de ihetusalem.

D edens lyon en trespuissant seigneur
E t en triumphe de bruit chenaleuteur
L e per sans per/de Vertus enseigneur
A lors se tint comme Victorieux
D ray pocesseur de renom glorieux
I ncomparable en decoration
S raue empereur/roy sans exception
N oble et inclit portant double couronne
E n son royaulme ou digne lisfloronne

Fig. 4.6. La Vigne's acrostic (emphasized), from *Le vergier d'honneur*, 1st ed.,
B.N., Réserve 4° Lb²⁸ 15α, fol. o vᵛ. © cliché Bibliothèque Nationale Paris.

G rave empereur, roy sans exception,
N oble et inclit, portant double couronne,
E n son royaulme ou digne lis floronne.

(fol. o v^v)

Into Lyons as a very powerful lord and in the triumph of chivalric reputation, the peer without peer, teacher of virtues, held himself victorious, true possessor of glorious renown, incomparable in decoration, stately emperor, king without exception, noble and famous, bearing a double crown, into his kingdom where the proud lily blooms.

In contrast to the unaccentuated acrostic signature in the previously discussed poem, this first edition of the *Vergier d'honneur* highlighted DE LA VIGNE in the same manner as the acrostics of noble names. This signature, however, does not work in quite the same way as its aristocratic counterpart. For the horizontal text generated by the author's name does not reflect back on the person associated with the vertically generated name by listing his virtues: this would have appeared too self-serving. Instead, DE LA VIGNE generated praise of the poet's patron, of his *nom* and *renom*, with the chronicler speaking in a third-person voice. Glorification flows from the author's name as it does from his pen. This association between the author's name and the generated text praising the "idealized Other" serves to convey the writer's subservient relationship to his patron, for the words emanating from La Vigne's name glorify Charles VIII. At the same time, the vertical advertisement of the author's presence reminds the reader that the king was dependent on his court secretary for the re-creation of his image in words. This adoption of the acrostic form for authorial signatures, with its vertical and horizontal modes, thus translated the developing relationship of exchange between patron and poet in late medieval French propagandistic literature better than the punning signature. Whereas punning signatures were generated from the verse, a product of carefully crafted words, the vertical arrangement of the poet's name at the head of each line reinforces the idea that the author engenders the text. Since his name does not figure in the poem's horizontal meaning, the acrostic signature remains more separate from the text than a punning signature, pointing more obviously outward to its personal referent. In this way, the acrostic plays a more crucial structural role, because each of its letters simultaneously serves horizontal and vertical functions.

La Vigne uses the same emphasized acrostic device to punctuate other compositions appearing in the *Vergier d'honneur* collection, including *Les louenges du roy faictes par l'Eglise, Noblesse, Prouesse et Honneur* (fol. p v^v),

Le temps de l'annee moralizé (fol. r i°), and *Chascun* (fol. r iii). In each case, extra spacing between the first and second letters of every verse highlights La Vigne's name. Moreover, the speaker does not assume the third-person stance of his earlier punning and acrostic signatures; he adopts instead the more personal and forceful first-person voice. In the *Louenges*, for example, the poet's vertically placed name, generating a horizontal diatribe against Italians in support of French military policy during the Italian Wars, acts as a "spokesman" for the king:

> D oncques Rommains, gros Lombars, Millannoys,
> E t vous Tuscans, qui[l] avez mil harnoys,
> L evez et pris pour (nu)yre en tout desroy
> A ux bons Francoys, qui le goust de la noys
> V ous a baillé, tant que plus dela ne oys
> J oindre ou hongner l'Itallye en charroy,
> G ardez, craignez, servez, aymez le roy
> N oble et entier soubz lequel apprendre a
> E t soyez seur que bien vous en prandra. (fol. p v°)

Therefore, Romans, stout Lombards, Milanese, and you Tuscans, who have raised and taken a thousand pieces of armor to destroy good Frenchmen, who gave you the taste of snow, so much so that beyond that you do not hear Italy threatening or grumbling in the streets: Watch out, fear, serve, love the noble and honest king under whom there is much to learn. And rest assured that he will take good from you.

La Vigne's acrostic signature likewise punctuates the work he wrote following his Parlement victory over Michel Le Noir, an account of Queen Anne of Brittany's entry into Paris in November 1504. The particular configuration of the author's name here offers evidence of yet another modification in La Vigne's use of the acrostic signature. It stands out all the more in this version because of its special, illuminated presentation (Figure 4.7):[33]

> D ame d'onneur, Royne par excellence
> E t Duchesse de grant magnifficence
> L a plus digne qui fut onc en noblesse,
> A Vous je viens soubz toute Reverence
> V ous apporter l'euvre qu'en Vostre absence

33. This work remained in manuscript form (see Stein, 268–304, and Waddesdon Manor, Rothschild Collection, ms. Delaissé 22, fol. 64).

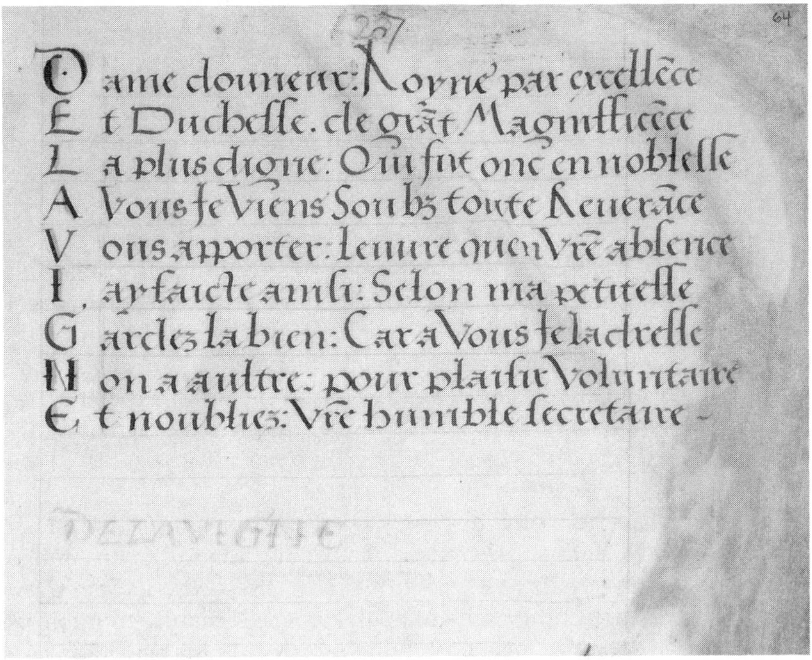

Fig. 4.7. La Vigne's illuminated acrostic, from *Le couronnement d'Anne de Bretagne*, Waddesdon Manor, ms. Delaissé 22, fol. 64. The National Trust, Waddesdon Manor.

> I'ay faicte ainsi selon ma petitesse.
> Gardez la bien: car a Vous je l'adresse
> Non a aultre, pour plaisir voluntaire
> Et n'oubliez Vostre humble secretaire.

Lady of honor, queen par excellence and duchess of great magnificence, the most worthy noble ever, I come to you in all reverence to bring you the work I wrote in your absence, according to my humble state. Guard it carefully: for I address it to you, to no other, out of voluntary pleasure. And forget not your humble secretary.

This highlighting of the author's name may be related to La Vigne's involvement in the *Vergier d'honneur* publications, which had accentuated DE LA VIGNE in a corresponding, albeit less ornate, manner. The writer's self-identification here resembles that found at the end of his *Voyage de Naples*, which had likewise marked a noble entry, Charles VIII's return to Lyons from Italy in November 1495. The strategy employed in La Vigne's description of Anne of Brittany's Parisian arrival nine years later is slightly different, however. While praise for Anne literally emerges from La Vigne's name, just as it had for Charles VIII, the poet also places emphasis on himself in these verses. Reference to the composition he has written in her honor and his appeal to be remembered as her secretary form an important counterpoint to the epideictic discourse that formerly dominated the horizontal text of La Vigne's and others' acrostics. Although the final reference, "Vostre humble secretaire," is formulated in the third person, La Vigne's overall perspective is that of a first-person speaker, which emphasizes all the more his presence. Thus, some of the meaning associated with the vertical representation of the author's name, which had heretofore remained distanced from the generated text, has penetrated the horizontal plane of this acrostic, signaling the infiltration of the poet's persona into his own narrative, a subject I will examine at greater length in the next chapter.

In the ten years between La Vigne's 1494 *Ressource de la Chrestienté*, in support of King Charles VIII, and his 1504 dedication to Queen Anne of Brittany, the author had come to sign in a more direct way. La Vigne's replacement of his punning name with an acrostic signature to publicize textually his authorship, instead of just the virtues of his patroness, and his appropriation of the form that had served to designate his patrons in earlier compositions reflect his growing self-confidence and self-awareness as a writer. The five works of La Vigne that were published during his tenure as secretary to Queen Anne contain no textual signature whatsoever. In every case, though, a prominent announcement of La Vigne as the author of the work and as the French queen's secretary figures on the title page (*L'atollite portas de Gennes* [1507], *Les ballades de Bruyt Commun* [1509], *Le libelle des cinq villes d'Ytallye contre Venise* [1509], *Epitaphes en rondeaux de la royne* [1514]) or in the preceding rubric (*La Patenostre des Genevois* [1507]).[34] In these works, which do not constitute narratives but rather a series of ballades or rondeaux, the author's voice plays no integral role within the text itself. It is as if at the very time La Vigne was detaching his voice from the fiction of his literary text to emphasize his external role as author, the paratext was becoming a more reliable space in which he could identify himself. Although La Vigne did not go to the extent of Jean Lemaire, who increasingly expanded the prefatory space of his works with letters of dedication and self-glorification and with prologues, the use of witty verse announcements about La Vigne's literary accomplishments in the service of the French court on the title page of the *Ballades de Bruyt Commun* and *Libelle des cinq*

---

34. See my *Shaping*, 163–86, and *Recueil de poésies*, ed. Montaiglon and Rothschild, 12:105.

villes d'Ytallye (see Figure 2.11*a–b*) attest to the successful outcome of his 1504 lawsuit, for his name had become a validated part of the publisher's enterprise (see my *Shaping*, 173, 179).

In signing his writings with an acrostic as he did at the end of his very first work, Pierre Gringore identified himself more literally than, though just as playfully as, Molinet and La Vigne had at the beginning of their careers. Gringore chose the acrostic form, perhaps, because his name did not lend itself to wordplay like his contemporaries' and because his audience, at least until 1518, encompassed a less sophisticated, non-courtly public. But the use of elaborate rubrics to alert the reader to the presence of Gringore's signature confirms that recognition of the author's name had become a defined goal of those involved in the printing of his works, including the poet himself. This continued action of ensuring name recognition, Gringore's acquisition of his first privilege in 1505 for the *Folles entreprises* and for many of his publications thereafter, and his strategy of overseeing the printing of the first editions of his works as a means of controlling later unauthorized editions may be related to an unusual incident that occurred in late 1500 in which the printer Michel Le Noir not only published Gringore's work without his authorization but appropriated his authorship of it through a manipulation of Gringore's acrostic signature.

It is in the last stanza of Gringore's *Chasteau de labour* of 1499 that the reader discovers the poet's name for the first time. The eight final verses of the work form a signature acrostic that will mark nearly all his subsequent writings:

L'acteur

Grace rendz au hault Createur
Regnant en triumphe haultaine,
Invocant le povre pecheur
Nourry en la gloire mondaine,
Gardien de nature humaine,
Omnipotent, plain de noblesse,
Resplendissant au hault demaine,
Estendant sur nous sa largesse.[35]

The Author: Grant favor to the Creator reigning on high in stately triumph, invoking the poor sinner, nourished in worldly glory, Guardian of human nature, omnipotent, full of nobility, radiant in His lofty domain, extending over us all His bounty.

35. Paris: Philippe Pigouchet for Simon Vostre, October 22, 1499, fol. f ix[v].

By inscribing his signature into his text, Gringore ensured that subsequent editions, which might bear paratextual details determined by others besides himself, would retain his name. In fact, this acrostic stanza was the sole means of authorial identification in the many editions of the *Chasteau de labour* published up through the middle of the sixteenth century. The use of the rubric "L'acteur" (The Author), which makes the final stanza an epilogue by isolating it from the preceding text, alerts the reader to the author's voice, even if it does not specifically indicate the presence of his name in the vertical register.

Even more regularly than Molinet and La Vigne, Gringore made his name an integral part of the texts he created. Unlike both of the CHARLES DE VALOIS acrostics that appeared in Vérard's printed version of Molinet's *Art de rhétorique* and La Vigne's *Ressource de la Chrestienté*, the horizontal text of Gringore's *Chasteau de labour* does not extol the virtues of the name that generates it. As in the case of La Vigne's acrostic signature at the end of his *Voyage de Naples*, written just a few years earlier (1495), it would not have been appropriate for the author to create a self-congratulatory text; such could be done, however, to glorify another. Yet, the words emanating from GRINGORE in the final stanza of the *Chasteau de labour* volumes do not serve an exclusively epideictic function. While the poet's voice offers extensive praise of God through his name, it also plays an exhortative role. For just as the acrostic signature mediates between the extratextual and textual worlds of the *Chasteau de labour*, just as it points simultaneously outward to the person behind the name and inward to the horizontal message, so too the author serves as an intermediary between the extratextual reader and the textual subject, in this case, God, urging the former to acknowledge the celestial goodness of the latter. In this way, the visual encoding of the author's name reinforces his poetic and rhetorical role as his words promote the Word of God. This same intercessory function characterizes the acrostics La Vigne placed at the end of *Le temps de l'annee moralizé* and *Chascun*, which appeared in print several years after Gringore's *Chasteau* (see p. 180 above).

The numerous editions of the *Chasteau de labour*, published between 1499 and 1529, indicate the work's great success in early sixteenth-century Paris. More surprising, perhaps, was its popularity in England, attested to by the six extant editions of the translated work that appeared in London between 1499 and 1510.[36] In these English versions, however, the French author's name was absent from the final verses. While one might expect Gringore's acrostic signature to disappear through translation, there is no sign of his authorship anywhere in the English edi-

36. For a bibliographical listing, see Appendix 5 below.

tions. Does this omission relate to the fact that the poet's name was absent from the title page and colophon of the French editions that doubtless served as the basis of the translation? Or does this constitute yet another example of a publisher's liberal "borrowing" of an author's work? Did a translator have any kind of obligation to the author of the text translated? Whatever the answer, another voice does claim proprietorship of the *Castell of Labour*. For the final acrostic in the *Chasteau de labour* has been replaced by an *"Actoris excusatio"* (my emphasis), presumably penned by the anonymous translator of the English version (see Pynson ed., ca. 1505, fols. 55ʳ–55ᵛ). While the English printers Richarde Pynson and Wynkyn de Worde took care to advertise their role in the publication of the *Castell of Labour* by placing their names in the colophon of their respective editions, they mentioned neither Gringore's nor the translator's name.[37] It is quite possible that Gringore was unaware of the English publications of his work. And yet it was supposedly his own compatriot, the publisher Antoine Vérard, who had initiated the translation venture and attempted to sell the books he had had translated and published in London.[38] Gringore would not have approved of Vérard's undertaking, which gave the author no credit whatsoever, but brought financial gain to the publisher. Even if he had been aware of Vérard's actions, though, the writer did not possess the necessary legal clout to rectify the situation.[39] Such adaptation of an author's works clearly benefited printers or publishers, but not writers. Although this manipulation of acrostic signatures could have—and may well have—occurred under manuscript reproduction, the stakes were clearly higher with print's more technologically advanced system.

The English version of yet another composition by Gringore that was published for the London book market, his *Complainte de Trop Tard Marié* of 1505, also eliminated the author's signature.[40] This time, however, the

---

37. The title page of Pynson's 1505 edition announces only the title, stating "Here begynneth the castell of laboure," while the phrase "Emprynted be me Richarde Pynson" follows the *"Actoris excusatio."* Wynkyn de Worde's 1506 *Castell of Labour* title page follows Pynson's strategy, but more information about his edition is provided in the added colophon: "Thus endeth the Castell of Labour wherin is rychesse, vertue, and honour. Enprynted at London in Fletestrete in the sygne of the sonne by Wynkyn de Worde. Anno domini. M.CCCCC.vi."

38. Pollard, ed., *The Castell of Labour*, xvii, suggests that Alexander Barclay translated the work for Vérard in Paris around 1503–4. Only a fragment of this edition still exists. The *"Actoris excusatio,"* which appears in the other complete English editions, presumably punctuated the last folios of Vérard's English version as well.

39. The jurisdiction of a French privilege, which was not even obtained for any of the *Chasteau de labour* publications, did not extend to foreign markets (see Armstrong, 1–20, 44).

40. *Complainte de Trop Tard Marié* (Paris: for Pierre Gringore, October 1, 1505), fol. 7ᵛ. For a bibliographical listing of the versions of this work, see Appendix 5 below.

translator, Roberte Copland, boldly substituted his own acrostic signature for the French poet's. This represented a more blatant appropriation of the work, because the *Complainte* editions, from which the English translation must have derived, had clearly advertised Gringore's
name in the colophon, where it reads: "Fait et composé par Pierre Gringore" (Written and composed by Pierre Gringore). The fact that Copland
adopted a signature acrostic all but confirms that he was aware of, and
probably inspired by, Gringore's. Like the translator of the *Chasteau de labour*, Copland is referred to in a rubric as the "auctour" of the *Complaynte
of Them That Ben To Late Maryed* (my emphasis):

The auctour
*R*ychenes in youth, with good gouernaunce,
*O*ften helpeth age whan youth is gone his gate;
*B*oth yonge and olde must have theyr sustenaunce
*E*uer in this worlde, soo fekyll and rethrogate:
*R*yght as an ampte, the whiche all gate,
*T*russeth and caryeth for his lyues fode,
*E*ny thynge that whiche hym semeth to be good.

*C*rysten folke ought for to haue
*O*pen hertes vnto God almyght,
*P*uttynge in theyr mynde thyr soule to saue,
*L*ernynge to come vnto the eternall lyght,
*A*nd kepe well theyr maryage and trouth plyght;
*N*othynge alwaye of theyr last ende,
*D*urynge theyr lyues how they the tyme spende.[41]

Thus the translator prominently announced his re-creation of the
Complainte, as did the printer, but the original author's name is absent.
Although certain authors, such as Molinet with his modernization and
moralization of the *Roman de la rose*, publicly acknowledged that they
were translators—this was especially the case with famous texts—these
English translations did not credit the original author of the *Chasteau de
labour* and *Complainte de Trop Tard Marié*. In point of fact, the translators
of these works were advertised as authors in their own right. Acknowledgment in the English versions of the authorship of Gringore, who was

---

41. Collier, ed., 1:18. The printer's name and address follow (my emphasis): "Here endeth the complaynt of to late maryed, / For spendynge of tyme or they a bordè. / The fayd
holy sacramente have to long taryed, / Humayne nature tassemble, and it to accorde. / Enprynted in Fletestrete by *Wynkyn de Worde*, / Dwellynge in the famous cyte of London, / His
hous in the same at the sygne of the Sonne" (19).

probably little known abroad, presumably would not have promoted book sales as much as the name of a local writer would have.

The disappearance of Gringore's acrostic signature in the translated versions of his works was perhaps understandable, even though the elimination of his identity was difficult to excuse. Its absence in French editions, however, can be attributed to sheer arrogance and greed, which doubtless motivated Le Noir in his publication of the *Chasteau d'amours.*[42]

As in nearly all his works, Gringore's name, though unannounced on the title page of his second publication, generated the last stanza of his text. Moreover, a rubric directed the reader of Pigouchet's and Vostre's edition of the *Chasteau d'amours* to reconstruct GRINGORE vertically, reflecting perhaps a concern about its possibly not being recognized in acrostic form:

> Le surnom de l'acteur qui a fait
> et composé ce livre par les premie-
> res lettres de ce couplet:
>
> Gens de bien qui lisez ce livre,
> Rememorez en voz couraiges
> Jeunesse qui maint assault livre:
> Nature conduit ses ouvraiges.
> Gardez tousjours le dit des saiges,
> Obtemperez a leur requeste,
> Recordez trestous ces passaiges
> En folle amour peu on acqueste.[43]

The last name of the author who made and composed this book [is to be known] by the first letters of this stanza: Good people who read this book, remember in your hearts youth, which wages many an assault; Nature leads its works. Always keep in mind the sayings of wise men, obey their request, record all these passages. In foolish love, one acquires little.

Thus, the author's name in its vertical register would have stood out on the last folio of the *Chasteau d'amours* to the eye of the potential buyer. As in the *Chasteau de labour*, the words generated by Gringore's name do not reflect back on the person behind the name but reach out in an intercessory way to the public, directly exhorting readers to ethical behavior.

42. Some of the following ideas have appeared in different form in my "Confrontation."
43. Paris: Philippe Pigouchet for Simon Vostre, n.d. [ca. 1500], fol. 44^v.

Once again the author-*acteur* plays the intermediary role of a moralist, one associated with the audience and somewhat above or outside it as well, just like the relationship between his name and the text it engenders. This change in the horizontal text from an epideictic, patron-oriented discourse (characteristic of earlier acrostic stanzas like those in La Vigne's *Ressource* and *Voyage de Naples*) to a public-directed, exhortative discourse recalls some of La Vigne's final acrostic stanzas examined above. It also characterizes the narrative function of the *acteur* in Gringore's texts (see Chapter 5 below).

But the writer's name was not the only one identified at the end of the *Chasteau d'amours*. In the stanzas preceding his signed verses, the names of the printer and publisher were also cast into acrostic form and announced through a system of similar rubrics. Like the Gringore acrostics, these verses incite the reader to exemplary conduct (Figure 4.8): "Le nom de l'imprimeur qui a imprimé ce livre congnoistrez par les premieres lettres de ce couplet . . . Le nom du marchant qui a fait faire ce livre . . . Le surnom dudit marchant" (You will discover the name of the printer who printed this book in the first letters of this stanza . . . The name of the merchant who had this book made . . . The last name of said merchant). The presence of acrostics identifying the printer and publisher as well as the author is rather unusual and suggests the same fear of misappropriation that the author may have felt.[44] In a sense, they replace the patron acrostics found in many earlier manuscripts and incunabula, and they signal the increasingly dominant role in book reproduction played by printer and publisher, who gradually came to provide an alternative to patronage. Gringore was in fact more dependent on publishers than on patrons at this particular time. And yet, since he presumably governed this textual space, it is apparent that in composing this series of acrostic verses, Gringore sought to control publicity from within the text by absorbing into it the colophon, normally a paratextual feature regulated by the printer or publisher. That he wrote his own and the other acrostics suggests that Gringore actually authorized the publication of the *Chasteau d'amours* under the auspices of Pigouchet and Vostre.

Such was not the case, however, with Le Noir's December 1500 edition of the *Chasteau d'amours*, in which dramatic alterations were made to the acrostics. While Le Noir had the verses that spelled out the names of Pigouchet and Vostre in earlier editions reprinted, perhaps because they

---

44. The printer Pigouchet was earlier associated with acrostic use, for he is named with his patrons and other collaborators at the end of the *Miroir d'or de l'ame pecheresse* of 1483. See Claudin, 1:296–97, and Pellechet, who calls attention to the acrostic signatures of four publishers' names associated with the printing of Pierre d'Ailly's *L'eschelle de penitance* (Antoine Caillaut, Louis Martineau, Geoffroi de Marnef, and Belart).

formed an integral part of the text, he omitted the rubrics that directed the reader to reconstruct them vertically. Le Noir obviously did not wish to draw attention to another printer and publisher. Remarkably, though, he modified the last lines of the *Chasteau d'amours* by replacing the eight-verse acrostic of Gringore's name with two stanzas that spelled out his own. Furthermore, rubrics before each stanza alerted the reader to the presence of *his* first and last names (Figure 4.9): "Le nom de l'imprimeur trouverez par les lettres capitales . . . Le surnom" (You will find the name of the printer by the capital letters . . . The surname). Daring to appropriate Gringore's acrostic idea for his own ends, Le Noir also appropriated his very words. For he lifted at least four of the verses in his two-stanza acrostic from different locations in Gringore's text, combining together without regard for meaning in such a way that the two stanzas do not appear related to each other (Brown, "Confrontation," n. 25). An artificial relationship between vertical and horizontal meanings results, for this printer did not create verses from his name but tried to reconstruct an acrostic from existing lines. Le Noir, then, stole the author's words to form his own acrostic signature, which in the end replaced the true writer's name. This printer's dramatic assumption of the authorship of a work is translated by his appropriation of Gringore's moralistic first-person voice in the very opening lines of these artificially added stanzas, when he states: "Monstrer ay voulu que amour n'est que follie" (I wanted to show that love is only folly). Clearly Gringore would not have authorized Le Noir's attempt to insert himself into the poetic text, especially since his own name was dissociated from the work he had composed. Le Noir's onomastic manipulation reveals a conscious attempt on his part to mask the author's identity, give himself sole credit for the work, and wrest control of the *Chasteau d'amours* from Pigouchet and Vostre.[45] His unauthorized printing and appropriation of Gringore's *Chasteau d'amours* in December 1500 anticipated in fact his pirating adventures involving Lemaire's *Temple d'honneur et de vertus*, Bouchet's *Regnars traversant*, and La Vigne's *Vergier d'honneur* in 1504. But it also precipitated a very important reaction on the part of these writers, who dared to challenge such practices in the legal arena. It is possible that Gringore served as one of La Vigne's witnesses against Le Noir in the June 1504 lawsuit, as did Bouchet, whose acrostic signature in the stolen *Regnars traversant* provided the only proof of his authorship (see Figure 1.2).

Although Gringore's name did not always appear paratextually in the

---

45. Le Noir probably chose to appropriate this particular work because it had already been favorably received. In fact, he published a second edition of the *Chasteau d'amours* on February 4, 1501, N.S., which closely follows the edition of six weeks earlier, except that an error in his acrostic signature in the December 1500 edition has been corrected.

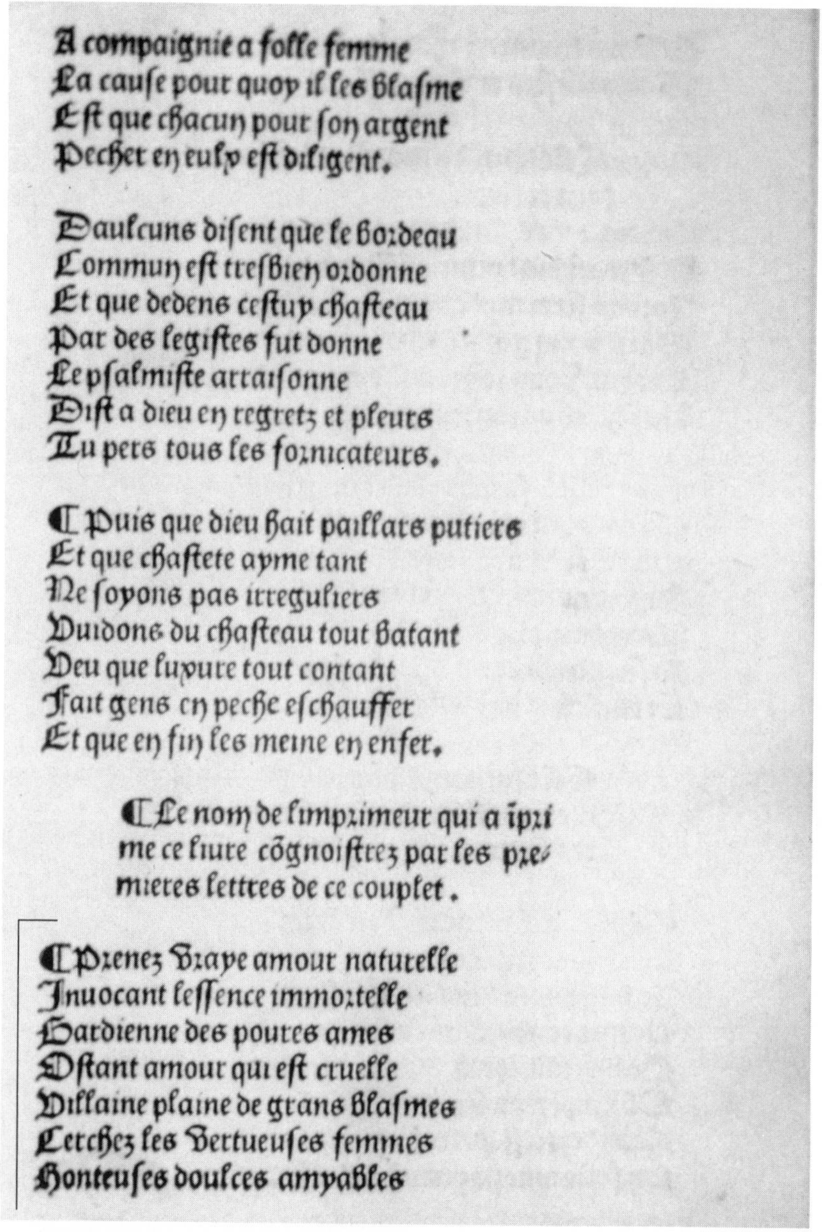

A compaignie a folle femme
La cause pour quoy il les blasme
Est que chacun pour son argent
Pecher en eulx est diligent.

Daulcuns disent que le bordeau
Commun est tresbien ordonne
Et que dedens cestuy chasteau
Par des legistes fut donne
Le psalmiste arraisonne
Dist a dieu en regretz et pleurs
Tu pers tous les fornicateurs.

C Puis que dieu hait paillars putiers
Et que chastete ayme tant
Ne soyons pas irreguliers
Vuidons du chasteau tout batant
Veu que luxure tout contant
Fait gens en peche eschauffer
Et que en fin les meine en enfer.

C Le nom de l'imprimeur qui a impri
me ce liure cognoistrez par les premieres lettres de ce couplet.

C Prenez vraye amour naturelle
Inuocant l'essence immortelle
Gardienne des poures ames
Ostant amour qui est cruelle
Villaine plaine de grans blasmes
Cerchez les vertueuses femmes
Honteuses doulces amyables

Fig. 4.8a. First 7 lines of Pigouchet's acrostic, from *Le chasteau d'amours*, 1st ed.,
B.N., Réserve Ye 1322, fol. 44ʳ. © clichés Bibliothèque Nationale Paris.

Et Vous trouuerez maintec dames
Tresßonneftes et Vertuaßles.

¶Le nom du marchant qui a fait
faire ce liure.

¶Seruez dieu principallement
Joyeuƥ ferez tant que aurez Vie
Mais Vous gardez difcretement
Du que Vous foyez nullement
Nayez deffus aulttruƥ enuye.

¶Le furnom dudit marchant.
¶Vous qui aymez oultre raifoɲ
Obtemperez a la faifoɲ
Si ferez reputez treffaiges
Tant auez ouy de blafoɲ
Refpandu fans nulle achoifoɲ
Et redoubtez peu les paffaiges.

¶Le furnom de lacteur qui a fait
et compofe ce liure par les premie⸗
res lettres de ce couplet.

¶Gens de bieɲ qui lifez ce liure
Rememorez eɲ Voz couraiges
Jeuneffe qui maint affault fiure
Nature conduit fes ouuraiges
Gardez toufiours le dit des faiges
Obtemperez a leur requefte
Recordez treftous ces paffaiges
Eɲ folle amour peu oɲ acquefte.

Fig. 4.8*b*. Pigouchet's (last 2 lines), Simon Vostre's, and Gringore's acrostics, fol. 44^v.

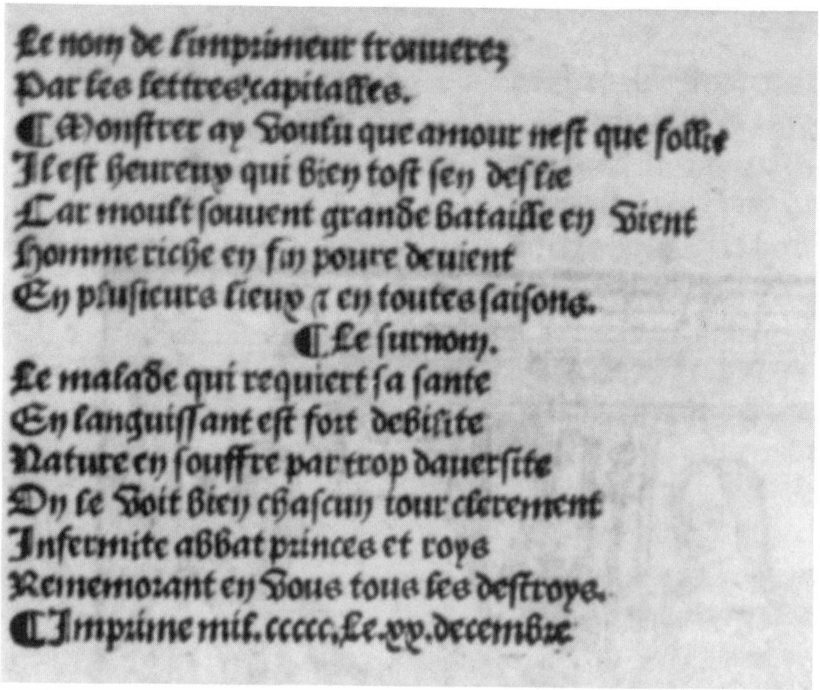
Le nom de limprimeur trouuerez
Par les lettres capitalles.
¶ Monstrer ay voulu que amour nest que follie
Il est heureux qui bien tost sen deslie
Car moult souuent grande bataille en vient
Homme riche en fin poure deuient
En plusieurs lieux & en toutes saisons.
¶ Le surnom.
Le malade qui requiert sa sante
En languissant est fort debilite
Nature en souffre par trop dauersite
On le voit bien chascun iour clerement
Infermite abbat princes et roys
Rememorant en vous tous les destroys.
¶ Imprime mil.ccccc.Le.xv.decembre

Fig. 4.9. Michel Le Noir's acrostic, from *Le chasteau d'amours*, 2d ed., B.N., Réserve Ye 1019, fol. 34ʳ. © cliché Bibliothèque Nationale Paris.

works he himself subsequently published,[46] in each of these and in fact in nearly all his other published writings, he signed with an acrostic stanza, whose ubiquity transformed it into a personal trademark much like the Mère Sotte woodcut (see my "Text," n. 39). As we discovered in the *Chasteau de labour*, the rubric "L'acteur" often set this final stanza apart from the rest of the verses in the text. Sometimes, however, more elaborate details direct the reader to look for the author's name or to reconstruct the vertical text containing his signature. The rubric "Le surnom de l'acteur sera trouvé par les premieres lettres de ce couplet" (The last name of the author will be found in the first letters of this stanza) announces the last stanza of the landmark *Folles entreprises*, whereas the *Notables enseignemens* offers these hints: "Fin et conclusion de ce present livre laquelle monstre et enseigne par la premiere lettre de chacun vers le surnom de l'acteur" (End and conclusion of this present book which

46. In some works, Pierre Gringore's name was announced either on the title page (*La chasse du cerf des cerfs; L'espoir de paix; Les heures de Nostre Dame; La paraphrase . . . Pseaumes*) or in a colophon at the end (*La complainte de Trop Tard Marié; Le jeu du Prince des Sotz; Les menus propos; Notables enseignemens*).

shows and indicates the last name of the author by the first letter of each verse). In *La quenoulle* one reads, "Incitation de l'acteur" (The Author's Incitation); in *La complainte de la cité crestienne*, "Conclusion de l'acteur" (The Author's Conclusion). The rubric "L'Acteur et surnom d'icel mys" (The Author and his last name placed herein) precedes the acrostic stanza in *La chasse du cerf des cerfs*. The timing of this change in signature rubrics suggests that they were motivated in part by Le Noir's alterations of Gringore's textual signature and, moreover, that they led to the author's acquisition of privileges and the decision to publish his own writings.

Unlike the more ambiguous metaphorical signatures characteristic of Molinet and La Vigne early in their careers, which risked greater anonymity once the text reached readers outside the literary circle that would have recognized them, Gringore's use of the acrostic, especially in its position of closure and in conjunction with a promotional rubric, reflects a growing concern to ensure that his authorship would be recognized and remain associated with the text. Gringore's textual signature—like Molinet's and La Vigne's eventually—became more and more accessible, ensuring that his public would recognize his name. Even when Gringore finally succeeded in obtaining patronage in 1518, which ultimately led to the disappearance of his Mère Sotte woodcut, he continued to sign with his famous acrostic stanza. Although paratextual praise was accorded his new patron's name in the works Gringore had published while working under his aegis, the poet never incorporated the duke of Lorraine's acrostic within the text. Gringore's initial independence as a writer had established a pattern whereby his own name was the one that he consistently publicized in his editions.[47]

Jean Lemaire's method of self-identification in his works provides evidence of how printing was gradually becoming an integral part of the authorizing process by the early sixteenth century. Whereas Molinet, La Vigne, and Gringore had experienced the loss of their authorial identities by dint of publishers' manipulation of their signatures in different circumstances during the late fifteenth and early sixteenth centuries, Lemaire was spared the same misfortune. His appearance on the Parisian literary scene in 1504—at precisely the moment when La Vigne, Bouchet, and Gringore were legally challenging or about to challenge the misappropriation of their works and names by publishers—was timely indeed and may explain why Lemaire never adopted a textual signature.

47. See Chapter 3 above for a discussion of Gringore's dedication to the lord of Ferrières in the *Folles entreprises*; for the author's reference to Antoine de Lorraine in the fourth edition of the *Fantasies de Mère Sotte*, see Frautschi ed., 43.

La Vigne's successful lawsuit, followed by Gringore's acquisition and advertisement of his own privilege a year later, served notice to publishers that writers had become aware of the need to play a more active role in the legal and practical appropriation of their works.

As we have seen, Lemaire often signed his writings with the device "De peu assez," which he placed outside the literary text.[48] But he adopted another strategy for ensuring recognition of his authorship, one which suggests that the paratext of imprints could legitimately authorize a writer's work through the advertisement of his name, especially when that writer supervised the reproduction and distribution of those imprints. By making extended use of introductory *épîtres*, as in the editions of his *Temple d'honneur et de vertus* (1504), *Epîtres de l'amant vert* (published 1511), and *Illustrations de Gaule et Singularitez de Troye* (1511–24), and of prologues, as in his *Concorde du genre humain* (1508), *Légende des Vénitiens* (1509), *Traicté de la différence des schismes et des conciles* (1511), and *Illustrations de Gaule*, Lemaire provided a more stable context for those paratextual features which were often lost in the manuscript tradition or in the transition to print. Because they first appeared in print, not in manuscript form like Molinet's *Art de rhétorique*, and because the author participated in the publication of many of these works, Lemaire's prefatory material tended to remain attached to the texts with which they were originally associated once he took over initial control of their publication. While the author's continued pursuit of privileges for his works from 1509 on confirms his commitment to obtaining legal control over their reproduction and distribution, his choice of the paratext rather than the text as the site of self-identification announces the growing relevance of this signature space for promotion of the author's identity and image. It symbolizes as well the writer's withdrawal from the fictional dimension of his text. In the end, the struggle between authors and publishers for paratextual presence on title pages and in colophons, in presentation motifs and author-images, together with writers' attempts to maintain control over their texts through the use of more accessible signatures in the late fifteenth and early sixteenth centuries accompanied authors' appropriation of prefatory space in imprints.

With the problem of misappropriation intensifying or, rather, becoming legally acknowledged for the first time in the early sixteenth century, authors changed earlier patterns associated with the manuscript culture's more limited circulation of writing. They began to sign their works in a more self-conscious and defensive fashion, adopting both the acros-

---

48. Besides his *Temple d'honneur et de vertus* (1504), see Lemaire's *Epîtres de l'amant vert* (1505; published 1511), *Concorde des deux langages* (1511; published 1513), the *Illustrations de Gaule et Singularitez de Troye* (Bks. 1–3), and *Le traicté de la différence des schismes et des conciles de l'Eglise* (1511).

tic and the straightforward proper name. Lemaire's reliance on a para-textual signature prefigures the situation of Renaissance writers such as Clément Marot, whose first authorized edition of the *Adolescence clémentine* of 1534 exemplifies how, during the sixteenth century, prefatory material had developed into an integral part of authors' published works.[49]

Authors' use of more-straightforward signatures in early sixteenth-century France was not just a sign of authorial self-consciousness and textual appropriation. Signatures had become marks of defiance as well, announcing a *prise de position* against unfair printing practices and the related misappropriation both of names and literary works. The inscription of one's signature into one's work was associated with the new artistic use of perspective and the so-called semiotic autonomy of the image (Lebensztejn, 46). Clearly the signature in a work, whether a painting or literary production, reflected the growing autonomy of the artistic creator in this period. How this new onomastic self-consciousness was reshaped into textual expression will be the subject of the next chapter, in which I trace the movement of the more independent, self-aware author-figure from the frame or margins of his canvas into its very texture.

49. For a discussion of Renaissance prologues, see Jeanneret, 279–89. Genette, *Seuils*, 116–26, discusses the ambiguity of dedications as paratextual forms.

AUTHORIAL AND
NARRATIVE VOICES IN LATE
MEDIEVAL VERNACULAR TEXTS

uthorial signatures, examined in the previous chapter, provided an important link in late medieval France between the paratext of a literary production, where their appearance was not necessarily controlled by the writer, and the text, in which writers purposefully anchored their names. More than any other feature discussed in this book, such signatures point to the crucial association between the growing paratextual advertisement of writers and their increasing authorial presence within the text. Both of the latter correspond to a new level of literary defensiveness and a new public awareness of the authorial presence.

I concentrate in this chapter on the textual portrayal of the author, the association between author and narrator, and the contrast between the fictionality of narration and the historicity of authorship. While supporting the contention that this period was marked by "intersecting crises of political and personal authority" (Brownlee and Stephens, eds., 12) and confirming the idea associated with Christine de Pizan that the practice of repeated self-naming "puts a distinctly different textual weight upon . . . the narrator's representation of [the author's] authority" (Quilligan, *Female Authority*, 28), my analysis offers evidence of an evolution from a marginalized, narrative voice enmeshed in the fiction of the *récit* to a more independent and aggressive first-person voice: that of the *acteur* who, standing apart from characters within the text, reacts instead with readers outside and identifies with the author himself. In my examination of Lemaire's poetic enterprise (see Chapter 1 above), I have already provided an example of such a development. Whereas the works of earlier medieval writers sometimes offered similar narrative strategies, their first-person narrators tended to remain more enmeshed in the fictional dynamics of the *récit* (see Hult, *Self-fulfilling Prophecies*, and Johnson) than those of their successors, whose *acteurs* came to assume increasingly defensive postures reminiscent of the author's own stance. This phenomenon may well be related to the gradual distancing of later writers from love-centered narratives, dream frameworks, and allegorical characters.

In order to situate this discussion properly, I wish first to reexamine two medieval terms that depict the idea of authorship and its related functions, because their shift in meaning during the Middle Ages coincides with a redefinition of the traditional roles of those participating in textual production. The classical and medieval distinctions and ambiguities relating to the Latin words *auctor* and *actor* (*aucteur* and *acteur* in French), meaning "authority" and "author," converged in a confusion of terms and overlapping of functions during the Middle Ages. These appear to have stabilized by the early sixteenth century with the widespread use of the single term *acteur*, which more or less absorbed the various meanings of both words before being replaced by *autheur/auteur* by the 1530s. I suggest that the appearance of the term *acteur* in print, not only in literary texts but also in the paratext, played a key role in this standardization. Because *acteur* maintained classical connections with the Latin term for "litigator" (*actor*), associations with the dramatic meaning of "actor" (*actor*) exist, although the French equivalent for an actor in a play, *acteur*, did not surface much before the seventeenth century.

Given their motivation to acquire legal protection for their works and their involvement in theatrical stagings in one form or another, La Vigne, Bouchet, Gringore, Lemaire, and their contemporaries were, I argue, playing out and playing on the ambiguous meanings of *acteur* and *aucteur* that will be discussed below. They were also playing the role of *acteurs*, in the legal sense of "demandeurs en justice,"[1] in a way never exhibited by their literary models. Their aggressively protective posture was transposed to the literary register in an implicit appeal that their works be recognized as authorized literary productions, an appeal that was sometimes veiled by an entreaty on behalf of a patron's political policies or in favor of adopting certain moralistic behavior. These associations are strengthened by the fact that both Jean de Meun, who assumed the roles of compiler and *aucteur* in a self-defensive strategy, and Alain Chartier, whose political experience bespeaks a forensic consciousness,

---

1. See Huguet, "Acteur," 1:60, who cites this usage in Calvin's *Ordonnances*, 10; Raynouard, "Actor, Auctor," 1/2:22, who refers to this term in the translation of the *Code de Justinien*; and Wartburg, 24:117. This usage also appeared in Latin throughout the Middle Ages (Blaise, "Auctor," 1:13; Du Cange, "Actor," 1:64).

served as authorities for late fifteenth- and early sixteenth-century writers. Instead of refusing responsibility for their texts, however, as both Jean de Meun and Chartier had at controversial moments, late medieval writers explicitly sought validation as authorities of their works.

Auctores were Latin authors, such as Ovid and Virgil, Priscian, Boethius, and Isidore of Seville, whose writings were granted special recognition or authority (*auctoritas*) by medieval scholars. With the high respect accorded the ancients, modern writers were generally not considered to be *auctores*. When these scholastic literary attitudes eventually reached the vernacular community, though, fourteenth-century writers like John Gower and Boccaccio sought to increase their own *auctoritas*.[2]

In the thirteenth century Vincent de Beauvais employed the term *actor* to maintain the distinction between ancients and moderns. Concerned about manuscript corruption and the difficulty of determining which *auctores* really said what, he introduced the term *actor* to contrast with *auctores*, whose works formed the basis of his *Speculum maius*, a compendium of excerpts from earlier pagan and Christian authors. The term *actor* was meant to signal Vincent's own opinion or that of contemporary scholars.[3] This clarification may have been a response to the long-standing confusion between these two words, which, despite their different etymologies (*auctor* deriving from *augeo*, *actor* from *ago*), had orthographic and semantic similarities. *Actor*, which had originally meant someone who did something, took on the meaning of *auctor*, author of a work, while *auctor*, originally someone who produced something, especially a book, acquired the more specialized meaning related to the idea of origins and the idea of authority, which recalled its association with *auctoritas* (Chenu, 81–83).

Vincent's *auctor*/*actor* distinction can be related to the differentiation made between *auctor*, commentator, compiler, and scribe by his contemporary Saint Bonaventure, who explained that

there are four ways of making a book, and only one is appropriate to an *auctor*. . . . The scribe is wholly subject to the materials of others, which he should copy as carefully as possible, adding or chang-

2. For details on these developments, see Minnis's *Theory*, an excellent study of scholastic prologues to late medieval commentaries on theological and philosophical works.

3. Minnis, *Theory*, 157, 193, 202. In the twelfth century William of Conches distinguished between *actores*, whose works did not pertain to philosophy, and *auctores*, whose works were "authoritative" because they related to philosophy through moral instruction (25–26).

ing nothing. The compiler puts together the materials of others, adding nothing of his own. . . . The commentator writes the materials of others, adding something of his own by way of explanation. Finally, the *auctor* writes mainly *de suo* but draws on the materials of other men to support what he is saying. (Minnis, "Discussions," 415–16).

Indeed, concerned about keeping ideas or opinions attributed to the correct "author," Vincent de Beauvais was essentially classifying his actions as compiler and commentator under the province of an *actor*. Although Vincent's contemporaries and successors more or less maintained his differentiation between author and compiler, they did not retain the terms *auctor* and *actor* for these distinctions, but rather *auctor* and *compilator*. Even though by the fourteenth century *auctores* were seen as those who asserted ideas and bore responsibility for their words, whereas compilers often denied such responsibility in their capacity as reporters or repeaters, the true function of the *auctor* incorporated the roles of both asserter and compiler (Minnis, *Theory*, 100–101).

Jean de Meun's work provides an example of the overlapping of these terms and functions and of the exploitation of their supposed distinctions.[4] In the *Roman de la rose* the narrator describes himself as a reporter or reciter of the written words of authorities, or *aucteurs* (my emphasis):

> ailleurs veill un petit antendre
> por moi de males genz deffandre. . . .
> s'il vos samble que je di fables,
> por manteür ne m'an tenez,
> mes aus *aucteurs* vos an prenez
> qui an leur livres ont escrites
> les paroles que g'en ai dites,
> e ceus avec que g'en dirai;
> ne ja de riens n'an mentirai,
> se li preudome n'en mentirent
> qui les anciens livres firent. . . .
> par quoi mieuz m'an devez quiter:
> je n'i faz riens fors reciter,
> se par mon geu, qui po vos coute,

4. Chenu, 84, n. 1, cites the *Roman de la rose* as an example of the assimilation of *actor* into the French *acteur* during the thirteenth century. According to the *Trésor de la langue Française*, ed. Imbs, 3:967, *auteur* (from *auctur*), meaning writer, dates back to the Anglo-Norman poet Wace (1160). Godzich and Kittay, 60–62, have a different understanding of the development of these terms, without, however, offering specific references.

quelque parole n'i ajoute,
si con font antr'eus li *poete*.

(vv. 15125–15210)[5]

I want to move aside a little to defend myself against wicked people. . . . [I]f it seems to you that I tell fables, do not consider me a liar, but apply to the authors who in their works have written the things that I have said and will say. I shall never lie in anything as long as the worthy men who wrote the old books did not lie. . . . For this reason you should the sooner absolve me; I do nothing but retell just what the poets have written between them . . . except that my treatment, which costs you little, may add a few speeches. (Dahlberg trans., 258–59)

The strongly defensive tone and juridical vocabulary ("pur moi . . . deffandre," "aus aucteurs . . . prenez," "m'an devez quiter") adopted in these lines suggests a conscious literary posture. Jean's narrator was obviously exploiting the so-called compiler's "disavowal of responsibility" trope (Minnis, *Theory*, 197–98) to attribute to authorities controversial ideas he supported. The would-be *auctor* thus manipulated a rhetorical convention that had paid tribute to the ancients in such a way that it would ultimately pay tribute to himself.[6] By deflecting responsibility for these ideas to classical *aucteurs*, by equating his actions with those of *poètes*, another term referring to ancient writers (see n. 15 below), Jean's narrator directed his readers to place the words he had written on a par with those of his revered predecessors. The trope thus devolved into a manifestation of false modesty as Jean de Meun, hiding behind the shield of a compiler, acted as an author (Minnis, *Theory*, 210). Indeed, as critics have noted, Jean did not consider himself inferior to the ancient *auctores*.[7] Unlike the scholastic compiler Vincent de Beauvais, whose effort to distinguish between ancients and moderns arose from a certain

5. Lecoy ed., 2:210–12. In Poirion's edition, based on a late thirteenth-century manuscript (Paris, B.N., f.fr. 25523), the word "actors," not "aucteurs" or "acteurs," is used (see v. 15218), demonstrating the interchangeability of these words at the time. Langlois's reconstructed edition of the *Rose*, 4:95–96, v. 15218, uses "aucteurs," whereas Baridon's edition of Marot's supposed version of the *Rose* employs "acteurs." Note the interaction of the written and oral modes of transmission here: the narrator functions orally ("dire," "reciter"), while the *aucteurs* express themselves in "escrites . . . paroles."

6. Minnis shows how others, such as Chaucer, exploited this topos as well (*Theory*, 190–210). Dante had succeeded in presenting himself as author as well as commentator or compiler in his thirteenth-century *Convivio* (Ascoli).

7. Huot, *From Song to Book*, 101–2, suggests that the *aucteur/acteur* ambiguity defined Jean's actions as both a compiler and an authority in the *Rose*, since he was known as a learned translator and described as a *poëte*, *docteur*, and *philosophe*. Dembowski, "Latin

modesty and respect for his forebears, Jean de Meun challenged tradition: as a modern writer he could now assume the status of *auctor* by making an indirect claim for his own *auctoritas*. In doing so, he set up his public to consider him—or his narrator—as an *aucteur*, not just an *acteur*.

It was the fictional framework of the *Rose*, adopted from Guillaume de Lorris and transformed into Jean's encyclopedia of knowledge, that facilitated such a move. Guillaume's narrative strategy conveniently served to complicate the relationship of authoritative, authorial, and narrative voices, of *aucteurs* and *acteurs*, in the *Roman de la rose*. The pseudo-autobiographical narrator, variously identified as "maistre," "auctor," "actor," and "amant" in the manuscript rubrics (Hult, *Prophecies*, 62, n. 103), had an ambiguous relationship both with the first author of the *Rose* and with its continuator, Jean de Meun.[8] Indeed, the narrative consciousness of the Guillaume narrator paved the way for the artistically self-conscious Jean de Meun narrator, whose famous discussion about authorship in the voice of Amor at the midpoint of the work supplies a metadiscursive commentary that lends still another level of *auctoritas* to the *Rose*.[9]

With the *Roman de la rose*, however, an important narrative modification took place, one that would affect the voice of the first-person narrator in literary texts for centuries to come. On the one hand, the narrator's voice gained prestige, not only through its association with the first-person voice of the protagonist, but also through a transfer of prophetic authority from the divine to the narrative mode. On the other hand, this shift to a writer-centered instead of a God-centered universe was accompanied by the development of a fictionalized creator-figure (Hult, *Prophecies*, 127ff.). Generally speaking, the first-person narrator-author, who came to be identified as the *acteur* by the fifteenth century, remained enmeshed in the fiction of the *récit* until dramatic extratextual events affecting authorship—such as the advent of print—inspired writers to reassess their literary positions both inside and outside their texts.

Hult's differentiation between passive scribes (copyists) and active scribes (editors) provides a useful clarification of the fact that Bonaventure's theoretical distinction between roles was not always maintained

---

Treatises," 261, claims that Jean considered himself just as learned and accomplished as the numerous *auctoritates* whom he paraphrased and cited. In her discussion of Jean's role as a translator, Copeland, 133–41, shows how he authorized his own works.

8. Huot, *From Song to Book*, 64, describes the narrator as a combination of the clerkly romance narrator, scribal editor, compiler, and amorous protagonist. This polyphonic first-person narrator has been studied by others, including Vitz, 49–75; Dahlberg, "First Person," 37–58; Dragonetti, "Pygmalion," 89–111; Nichols, "Rhetoric," 115–29; Pickens, 175–86; Strohm, 3–9; Uitti, "*Clerc* to *Poète*," 209–16; and myself, "Rise," 51–52.

9. See Poirion ed., vv. 10526–10678. Minnis, *Theory*, 210, points out how Boccaccio employed a similar strategy by providing a commentary on his own *Teseida*.

in practice.[10] A scribe, like the copyist of a *Rose* manuscript, could in fact play a role approaching that of an author, as could a compiler and continuator (Hult, *Prophecies*, 60–61).[11] Again, the ambiguities in the *Rose* serve as an early example of a tacit *mise-en-question* of traditional literary conventions regarding authorial and narratorial roles. Such questioning was to become more pointed and defensive with later modifications associated with print.

Although, as M. D. Chenu claimed, the distinction between the Latin terms *auctor* and *actor* became more clearly marked in the Middle Ages (82–83), the difference between an *aucteur* and a compiler, or transmitter of others' words, became less and less clear in the later Middle Ages (Minnis, *Theory*, 210), a phenomenon that Sylvia Huot has suggestively linked to the vernacular poet's changing status at that time (*From Song to Book*, 101–2). While certain writers and/or scribes seemingly employed the terms *acteur* and *aucteur* interchangeably in the thirteenth and fourteenth centuries, especially to refer to the author-narrator function, the more systematic use of *acteur* by the fifteenth century to identify the first-person speaker of a narrative suggests that the latter term had overtaken *aucteur* as the accepted form.[12] Other terms, such as *faiseur, faiteur,* and *facteur*, French words related to *acteur* (*faire* being a translation of *agere*), were also commonly employed to refer to a writer, and particularly to a poet.[13] By the early sixteenth century, Lemaire used *acteur* to refer both to authors of books and to classical authors whose works were accorded a

10. There are many instances in medieval literature in which the scribe crossed over the supposedly defined boundaries between transcription and authorship. See, for example, the case of Godefroi de Leigni's continuation of Chrétien de Troyes's *Chevalier de la charrette* (Brownlee, "Transformations") or Gui de Mori's transcription of the *Roman de la rose* (Huot, *Rose and Its Readers*, 85–129, and Hult, "Author/Narrator/Speaker"). See also Hult, *Prophecies*, 34–55, and Poirion, *Poète*, 172–73.

11. See also Huot, *From Song to Book*, 84, and her "Scribe as Editor." Huot also speaks of an analogy between author and rubricator in *From Song to Book*, 72, while Copeland, chaps. 4–5, points out the authorial-like functions of medieval vernacular translators in their roles as expositors, exegetes, allegorists, compilers, glossators, and mythographers.

12. For example, *acteur* appears in Machaut's *Jugement du roy de Navarre* (see Œuvres, ed. Hoepffner, 1:225, 229, 254); the works of Alain Chartier (see n. 18 below); Antoine de la Sale (*Jehan de Saintré*, ed. Misrahi and Knudson); Chastellain (*Œuvres*, ed. Lettenhove, vols. 1–3); Jean Robertet (*Œuvres*, ed. Zsuppan); Cretin (see n. 17 below); and Arnoul Gréban's *Mystère de la Passion* (ed. Paris and Raynaud). Enders's claim, 8, n. 16, that Gréban used *acteur* and *aucteur* interchangeably is to be understood in terms of the *implied* theatrical and legal associations related to the word *acteur*.

13. See, for example, La Vigne's description of himself as the "facteur du roy" in a 1496 document related to the presentation of his *Mystère de Saint Martin* and a 1514 document referring to Gringore as "historien et facteur" (Julleville, 2:68, 205). Vérard uses the term "facteurs" on the title page of his 1504 edition of Bouchet's *Regnars traversant*, and Bouchet uses it in one of his attacks on printers (see p. 27 above). See also Poirion, *Poète*, 168.

certain *auctoritas*.[14] This usage suggests that a formalized consolidation of the overlapping meanings of *aucteur* and *acteur* had taken place before 1511 and that Jean de Meun's defensive gesture, aimed at equating his authority with that of the ancients, had been achieved through the single term *acteur*. Lemaire explicitly assimilates these ambiguous but related authorial dimensions, roots, and meanings in the prologue to his *Concorde des deux langages* (1511), authorizing his Italian predecessors, with whom he implicitly aligns himself (my emphasis): "Et pour ce prouver, mettoit en avant plusieurs *acteurs* renomméz et *auctoriséz*, si comme Dante, Petrarque et Bocace" (And to prove this he put forward several renowned and authorized authors, such as Dante, Petrarch and Boccaccio) (Frappier ed., 4). An *acteur* had come to stand for an authorized vernacular writer, even as the term continued to be inscribed into literary texts to identify the first-person narrative voice.[15]

Thus, shortly after authors such as La Vigne and Gringore acquired legal control over the reproduction and dissemination of their own poetic words, a convergence of the two terms denoting an author as an authoritative figure was taking place. In fact, the presence of *acteur* in the privilege announcement that appeared in the colophon of Gringore's 1505 *Folles entreprises*—the term also identified the narrator within the text—may have been the first time it was printed in a legal context.[16] By at least the 1530s *autheur*, or *auteur*, was replacing *acteur*, as suggested by the use of *autheur* to identify the narrator in the rubrics of Guillaume Cretin's *Apparition du mareschal sans reproche . . . Jacques de Chabannes* (1525) and in Clément Marot's editions of his *Adolescence clémentine* (1532) and Villon's poetry (1533).[17]

14. Compare the following passages from Lemaire's *Illustrations* of 1511 (*Œuvres*, ed. Stecher, 1:86, 16) (my emphasis): "De luy [Belgius] est denommee la grande et noble, et populeuse prouince de Gaule Belgique, dont *lacteur* de ce liure est natif" (After him is named the great and noble and populous province of Belgian Gaul, of which the author of this book is a native) and "Desquelles choses ie prens à tesmoings trois bons *acteurs*, cestasavoir Xenophon en ses equiuoques, Isidore en ses etymologies, et saint Hierome, sur les interpretations des noms Hebraïques" (For which things I take as witness three good authorities; that is, Xenophon in his equivocations, Isidore in his etymologies, and Saint Jerome in his interpretations of Hebrew names).

15. See the rubrics on pp. 7, 34, and 43 of the *Concorde de deux langages* (Frappier ed.). Brownlee, *Poetic Identity*, 3–23, uncovers Eustache Deschamps's 1377 use of *poète* to identify not a classical writer, as tradition had dictated, but a contemporary figure, Machaut. The term *poète* was not much used, however, until the sixteenth century. Although Godzich and Kittay, 63–66, make a convincing claim that the term *acteur* was a textual device that marked the neutral "voice" of prose, they do not account for its use in other contexts, such as those in which the author's name is directly associated with the term.

16. The term did not appear in La Vigne's lawsuit or Bouchet's attacks on printers.

17. See Marot's edition of Villon, fol. A iv, and his letter "A ung grand nombre de Freres," which prefaces his *Adolescence clémentine* (*Œuvres*, ed. Defaux, 1:17). Cotgrave,

The Middle French term *acteur*, then, evokes the overlapping meanings of *auctor* and *actor* examined above: classical authority, compiler-commentator, and author. But, as Leonard Johnson suggests, it also evokes a dramatic function.[18] So how can we account for the apparent anachronistic use of *acteur* as actor in a play, when there is little evidence of this meaning before the later sixteenth century? We can do so through the classical and medieval assimilation of "actor" and "litigator" in the Latin term *actor*, brought to light so compellingly by Jody Enders in her recent study of rhetoric and performance in medieval drama. The long-standing analogy between *orator* and *actor*, between lawyer and actor, that she uncovers can help modern readers understand yet another dimension of the term *acteur*.[19] Although the French use of *acteur* to designate an actor in a play does not commonly appear before 1663, other words such as *joueur* being employed instead, one can make a case that for most intellectuals, versed in Latin as they were, the move from *actor* to *acteur* was a latent gesture (Godzich and Kittay, 61).[20] Moreover, many

---

who provides no entry for *acteur*, *aucteur*, or *auteur*, defines *autheur* as "an author, actor, causer, founder; th'originall inuentor, the first deuiser, of a thing; also, an author, or writer of bookes; also, he that sels with warrantie" (fol. H ii). In Cretin's earlier works, such as his *Déploration . . . Okergan*, *Plainte . . . Byssipat*, *Débat entre deux dames*, *Plaidoyé de l'amant doloreux*, and *Nativité de Monseigneur François Daulphin*, the term *acteur* is used in rubrics to refer to the author-narrator (see Chesney ed.). See R. Chartier, *L'ordre des livres*, 49–52, for a study of the term *auteur* in the late sixteenth and seventeenth centuries.

18. In his discussion of Alain Chartier, 106–66, Johnson makes an implicit association that late medieval critics have heretofore avoided: between *acteur*-author and *acteur*-actor. By describing the narrator-*acteur* in certain narrative poems of Chartier as a "dramatic monologuist" (118), Johnson (re)introduces the idea of performance into the discussion of literary authorship, an idea that the title of his work (*Poets as Players*) and the thrust of his argument reinforce. His distinction between *acteur* and *aucteur*, however, differs from that of Vincent de Beauvais. According to Johnson, the narrator-*acteur* offers his own point of view assertively, whereas the narrator-*aucteur*, serving as reporter, hides behind the mask of the scribe-recorder in presenting others' points of view (117–21). Although Vincent did not consider works of fiction, the function of Chartier's narrator in these particular examples recalls that of Vincent's *actor*-compiler rather than the authoritative *auctor* of the Latin scholastic tradition.

19. Enders calls for a restoration of *actio* to medieval studies, arguing that "delivery," whose source is located in classical forensic rhetoric, formed an essential component of medieval literary texts, particularly theatrical works. Although Enders associates the offensive role with the term *actor-acteur* by defining it as "prosecutor," medieval Latin, Old French, and Middle French definitions often associate the defensive role with this term (see n. 1 above).

20. One of the earliest uses I have found of the term *acteur* to mean actor in a play dates from Molière's *Impromptu de Versailles* of 1663 (*Trésor*, ed. Imbs, 1:593). See the documents pertaining to medieval theatrical presentations in Julleville, vol. 2, and Meredith and Tailby, eds., in which the use of *acteur* at this time is absent. I am grateful to Jody Enders for calling my attention to the latter publication. The term *acteur* or *autheur* does not appear to have been used to depict the playwright, who was referred to as "originateur et es-

late medieval vernacular authors are known to have participated in theatrical productions.[21] It was very likely the conjunction of his theatrical and narrative experience that inspired La Vigne to adopt the term *acteur* to refer to Parisian actors presenting street dramas to Queen Anne of Brittany on the occasion of her entry into the capital in 1504.[22]

Having examined the evolution of the terms *acteur* and *aucteur*, I will now turn to some late medieval literary examples that illustrate these modifications. It is particularly with Alain Chartier that the modern reader finds both historical and literary evidence of the rhetorico-dramatic dimension of *acteur*. Preparing the way for his successors through the creation of a fictional defensive narrator, Chartier anticipated the new sense of authorship that I have associated with the advent of print; at the same time, he continued to adopt traditional medieval patterns such as a dream framework, an allegorical cast of characters, and a love-centered narrative.

As notary, secretary, ambassador, and orator to Charles VII during the early fifteenth century, Chartier represents an especially illuminating ex-

---

cripveur" or "fabricateur selon le arth de rethorique de la plus grande partye des jeux et originateur" as late as 1547 (Julleville, 2:146ff.). Oulmont, in "Pierre Gringore et l'entrée," 387, cites a document that refers to Gringore and other writers of "mystères mimés" as "facteurs et inventifs d'iceulx mistaires et esbatemens." Godzich and Kittay, 62, claim that "fatiste" defined a director who supervised theatrical performances, but they offer no details. Alan Knight has called my attention to the definition of "actor" in the *Oxford English Dictionary*, 1:131, which shows that "actor" in the sense of "stage-player" first appeared in 1581 in Sir Philip Sidney's *Defense of Poesie*.

21. In October 1496 La Vigne directed the presentation of his *Mystère de Saint Martin*, *Moralité de l'aveugle et du boiteux*, and *Farce du meunier* in Seurre; his 1501 *Complaintes et épitaphes du roy de la Bazoche* suggests an association with the Basoche. Gringore's involvement as an actor with the Enfants Sans Souci complemented his co-organization of at least six royal entries into Paris between 1502 and 1517, which always involved the composition of a *mystère* (Julleville, 2:201–2, 205–6). He wrote at least two plays, the *Jeu du Prince des Sotz* (1512) and the *Mystère de Saint Louis* (ca. 1514). Lemaire was involved in the organization of Louis XII's *entrée royale* into Lyons in 1509 (see Chapter 1, n. 52 above). And Bouchet, a member of the Parisian Basoche in the early sixteenth century, gained a reputation later in life as a director of mystery plays and an organizer of royal entries (Britnell, 1, 11–15).

22. On pp. 72–73 of Waddesdon Manor, Rothschild Collection, ms. Delaissé 22, the entry account that La Vigne offered to the queen, one reads (my emphasis): "Et devantaige pour declairer a ladite dame [Anne of Brittany] et a tout le surplus de sa compaignye La cosequence dudit mistere avoit ung *Acteur* qui disoit ce que s'ensuit" (And, moreover, to declare to the said lady and to her entire entourage the importance of the representation, there was an actor who said what follows). See also pp. 99 and 101 of ms. 22. In these examples, La Vigne seems to make a distinction between allegorical "personnages" in these dramas and an *acteur* who had the role of explaining the meaning of the scene. But given the consistent use of the indefinite pronoun "ung" in association with this term, *acteur* clearly did not refer to the author, as it did in Gréban's *Mystère* (see n. 12 above). La Vigne's usage seems to stand midway between *L'Acteur* of Gréban and the *acteur* of Molière's time (see n. 20 above).

ample of a literary figure arising out of the ranks of the *fonctionnaires* in the fourteenth and fifteenth centuries.[23] His direct participation in the international arena would have exposed him to various juridical matters and aligned him with the forensic mode. Indeed, Chartier, whose repertoire included a number of Latin *epistolae, invectivae,* and *orationes,* characterized himself in 1422 as a "lointaing immitateur des orateurs" (distant imitator of the orators).[24] When La Vigne identified himself to Charles VIII as "Vostre treshumble orateur, De la Vigne," in the printed *Vergier d'honneur* versions of his *Ressource* some eighty years later (*Ressource,* 149), he may have had in mind either Chartier or another illustrious model, Georges Chastellain, who was commonly referred to as an "orateur" by his contemporaries.[25] The very rhetorical and performative nature of Chartier's works also provides fertile ground for the appearance of a new kind of defensive voice, which emerges through the combined polemical dimension of many of his writings and the dramatic staging of his various allegorical characters.

Chartier's *Excusacion aux dames,* for example, written in 1425 in response to the court audience's negative reaction to his *Belle dame sans merci* (1424), testifies to the forensic character that marks much of his corpus.[26] Moreover, by the time Chartier wrote the *Excusacion,* his narrator had distanced himself from love service,[27] prefiguring the absence of a personal love quest on the part of the *acteur*[28] that contributed to the increasingly self-defensive, self-conscious, and less fictionalized posture of later vernacular narrators. In much of the literature dating from the late fifteenth and early sixteenth centuries, the lover-protagonist was replaced by a first-person voice that defended his patron's political enterprise while seeking a way to defend his own poetic enterprise. Oftentimes the notion of a defense intersects with the creative process through the symbol of the book. In fact, it is the object of the book that

23. See Poirion, *Poète,* 173–77. One of the meanings of the medieval Latin term *actor,* in fact, is "fonctionnaire royal" (Blaise, 1:13). For biographical details on Chartier, see Walravens, 21–34, and Laidlaw, ed., *Poetical Works of Alain Chartier,* 3–15.

24. *Quadrilogue invectif,* ed. Piaget, 1. Several of the orations that Chartier delivered while on ambassadorial missions have come down to us (Walravens, 92–93). For examples of Chartier's reproaches and exhortations, see his *Dialogues familiaris, Epistola de detestatione,* and *Libellus curialis.*

25. See, for example, Jean Robertet, *Œuvres,* 115, 118, 119, 159, 160, 161, 171, 176.

26. See also his *Débat des deux fortunés d'amours, Débat de réveille-matin, Débat du hérault, du vassault et du villain, Livre des quatre dames, Belle dame sans merci,* and *Quadrilogue invectif.*

27. The *Belle dame* narrator had already adopted this stance, having just renounced love upon the death of his lady (vv. 1–56), as had the narrator of Chartier's *Quadrilogue invectif.* See also his *Lay de paix, Débat du hérault, Débat de réveille-matin,* and *Livre des quatre dames.*

28. Laidlaw, ed., *Poetical Works,* always uses the rubric "acteur" in his edition of the *Excusacion.* All citations will be taken from this edition.

serves to crystallize the defensive gesture on the part of Chartier's narrator in the *Excusacion*. Though not having to stand up to the excessive improprieties associated with aggressive printers after the advent of the press, Chartier, challenged in a different way, nonetheless placed on center stage, albeit in a fictional framework, a debate over literary responsibility and the author's relationship to his text.

In the *Excusacion*, the *acteur*'s defense of Chartier's *Belle dame* consists of a refutation against an inquisition of pseudo-religious proportions, as the God of Love threatens to burn "[s]on livre infame" (his reproachful book) (v. 85):

> Tu mourras de ce peché quicte;
> Et se briefment ne t'en desdiz,
> Prescher te feray comme herite
> Et bruler ton livre et tes diz.
> En la loy d'Amours sont maudiz . . .
> Les lire est a tous interdiz
> De par l'inquisiteur d'Amours.
>
> (vv. 41–48)

You will die of this sin and if you don't renounce it in short order, I will have you branded a heretic and your book and poetry burned. Under Cupid's law, they are denounced. . . . All are forbidden to read your works by Cupid's inquisitor.

Essentially a fictionalized trial staged within an allegorical dream concerning who is responsible for the written word, this literary prosecution and defense are controlled by Chartier, often in an ironic mode, as he places on his literary stage his accuser(s) and his *acteur*-defender, an alter-ego spokesman. What Chartier was negotiating in literary form before his resistant court public was in reality the rejection of love service by the first-person lover-protagonist, a role long associated with the speaking "I" in vernacular narrative.[29] Such a stance is reflected in the voice of the *acteur* in both the *Belle dame* and the *Excusacion*, although

29. In explaining why he wrote the moralistic *Livre de l'Espérance* in 1429, Chartier states the following (Rouy ed., p. 2, vv. 47–50): "Je souloye ma jonnesse acquiter / A joyeuses escriptures dicter; / Or me convient aultre ouvrage tissir: / De cueur dolent ne pourroit joye issir" (I used to spend my youth composing joyful writings; now it behooves me to write another work: joy cannot come out of a dolorous heart). Poirion, "Lecture," 703, argues that skepticism was introduced into literary love couples after Chartier. In fact, Christine de Pizan had introduced this idea in her 1409 *Cent ballades d'amant et de dame*. See Huot, *From Song to Book*, 271, who discusses Machaut's redefinition of the lyric persona from lover to poet-codifier of love.

Chartier compromises this position by claiming to continue to serve women. Perhaps this strategy was deemed necessary to obtain his critical public's sympathy; it turned out to be ineffective, however.

In the *Excusacion*, the *acteur* is on the defensive as he adopts the conventional disavowal-of-responsibility topos. It is to his fictional characters, the Amant and the Dame of the *Belle dame sans merci*, not to cited *auctores*, that Chartier, in his guise as scribe, attributes independent responsibility:[30]

> Mon livre, qui peu vault et monte,
> A nesune autre fin ne tent
> Si non a recorder le compte
> D'un triste amoureux mal content. . . .
> Et qui autre chose y entent,
> Il y voit trop ou n'y voit goute. . . .
> J'ay voulu ses plaintes escrire
> Sans un seul mot en trespasser
> S'en doit tout le monde amasser
> Contre moy a tort et en vain,
> Pour le chestif livre casser
> Dont je ne suis que l'escripvain?
>
> (vv. 193–216)

My book, which is of little value or worth, aims toward no other goal than to record the tale of a sad, unhappy lover. . . . And he who understands anything else sees in it too much or nothing. . . . I wanted to write his complaints without omitting one word. Must everyone assault me, wrongly and in vain, in tearing apart this poor little book of which I am only the scribe?

By identifying himself as the copyist, or "l'escripvain," who has merely transcribed someone else's spoken word, Chartier's *acteur*, with tongue in cheek perhaps, willfully blurs the distinctions between fiction and reality on more than one level.

In its close affiliation with historical reality, this fictionalized trial differs from other literary narratives. Although such a *procès* never took place in actuality (Laidlaw ed., 5–9), what apparently gave rise to the *Excusacion* was a real display of audience dissatisfaction, especially on the part of the female public, about the ending of the *Belle dame*. Extant documents such as *La requeste baillee aux dames contre Alain, Les lectres envoyees*

---

30. Jean de Meun's supporters adopted this tactic as well in their early fifteenth-century defense of the *Roman de la rose* (see Hicks, ed., *Débat*).

par les dames a Alain (Laidlaw ed., 360–62), and *La Réponse des dames faicte a maistre Allain* (Piaget, 30:31–35) provide evidence of an extratextual context for Chartier's poem. The goal of these metacommentaries, however, was not to authorize Chartier's work but to devalorize it.

Sent presumably by the men of Charles VII's entourage, who feared losing the amorous favors of their female counterparts as a result of the *Belle dame*, the *Requeste* begs those very ladies not to read and even to tear up and destroy ("rompre et casser partout") Chartier's unreasonable writing ("desraisonnables escriptures"). The ladies' somewhat sympathetic letter to Alain, dated 31 January [1425] and signed by "Les voustres, Katherine, Marie et Jehanne," reinforces this prosecutory tone by advising the author to disculpate himself at a trial, whose date they have set for the first of April. Here the line between fact and fiction becomes increasingly unclear: on the one hand, real women's first names have been attached to this document (Walravens, 79); on the other hand, the Court of Love, to which implicit reference is made, was more or less a literary game (Poirion, "Lecture," 692–93). The fictional account offered by Chartier in his *Excusacion* represents his attempt to control an apparently genuine controversy over his *Belle dame sans merci* by placing it within literary confines. Perhaps he hoped to charm and appease the "plaintiffs" with a witty defensive gesture. And yet, Chartier's signature in the final lines of this work, "Voustre humble serviteur Alain," indicates a conscious narrowing of the gap between reality and fiction, between his historical position as author and that of his fictional *acteur*. The customary omission of Chartier's name from his texts or from the rubrics of his works makes its textual and paratextual presence here all the more remarkable.[31]

Although the *Excusacion aux dames* featured no final judgment, the ladies indicted the author for his "faulx mensongier livre" (false and lying book) in their *Response*, a gesture that, by ordering the author to appear again in court and by naming "Dessarteaulx et Chastel" as their lawyers (vv. 103–4), kept Chartier's fictionalized literary debate anchored in reality. Their severe sentence—that the author be burned for his "heretical actions"—recalls the fictive scenario that Chartier had created in the *Excusacion*, except that Chartier had attributed to the God of Love the desire to burn his book, whereas the court ladies threatened to burn (or hang) the author himself:

31. The author's name appears in the *Débat des deux fortunés d'amours* (v. 1245), *Débat du hérault* (v. 429), and the prologue to his *Quadrilogue invectif* (Piaget ed., 1). Although Chartier's name appears in many rubrics of the *Excusacion*, it is found in only seven (three of which are copies of others) of the thirty-one *Quatre dames* manuscripts (see *Poetical Works*, Laidlaw, 329).

Puis qu'ainsy est, Alain, feu nostre amy,
Qu[e] . . . tu escrips que dame est sans mercy . . .
Qu'on te pendist ou que l'on te brullast.

(Piaget ed., vv. 1–9)

Sy t'en desdiz et humblement demandes
Grace et pardon, et ton faulx livre amendes;
En ce faisant tu respites la mort;
Ou aultrement gaigeras les amendes
D'un herite qu'a herese s'amort.

(Piaget ed., vv. 92–96)

Since it is so, Alan, our former friend, that. . . . you write that a lady is without pity . . . may you be hanged or burned. . . . If you recant [your error] and humbly ask for grace and pardon, and if you correct your false book, you will stave off death by your action; otherwise, you will pay the penalties of a heritage that has become heresy.

In criticizing Chartier's portrayal of the *Belle dame* and in rewriting the terms of his literary defense in a way that defictionalizes the debate and makes the author directly responsible for the characters he has created, the court ladies have attempted to dictate the terms of poetic creation.[32] History leaves no traces of Chartier's reaction to their *Response*, although subsequent writers joined the controversy by offering a variety of literary sequels (see Piaget).[33] The fictional trial that the author had created and sought to control clearly did not meet with the approval of his public; nor did the latter's attempt to rewrite Chartier's narrative elicit any acceptable meeting of minds. With the debate over textual ownership staged within the boundaries of a fictional framework and directed to a court audience desirous of maintaining associations between the narrator and questions pertaining to love, with the *acteur* refusing responsibility for his own words, we are still quite distant from the extratextual

32. On the legal and sociological implications of these various reactions for the women involved, see Solterer's very insightful chapter 7. I am indebted to the author for providing me with a typescript copy of these pages before publication. Although my analysis of the text comes from a different angle, I agree with Solterer that the *Belle dame sans merci* controversy should be interpreted as more than a literary game. Even if one were to claim that remarks made both by the *acteur* of the *Excusacion aux dames* and by the ladies are essentially ironic, it is nonetheless revealing that Chartier was drawn into "playing" a defensive role concerning his work.

33. Poirion, "Lecture," 692–95, argues that the meaning of the *Belle dame sans merci* was falsified and maintained in the many continuations, beginning with the *Requeste*.

validation of the author that La Vigne would receive through his historic lawsuit some eighty years later. Despite his fictionalized staging of the issue, Chartier, whose influence on later vernacular writers was legendary, does anticipate the defensive authorial voice of his successors.

Although Chartier's consciousness of the bookmaking and creative enterprise is thematized in the *Excusacion aux dames* and intersects with defensive gestures on his part, there is no evidence that he was involved in the actual production of his works. Much recent scholarship confirms, though, that earlier writers such as Guillaume de Machaut, Jean Froissart, Christine de Pizan, and Antoine de la Sale played key roles in the production of their works and that this involvement informed their literary enterprise in significant ways.[34] Indeed, subsequent to Machaut's involvement in the organization of his own compositions, compilation and ordering became part of a poet's work (Huot, *From Song to Book*, 274). It is the high level of sophistication associated with the function of the compiler (Minnis, *Theory*, 97) that provided impetus for this assimilation of roles by authors from the late fourteenth century on. Some writers, such as Christine de Pizan and Charles d'Orléans, went so far as to become their own scribes, thereby embodying the conflation of *scribere* (transcribe) and *dictare* (compose).[35] The growing consciousness about the vernacular literary work as an artifact more than as oral performance, which Sylvia Huot has so brilliantly demonstrated in her discussion of manuscripts, contributed to an increasing convergence of the roles of scribe, compiler, and author by the end of the Middle Ages and a growing authorization and validation of vernacular writers.

Just as fourteenth- and early fifteenth-century poets became compilers of their own works, and not long before Clément Marot provided the first-known critical edition of a French vernacular work with his publication of Villon's poetry, so too did late fifteenth-century writers in-

34. See Williams; Brownlee, "Transformations"; Looze, "Machaut"; Huot, *From Song to Book;* Desonay's introduction to his critical edition of La Sale's *Œuvres*, 1:ix–x; and Jeay, "Theorie." Hindman, *Epistre Othéa*, 13, 77–89, describes Christine's role as the first female publisher, detailing her involvement in all stages of book production; Quilligan, *Female Authority*, 33, 46, studies Christine's role as a compiler. Although it is true that Christine de Pizan assumed a defensive posture in the prologue to her *Cent ballades d'amant et de dame* and in strategic places of her *Cent ballades,* clearly distancing herself from her first-person protagonists in a way that anticipates late fifteenth-century writers more than Chartier, her defensiveness relates more to her obligations toward patrons than to the protection of her word. In fact, there is no evidence that she had any influence on Molinet, La Vigne, Lemaire, or Gringore. Moreover, in most of Christine's narratives, her authorial voice is inextricably enmeshed within the allegorical dream fiction.

35. See Ouy, 221–38; Reno, 3–20; Willard, 45; Champion; and Jeay, "Théorie," who discusses Antoine de La Sale's active interventions in the manuscript of his *Jehan de Saintré*. In her compelling study, Carruthers discusses the authorial and scribal phases of bookmaking at an earlier date (see esp. chap. 6).

volved in the publication of their works come to serve as their own compilers and publishers. As we saw above, Molinet likely played a key role
in the organization of a manuscript anthology of his works in the early
sixteenth century and in fact did publish several of his own works, including the *Naissance de Charles d'Autriche*. La Vigne was one of the first
well-known writers to compile a printed anthology of his (and others')
writings, *Le vergier d'honneur*, and Lemaire's 1498 manuscript compilation of Latin and vernacular texts, including several of his own (Jodogne, "Recueil"), anticipated his active role as publisher-editor of
nearly all his works from 1509 on. Indeed, it is the defensive and even
the aggressive character of these late medieval writers, who assimilated
and assumed such a great variety of roles, that so markedly distin-
guishes them from their predecessors and characterizes their work as
what one might call a more printerly kind of poetics. If the writer had
come to assume more of the activities of a scribe-compiler and manuscript editor by the early fifteenth century, if at the same time the scribe
was becoming more of an editor and rewriter (author), then with the advent of print it was perhaps inevitable that the functions assumed by the
printer, bookseller, and publisher would come into direct conflict with
the ever-expanding role of authors. What might have led to a cooperative enterprise, as was sometimes the case, developed into a legal confrontation with the authors under discussion here, particularly when financial losses and gains were at stake. La Vigne's challenge to Le Noir
involved precisely this potentially incompatible sharing of a compiler's
and publisher's duties by author and printer, as did Bouchet's criticisms
of publishers and printers. Rita Copeland's statement that "the power of
the *compilator* lies in the way that he can retreat behind the *ipsissima verba*
of the texts and conceal the very control that he exerts as orchestrator of
auctoritates" (118), though made in another context, crystallizes the elements of the struggle that late medieval vernacular authors experienced
vis-à-vis a new kind of *compilator*—namely, the maker and producer of
early printed books—who often did not even try to conceal his power
and control.

To summarize the preceding argument, we can see that Vincent de
Beauvais's move in the thirteenth century to credit *auctores* with their
ideas represents an early concern for "literary property." Jean de Meun's
transparent disavowal of responsibility in the *Roman de la rose*, coupled
with his more self-conscious narrative voice and the interchangeable use
of *auctor* and *acteur*, went further to establish the vernacular author's authority. In initiating and supervising the material and literary development of anthologies of their own works, late fourteenth- and early
fifteenth-century writers brought greater credibility and visibility to the
notion of vernacular authorship. At the same time, the term *acteur* was

starting to prevail over *aucteur*. Such narrative personae, however, still existed to a great extent within the framework of a love quest.

Although Alain Chartier's authorial self-consciousness remained inscribed within the fiction of his narratives and was often thematized around the Court of Love, the increasingly litigious framework of his texts paved the way for the more defensive posture of his successors, who had almost completely distanced themselves from the courtly love tradition. Motivated perhaps by greater materialistic concerns, many late fifteenth- and early sixteenth-century authors sought to protect their association with their words, a development announced by their predecessors and intensified by the new print technology. The predominance of the *acteur* as the principal narrative voice of works that were to become more polemical and moralistic accompanies this particular shift, resonating as it does with authoritative, authorial, forensic, and even dramatic meanings. Close readings of the text, paratext, and narrative voices in these later works offer insight into the working out of such changes.

The defensive posture fictionalized in Chartier's texts assumed a more authentic dimension in later works with its appearance in the paratext of printed editions and through more author-like textual voices. The shift from an erotic to a polemical dynamic in literary writings at this time played no small role in this development. The subject of love and the presence of a lover-protagonist are almost completely absent from Molinet's repertoire,[36] in which he attempts to thematize bookmaking by focusing on the specific tools of textual reproduction and the dynamics of the manuscript page within a political and sociological framework.[37] Mo-

36. Molinet wrote a few ballads, some of which deal with love, but usually in a satricial or an obscene way. See *Faictz et dictz*, ed. Dupire, vols. 1–2. All subsequent references will be taken from this edition, unless otherwise noted.

37. In at least ten instances, the author marks his intimate association with the craft of manuscript reproduction by invoking within his verses the tools of the trade: "encre et plumes," "blanc parchemin ou papier," "mon cornet petit," "lume," "lettres d'or, d'azur, d'argent, d'arain." See *Chappellet des dames* (v. 157), *Dictier sus Franchois et Gantois* (vv. 81–82), *Lamentables regrés pour le . . . duc de Zassen* (vv. 90, 92–93), *Débat des trois nobles oiseaux* (vv. 154–55), *Miroir de vie* (vv. 328–29), *Gaiges retrenchiés* (vv. 19, 22), *Lettres a Fenin* (v. 19), *Revid a ung nommé Maistre Pol* (v. 23), *Balade figurée* (v. 23), and *Lettres a Robertet* (v. 36). In one passage, Molinet uses manuscript imagery in such an obscure manner, not to mention the accumulation of interior rhymes, that its meaning is almost inaccessible (see *Lamentables regrés . . . Zassen*, vv. 89–95). The poet's nightmarish vision in the conditional voice apparently depicts an obsessive fear that the world might turn into an indecipherable manuscript page: were the land to change into parchment or paper, the seas and nourishing liquids into a red ink, and the forest into the writer's quill, his hand would fail to write before the incomprehensible "grand bien." Is this end-of-the-world scenario designed to invoke the Book of Nature that the subject of this lament, the recently deceased duke of Zassen, now reads?

linet's incorporation of such details associated with the manuscript page into his works often intersects with his self-defensive posture, which is most obviously expressed through the changing role of the *acteur*-narrator. In his *Gaiges retrenchiés* (1496) and *Naissance de Charles d'Autriche* (ca. 1500), these codicological concerns accompany a call for authorial recognition within the text itself, a development that coincided with Molinet's increasing extratextual control of his literary production. A single, more authoritative voice that coincides with Molinet's author-centered signature eventually replaced the fragmented narratorial voices of the earlier, more conventional works, emblematized by Molinet's bivalent punning signature. At the same time, allegorical dream-vision frame-works disappeared from these narratives. We can best understand this evolution against the background of the poet's more traditional *Trosne d'honneur* (after June 1467).

The *Trosne d'honneur*, a glorification of the house of Burgundy, the *Gaiges retrenchiés*, in which Molinet wittily argues for his complete pension, and the *Naissance de Charles d'Autriche*, which simultaneously celebrates the birth of his patron's son and the construction of the author's own poem, represent key moments in the development of the authorial-narrative role of this first-generation *rhétoriqueur*. The changes in the interaction between poet and patron and between the author and his book signaled in these works surface, not coincidentally, at moments of financial threat for Molinet. In the *Trosne d'honneur* the narrator plays a conventionally marginal role as fiction and history are allegorically linked. Internal textual signs remind the reader of the traditional relationship between patron and poet, characterized so compellingly by Paul Zumthor (*Masque*) and Richard Green, as the verbally illuminated patron's image and name overshadow the poet's. In the second work, admittedly unusual in Molinet's repertoire in that the poet puts himself on stage, narratorial and authorial voices all but coincide, although a certain distance between the two is maintained through third-person usage. A questioning of authority, of his patron's failure to pay his salary, permeates this work, whose manuscript allusions remind the reader of the centrality of bookmaking to the neglected poet's enterprise. The third work offers a synthesis of the first two, with authorial and narrative voices barely distinguishable and with a focus on author and patron, who are placed on more equal terms in both text and paratext. The juxtaposition of verbal metaphors of manuscript illumination with the printed words and woodcuts in this rare, author-directed publication alerts the reader to the transitional nature of this period, involving changes from manuscript to imprint, from court-oriented to public-oriented literature, from patron-controlled to author-controlled texts.

The *Trosne d'honneur*, which praises Molinet's recently deceased patron, Philip the Good, is addressed to Philip's son and successor at the Burgundian court, Charles the Bold, whose patronage Molinet seeks to obtain. In this conventional, propagandistic text, the relationship between the multiple, marginalized narrative voices and the allegorical protagonists calls to mind the hierarchical rapport between poet and prince outside the fictional narrative.[38] For the abstractions linked to the deceased patron and the house of Burgundy hold the most authority in the narrative of the *Trosne d'honneur*; their actions eclipse those of the human narrator. While the first-person voice of the opening lines, later identified as the *acteur*, establishes a strong presence through the use of first-person pronouns and pronominal verbs of action as he initiates the dream sequence (1:36, ll. 8–10), his immediacy fades into the background when he becomes a distant observer of what occurs (1:37, ll. 24–30), describing the action in prose and announcing the speeches delivered by Nobility, Virtue and Honor.[39] In essence, the narrator serves as a witness to the death, mourning, and subsequent glorification of the "tres noble fleur de lys," Philip the Good, through an exploitation of his name, from which the inspiration for much of the text derived. Each letter of PHILIPPVS, standing for an allegorized virtue, illuminates the nine heavens through which one must pass to reach the "trosne d'honneur." Within the dream-generated narrative, then, nonhuman characters hold greatest authority. Moreover, the dazzling presence of PHILIPPVS, whose once earthly form has been translated into noncorporeal heavenly script in a veritable codicological drama, completely diminishes the stature of the human narrator. Indeed, the textual relationship between the narrator and the "protagonists" resembles the association between author and protector outside the text, where the first supposedly creates publicity for the second.

Contrasting with the main body of the *Trosne d'honneur*, yet symmetrically echoing its opening lines, the final passage of the work stands out because the *acteur*, speaking for the first and only time in verse (like those just declaimed by Honneur), redirects attention to himself as protagonist (1:51, vv. 33–34). As in the opening lines, the narrator dominates the action only when it occurs outside the borders of the dream world. His function here differs, nonetheless, from that of the beginning

38. Some of the following ideas appear in different form in my "Poètes, mécènes et imprimeurs."

39. Tournai, Bibl. Communale, ms. 105, lost through fire during World War II, apparently displayed a miniature on the folio immediately preceding the *Trosne d'honneur*, depicting in the upper space a throne of honor and in the lower space a mourning female figure (Dame Noblesse?) and a poet asleep under a tree (Dupire, *Etude critique*, 12). To my knowledge this is the only decorated version of the work, one with which Molinet was probably associated. For bibliographical details, see Appendix 4 below.

passage, where he set the stage by insinuating himself into the narrative action as a witness-narrator of his own dream. Here the business of re-membering and recording that dreamed action, at once the task of the chronicler and the scribe, is detailed. This involves another level of per-formance on the part of the speaker, one further removed from, yet still connected to, the narrative action, one that draws closer to the role of the true author: Molinet.

Despite a rapid series of first-person verbs, the repeated absence of the subject pronoun "je" (1:58, vv. 35–38) subtly undermines the narra-tor's presence in those first lines leading out from the dream, as does the diffused nature of the task of writing. It is because of a divinely induced wind that the poetic windmill, an object possessed by the narrator, turns:

> Du vent tel que Dieu donna
> Au limeur de gros limage,
> Mon gros molinet tourna
> Et rima ce gros rimage.
>   (1:58, vv. 40–43)

With the wind like the one God gave to the filer of big filings, my big mill/Molinet turned and rhymed this big rhyme.

At the same time that Molinet's name marks the text as a work he cre-ated, the metaphorical association of the word "molinet" with a small mill draws attention away from the author to the object, which has a function in the text. In fact, the writer fragments himself into a gram-matical and concrete object, a big mill (*gros molinet*), and a human sub-ject described in the third person (*limeur*). Through the third-person stance of his *acteur*-narrator, he seems on one hand to deride his accom-plishment by qualifying it in derogatory terms as a "gros rimage" and by asking the reader's forgiveness for any flaws (1:58, vv. 44–46). The as-sociation of his work with the "gros limage" of a "limeur" implies, on the other hand, that the hard work of a craftsman was involved in this poetic creation.[40] At the same time, the large size of the mill ("Mon gros moli-net") doubtless constitutes a humorous, self-critical reference to Moli-net's own body size. Despite the author's aggressive move to advertise his own literary presence, the overall self-mocking tone of this stanza tends to play down the importance of his authorship, especially in com-parison with the enhanced presentation of his patron.

40. Artisan images are typical in *rhétoriqueur*, poetry but different from those in Renais-sance poetry, in which a collective self-consciousness based on classical sources allows for a more glorified poetic role.

Thus, it is only at the boundary of the allegorical dream that the narrator's comments acquire a certain authority, and that authority is self-consciously belittled and fragmented into multiple narratorial voices. Unlike the narrator-witness who presents the allegorical characters' speeches, the first-person voice that speaks at the margin of the text plays the role of a scribe-chronicler who remembers and records the witnessed action[41] and who owns the poetic mill. Both the fragmentation and the multiplicity of the first-person voices here (and in many works of the period) undermine the writer's image, which is related to this narrator's persona, because of the absence of any strong, unified presence.[42] This narrative strategy may reflect the author's consciousness about the tenuousness of his poetic identity and status.

In the final stanza of the *Trosne d'honneur*, the action moves to yet another plane of discourse as the first-person voice of the author himself emerges. He is neither the narrator-dreamer nor the narrator-witness nor the chronicler-scribe, the mill owner nor the divinely inspired *limeur*, all of whom have peopled the allegorical and metaphorical landscape of the text. Instead, in the final scene, often rendered in manuscript dedication miniatures, Molinet portrays himself as dedicator of his work. Stepping completely outside the poem's narrative framework, the author presents his poem to Duke Charles the Bold. The relationship between poet and future patron is thereby highlighted:

> A toy, duc resplendissant,
> Mon ouvrage je presente,
> Ou ton pere tres puissant
> A gloire tres exellente.
> (1:58, vv. 47–50)

I offer to you, resplendent duke, my work, in which your very powerful father is glorified to the highest degree.

The author's clearest representation of himself, then, occurs only in connection with his past and future protectors, whose family he has

41. He thereby approaches the voice of the author himself, who, eight years later, would become the official chronicler of the house of Burgundy.

42. See Jeay, *Donner la parole*, 39–51, 113, 144–45, who analyzes the role of *acteur* and author in the *nouvelle* of the fifteenth and sixteenth centuries. She defines the history of narration during this period in terms of a refusal of univocity and a resistance to textual coherence, accomplished through a conscious and constant variation on all the different combinations and possible interferences among narrator, author, and characters. See also my comments regarding Godzich and Kittay, n. 15 above.

just defended and to whom he proffers some final advice regarding that heralded image: "Prens de vertu telle sente / Qu'apprés luy ton guerdonneur / Te doint le trosne d'honneur" (Follow such a path of virtue so that after him your rewarder might give you the throne of honor) (1:58, vv. 51–53). Defending the honor and virtue of the house of Burgundy, the author implicitly accords himself the very important function of "guerdonneur" of the *Trosne d'honneur*. In doing so, he creates a conscious confusion of worldly and divine authors, since presumably both God and Molinet will play a role in the glorification of the duke. The writer literally and metaphorically rewards his future patron with the "throne of honor"—that is, both his book bearing that title and the abstract quality of honor itself—which the dedicatee will attain if he follows his father's model behavior, so extensively lauded by Molinet. The author thereby implicitly defines his writing as an object of commerce: continued glorification, honor, and defense of the Burgundian name in exchange for a court pension.

The work's paratext likewise reproduces the hierarchical dynamic of power between prince and poet. For example, in one of its three extant fifteenth-century manuscript versions, B.N. nouv. acq. f.fr. 21532,[43] a title that emphasizes the identity of the patron for whom the *Trosne d'honneur* was written announces the text in the following way (fol. 2ʳ): "La vigne d'honneur faitte au mariage de Charles le Hardy, duc de Bourgogne, avec la seur du roy d'Angleterre" (The vine of honor made for the marriage of Charles the Bold, duke of Burgundy, with the sister of the king of England). Molinet never appears as author of the *Trosne d'honneur* in these versions.[44]

The *Trosne d'honneur*, in which a secondary narrator-figure witnesses the allegorical action of the dream narrative, thus represents a conventional example of "authorial" presence at work in late medieval French literature. It is only in positions framing the narrative that the reader finds comments regarding the composition of the poem and the identity of the narrator-figure. This configuration reveals also that the author, in his multiple fictionalized forms, existed only in relationship to his patron. As at court, the patrons—one deceased, one living—

---

43. The *Trosne d'honneur* is the only work in this manuscript and in Bibl. Royale II.2604 (see Dupire, *Etude Critique*, 50–51, and Appendix 4 below for details).

44. The presence of the poet's name in the four sixteenth-century manuscripts of the *Trosne d'honneur* can be explained by the fact that Molinet compiled or had compiled the Tournai manuscript (Bibl. Communale, ms. 105), as discussed above in Chapter 2, p. 74. Arras ms. 692, Rothschild ms. 471, and probably B.N. ms. f.fr. 12490 postdated the Tournai anthology. For similar conclusions about Molinet's *Temple de Mars*, see my "Du manuscrit à l'imprimé," 104–12.

dominate the narrative, while the poetic voice remains on the outside looking in.

Numerous other works composed by Molinet and his contemporaries follow similar patterns and reflect the same association between poet and protector, including the *Lyon couronné*, Chastellain's *Outré d'Amour*, *Déprécation pour Pierre de Brézé*, *Advertissement au Duc Charles*, and *Livre de paix*, and Lemaire's *Temple d'honneur*, analyzed in Chapter 1 above.[45] Borrowing their narrative and rhetorical structure from the *Roman de la rose* and their political, even polemical, tone from Chartier's *Quadrilogue invectif*, these late medieval poets were at once more beholden to their patrons than their predecessors and, perhaps for that very reason, seemingly more anxious about their relationship with their own works. Through them we are reminded of the rather closed and self-perpetuating patronage system in which the person who commissioned the poetic enterprise or to whom the literary work was dedicated, along with his or her entourage, read the work designed to praise them (see Zumthor, *Masque*).

Whereas the potential loss of his court position through the death of his patron had inspired Molinet's composition of the *Trosne d'honneur*, it was the lack of earned wages that precipitated the writing of his *Gaiges retrenchiés*. The defense of the reputation of Molinet's patron through linguistic, allegorical, and poetic means in the *Trosne d'honneur* and other works is transferred to Molinet's own self-defense in this poem, which was obviously not a commissioned work.[46] Though following in the tradition of earlier poets, such as Colin Muset, Rutebeuf, and Villon, who versified their appeals to nobles for financial support, Molinet was, unlike his predecessors, an established court writer with a more-or-less secure income. In 1496, however, the date of this poem, he did not receive half of his "promised" pension.[47]

Changing the "rules of the game" with his *Gaiges retrenchiés*, the author brings to the fore *his* perspective of the patron–poet relationship by exploiting his polysemous name, which had remained marginalized in

45. See Molinet's other principal works, such as his *Naufrage de la pucelle, Resource du petit peuple, Complainte sur la mort Madame d'Ostrisse, Chappellet des dames*, and *Arbre de Bourgogne*, for a similar scenario.

46. This probably explains the poem's survival in only two manuscript versions. The *Gaiges retrenchiés* is not found in any early printed editions. See Appendix 4 below for details.

47. See above, Chapter 3, n. 12, for a discussion of Molinet's financial woes. One wonders if Molinet's *Voyage de Napples*, written after September 1496 in praise of Charles VIII's Naples expedition and dedicated to the French king, represented the author's attempt to obtain patronage at the house of France at a time when the financial security of his position with Philip the Handsome was in jeopardy (see ll. 1–21).

the *Trosne d'honneur*. Though stamped on a limited number of his main-stream court works up to this date (1496), either in the opening or the final lines,[48] Molinet's name or a symbol thereof, the windmill, insinuates itself into the eighty verses of the *Gaiges retrenchiés* some eight times (vv. 3, 33, 41, 58, 61, 70, 73, 79). Woven into this double-level appeal of a poet lacking funds and a windmill lacking wheat is the metaphorical play on the name Bauduin de Lannoy, before whom Molinet's narrator pleads his case. This first-person speaker sounds different from that of other works by Molinet, in part because the true author's voice comes through more clearly than ever.

Molinet's focus on himself in the *Gaiges retrenchiés* is consciously indirect, most likely in an attempt to follow the modesty and decorum appropriate to a hired court writer. Although the poem's extraordinary alliteration, rhyming, and rhythmic play attest to the writer's technical prowess,[49] they simultaneously draw attention away from the self-centered perspective of the text. Furthermore, the fragmentation of narrative voices that characterized the *Trosne d'honneur* reappears in slightly different form in the *Gaiges retrenchiés*, for the focus continually switches back and forth between the metaphorical *object* of the "moulinet" and the writing *subject* himself. While the image of the inactive windmill, lacking grain to grind, dominates the first of ten stanzas, with the second stanza centering on the improperly compensated writer himself, the reader discovers from the outset a purposefully ambiguous and playful enmeshing of the two worlds. This intersection is drawn most stunningly in the third stanza, which shows in a curious interaction of crafts how the mill's functions have ground out poetic works. The result is the unexpected production of illuminated manuscript letters from "gros grain" with the aid of hammer and quill, anvil and ink, iron and paper:

> Il a mollut, tout net jusque a l'estrain,
> De Mars le train qui gens d'armes alume,[50]
> En lettres d'or, d'azur, d'argent, d'arain;
> Tant le derrain que le premier gros grain
> Noble et purain a mys a son volume;

---

48. See, for example, *La complainte de Grèce, Le trosne d'honneur, Le temple de Mars, Le chappellet des dames, La ressource du petit peuple, Complainte sur la mort Madame d'Ostrisse, L'arbre de Bourgogne, Collaudation à Madame Marguerite*, and *Le voyage de Napples*.

49. It is perhaps the poet's own emotional distress and personal intensity about his threatened economic situation that comes through in every stanza of the *Gaiges retrenchiés*.

50. Note the publicity for the author's earlier work, his popular *Temple de Mars*, discussed above in Chapter 2.

> Mais que vault plume, encre, papier et lume,
> Martel, englume, achier, fer ou souflés?
> Quant argent fault.
>
> (2:769, vv. 17–24)

He has ground, completely through to the straw, the cortege of Mars which illuminates men of arms in letters of gold, blue, silver, and brass. He has put in his book the last as well as the first large, noble, and pure seed. But what are the quill, ink, paper and file, hammer, anvil, steel, iron, or bellows worth when money is lacking?

A similarly ambiguous image of man and object surfaces in the sixth stanza, as attention moves from the windmill, worm-eaten for lack of "monnee" (milling), back into the human realm through the pun created with "monnaie," a direct allusion to the poet's loss of wages. This fragmentation of the poet into subject and object intensifies throughout the work with the role of its first-person narrator, who acts as defender of poet and mill:

> Il cline en bas, ame ne le soustient,
> Ni entretient, ne scet a quoy il tient
> Qu'on luy retient une demye annee;
> Sa destinee est d'avoir une annee
> D'orge vanée.
>
> (2:769, vv. 43–47)

It's/He's declining, no one supports it/him, nor maintains it/him, nor knows why a half of a year is withheld from it/him. It/He is supposed to have one year of winnowed barley.

Just as he created his self-defense in the first half of the *Gaiges retrenchiés* through wordplay, so too in the second half of the composition, Molinet invokes through linguistic punning the presence of the figure to whom his appeal is addressed. Using a metaphorical image—the "*baudet de l'annoy* verd issus" (my emphasis) (the ass issued forth from youthful difficulty) (v. 65), an ass that will bring grain to the mill to grind—the author has his narrator present his case before Bauduin de Lannoy, a powerful noble of Molembaix and captain of the Château of Lille. Through the forceful use of imperatives and interrogatives, the speaker directly urges Bauduin to intercede on the writer's behalf before Archduke Philip the Handsome, whom Molinet had served as official chronicler since 1494:

Vers l'archiduc fays le molin tourner
Pour l'atourner de telz dictz, par tel tour,
Que cent escus luy puissent retourner,
Sans bestourner, et se luy fais donner
Et ordonner habis de riche atour.

(2:770, vv. 73–77)

Have the archduke activate the mill so as to equip it with such expressions, by such a course, that one hundred ecus can return to it/him, without destruction. And have him give and order for it/him [?] finely made clothes.

In a sense, the author's exploitation of both his own and his possible intercessor's name, associating one with the material world of objects and the other with the realm of animals,[51] places the plaintiff (Molinet), the public defender (the *acteur*), and the judge (Bauduin) on a near-equal footing. In the penultimate stanza, the author identifies himself directly for the first time with his proper name: "Soustiens a ton Molinet le menton" (Support your Molinet's chin) (2:770, v. 70). Up until this point, his name, mentioned in the third person, referred only to the object of the mill itself. This direct allusion to the human writer himself is maintained in the final stanza, where the narrator reiterates his plea for "pouvre Molinet, / Qui n'a deja plus d'encre en son cornet" (poor Molinet, who no longer has any ink in his horn) (2:771, vv. 79–80).

Though occupying the spotlight, then, Molinet is still conservative in his demands in the *Gaiges retrenchiés*, placing himself on stage in a fragmented manner that subtly undermines the potentially aggressive tone of the work and the strong, coherent image of the author himself: he is the first-person voice of the defender, the unproductive poet-plaintiff lacking wages described in the third person, and the decrepit object that sees no action. Such a scenario, while playful, is not nearly so direct as the strategy earlier employed by Villon in his request to Duke Jean II of Bourbon or by Clément Marot when he appealed to King Francis I some twenty-five to thirty-five years later.[52] Nonetheless, the poem's subject does call direct attention to the predicament of an author financially dependent on the patronage system. The absence of any dream vision or staging of allegorical characters reinforces the directness of this mes-

51. A reference to Balaam (v. 54) signals an implicit comparison between the disloyal prophet and Archduke Philip, both of whom must be talked into rectifying their behavior by a "baudet."

52. Compare Villon's *Requête à Mons. de Bourbon* (1461) with Marot's *Petite épistre au roy* (1518–19), *Marot, prisonnier, écrit au roy pour sa délivrance* (1527), and *Au roy, pour avoir été dérobé* (1531).

sage. In the end, Molinet's poem achieved its purpose, for he regained his lost wages the following year. But the insecure status of his dependence on the archduke continued to undermine the financial stability of the poet, as his loss of a complete pension for the years 1498 and 1499 suggests. It was most likely this recurrent state of affairs that motivated Molinet to publish his *Naissance de Charles d'Autriche* between the spring and fall of 1500.

An examination of this later writing provides insight into the changes that had taken place in textual production some thirty years after the *Trosne d'honneur*. Like the latter work, Molinet's *Naissance* glorifies his patron's family. No dream vision precipitates the action, though. The author's abandoning of this allegorical veil in his later works, as did so many of his literary compatriots, signals that Molinet no longer needed the validation of a conventional dream framework to promote his and his patron's views and that he was freer to assume greater extratextual authority over his own literary production. Indeed, signs of artistic self-consciousness pervade the *Naissance* from the outset, in such a way that the reader's awareness of the writer's artistic consciousness is much more heightened than in the *Trosne d'honneur*. For in speaking about the arch of peace that symbolizes the momentous birth of Charles of Austria, the poet sets up an implicit comparison between this monument and his own literary work. Can these new developments be related to the fact that Molinet himself took charge of the publication of the *Naissance*? I believe so.

In contrast to the *Trosne d'honneur* and the *Gaiges retrenchiés*, the *Naissance* was printed shortly after having been composed: it exists in two single editions, dating from circa 1500 and 1503, and in the posthumous editions of Molinet's *Faictz et dictz*. All the extant manuscript versions appear to postdate the first, and perhaps even the second, edition (see Appendix 4 below). The *Naissance* is thus primarily an imprint or, at the very least, a product of the transitional period from script to print.

Although the title page of Molinet's edition announces the name of his protectors, and not his own,[53] the swan emblem of Valenciennes (a pun on "val en cygnes") that dominates the first folio relates more to the author, who lived in that city, and to his book, which was printed there by Jean de Liège, than it does to the archduke (see Tchémerzine, 8:368). This same balance of identities is maintained visually elsewhere: the author's mark on the last folio advertises Molinet's new role as his own publisher (see Figure 3.12), and the arms on the title page verso an-

53. It reads: "Le tersdesiree [sic] et proufitable naissance de tresillustre enfant Charles d'Austrice, filz de monseigneur l'archiduc nostre tresredoubté prince et seigneur naturel" (The much desired and profitable birth of the very illustrious child Charles of Austria, son of my lord the archduke, our much revered prince and natural lord).

nounce the political power of the house of Austria (see Tchémerzine, 8:368).

Molinet's new paratextual presence coincides with his more manifest textual presence. It is again the poet's playful use of language, particularly his extraordinarily rich rhymes, that allows him to stretch the implicitly imposed limits of a court propagandist. In this case, the author's poetic talent affords him the opportunity to speak at once of the symbol of his patron's son's birth and of his own poetic composition. Thus, the juxtaposition of political and poetic emblems of authority that appeared visually in the paratext of Molinet's edition of the *Naissance* is textually translated through a superposition of discourses: one publicizes the glory of the newborn Charles; the other advertises the poet's literary endeavor. The first stanza sets the stage for these concurrently expressed voices of authority, offering a kind of politico-poetic palimpsest that imitates the coexisting woodcuts of the patron's and poet's emblems of authority:

> L'arche de paix, des aultres l'outrepasse,
> Forte que passe, ou Dieu veult reposer,
> Resplendissant comme clere topasse,
> En briefve espasse au compas je compasse,
> Mes pas j'apasse a le bien composer;
> Sans despasser, passer ne rapasser,
> Pour temps passer, arrestez vostre pas:
> L'or est de l'oeul le gracieux repas.
>
> (1:352, vv. 1–8)

The arch of peace, the paragon of all others, strong as a tower where God wants to repose, gleaming like clear topaz, in a short time I measure it with a compass, spacing out my steps to compose it carefully without exceeding, overreaching, or being extreme. To pass time, halt your steps [before it]: gold is the lovely feast of the eye.

The very rich rhymes and sounds in this opening passage incorporate a great variety of political and poetic, sculptural and linguistic, princely and public dimensions. While the peace arch ultimately designates the house of Austria and its newborn heir on its first level of meaning,[54] such specific reference is not directly articulated until verse 16, which finally

---

54. See *Faictz et dictz*, 3:1019, for Dupire's description of the construction by the people of Ghent of what must have been the arch of peace in honor of Charles of Austria. Other allusions are found in *L'arche ducalle* (1:367–70), *A Nicolas de Ruttre* (1:386–88, vv. 1–8), and *Chroniques*, ed. Doutrepont and Jodogne, 2:468–71.

mentions "L'empire, Espaigne, Austrice avec Bourgoigne" (The empire, Spain, Austria as well as Burgundy). In the meantime, the poet has "contaminated" this memorial through so many associations with himself and his poetic enterprise that subsequent mention of the arch of peace elicits his as well as his patron's connection with the edifice.

Consequently, it is not only the symbol of the house of Austria that surpasses all else—"des aultres l'outrepasse"—it is the poet's creation that does so as well. For thanks to his own words, fixed in print, as they are, for posterity, the "arche de paix" is monumentalized, remembered, and immortalized. The very richness and density of Molinet's vocabulary in these opening stanzas, metaphorically translated into the gold and resplendent "clere topasse" of the symbolic edifice, finds its concrete manifestation in the implied allusions to manuscript decoration. Whereas the centrality of the book image as an emblem of Molinet's defense of his artistic enterprise did not surface until the very end of the earlier *Trosne d'honneur*, from the outset of the *Naissance* the author's poetic endeavor, expressed metaphorically in codicological terms, receives equal space with his patron's endeavor. This association of illuminated book and authorial defense, already announced a few years earlier in the less publicized *Gaiges retrenchiés*, had thus found its way into the mainstream of Molinet's work written and printed for the glory of his protector.

While Molinet's manipulation of the rich, complicated linguistic and rhyme system throughout the *Naissance* was very likely meant to dazzle a court audience, his more straightforward presentation of events, uncomplicated by a dream framework or an elaborate allegorical scenario, made his work—and himself—more accessible to a wider audience.[55] Moreover, in signing the *Naissance*, Molinet presents himself as subject of the action, without fragmenting his authorial voice, as he had commonly done in earlier works: "Et sans amere orge ait en son van net / Grain et bon vent vostre humble Molinet" (And may your humble mill/ Molinet have grain and good wind without bitter barley in its/his clean winnowing sieve) (1:358, vv. 183–84). Whereas the Valenciennes edition maintains the ambiguity between object and human, because the very last word of the text, "molinet," is not capitalized, the Lyons edition's capitalization of the author's name in the final verse marks "Molinet" as

---

55. Molinet's account of the important events surrounding Charles's arrival on the scene, including his birth and baptism, the arrival of Margaret of Austria in Ghent (vv. 97–104, 153–60), as well as his praise of the city of Ghent, where the future Holy Roman emperor was born, his glorification of the archduke and his son at the very center of the poem (vv. 73–96, 137–60), and his direct exhortation to Flanders to celebrate (vv. 121–28) are rendered in chronicle-like fashion. For a discussion about the changing structure of dreams in late medieval narratives, see Cornilliat, "Aspects du songe."

a man running his own poetry mill. This subtle alteration reflects the printer's consciousness of a newly expanding, less sophisticated public, which did not yet know Molinet or which may not have sought to decode names as a court audience would have. In fact, as revealed in Chapter 4 above, Molinet's more directly accessible signature punctuated all of his works written in the last decade of his life.

Without an allegorical dream framework, but with the persistent double presence of the patron's and the author's monument as subjects of discussion, and with the refusal to fictionalize the first-person voice and the use of an increasingly accessible signature, Molinet's narrator had evolved from the fragmented and multiple secondary voices of his *Trosne d'honneur* and *Gaiges retrenchiés* to the one-dimensional, more self-centered narrator persona that coincides with Molinet himself in the *Naissance*. This development marks a significant change in the sociopolitical role of the writer since his composition of the *Trosne d'honneur* thirty years before. Instead of accepting a marginal position both at the court and in the propagandistic text, Molinet has taken control of the publication of his writing, advertised his own arms in the paratext, and called attention to his poetic qualities and presence in the text itself. Both text and image, ingeniously combined in verbal illumination and in print form, reflect the author's simultaneous focus on political and poetic authority.

In conclusion, a study of the relationship between the text and paratext of Molinet's *Trosne d'honneur*, *Gaiges retrenchiés*, and *Naissance de Charles d'Autriche*, each written at a critical financial juncture in his career, suggests a strong correlation between the author's questioning of the patronage system, his involvement in the new form of book production, and the appearance within his texts of an increasingly accessible authorial signature and a less fictionalized, less fragmented narratorial voice. With an apparent loosening of the binding ties between author and patron that had characterized the manuscript culture came a more interactive relationship between author and text. Molinet thus represents a key transitional figure in the shift from manuscript to print.

Many of Molinet's contemporaries and successors followed similar patterns, although the shift from script to print production occurred at an earlier stage of their careers, as Lemaire's works reveal. I have discussed elsewhere the dynamics of such an evolution in the case of La Vigne, through a study of the relationship between the physical presentation of the various versions of his *Ressource de la Chrestienté* and the image he draws of himself in it (*Shaping*, 10–18, and "Text"). Over a period of some thirty years, dating from the first known manuscript version of this work (1494) to its last extant edition (ca. 1525), La Vigne's status as author gradually emerged from the conventionally self-effaced position of a late medieval narrator-witness, anchored in the text's *récit*, into a growing authoritative presence that was increasingly advertised in the work's paratext.

After the publication of the *Vergier d'honneur* editions—or, one might say, after the 1504 lawsuit concerning that volume—La Vigne never again composed a work like the *Ressource*, in which the *acteur*, enmeshed in the allegorical story line, plays a secondary narrative role and in which the authorial voice is anonymously or ambiguously depicted.[56] From this point on he maintains a careful distance between himself as author and his textual characterizations. Even in those works of La Vigne which still presented a theatrical staging of allegorical characters, such as *Atollite portas de gennes* (1507), *Ballades de Bruyt Commun* (post 1508), and *Libelle des cing villes d'Ytallye contre Venise* (1509), no narrator ever appears. The title pages of these publications, moreover, prominently display the author's identity and position as the queen's secretary.

Even more-aggressive, single-voiced narrators surface in the writings of Gringore. There the visual and the verbal, paratextual and textual, dovetail in such a way that the image of an ever-present authorial figure dominates this poet's works.

Anticipating his contemporary Jean Lemaire de Belges by a few years and following in the footsteps of André de la Vigne, whose *Ressource de la Chrestienté* had appeared in print in its second stage of reproduction around 1495 (*Ressource*, 82–83), Pierre Gringore announced a new generation of authors with his *Chasteau de labour* in 1499, for it marked the publication of his very first writing. Signs of an emerging authorial speaker in the text of the *Labour* announce an evolution in Gringore's literary output from a multivoiced *acteur* enmeshed in the textual web of allegorical interactions to a less fictionalized, moralizing first-person voice that coincides increasingly with the historical figure outside the text who penned the verses. Indeed, Gringore came to distinguish more carefully between the voice of the *acteur*, which grew increasingly distant from the narrative action, while gaining more control of its development, and that of the protagonist, firmly anchored in the fiction of the text. The author's gradual abandonment of the continuous narrative form reinforced this distinction, creating a more coherent image of the author within the text.

---

56. La Vigne's *Epitaphes du roy de la Bazoche* (ca. 1501) does portray an *acteur*-narrator who records the complaints of La Bazoche, whom he overhears in a vision. This fascinating, dense work, which has received very little critical attention, will be the subject of a future study. See *Recueil de poésies*, ed. Montaiglon and Rothschild, 13:383–413.

Such textual prominence of the authorial voice coincides with Gringore's increasing authority in the bookmaking enterprise. As actor, author, and moralizing prosecutorial voice, all of which the famous Mère Sotte image embodied, Gringore represents one of the clearest examples of a late medieval writer who (re)invested the term *acteur* with all its latent meanings, as he set out to protect, validate, and bring a new authority to his writings. These developments will be traced through his *Chasteau de labour, Folles entreprises* (1505), and *Chasse du cerf des cerfs* (1510), which offer insight into how Gringore increasingly empowered the voice of his *acteur*.

The admonishment to virtue that had merely punctuated the central encomium of the *Trosne d'honneur* became the main theme of the *Chasteau de labour* and subsequent works, thereby placing Gringore in the didactic camp of Jean Meschinot, whose *Lunettes des princes* (1461–65) may have influenced him.[57] Placed within a dream framework, the narrative promotes reason and the virtue of hard work over sloth and other vices as the way to the Castle of Wealth. With the aid of Reason and Understanding, the protagonist frightens away an astounding number of personified worries and cares that beset him one night. He then makes his way to the Castle of Labor, where his hard work is rewarded with rest at the House of Repose and the release of all his troubles.

With direct ties to the manuscript tradition through its unacknowledged source—Bruyant's fourteenth-century *Voie de povreté et de richesse*—the *Chasteau de labour* served as an important work in the transition from manuscript to print.[58] As seen in Chapter 2 above, the evolving features of the paratext of Gringore's *Labour* underscore the visual and verbal dominance of the printer and bookseller over the author throughout the entire period of this work's early publication (1499–1532). Pigouchet's large printer's mark dramatizes the title page of his four editions of what must have been an immensely popular publication and is

---

57. Although the *Lunettes des princes* was printed more than thirty times from 1493 until the mid-sixteenth century, making Meschinot the most frequently published author of that time, he has not been considered in this book, because he did not live to see his works published.

58. Gringore's title and the scenes for the woodcuts in his first edition appear to have been inspired by a fifteenth-century manuscript, which belonged to the library of George C. Thomas in 1909, or by a closely related version. Unlike every other manuscript but one, which postdates Gringore's edition (Stockholm Royal Library, fr. LV), this privately owned copy bears the title *Le chastel de labour*. As the only single version of Bruyant's work (in all other known manuscripts, the text appears as part of an anthology or as an interpolation in the *Ménagier de Paris*), it is also the only one of the eleven extant manuscript versions that bears illustrations. For details about this manuscript, see Bruyant, *Le Livre du Chastel de Labour*, and Långfors. For the most recent details about the *Ménagier* manuscripts, see Brereton and Ferrier, eds., xii–xviii.

accompanied by the publisher's name, Simon Vostre (see Figure 2.8). The numerous woodcuts of the Pigouchet-Vostre editions, specially designed for this work and apparently based on miniatures from the fifteenth-century Thomas manuscript (see n. 58), illustrate allegorical scenes from the narrative. None of the woodcuts in the early editions of the *Labour* relates in any way to the author himself.[59] In a mode reminiscent of manuscript convention, Gringore's name never figures in the paratextual features of any of the *Labour* imprints. Indeed, the second-rate status accorded the author in the paratext of the *Labour* announces the *acteur*'s secondary function throughout the principal narrative. Gringore's acrostic signature in the last stanza of the work, however, coincides with a strong authorial presence in the work's prologue, a voice that stands apart from the traditional *acteur*-narrator and that eventually will overtake it in Gringore's later works. Thus, the presence of Gringore's name within the *Labour* text marks a midway point between the general anonymity of the extant fourteenth- and fifteenth-century manuscripts of his source, the *Voie de povreté*, and the clearly emphasized identification of Gringore in the paratext of his later works.[60]

In this moralistic allegory, the reader can identify several first-person voices that are distinct from one another and yet at times overlap, resulting in a multivoiced narrative perspective that is reminiscent of many other late medieval French texts: the narrative voice of the prologue, the first-person voice of the protagonist, and the *acteur*-witness. The juxtaposition of the last two voices within the narrative sometimes results in an awkward transition between first- and third-person accounts, while the transitions between the voices of the prologue narrator and the protagonist voices or between those of the prologue narrator and the *acteur* are often ambiguous.

The complex network of speakers in Gringore's *Labour*, attributable in part to its traditional allegorical construct, is further complicated by the fact that the author himself added, at different moments, two narrative layers to the first-person protagonist voice of Bruyant's *Voie de povreté*. The significance of this gesture cannot be overemphasized, for it is particularly in the creation of other first-person voices that Gringore distanced himself most markedly from his source. While he borrowed the work's principal concepts and the main plot elements from Bruyant, as several critics have noted, no one has recognized how dramatically Grin-

---

59. See above, Chapter 3, n. 46, for details about the authorial images in the later *Labour* editions.

60. Only two of the eleven manuscript versions of *Voie de povreté* mention the original author's name as Jean or Jacques Bruyant (Långfors, 73). The Thomas manuscript, which has strong ties with Gringore's work, does not identify the author, suggesting that Gringore never knew Bruyant had written it. See also Chapter 1, n. 20, above.

gore altered the fourteenth-century work by embroidering on its single narrative-protagonist voice with his development of a strong, authorial prologue-speaker and with several third-person insertions of the *acteur* into the main narrative.[61] A further complexity surfaces in Pigouchet's third edition of the *Labour*, because of its six hundred or so additional verses, which I will discuss below.

The superior attitude and accusatory language of the speaker who opens the prologue of Gringore's *Chasteau de labour*, as he addresses a wide-ranging public of "Hommes et femmes," "gens oyseux," and "seigneurs," characterizes him as a prosecutor-moralist:

> Hommes et femmes qui desirez auoir
> Les biens celestes, et acquerir auoir
> Au mortel monde: estudies ce liure. . . .
> L'homme n'aura iamais peu en ce monde,
> Mais que raison dedens son cueur habonde. . . .
> Pour ce, seigneurs qui ce liure lisez,
> A vostre cas pensez et aduisez,
> En contemplant vostre vie, qui est brieue.[62]
> (vv. 1–3, 49–50, 61–63)

Men and women who wish to obtain heavenly wealth and acquire goods in this mortal world, study this book. . . . Man will never have little in this world provided that reason abounds in his heart. . . . For this reason, lords who read this book, think and consider your situation in contemplating your life, which is brief.

This constitutes not a dedication to a specific patron, but a prologue aimed at reaching a general reading public, as the speaker's desire to "demonstrer . . . a tous publiquement" (v. 69) signals.[63] He is indeed

61. On Gringore's debt to Bruyant as well as certain stylistic differences between the two works, see the following: Långfors, 80–83; Oulmont, *Gringore*, 96–107; and Pollard, ed., *Labour*, xxx–xxxiv. I have relied on Pichon's edition of Bruyant's *Voie de povreté*, which is based on three manuscripts of the *Ménagier de Paris* and B. N. ms. fr. 808, fols. 51–72 (all references will be to this edition). The most recent editors of the *Ménagier de Paris*, Brereton and Ferrier, omitted Bruyant's work from their volume, mistakenly believing that Långfors had re-edited the poem in his article (300, n. 117. 18).

62. All verses cited from Gringore's *Chasteau de labour* are taken from Pollard's 1905 edition, the only known modern version of the work. It is based on Wynken de Worde's 1506 edition and also contains the French text of Pigouchet's and Vostre's third edition of March 31, 1501.

63. Compare, for example, with the opening prologue dedication to Charles VIII in Octavien de Saint-Gelais's *Séjour d'honneur* or with the dedication that prefaces Molinet's *Art de rhétorique* in the manuscript versions (see p. 159 above).

aware of both the diversity of his readership ("a tous") and the "public-ness" of his literary and moralistic act (see also vv. 992–99). In fact, the author consciously makes a dedicatory offering of his book to his general reading audience: "En le lisant que chascun soit tachant / Laisser oyseuse et prendre diligence" (May each one reading it try to leave aside sloth and take on diligence) (vv. 11–12). Like Molinet's *Naissance*, then, this imprint reaches out to a public broader than an official royal audience. This is not a surprising strategy to find in an edition of Gringore, who did not hold a court position at the beginning of his literary career. Modeled perhaps on dramatic *crys*, or public announcements of upcoming theatrical productions, but influenced also by the new technology of printing, this prefatory space assumes a publicity-like character, for the author essentially hawks his book in an effort to attract an audience. This tactic was probably necessitated by the economics of publication, a move, moreover, that seems to have paid off well, given the numerous re-editions of the work in a rather short period of time.[64]

These details and others in the prologue of the *Labour* call attention to Gringore's and Bruyant's different narrative strategies. For in the *Voie de povreté*, no separate prologue exists, no publicity tactics are in evidence (see Pichon ed., 2:4). In its first ten lines of introduction, the first-person speaker briefly criticizes a self-centered, worldly materialism, as does the *Labour* prologue voice. But Gringore has expanded the short passage into seventy-two sermonizing verses that exhort readers to adopt strict, ethical behavior.

The Gringore prologue, moreover, includes a self-conscious passage about artistic adequacy, which had no place in Bruyant's work. Indeed, the narrator's demonstrated concern about the language of his "propos" all but confirms an identification between this voice and that of the author:

> Affin doncques que mon propos acheue,
> Et que par tout y a commencement,
> Demonstrer vueil a tous publiquement,
> En excusant ma petite simplesse,
> Les deux chemins, dont l'ung va iustement
> A pourete: l'autre va a richesse.
>
> (vv. 64–72)

64. Five editions are known to have appeared in the first year and a half, and there were at least nine during the first five years, with editions appearing until 1560. See Appendix 5 below for details.

So that I might conclude my remarks and begin, I wish to demon-strate to everyone publicly, in apologizing for my plainness, the two paths: one which leads straight to poverty, the other to wealth.

Completely separated from the work's main action, this prefatory space allows Gringore not only to establish immediate contact with his readers but to cast a light on his own authorship in a way that the paratext, which does not refer to him, fails to do. In this way, Gringore stamps his authorial imprimatur on the writing from the outset.[65]

The prologue of Gringore's *Labour*, then, presents a speaker conscious of his role as public teacher and writer. This more extrovert, less fiction-alized voice does not reappear until the final stanza of the work, where it again exhorts the reader to acknowledge his debt to God (my emphasis):

> Grace rendz au hault createur
> Regnant en triumphe haultaine,
> Inuocant le poure pecheur
> Nourry en la gloire mondaine;
> Gardien de nature humaine,
> Omnipotent, plain de noblesse,
> Resplendissant au hault demaine,
> Estendant sur nous sa largesse.
>   (vv. 3034–41)

Praise the Creator on high, reigning in lofty triumph, calling upon the poor sinner, nourished upon earthly glory; Guardian of human nature, omnipotent, full of nobility, shining in His lofty domain, ex-tending to us His generosity.

Expanding the final verses of the *Voie de povreté* as he had its initial lines (see Pichon ed., 2:42), Gringore reintroduces into the text his own exter-nal authority, this time through his acrostic signature. The rubric "Ac-teur" that announces these verses establishes, moreover, a critical link between the author, whose name is spelled out vertically, and the sec-ond level of narrative voice, announced in textual rubrics as that of the

65. Molinet's self-reflexive references to the difficulties of his creative enterprise, through use of his punning name in the opening lines of a few of his works (e.g., the *Res-source du petit peuple* and *Voyage de Napples*), anticipate Gringore's gesture, but these pas-sages form a much more integral part of the remaining narrative than does Gringore's prologue.

acteur. Although the assertive authorial voice that the reader encounters here appears in positions of closure in many other late medieval works, its rhetorical force has not been quite so strident as in the *Labour*.

After the prologue in most editions of the *Labour*, the reader is led immediately, almost abruptly, into the narrative by the first-person protagonist. The dramatic difference here from the voice of the prologue narrator is all the more striking because of the absence of any conventional signs of transition in the prologue. This is the voice of the protagonist who had narrated Bruyant's work, where a more natural transference of the first-person voice occurred because the prefatory verses were not developed at great length (see Pichon ed., 2:4). This natural association between narrator and protagonist breaks down with Gringore's more developed prologue because, instead of preparing the narrative background by pointing inward to the allegorical action, it focuses on the author's artistic concerns and his extratextual connection with his readers. As a result, the passage from the authorial to the protagonist's first-person voice is awkward and artificial. Indeed, it may be the absence of a smooth transition between the two narrative levels that gave rise to the addition of some six hundred verses at this very point (v. 73) in Pigouchet's third edition, which appeared one and half years after the first. Given Gringore's presence in Paris at this time and the fact that Pigouchet's and Vostre's publication of the *Chasteau d'amours* (sometime before December 20, 1500) indicated a continued, amicable working relationship between author and publishers, one may assume that it was Gringore who penned these additional verses.[66]

The author's motives for inserting this second prologue before the original narrative are not entirely clear. Was it for stylistic, structural, or even economic reasons? The interpolation does create a cleaner distinction between the first-person authorial speaker of the prologue and the voice of the Bruyant protagonist by introducing earlier into the work the *acteur*, whose identity was not established in Gringore's first edition until some thousand lines into the action (see v. 1740).[67] In the interpolated passage, the *acteur* presents in the third person another allegorical scenario (entirely absent from Bruyant's fourteenth-century writing) that prepares the reader for the main action of the narrative, where the married protagonist presumably represents the adult version of the child

66. Oulmont, *Gringore*, 105–6, and others take this for granted.

67. The *acteur* does not appear in the extant manuscript versions of Bruyant's *Voie de povreté*, for the first-person voice is that of the protagonist. In fact, the Thomas manuscript, one of only two to employ rubics (see also Stockholm, Royal Library, fr. LV), consistently announces the protagonist in the third person as "le nouvel mesnagier," suggesting that this manuscript derived from a version of the *Ménagier de Paris* (see the description of the rubrics in the Thomas manuscript in Bruyant, *Le Livre du Chastel de Labour*, 8–19).

presented in this second prologue. The transition is not, however, entirely smooth, especially since no voice is ever given to the child. But it is somewhat more satisfactory than that of the first editions.

With the appearance of the "I" protagonist,[68] the narrative perspective of the *Labour* changes again, this time from the third-person account of the *acteur* to the first person, as the speaker—again, presumably the matured "enfant" of the second prologue—relates directly his decision to marry and his subsequent concerns. Oddly enough, however, the voice and rubric of the *acteur* suddenly reappear some thousand lines later (vv. 1740–63). This narrative interruption recurs six more times, with the result that first- and third-person perspectives often become awkwardly juxtaposed.[69]

The six-hundred-verse interpolation also has the effect of delaying the dream sequence of the main action; and the appearance of the dream so late in the narrative of Gringore's revised version, its cursory treatment (vv. 696–98), and the abruptness of the protagonist's awakening minimize its conventionally dominant character. Moreover, the dream is the protagonist's, not the *acteur*'s; thus, it is not related in any way to the *acteur*'s recording of the action, as it is in nearly all other narratives of this period.

As I have already suggested, the *Chasteau de labour* recalls Meschinot's *Lunettes des princes* in many ways. As a rather long doctrinal poem in which a first-person narrator recounts a dream, it possesses many of those characteristics of continuous allegorical narratives defined by Leonard Johnson (170–72). Like Meschinot's narrator, the protagonist falls prey to similar worries and he experiences a rehabilitating visit by Reason and her followers. Unlike Meschinot's work, however, there is no personalized pseudo-autobiographical confession of the speaker's own grief and distress; this is because of Gringore's peculiar play with narrative voices. The "I" narrator in the *Lunettes* is a very different first-person construct from Gringore's, in part because it is both personal and public, associating with the "I" of Everyman while at times withdrawing into its own personal shell (Johnson, 194–98). Instead of embodying the voices of a poet revealing himself both in his singularity and as a member of the community (Johnson, 229), the poet's voice in the *Labour* sets itself above the community, as it will in Gringore's *Folles entreprises* and in the series of moralistic works he wrote at the end of his career. In other words, where Gringore's work differs from the allegorical didactic narrative described by Johnson is precisely where Gringore deviates from

68. This occurs immediately following the prologue, at v. 73, in all but Pigouchet's March 1501 edition and Augereau's 1532 edition, in which the passage appears at v. 656.

69. Compare the following verses: 1740 (3°) and 1768 (1°); 2052 (3°) and 2071 (1°); 2484 (3°) and 2508 (1°); 2564 (3°) and 2604 (1°).

Bruyant's fourteenth-century text. Gringore does indeed "play with his statute as author," as did Meschinot and others before him like Machaut, Christine de Pizan, and Chartier (Johnson, 203). But he plays differently than his forebears, presenting most prominently not the personal, poetic "I" of Villon, Meschinot, or Saint-Gelais, but the exhortative, authorial "I" of the prologue and the acrostic stanza. The more personal "I" of the protagonist is in fact confused with the *acteur*'s voice which, though enmeshed in the narrative, succeeds in distancing itself from it as well. This difference can perhaps be attributed to the author's more self-conscious posture, resulting from his direct involvement in the publication of his writings.[70]

The authorial voice of the *Labour* prologue takes center stage in Gringore's *Folles entreprises*, the work whose paratextual features signaled such a dramatic shift in the poet's involvement in the bookmaking process. In the *Folles entreprises*, which provides examples of human behavior that are designed to upbraid the misguided for their immoral exploits, the author, through his first-person speaker, attacks all kinds of political, religious, and social abusers of power, including imperialistic leaders, covetous "fools," deceptive lawyers, ambitious pastors, religious women seeking too much knowledge (!), hypocrites, and heretics. As a voice for the people, who are depicted as victims of the powerful, Gringore attributes much of the world's ills to war, arrogance, and greed, locating their source in the immoral behavior of princes and preachers.

Although Gringore sets up the *Folles entreprises* to resemble a conventional, late medieval scenario through the *acteur*'s nightmarish vision, which he records after awakening, in fact this traditional dream framework, including the cast of allegorical figures, is a superficial veneer. This coincides with a weakening both of the continuous narrative structure and the conventional *acteur*-narrator role, which, adumbrated at the outset, disappear throughout most of the text, only to return in a somewhat incongruous manner at the end. For the *acteur* breaks through this artificial staging as early as verse 17 of the work (*Œuvres*, ed. Héricault and Montaiglon, 1:13) and does so repeatedly thereafter, abandoning his narrative and directly addressing his general public in a prosecuto-

---

70. A similar development characterizes Gringore's second work, the *Chasteau d'amours* (1500), in which the first-person roles of moral teacher and witness-recorder merge under the rubric of "L'acteur," who nevertheless maintains close ties with the protagonist through his various adventures. Although personified characters speak in Gringore's *Complainte de la Terre Sainte* (ca. 1500) and *Complainte de Trop Tard Marié* (1505), both are typified by a sharp, moralizing tone and by a strong association with the *acteur* voice that generates Gringore's acrostic signature.

rial tone that echoes that of Gringore's prologue narrator in the *Labour*.[71] Assuming a defensive posture, he describes his motives for undertaking this enterprise, explaining that despite his lack of a university degree and despite the high stakes, he feels compelled out of a sense of justice to follow through, even if he meets with criticism. Here, then, is the voice of the author speaking:

> Je m'entremis de faire et composer
> Ce traictié cy, que laisse pour gloser
> A tous liseurs, car, sans difficulté,
> Je n'ay degré en quelque faculté;
> Et toutesfois, pour l'onneur de justice,
> L'ay composé, posé que soye nice
> D'entreprendre œuvre de si hault pris;
> Mais, s'ainsi est que de ce soye repris,
> Pas trop courcé ne seray des reprises
> Veu que ce sont les *Folles Entreprises*.
>
> (p. 13)

I began to write and compose this treatise, whose interpretation I leave to all readers, which should not be difficult, because I have no university diploma. Nevertheless, I have written it in the name of honor and justice, even though I might have been foolish to undertake a work of such great import. But if it happens that I am criticized for that, I shall not be too angry about any reprisals, given that these are *Foolish Undertakings*.

Characterizing his poetic act as an honorable undertaking, Gringore, in a modest, ironic, and even humorous way, compares it with the many foolish "entreprises" he will subsequently attack in his text. The presence of Latin quotations in nearly all editions of the *Folles entreprises*, signposts for the educated reader and publicity for the author's biblical

71. The wide range of readers targeted by Gringore is indicated by the various terms of direct address used throughout the *Folles entreprises*, including "Princes, qui guerre entreprenez" (17), "Empereurs, roys, ducz, contes et marquis, / Cadetz, seigneurs, vicontes, mareschaulx, / Princes, barons" (22), "Seigneurs mondains, à vices adonnez" (23), "messieurs les lisans" (27), "gens ingratz" (32), "gens lettrez" (49), "justiciers, qui ministrez Justice" (50), "Gens aveuglez, à discords adonnez" (57), "nobles, preux et gentilz" (59), "Pasteurs" (65), "Vous qui faictes les venditions folles" (93), "mondains pasteurs, pecheurs, / Prescheurs, pescheurs, loups rampans" (94), and "gens despitz, felons, blasphamateurs, / Jureurs, menteurs" (132). All my references are to Héricault and Montaiglon's edition, 1:11–144.

and classical erudition,[72] reveals, however, that Gringore is merely assuming the conventionally modest stance of a medieval writer.

With this publication, Gringore, consciously or not, replaces conventional third-person narratives and allegorical disputations with an ever-present admonishing first-person voice, whose speeches and diatribes aim at engaging the reader directly. The rhetorical dynamics between staged personifications that had previously dominated late medieval texts have shifted here to secondary status.[73] The entire narrative mode, disrupted by a dominating first-person authorial speaker, who adopts a superior rhetorical stance in subsuming all other voices,[74] essentially disappears. It is replaced by a dramatic tension that directly links narrator and reader as they become the new players on the literary stage. Aware of his moralistic role and even his persuasive "power" in this honorable enterprise, the *acteur* explains in a personal note his motivation for writing:

> Mais qui me meult de m'enquerir des choses
> Incongnues au cueur d'autruy encloses,
> A vostre advis, messieurs les lisans?
> Se ce n'est ce que j'ay veu puis douze ans.
>
> (p. 27)

But what moves me to inquire about unknown things, hidden in the hearts of others, in your opinion, Messrs. readers, if not what I have seen for the past twelve years?

He also exhorts his audience to learn the moral lesson he teaches: "Se retenez mes ditz, et apprenez, / Endoctrinez serez en general" (If you keep my words in mind, and learn them, you will be generally taught) (23).

---

72. The Latin quotations appear in the margins of all of the known editions of the *Folles entreprises*, save two issues of the 1505 Le Dru edition (B. N., Rés. Ye 1321, and ENSBA, Rés. Masson 428[1]), which were apparently sold by the author, who presumably had a different clientele than Le Dru.

73. Only twice are the words of others briefly quoted—Saint Gregory's (85) and Saint Augustine's (89)—before the traditional allegorical drama that occupies pages 107–42.

74. At times this figure sermonizes (15, 17, 55), moralizes through rhetorical questioning (15, 17, 19, 23, 27, 51, 71, 85, 90, 95), offers his opinion and interpretation, but refuses to judge (16, 44–46, 49, 74, 77, 79, 96), explains his function (23, 27, 43–44, 52, 80, 82, 107, 142), directly addresses and sometimes attacks (17, 20, 21, 22, 23, 26, 33, 37, 54), admonishes (20, 32, 59, 65, 93, 103), remonstrates (23, 33, 49, 57, 88, 94, 97, 131, 140), demonstrates through example (18, 28, 71, 78, 84, 86 91–92), and counsels (37, 38, 39, 41, 42, 50–51, 52, 66, 69–70, 86). These moments are punctuated by numerous lyric insertions, which provide in encapsulated form the same kind of rhetorical strategies (see 17–18, 40, 53–54, 55–56, 57–59, 60–62, 72–73, 104–7, etc.).

Like the "sotz" of the theatrical troupe with whom Gringore actually performed and whose repertoire he composed, the *acteur* of the *Folles entreprises*, closely aligning himself with the author, speaks out boldly, remonstrating with political, legal, and religious leaders, though not wearing the protective, satirical mask of Mère Sotte.

An elaborate system of rubrics, which Gringore, as publisher, doubtless oversaw, advertises the *acteur*'s constant presence and his demonstrative and exhortative role in the *Folles entreprises*, facilitating the reader's ability to follow a somewhat disorganized exposition.[75] Likewise, the twenty or so woodcuts that depict the *acteur*'s descriptions of various allegorical interactions offer the reader a visually dramatic preview or reminder of the moral message, designed perhaps as a conscious appeal to a more popular audience.[76] In fact, the illustrations allegorize Gringore's message much more than the text, which remains relatively literal, until the final scenario of the *Folles entreprises* (107–42), with which the woodcuts are more compatible and which marks a return to a more conventional allegorical debate. It is as if the author still felt a need to enclose his sermonizing within a familiar narrative framework. Even though the *acteur* plays the traditional role of narrator-witness in this allegorical staging, the exhortations delivered by Faith and Devotion recall his own earlier diatribes. That is to say, the *acteur*'s dominant moralistic persona is echoed and remembered through these allegorical voices.

Drawing attention to the problem of patronage in a manner that echoes Lemaire in the printing of his *Temple d'honneur* one year earlier, Gringore's dedication to Pierre of Ferrières at the end of the *Folles entreprises* reminds us of his continued need for support.[77] Like the opening autobiographical allusion that justifies the composition, the reference in these verses to Gringore's own relatives brings an authority to the moralizing voice of the *acteur*.[78] This is reinforced in a crucial way by the use

75. See, for example, "Remonstrances par l'acteur" (23), "Advertissement aux princes par l'acteur" (26), "Des quatre Vertuz Principalles que les princes doyvent tousjours avoir en eulx et se gouverner par icelles" (38), "Valère dit et recompte une hystoyre Que j'ay voulu rediger en memoire" (43), "Comment l'acteur de ce present livre le presente à Noble et Puissant Seigneur sire Pierre de Ferières, Chevalier, Seigneur et Baron dudit lieu de Ferières et de Thuri, et Seigneur de Dangu" (142).

76. These woodcuts appear on folios 10^v, 13^v, 14^r, 16^v, 19^v, 21^r, 22^r, 25^v, 26^v, 28^r, 30^r, 34^r, 41^v, 42^r, 49^r, 52^v, 54^r, and 59^v of the B. N. Rés. Ye 1321 version of the 1505 *Folles entreprises*.

77. See also the interpolated ballad to the Virgin Mary, which, the rubric explains, could also be interpreted as a poem in honor of the French queen (60–63). Was this Gringore's attempt to get into Anne of Brittany's good graces so as to obtain her patronage? The author's reference to her distribution of alms (61) suggests that the answer is yes.

78. Gringore's statement in these lines that his predecessors had served in the house of Ferrières (143) furnishes evidence that he came from Normandy (Oulmont, *Gringore*, 3–7). See pp. 142–43 above for a discussion of the dedication.

of the term *acteur* to refer to the author in the announcement (which follows the text; see pp. 35–36 above) of the first French privilege known to have been obtained by a vernacular author. Lending, perhaps for the first time, a legalized, nonfictional status to the term *acteur*, appearing as it does in the paratext, this usage doubtless validated in a new way the voice of the *acteur* within the text, which here appears in a much less fragmented form than in Gringore's *Labour*. The twenty-verse elaboration on the traditionally more modest dedication disrupts all the more noticeably the action of the literary text, as does the lengthy rubric advertisement (see n. 75 above) that refers to "l'acteur de ce present livre" (the author of this present book).

Announced by a similar rubric, which clearly informs the reader how to reconstruct the author's (*acteur's*) name,[79] the final acrostic stanza reflects how Gringore has absorbed the aggressive public relations strategy of the paratext of the *Folles entreprises* into his text. As in his *Labour* prologue, Gringore encourages everyone to buy his book, even as he maintains the *acteur's* superior, moralistic tone, and then centers on his poetic enterprise once again, acknowledging a debt of inspiration to God:

> Le surnom de l'Acteur sera trouvé par les
> premières lettres de ce couplet.
>
> G rans et petitz, le livre en gré prenez,
> R ongez ces motz à vostre entendement;
> J oyeusement les faultes reprenez;
> N otez que l'ay composé simplement.
> G races en rens à Dieu devotement,
> O ù j'ay recours en composant tout œuvre,
> R ememorant que sans luy nullement
> E ntendement choses offusques n'euvre.
>
> (p. 144)

The author's last name can be found in the first letters of this stanza: Great and humble, receive this book willingly, set your minds to studying these words; check the errors joyfully, note that I have written it simply. I thank God devoutly, to whom I have had recourse in writing this work, remembering that without Him in no way can intelligence discover obscure things.

79. In many versions, the acrostic is emphasized by means of spaces between the first and second letters of each verse, thereby setting off the vertical letters that spell out GRINGORE.

With a significant weakening—and at times disappearance—of the traditional continuous-narrative structure, dream framework, allegorical characters, and secondary witness role of the *acteur*-narrator, Gringore thus marks a new phase in his narratorial experimentation with the *Folles entreprises*.

The domineering narrator has gained complete control of the text with the publication of Gringore's *Chasse du cerf des cerfs* (ca. 1510), the first of Gringore's works to bear his name on the title page.[80] More of a political than a moralistic diatribe, the *Chasse* satirized Pope Julius II's militancy and propensity for dishonest strategems during a confrontation with the French at Bologna in the autumn of 1510. The entire episode of an apparently feigned papal illness in order to gain military advantage over France is recounted in the metaphorical terms of the hunt, with the protagonist, identified as the "cerf des cerfs" and the "serf des serfs" (a pun on the pope's designated role as *Servus servorum Dei*), tricking the "francs veneurs," or French forces, who are hunting him.[81]

Contrasting with his earlier political tracts and with other contemporary polemics about the same issue (Brown, *Shaping*, 91–146), Gringore's *Chasse* has no dream structure, no protagonist is given voice, nor does the author stage allegorical speakers. Only the first-person narrator controls the third-person *récit*, intermittently breaking into it to address a prospective patron, sympathize with his French readers, pass judgment indirectly on the behavior of the "serf des serfs" (163), or directly take to task the pope's alter ego (165). The moralizing, authoritarian voice of the *Labour* prologue's narrator strikingly resurfaces to attack the pontiff at a particularly dramatic moment, set off from the narrative by the rubric announcing an "Exortacion au cerf des cerfz":

> Sainct Gregoire n'apétoit seigneurie
> Quand il se dist serf des serfz; si vous prie,
> Puisqu'il vous plaist comme luy vous nommer,
> Que vous facez selon son industrie;
> Soyez ainsi que une biche serie,
> Sans porter cors; bien serez estimé. . . .

80. The title page reads: "La chasse du cerf des cerfz Composé par Pierre Gringore" (*The Hunt for the Deer of Deer / Serf of Serfs*, written by Pierre Gringore). The only extant edition of this work, currently housed in the Bibliothèque Nationale (Rés. Ye 1319), was reprinted by Héricault and Montaiglon in *Œuvres*, 1:157–67; all my citations are from this edition.

81. The actions of the "cerfs marins Adriatiques" (i.e., Venetians) and "cerfz ruraux" (i.e., Swiss) are likewise criticized in the narrative. Several woodcuts in this publication, including the one placed on the title page (see Tchémerzine, 6:75), depict scenes related to this hunt (fols. 1^v, 2^r, 8^v).

Posé qu'avez esté durant la ruyt
Fort eschauffé en faisant noyse et bruit,
C'est assez fait, cela vous doit suffire;
Vostre buisson gardez de jour, de nuyt. . . .
Car les veneurs Françoys, à bref vous dire,
Vous ont remis bien souvent au buisson.

(p. 166)

Saint Gregory did not covet territory when he called himself the servant of servants; I beg of you, since you like being named after him, that you adopt his vigilance. Act like a mild female deer without antlers; you will be well esteemed. . . . Even if you were very heated during the mating season, making much trouble and discord, it is enough, that should suffice. Stay in your territory day and night . . . for the French hunters, in short, have often put you back in the bush.

Written as much to berate the pope for his actions as to convince the French public of his inappropriate behavior, the *Chasse* introduces a humbler version of the morally superior *acteur* of the *Labour* and the *Folles entreprises*: one who openly sympathizes with his audience, explicitly identifying with them at times through his use of the first-person plural (158). Indeed, this first-person voice coincides with that of Gringore, for from the outset he clearly defines his role as *author*, not as narrator-witness of events, drawing attention to his dedication to the "prelat de Cahors," which has been strategically moved from its location at the end of the *Folles entreprises* to the beginning of the *Chasse*:

Je passoye temps en ung petit village
Nommé Estiolles. . . .
Et au plus près de ce lieu je choisy
Ung beau chasteau qu'on appelloit Soysy,
Où reposoit le prelat de Cahors,
Qui d'avec luy chasse mauvais cas hors.
Lors m'ingeray luy presenter ce livre
Que de bon cueur luy transmetz et luy livre,
Intitulé *le Livre de la chasse*
Du serf des serfz; bien a qui le pourchasse.

(pp. 158–59)

I spent time in a small village called Estiolles . . . and very near this place I saw a beautiful castle called Soysy, where the prelate of Cahors, who chases out bad things, lived. So I took it upon myself to offer him this book, entitled the *Book of the Hunt for the Deer of Deer / Serf of Serfs*, which I transmit and deliver to him in good faith. Good wishes to the one who pursues it.

While implicitly calling attention within the text to Gringore's need for financial support, this dedication also serves to authenticate the writer's success at establishing ties with a powerful leader. Although no evidence suggests that the dedicatee ended up supporting the author,[82] Gringore's "targeting" of an ecclesiastical figure as the potential patron of a work that attacks the pope was probably designed to elicit public support for the French king against the pontiff's militant actions at the time—or at the very least to impress his potential audience so that they would buy his book.

Nevertheless, the juxtaposition of a more authorial speaker with this explicit request for patronage reflects again the conflicting needs of late medieval authors, who were striving for a certain literary independence while still remaining dependent on the financial support of nobles. This contradiction surfaces again at the end of the work. In a renewed effort to obtain support, the author flatters, almost submissively, his prospective patron and, through a play on the "serf des serfs" expression that implicitly criticizes the pope's failure to *serve* his people well, demonstrates his own willingness to *serve* the bishop in this search.

> Gubernateur et pillier de l'esglise,
> Reveramment par devant vous m'adresse;
> Je congnois bien qu'estes plain de franchise,
> Noble de cueur en vivant sans reprise,
> Glorifiant de Jhesus la haultesse;
> Or suis-je serf à la vostre noblesse;
> Rurallement ay parlé de la chasse,
> En esperant d'acquerir vostre grace.
>
> (p. 167)

Governor and pillar of the Church, I reverently stand before you and address you. I know well that you are full of kindliness, noble in heart, living without reproach, glorifying the greatness of Jesus. Now, I am a servant of your nobility; I have spoken in rustic terms about the hunt, hoping to obtain your grace.

82. Although Héricault and Montaiglon, eds., *Œuvres*, 158–59, n. 2, suggest that these lines refer to Gringore's protector, whom they have identified as Germain de Ganay, bishop of Auch, the lack of extratextual confirmation of this association makes it more likely that this passage represents the author's *effort* to obtain patronage.

Still, the rubric preceding this acrostic stanza directs the reader to reconstruct Gringore's acrostic signature—"L'Acteur et surnom d'icel mys" (The author's surname herein placed)—an obvious, recurring sign of the author's consciousness of the importance of clearly identifying himself with all his works.

Moreover, while the privilege announcement following the final stanza of the *Chasse* reminds the reader of Gringore's increasing direction of the production of his works, it also recalls the controlling and demonstrative *acteur* of the text (my emphasis):

> Congé est donné par justice a l'*acteur* de ce present livre le faire imprimer, et deffenses faictes à tous imprimeurs de ne le imprimer ne vendre jusques au jour de Noel prochain venant, fors à ceulx à qui il les baillera à vendre et distribuer. (167)

> Permission is granted by the court to the author of this present book to have it printed, and all printers are forbidden to print or sell it until next Christmas Day coming up, except those to whom he gives it to sell and distribute.

Given its repeated appearance in a legal context outside the text and the increasing distancing of the *acteur* from the narrative action within the text, the term *acteur* had clearly broadened in usage and meaning by the second decade of the sixteenth century, as it both designated the author outside the text and announced the nonfictional, first-person voice within it.[83] In fact, the term appears only once in the *Chasse*, in the rubric announcing the final acrostic.

Thus, the *Chasse du cerf des cerfs* provides yet another example of how the increasingly prominent paratextual image of Gringore was taking over the traditional textual image of the *acteur*. The first-person speaker's identification with Gringore as author from the outset, his absolute control of the narrative (no other voices speak), his exhortatory and moralizing stance vis-à-vis the pope, his sympathetic identification with his French audience, his acrostic signature—all these furnish evidence of the encroachment of Gringore's controlling paratextual image into his text. At the same time that Gringore was assuming nearly complete con-

---

83. Pierre Gringore is also referred to as the "acteur" of his book in the privileges of the *Folles entreprises* (1505) and the *Union des princes* (ca. 1509). The privilege of the *Abus du monde* of 1509 employs the expression "acteur et compositeur," as do the privileges found at the end of *Entreprise de Venise* (ca. 1509), the *Coqueluche* (1510), and the *Espoir de paix* (1511).

trol of the composition, printing, distribution, and sale of his works, his authorial voice was coming to dominate their textual dynamics. As a result, the image promoted in his later works is that of a more clearly defined, single-minded, unified, moralizing *acteur* who increasingly distances himself from traditional scenarios while directly exhorting his readers and potential protectors. This is not the ambiguous, ever-changing first-person speaker of Molinet's *Trosne d'honneur*, La Vigne's *Ressource de Chrestienté*, Lemaire's *Temple d'honneur et de vertus*, or Gringore's *Labour*. A clearer distinction between *acteur*-narrator and fictional protagonist has emerged along with a coincidence of the *acteur* inside the text and the author outside it.

The preceding examination of late medieval works reveals that the increasing self-awareness of vernacular authors and the related changes in public perceptions of them are linked to important textual modifications. With the gradual disappearance of the dream framework and of staged allegorical characters, the multivoiced, fictionalized *acteur*-narrator tends to disappear as well. It is the external authoritative figure of the *acteur* as author that comes to dominate the text.

Gringore, like La Vigne and Lemaire, eventually abandons medieval-like narrative voices altogether. Whereas the narrator figure essentially fades out of those works written by La Vigne after the *Ressource de la Chrestienté* and the *Vergier d'honneur*, the author's moralistic exhortations, increasingly punctuated by autobiographical references, dominate the narrative of most of Gringore's works, while Lemaire's artistic voice invades his polemical texts in a move that develops more explicitly the pattern set by Molinet in the *Naissance*. At the same time, the paratext, particularly in those volumes whose publication the writers themselves controlled, focused more and more sharply on the author. The verbal announcement of La Vigne's identity on the title page of the *Vergier d'honneur* editions is followed by a generic author-woodcut that highlights the idea of authorship, instead of patronage as the manuscript version had. Gringore's presence, visually publicized through the appearance of his personalized Mother Folly woodcut on the title page of many of his works, accompanied the verbal advertisement of his role as author, bookseller, publisher, and legal protector of his work. Anticipated by the coat of arms printed at the end of Molinet's self-published *Naissance*, Lemaire's "aristocratic" authorship is visually emblazoned on the title page of certain editions of his *Légende des Vénitiens*, and of other works he oversaw, and is verbally reinforced by the entire text of the privilege granting him control over the publication and distribution of his works. These actions reflect the aggressively defensive behavior of late medieval writers who were seeking to protect their authorship but also to validate and advertise publicly their newly obtained legal status as *acteur*—as original owners, composers, and controllers of their works.

In many ways, the actions of Molinet, Lemaire, La Vigne, Bouchet, and Gringore set the stage for the next generation of writers, in particular for Clément Marot, the first Renaissance heir to their legacy of protecting and defending authorial rights. As poet, translator, compiler, and editor, Marot, conscious of printers' unauthorized appropriation of texts, was able to seek protection against them, thanks to his predecessors. Like his forebears, Marot manipulated paratextual information for the benefit of his own image; his narrative presence matched his authorial position. But a new dynamic developed with the next generation of writers, because they obtained stronger support from the nobles associated with the court of Francis I, and because humanists, who were also active as authors, became printers. Increasingly, such cooperative publication ventures as the 1538 edition of Marot's *Œuvres*, printed by Etienne Dolet, came to characterize the relationship between publishers and authors.

Although critics have examined the continuation and, more often, the rejection of the literary tradition bequeathed by the *rhétoriqueurs*, no one has examined and defined the late-medieval French vernacular legacy of authorial protection and projection that so benefited Renaissance writers. This inheritance is one they never acknowledged, perhaps because it had already become institutionalized. I wish to call attention to this important but neglected contribution by late medieval literati.

AFTERWORD

on July 31, 1538, the first edition of Clément Marot's *Œuvres* was published in Lyons by Etienne Dolet under the author's supervision. It was not his first publication, but according to Marot's own claim, it was the best edition of his works to date.[1] Although Marot's literary indebtedness to his predecessors has been duly recognized,[2] their persistent defense of vernacular authorship was an equally important influence on this first major poet of the French Renaissance, one that has not yet been acknowledged. Certainly an examination of the paratext of the 1538 *Œuvres* confirms Marot's debt to La Vigne, Bouchet, Lemaire, and Gringore.

Because certain publishers continued to challenge writers for control of their works during the third and fourth decades of the sixteenth century, Marot shared, and indeed profited from, his predecessors' concern for protecting authors against the careless and often unauthorized propagation of their words. Indeed, it was a concern that led to his own direct involvement in the book industry; he, too, railed against the profits publishers reaped at the expense of writers. But whereas La Vigne's 1504

1. Many of Marot's writings had appeared in print earlier, some with his authorization, such as Pierre and the Widow Roffet's editions of his *Adolescence clémentine* of 1532–36. Others were printed without the author's sanction. For details see Mayer, 2:11–35. Defaux's edition of Marot's *Œuvres* is based on Dolet's 1538 edition. All citations of Marot will be from Volume 1 of Defaux's edition, unless otherwise noted.

2. In his *De Monsieur le Général Guillaume Preudhomme*, Marot pays homage to Molinet, Chastellain, Chartier, Octavien de Saint-Gelais, Cretin, the two Grébans, and Lemaire (Defaux ed., 1:xxvi). The direct influence of Lemaire on Marot can be traced to their 1512 meeting at the court of Anne of Brittany. In a letter that prefaces his *Adolescence clémentine*, Marot praises Lemaire, who had taught him the importance of "Couppes feminines" (18). The poet may have met Gringore too, since both had ties with the Enfants Sans Souci, and perhaps with the Basoche, at around the same time.

lawsuit against Le Noir had set a remarkable precedent, in that no established tradition of authorial protection previously existed on which to base his dramatic challenge, Marot could rely on an important outcome of La Vigne's actions: namely, the increasingly standardized use of author-privileges, which had come to provide protection for a longer period of time. Marot had inherited this new state of mind about authorship and its inherent rights.

This state of mind, in fact, may have contributed to the formulation of one of the most recognizable hallmarks of Marot's work, the direct expression of his "moi." For Marot's poetry became the privileged, if not unique, site of the inscription and expression of his voice (Defaux ed., 1:c). It is not a coincidence that the form through which Marot best succeeded in expressing his personal lyricism, the *épître*, served also as a vehicle for his self-defense. Like that of his precursors, Marot's self-assertive and defensive posture was related in large measure to the unauthorized production of his writings.

Yet the stakes and atmosphere were decidedly different. For example, Marot enjoyed a closer, more compatible relationship with his publisher, who represented a new generation of humanist printers who had an innate interest and personal involvement in textual production, for they were authors themselves. Other forces motivated Marot in his dealings with publishers. While his father, Jean Marot, as secretary-poet at the French court, had chosen not to put his words into print, Clément was obliged to involve himself in the book industry—as much to protect his life as to preserve the integrity of his works.[3] For the unsupervised publication and circulation of certain of his potentially heretical writings, such as *L'enfer*, were a very real threat to his person.[4]

These old and new dynamics are in evidence on the title page of Dolet's edition of Marot's *Œuvres*, and in other parts of the paratext, which includes the publisher's exhortation to the author's book and Marot's letter to Dolet. These are followed by the prefatory material of the first part of the volume, the *Adolescence clémentine*, material that had appeared in earlier editions supervised by Marot: Nicolas Bourbon's and Nicolas Bérault's Latin epigrams, Marot's verses to his book and to an

---

3. Clément's father did not participate in his literary contemporaries' defense of their rights against printers, in part because of his stable court position (see pp. 43–45 above). Although Clément's status as court poet was secured upon the death of his father in 1528, albeit not without some aggressiveness on the author's part, the religious difficulties that he encountered, which forced him to flee France in 1534, resulted in a somewhat more precarious situation than that of his father. Clément, though, did resume his duties on his return, even obtaining two years' back wages.

4. Etienne Dolet was burned at the stake in 1546 for having published, among other works, Marot's *Pseaumes* and *L'enfer*.

unknown female dedicatee, and the author's letter to his fellow poet-readers.[5] Anticipated already by the developing paratextual space of his predecessors' publications, this accumulation of prefatory material reflects the increasingly defensive strategy adopted by authors and certain publishers in a seemingly new cooperative effort to secure the protection and marketability of literary works. The anonymous reader, whom the author and his sponsors or authorizers address time and again as directly and intimately as they would a patron, was coming to enjoy a more noticeable presence in book production, as purchasing capabilities translated into greater economic power.[6]

By this time, the name of the author had assumed a secure position on title pages. This was especially true in the case of Marot who, as the king's valet for the previous ten years, had become a very popular figure.[7] In fact, he had acquired such a reputation that, in order to attract as many book purchasers as possible, the title page of the Dolet edition conspicuously announced the inclusion of some of his previously unpublished works. Marot's role as editor and reviewer of his collected works likewise served to authorize this publication, as the prominent notice on the title page indicates:[8] "Les Oeuvres de Clement Marot de Cahors, valet de chambre du Roy. Augmentées de deux Livres d'Epigrammes, Et d'ung grand nombre d'aultres Oeuvres par cy devant non imprimées. Le tout songneusement par luy mesmes reveu, & mieulx ordonné" (Mayer, 2:35). (The *Works* of Clément Marot of Cahors, valet to the king. Augmented by two books of epigrams, and a great number of other works not heretofore printed. The entire [volume] carefully reviewed by himself and better organized).

5. The second part of the publication, entitled *La suite de l'adolescence*, is similarly prefaced by Salmon Macrin's Latin poem (with translation) addressed to the reader and by Latin verses in praise of Clément, between which is inserted Nicolas Bourbon's short Latin poem. For details, see Defaux ed., 1:205–6, 607–8.

6. See Marot's letter to Dolet, in which he also addresses his reader (9–11); Nicolas Bourbon's poem *Ad Lectorem*, which prefaces the *Adolescence clémentine* (12); Bérault's Latin epithet (16); and Marot's entreaty to his fellow poets (17–18).

7. The 1532 edition of Marot's *Adolescence clémentine*, which aimed at curtailing the numbers of unauthorized versions of his works, proved to be a monumental success for booksellers and publishers (Defaux ed., 1:x–xi, xxxv, cxviii).

8. These claims echo those made in the authorized editions of Marot's *Adolescence:* that the author had played a role in the correction of the edition and that additional works of his were available. The title page of the first edition, printed by Geoffroy Tory for Pierre Roffet in 1532, features the following information: "Le tout reveu, corrigé et mis en bon ordre" (The entire volume reviewed, corrected, and well ordered) (Mayer, 2:13). Roffet's editions of November 13, 1532, and February 12, 1533, added the following title-page announcement: "Plus amples que les premiers imprimez de ceste, ny autre impression" (More substantial than the first imprints of this or any other printing) (Mayer, 2:14). For further details, see Tchémerzine, 7:474–75).

Thus, the author's involvement in the final arrangement and correction of his edition had become a new way to validate his work.[9] Not only was it in the interest of the publisher to obtain the author's complicity in the publication enterprise; he also profited by advertising that fact. Marot himself reveals the importance of his participation in such activities in his letter to Dolet, which speaks as well to "vous aultres Lecteurs debonnaires" (10–11) (you other gentle readers): "de tous les Livres, qui par cy devant ont esté imprimez soubz mon nom, j'advoue ceulx cy pour les meilleurs, plus amples, et mieulx ordonnez. Et desadvoue les autres, comme Bastardz, ou comme Enfans gastez" (11) (of all the books that have heretofore been printed under my name, I claim that these here are the best, most complete, and best arranged. And I disavow the others, as bastards or spoiled children). In his effort to control the form in which subsequent printers and booksellers would gain access to his works, he enlists the aid of his publisher and friend:

> Si te prie de tout mon cueur y vouloir vacquer en Amy, m'aydant à garder diligemment les Imprimeurs, et Libraires, que desormais ilz n'y adjoustent rien sans m'en advertir. . . . Car si j'ay aulcunes Œuvres à mettre en lumiere, elles tumberont assez à temps en leurs Mains, non ainsi par pieces comme ilz les recueillent ça et là, mais en belle forme de Livre. (10)

> And so I beg you with all my heart, please, as a good friend, to attend to helping me diligently prevent printers and booksellers from ever adding something without warning me of it. . . . For if I have works to publish, they will in due time fall into their hands, not however in pieces collected here and there, but in the beautiful form of a book.

It would be ten years later, one might presume (for his privilege was then due to expire), that Marot would lose control over the *Œuvres*. Yet, even though the length of time that could now be obtained for protection of a work had significantly increased since La Vigne's 1504 lawsuit, evidence suggests that some printers, particularly those in a different city from the one in which a privilege originated, did not respect its author-

9. Marot spells out the nature of his editorial activities in his letter to Dolet: elimination of all those works not penned by himself; a twelvefold increase in the number of his previously unpublished works, including a book of epigrams; a better organization of the material; and the correction of some thousand previous printing errors (10). In Marot's address to his book, preceding the *Adolescence clémentine*, the author raises similar issues (15).

ity. For example, the Roffet editions of Marot's *Adolescence clémentine*, published in Paris beginning in 1532, were supposedly protected by a privilege for the period of three years. Nonetheless, François Juste printed unauthorized versions of that work in Lyons in February 1533, July 1533, December 1534, and February 1535. And, despite the three-year privilege protecting the widow Roffet's Paris publication of Marot's *La suite* at the end of 1533 or beginning of 1534, the Lyons bookseller Guillaume Boulle was able to obtain a privilege for his own edition of the *Suite*, which he printed in 1534 along with other works that were not Marot's. The poet's comments in the passage quoted above and the title-page announcements of authorized editions of the *Adolescence*, in fact, confirm that the author was well aware of this situation.[10] Thus, because privileges did not provide fail-safe protection, especially in cities other than the one of the original privilege, authors had to rely on honest publishers. Marot turned to a fellow intellectual, who was doubtless more versed in textual production than he was.

That publisher, Etienne Dolet, whose name appears on the title page of the *Œuvres* along with the author's, played an important role in the new dynamics of the book trade. His charming six-verse Latin poem of encouragement, praise, and friendship, addressed to Marot's book (6), and the author's respectful letter to him (9–11) not only provide evidence of the amicable interaction that could characterize the relationship between publisher and author, but reveal as well the fact that the advertisement of this mutual support and admiration could enhance the marketability of a volume. Of course, as Marot's letter suggests, all printers were not so favorably judged as his "cher Amy Dolet" (9) (dear friend Dolet), whose great admiration for Marot and his writings was legendary (Defaux ed., 1:cliii). For his part, Marot publicizes his great friendship and respect for the "docte Dolet" (10) (learned Dolet), who is praised for his "scavoir" (knowledge).

This more or less positive experience aside,[11] it is the impropriety and lack of scruples on the part of certain printers and publishers that served as the explicit or implicit theme of nearly all the paratextual material of the *Œuvres*. Marot opened his letter to Dolet with an attack on the out-

10. The title page of the authorized 1536 edition of the *Adolescence clémentine* underscored for the first time the evasion of privilege dictates by printers and booksellers outside Paris, in this case Lyons: "contrefaictes tant a Paris que a Lion. . . . Et sont toutes aultres faulces & erronicques contrefaictes & sans adveu" (pirated both in Paris and in Lyons. . . . And all others are false and erroneous, pirated and without approval) (Mayer, 2:25).

11. As it turned out, a mysterious rift developed between Dolet and Marot at the time the *Œuvres* were to be printed, and Marot apparently authorized Gryphius to publish the book shortly thereafter (Defaux ed., 1:clii–cliii).

rageous wrong done to him and the dishonor and personal danger caused by those who had carelessly and inappropriately published his works:

> [C]ar par avare couvoitise de vendre plus cher . . . ont adjousté à icelles miennes Œuvres plusieurs aultres, qui ne me sont rien: dont les unes sont froidement, et de maulvaise grâce composées, mettant sur moy l'ignorance d'aultruy: et les aultres toutes pleines de scandale, et sedition. (9)

> For, out of avaricious desire to sell at a higher price . . . they have added to my works several others that are not mine: some of which are coldly and gracelessly written, attributing to me another's lack of skill, while others are completely scandalous and seditious.

Marot complained here of the same injustices that Bouchet had earlier decried in his confrontation with Vérard: namely, the unauthorized addition of others' words to his. Unlike his predecessor, though, the more trusting Marot had actually furnished publishers with copies of his work.

These attacks echo concerns Marot had voiced in a 1530 letter, which had figured in his *Adolescence clémentine* edition and reappeared in his 1538 *Œuvres*.[12] They also reformulate at greater length the title-page announcements of the authorized *Adolescence* publications. In the 1534 edition of the latter, Marot publicly disavowed works falsely attributed to him, legitimizing his complaint through his legal procurement of a privilege: "Et ne sont en ce present livre autres meschantes œuvres mal composees, que on impose estres dudict acteur, les quelles il reprouve & desadvoue, comme il appert par le privilge par luy obtenu pour ceste presente impression" (And this present book does not contain any other unworthy, badly written works, which have been imputed to the said author, which he condemns and disavows, as is manifest by the privilege obtained by him for this present printing) (Mayer, 2:17).

Marot's increasing stress can be measured by the more strongly worded condemnation of the 1535 edition of the *Adolescence*. The adoption of the word "contrefaicte" here may be one of the earliest uses in print of an expression that essentially meant "pirated":

12. See the opening lines of this letter, in which Marot refers to "le desplaisir, que j'ay eu d'en ouir crier, et publier par les Rues une grande partie toute incorrecte, mal imprimée, et plus au proffit du Libraire, qu'à l'honneur de l'Autheur" (17) (the displeasure that I felt on hearing a great part [of my works] advertised and publicized in the streets in an incorrect form, poorly printed, and more profitable for the bookseller than honorable for the author).

Revues & corrigées selon sa dernière recognoissance oultre toutes autres impressions contrefaictes auxquelles a son grant deshonneur ont este adjoustees aulcunes oeuvres scandaleuses mal composees & incorrectes desquelles craignant yceluy non seullement le blasme de chose mal faicte, aussy le grant dommage qui luy pourroit venir a cause desdictes oeuvres scandaleuses apres avoir desavoué lesdictes oeuvres a obtenu privilege oultre les troys ans premiers deux aultres ans qui sont cinq ans, commencant a la datte de la premiere impression . . . Avec privilege pour cinq ans. (Mayer, 2:24)

Reviewed and corrected according to his last appraisal, omitting all other pirated editions to which have been added, to his great dishonor, other scandalous, poorly written, and incorrect works, of which he fears not only the blame for a badly done thing but also the great damage that could come to him because of these scandalous works; after having disavowed these said works, he obtained a privilege for two years beyond the first three years, which makes five years, beginning with the date of the first edition . . . with a five-year privilege.

Such announcements confirm that the title page had become the site of the direct and public prosecution of unscrupulous book producers, whose activities were not being controlled by the state. It was the author who had to continue waging the battle for his rights, his readers becoming the jury.

Marot's anxieties take on even greater significance in the ever more dangerous climate in which his outspoken religious opinions were being aired. In his *épître* to Dolet that prefaces the *Œuvres* of 1528, Marot develops these points in the form he had done so much to popularize. Calling into question the profits publishers gained from his labors, the poet reiterates his disturbance at the wrongful attribution of mediocre works to himself and to others: "J'ay planté les Arbres, ils en cueillent lers fruictz. J'ay trayné la Charrue, ilz enserrent la moisson: et à moy n'en revient qu'un peu d'estime entre les hommes: lequel encor ilz me veulent estaindre, m'attribuant Œuvres sottes, et scandaleuses" (9) (I have planted the trees, they pick the fruits. I have dragged the plow, they hoard the harvest; and I receive only a little esteem among men which, to make matters worse, they want to extinguish by attributing to me foolish and scandalous works). It is not only that the pedestrian writings of others have been imputed to Marot. Just as troubling to Marot is the fact that he has been made an unwilling "usurpateur de l'honneur d'aultury" (usurper of another's honor); for the works of other, excellent poets have also been wrongfully ascribed to him. Marot's strong moral

sense of propriety and literary property, which may have been significantly shaped through his role as a critical editor of the *Roman de la rose*
(1526), the works of Villon (1533), and those of his father (1534), are
underscored in this important letter.

Marot's public call here for the rightful designation of authorship by
printers and publishers marks another singular moment in the struggle
for authorial recognition that was initiated by late-medieval French vernacular writers, beginning with La Vigne and Bouchet. Although Marot
did not make his stand in a court of law, his airing of the issue in the paratext of his *Adolescence* and *Œuvres* forced the public, his readers, to bear
witness to the injustices of the capitalistic world of book production and
to take to task the unscrupulous actors in this affair. Although writers
were still a long way from obtaining full legal protection in the publication enterprise, the seeds of authorial rights had been planted. Marot
had begun to reap some of the benefits of their fruits and, in turn, to sow
yet more seeds for future generations. Through his efforts, what had
been a struggle was growing into a battle, one that had been moved to
the title page of his publications and one that, in the expanding use of
prefatory letters and other paratextual material, had come to engage the
reader directly.

{ APPENDIX 1 }

DOCUMENTATION OF
ANDRÉ DE LA VIGNE'S 1504 LAWSUIT
AND BIBLIOGRAPHICAL DATA

Documents concerning André de la Vigne's lawsuit against Michel Le Noir in April–June 1504:

Entre Maistre André de la Vigne, escolier estudiant en l'université de Paris, demandeur et requerant l'enterrinement de certaine requeste par luy baillé à la Court le dernier jour d'avril dernier passé. Et en ce faisant que pour recouvrer certaines attestations et autres pieces pour produire ou procés pendant en ladite Court entre ledit demandeur et Michel Le Noir, delay luy fut donné de quinzaine, pendant lequel delay peut faire interroguer plusieurs tesmoings pour monstrer et faire apparoir du contenu en sadite requeste d'une part, et le dit Michel Le Noir, imprimeur de livres a Paris, defendeur sur l'enterrinement de ladite requeste et requerant que permission luy fust faicte de parachever les livres par luy commencez a imprimer non obstant certaines defenses a lui faictes a la requeste dudit De La Vigne, d'autrepart, veu par la Court ladite requeste, l'acte accordé des dites parties et tout ce qu'elles ont mis et produit par devers certain commissaire de ladite Court commis a les oÿr ou son rapport. Et tout consideré, il sera dit que ladite court a donné et donne audit demandeur ledit delay de quinzaine pour produire tout ce que bon luy semblera audit procés pendant en ladite Court, entre lesdites parties, pour tous delays, pendant lequel delay icelle court a permis et permit audit Le Noir, defendeur, de parachever d'imprimer lesdits livres ja par luy commancés, sy achevés ne sont, en luy defendant l'alienation et vendition d'iceulx livres jusques a ce que par ladite Court autrement en ait esté ordonné, les despens de ceste instance reservee en definitive. (Archives Nationales, Conseil 1509 [12 novembre 1503–7 novembre 1504], le 11 mai [1504], fols. 154–154^v)

Entre Michel Le Noir, libraire et imprimeur demourant en ceste ville de Paris, demandeur et requerant l'enterrinement de certaine requeste par luy baillée a la Court le second jour d'avril dernier passé, d'une part, et André de la Vigne, escolier en l'Université de Paris, defendeur d'autre, veu par la Court le plaidoyer fait en icelle le xxvie jour d'avril dernier passé et tout ce que lesdites parties ont mis et produict par devers ladite Court et tout consideré: Il sera dit que ladicte Court a debouté et deboute ledit demandeur de l'enterrinement de sadite requeste et fait defenses audit demandeur et a tous autres libraires et imprimeurs de ceste ville de Paris, autres que ledit defendeur, de ne faire imprimer ne vendre les livres appellez le Vergier de honneur et les Regnars traversans, jusques au premier jour d'avril prochain venant, et ce sur peine d'amende arbitraire et confiscacion desdits livres; et si condamne la Court ledit demandeur es despens de ceste instance, la tauxacion d'iceulx reservee par devers elle. (Archives Nationales, Conseil 1509, le 3 juin [1504], fol. 171)

The dates referred to in the second document are at odds with those of the first document. The references here to "the second of April" as the day Le Noir filed a suit against La Vigne and to "April 26" as the date of the trial itself should probably read "the second of *May*" and "*May* 26." The earlier document, dated May 11, 1504, states that La Vigne had filed his lawsuit on April 30 and that the decision to honor both his requested two-week delay to obtain evidence for the *upcoming* trial and Le Noir's request to continue printing the works in question was made on May 11. The trial date of May 26 would have fallen about two weeks after that preliminary decision and just ten days before the official entry was made (June 3, 1504).

Extant versions of André de la Vigne's *Ressource de la Chrestienté*, published as part of the *Vergier d'honneur* from 1502–3 on (see nos. 4–9), with specific references to those copies examined:

1. Paris, B.N., ms. f.fr. 1687 [1494].
2. Paris, B.N., ms. f.fr. 1699 [1494–95].
3. [Angoulême: André Cauvin and Pierre Alain, ca. 1495] (Aix-en-Provence, Bibl. Méjanes, D.14–15; Paris, B.N., Rés. 4° Lb²⁸ 15E [fragment]).
4. [Paris: Pierre Le Dru, ca. 1502–3], fols. 2ʳ–12ʳ (Paris, B.N., Rés. 4° Lb²⁸ 15α; B.N., Rés. 4° Lb²⁸ 15 [incomplete]; Baltimore: Walter's Art Gallery, Stillwell V128).
5. [Paris: Pierre Le Dru, post 1504], fols. 2ʳ–14ᵛ (Paris, B.N., Rés. 4° Lb²⁸ 15A; B.N., Rés. Vélins 2241; Lyons, Bibl. Mun., Incunable 301; Oxford, Bodleian Douce 0168; New Haven, Yale University, Beinecke Library Zi. 8320.5).
6. Paris: Jean Trepperel, [1606–9], fols. 1ᵛ–12ʳ (Paris, B.N., Rés. 4° Lb²⁸ 15B; Chantilly, Musée Condé, 1741; Versailles, Bibl. Mun., Incunable M 44; Aix-en-Provence, Bibl. Méjanes, Rés. o.45; Washington, D.C., Library of Congress, Rosenwald Collection 456, Incunable X.S135).
7. Paris: for Jean Petit [and Jean Frellon, ca. 1512], fols. 2ʳ–12ʳ (Paris, B.N., Rés. 4° Lb²⁸ 15D; Paris, Bibl. Mazarine, Inc., 1200; Paris, Bibl. de l'Arsenal, Rés. Fol. H 1742; Madrid, Biblioteca Nacional, Inc. 1431; Cambridge, Harvard University, Houghton Library, FC. Sa 233.500.VC; Liège, Bibl. de l'Université, XVᵉ B 89 [incomplete]).

8. Paris: Philippe Le Noir for himself and for Jean Jehannot [Edition shared with Jean Petit? ca. 1521–22], fols. 2^r–10^v (Paris, B.N., Cat. Rothschild 479; B.N., Rés. Smith-Lesouëf 149; Paris, Bibl. Mazarine, Rés. 5887B; Lyons, Bibl. Mun., Incunable 609; London, B.L., Cottonian 107.e.1; The Hague, Rijksmuseum Meermanno-Westreenianum, 6 B29).

9. Paris: [Philippe Le Noir, ca. 1525], fols. 2^r–10^v (Paris, B.N., Rés. K.70 [2]; B.N., Rés. 4° Lb^{28} 15C [incomplete]; Paris, Bibl. Mazarine, Incunable 1199; London, B.L., Cottonian 8.i.II.

10. Montreal: CERES, 1989 (ed. Cynthia J. Brown).

{ APPENDIX 2 }

BIBLIOGRAPHICAL DATA
FOR JEAN LEMAIRE DE BELGES

Extant editions of Jean Lemaire's *Temple d'honneur et de vertus*, with specific references to those copies examined:

    1. [Paris: Antoine Vérard, 1504] (Bern, Bibl. de la Ville, Inc. III, 112).

    2. Paris: Michel Le Noir, 6 April 1504 (Paris, B.N., Rés. Ye 846); one printing of this edition bears no date (B.N., Rés., Ye 219).

    3. [Paris: Philippe Le Noir, ca. 1520] (Paris, B.N., Rés. Ye 859; Washington, D.C., Library of Congress, PQ 1628.L5A75).

    4. Paris: Alain Lotrian and Denys Janot, n.d. [1535] (London, B.L., C.39.b.14).

    5. Louvain: Lefevre, 1891, in *Œuvres*, 4:183–242 (ed. J. Stecher).

    6. Geneva: Droz, 1957 (ed. Henry Hornik).

Extant editions of Jean Lemaire's *Légende des Vénitiens*, with specific references to those copies examined:

    1. Lyons: Jean de Vingle, 1509 (Paris, B.N., Rés. Lb^{29} 27; London, B.L., C.32.a.10).

    2. Paris: Geoffroy de Marnef, [1512] (Paris, B.N., Rés. La^2 3 (1); B.N., Rés. La^2 4 [5]; London, B.L., 492.i.1 [2]).

    3. Paris: G. de Marnef, [1512] (Paris, B.N., Rés. La^2 3A [1]; B.N., Rés. 3Aa).

    4. Paris: G. de Marnef, [1516] (Paris, B.N., Rés. La^2 5 [6]).

    5. Louvain: Lefevre, 1885, in *Œuvres*, 3:361–409 (ed. J. Stecher).

{ APPENDIX 3 }

BIBLIOGRAPHICAL DATA
FOR JEAN BOUCHET

Extant editions of Jean Bouchet's *Regnars traversant*, with specific references to those copies examined:

1. Paris: for Antoine Vérard, [inter September 1503 and May 1504] (Paris, B.N., Rés. Yh 7).
2. Paris: for Antoine Vérard, [n.d.] (Paris, B.N., Vélins 1103; B.N., Rés. 8° Z.Don.594 [321]).
3. Paris: Michel Le Noir, 21 May 1504 (Paris, B.N., Rés. Yh 61; Washington, D.C., Library of Congress, Rosenwald Collection 919).
4. Paris: Philippe Le Noir, 23 July 1522 (Paris, Bibl. de l'Arsenal, 4° BL 2146; Paris, Bibl. de Sainte Geneviève, 4° Y426²⁵ [589 Rés.]).
5. Paris: Philippe Le Noir for Denis Janot, 25 January 1530 (Paris, B.N. Rés. Yh 60).

For further details, see Britnell, 305–6.

Verses forming Bouchet's acrostic signature; located on folio fii^v of Vérard's circa 1504 edition of the *Regnars traversant*, they spell out IEHAN BOVCHET NATJF DE POICTIERS (see Figure 1.2):

Exhortacion ou par les premieres lectres des lignes trouverez le nom de l'acteur de ce present livre et le lieu de sa nativite:

> Incensez folz qui Dieu mescongnoissez
> Et en ses faitz ne pensez nullement,
> Helas! temps est que vous recongnoissez
> Avoir peché contre luy grandement.
> Ne voyez vous qu'il fait amerement
>
> Bransler sur vous de sa fureur vengence?
> O aveuglez! vous pouez clerement
> Voir maintenant qu'il nous veult promptement

Constituer en mortel indigence.
Honte n'avez de vostre negligence,
Et de bien faire ne semblez curieux:
Traistres estes a la Haulte Regence.

N'en doubtez point et aux saintz glorieux
A bien parler semblez gens furieux,
Tous promptz et prestz de guerroyer les cieulx;
Je le congnois a l'oeil sans en enquerre:
Faulz Chrestiens voz faitz tant vicieux,

De peste et mort sont cause et conscieux
Et de famine et de mortelle guerre.

Pour quoy doncques sans autres signes querre
On ne s'amende? Ou pensez vous humains?
Ignorez vous que le ciel et la terre
Contre vous soyent pour voz maulx inhumains?
Tendez les bras chascun, joingne les mains
Incessamment cryant misericorde,
Et delaissez les maulx dont estes taintz,
Rem[em]orant les faitz de Dieu haultains,
Si avec Luy avoir concorde.

{ APPENDIX 4 }

BIBLIOGRAPHICAL DATA
FOR JEAN MOLINET

Extant manuscripts and editions of Jean Molinet's *Temple de Mars*, with specific references to those copies examined (the manuscript preceded by an asterisk has not been studied):

1. Paris, B.N., ms. f.fr. 1642 [15th c.], fols. 456^r–460^v.
2. Paris, Bibl. de l'Arsenal, ms. 3521 [15th c.], fols. 288^r–292^v.
3. Brussels, Bibl. Royale, ms. II. 2545 (1476), fols. 275^r–280^v.
4. Tournai, Bibl. Communale, ms. 105 [early 16th c.], fols. 119^v–126^r.
5. Paris, B.N., ms. f.fr. 1717 [16th c.], fols. 70^v–76^v.
6. Paris, B.N., ms. f.fr. 12490 [16th c.], fols. 148^r–154^v.
7. Paris, B.N., ms. nouv. acq., f.fr. 10262 [16th c.], fols. 194^r–201^v.
8. [Flanders or Lowlands, ca. 1476] (Chantilly, Musée Condé, IV.G.15).
9. Paris: Le Petit Laurens, [ca. 1491] (New York, Pierpont Morgan Library, PML 75124).
10. Paris: Jean Trepperel, [ca. 1497–98] (Paris, B.N., Rés. Ye 1127, Cat. Rothschild 473).
11. Lyons: [Jean de Vingle], 18 December 1502 (Paris, B.N., Cat. Rothschild 2580).
12. [Paris: Michel Le Noir, inter 1501 and 1505] (Paris, B.N., Rés. Ye 220).
13. [Paris]: Jean Trepperel, [inter 1506 and 1509] (Paris, B.N., Rés. Ye 273).
*14. Arras, Bibl. Mun., ms. 692 [ca. 1520], fols. 157^v–162^r.
15. Paris: [ca. 1520] (Paris, B.N., Rés. Ye 1282; Tournai, Bibl. Mun., 11632).
16. Paris: [Alain Lotrian, ca. 1520] (Paris, B.N., Rés. Y² 2579).
17. Paris [Alain Lotrian, ca. 1520] (Paris, Bibl. de l'Ecole Nationale Supérieure des Beaux-Arts, Rés. Masson 469).
18. Paris, Anthoine Couteau for Galliot Du Pré, 8 February 1526 N.S., in *Traictez singuliers* (Paris, B.N., Cat. Rothschild 487).
19. Paris, Jean Longis, 1531, in *Les faictz et dictz*, fols. 61^v–64^r (Paris, B.N., Rés. Ye 41 and Ye 42).
20. Paris, Jean Longis, 1537, in *Les faictz et dictz* (Paris, B.N., Rés. Ye 1339).
21. Paris, Alain Lotrian, 1540, in *Les faictz et dictz* (Paris, B.N., Rés. Ye 1340).

22. Paris: Lefrançois, 1923 ("Le Temple de Mars par Jehan Molinet, vers 1476," ed. Emile Picot and Henri Stein).

23. Paris: Société des Anciens Textes Français, 1936, *Les faictz et dictz*, 1:65–76 (ed. Noël Dupire).

For further details, see Picot and Stein.

Extant manuscripts and editions of Jean Molinet's *Art de rhétorique*, with specific references to those copies examined:

1. Paris, B.N., ms. f.fr. 2159 [15th c.], 32 fols.
2. Paris, B.N., ms. f.fr. 2375 (5), fols. 14–38 [16th c.].
3. Paris: Vérard, 10 May 1493 (Paris, B.N., Rés. Ye 10; Rés. Vélins 577; Paris, Bibl. Mazarine, Inc. 708A; London, B.L., IB.41139).
4. Paris: Trepperel, 9 May 1499 (Chantilly, Musée Condée, IV.E.68).
5. Paris: Trepperel, n.d. [ca. 1505] (Cambridge, Harvard University, Houghton Library, *FC.C8865.493ac).
6. Toulouse: Guerlines, n.d. [ca. 1513?] (Paris, B.N., Rés. Ye 1201).
7. Paris: [Trepperel, n.d. (ca. 1515?)] (London, B.L., 87.b.18.[2]).
8. Paris: [n.p., n.d. (ca. 1520)] (Paris, B.N., Cat. Rothschild 2795).
9. Paris: [n.p., n.d.] (Aix-en-Provence, Bibl. Méjanes, Rés. 040 [1]).
10. Poitiers: [Marnef, ca. 1550].
11. Paris: Imprimerie Nationale, 1902, in *Recueil d'Arts de seconde rhétorique*, 214–52 (ed. Ernest Langlois).

Extant manuscripts and editions of Jean Molinet's *Roman de la rose moralisé*, with specific references to those copies examined:

1. The Hague, Koninklijke Bibliotheek, ms. 128 C5 [1500].
2. Paris, B.N., ms. f.fr. 24393 [30 April 1500].
3. Paris: Antoine Vérard [ca. 1500] (Paris, B.N., Cat. Rothschild 438; Rés. Vélins 1101; Rés. Vélins 1102; London, B.L., C.22.C.2).
4. Lyons: Guillaume Balsarin, 1503 (Paris, B.N., Rés. Ye 167; Rés. Ye 23; Paris, Bibl. de Sainte Geneviève, Y fol. 140⁸ inv. 198 Rés.; Chantilly, Musée Condée, 1718 VI.A.32); Washington, D.C., Library of Congress, Rosenwald Collection 917.
5. Paris: Michel Le Noir's widow, 17 August 1521 (Paris, B.N., Rés. Ye 16; Rés. Ye 17; Paris, Bibl. de l'Arsenal, 4° BL 2841 Rés.; Chantilly, Musée Condé, XVI.B).

Extant editions of Jean Molinet's *Naissance de Charles d'Autriche*, with specific references to those copies examined:

1. Valenciennes: Jean de Liège for Jean Molinet, [post 7 March 1500] (Paris, B.N., Rés. Ye 1077).
2. [Lyons: Guillaume Balsarin, ca. 1503] (Paris, B.N., Rés. Ye 221).

3. Paris: Jean Longis, 1531, in *Les faictz et dictz*, fols. 81^v–83^r (Paris, B.N., Rés. Ye 41 and Ye 42).

4. Paris: Jean Longis, 1537, in *Les faictz et dictz* (Paris, B.N., Rés. Ye 1339).

5. Paris: Alain Lotrian, 1540, in *Les faictz et dictz* (Paris, B.N., Rés. Ye 1340).

6. Paris: Société des Anciens Textes Français, 1936, *Les faictz et dictz*, 1:352–58 (ed. Noël Dupire).

Extant manuscripts and editions of the *Trosne d'honneur*:

1. Brussels, Bibl. Royale, ms. II.2604 (end 15th c.), 16 fols.

2. Paris, B.N., ms. nouv. acq. f.fr. 21532 (end 15th c.), 12 fols.

3. Brussels, Bibl. Royale, ms. 21521–21531 (15th c.), fols. 202^r–207^v.

4. Tournai, Bibl. Communale, ms. 105, fols. 70^r–80^r (early 16th c.).

5. Arras, Bibl. Mun., ms. 692 (ca. 1520), fols. 25^r–33^v.

6. Paris, B.N., Cat. Rothschild 471 (ca. 1526), fols. 49^r–56^v.

7. Paris, B.N., ms. f.fr. 12490 (16th c.), fols. 138^r–142^v (incomplete).

8. Paris: Jean Longis, 1531, in *Les faictz et dictz*, fols. 35^r–41^r (Paris, B.N., Rés. Ye 41 and 42).

9. Paris: Jean Longis, 1537, in *Les faictz et dictz* (Paris, B.N., Rés. Ye 1339).

10. Paris: Alain Lotrian, 1540, in *Les faictz et dictz* (Paris, B.N., Rés. Ye 1340).

11. Paris: Société des Anciens Textes Français, 1936, *Les faictz et dictz*, 1:36–58 (ed. Noël Dupire).

Extant manuscripts and modern edition of Jean Molinet's *Gaiges retrenchiés*:

1. Tournai, Bibl. Mun., ms. 105 (early 16th c.), fols. 67^r–68^v.

2. Bibliothèque James de Rothschild, ms. 471 (October 1526), fols. 2^v–3^r.

3. Paris: Société des Anciens Textes Français, 1937, *Les faictz et dictz*, 2:768–71 (ed. Noël Dupire).

For details, see Dupire, *Etude Critique*, 12, 37.

{ APPENDIX 5 }

BIBLIOGRAPHICAL DATA
FOR PIERRE GRINGORE

Extant French editions of Pierre Gringore's *Chasteau de labour*, with specific references to those copies examined (editions preceded by an asterisk have not been located or studied, but relevant references are provided; "Oulmont" refers to the bibliographies provided in Oulmont, *Pierre Gringore* for each of Gringore's works [29–66] and the following number refers to Oulmont's list of editions for each work):

1. Paris: Philippe Pigouchet for Simon Vostre, 22 October 1499 (Paris, Bibl. Mazarine, Inc. 1055).

*2. Paris: Philippe Pigouchet for Simon Vostre, 31 December 1499 (Cat. Fairfax-Murray 205; Brunet, 2:1742–43).

3. Paris: Philippe Pigouchet for Simon Vostre, 31 May 1500 (Paris, B.N., Rés. Ye 1330).

4. Rouen: Jacques Le Forestier, 5 November 1500 (Paris, B.N., Rés. Ye 301).

5. Paris: Philippe Pigouchet for Simon Vostre, 31 March 1501 N.S. (Paris, B.N., Rés. Ye 1331); Chantilly, Musée Condé, 851 VII.B.67; London, B.L., I.A. 40361).

6. [Paris: for Guillaume Le Rouge, post 1500] (Paris, B.N., Rés. Ye 4107 [fragment]).

7. Paris: Gaspard Philippe [and N. de la Barre?], n.d. [1502–March 1505] (Paris, Bibl. de l'Ecole Nationale Supérieure des Beaux-Arts, Rés. Masson 703³).

8. Paris: Gilles Couteau, n.d. [ca. 1505] (New York, Public Library, Spencer Collection, French 1505).

9. Paris: Jean Trepperel, n.d. [after 31 May 1504–1511] (Aix-en-Provence, Bibl. Méjanes, Rés. o.40; Washington, D.C., Library of Congress, Rosenwald Collection 946).

*10. Paris: Jean Trepperel, n.d. (Brunet, 2:1744; Tchémerzine, 6:35a; Oulmont, no. 8).

*11. Paris: Alain Lotrian, [ca. 1511] (Tchémerzine, 6:36a; Oulmont, no. 10).

*12. Lyons: Barnabé Chaussard, [ca. 1515] (Tchémerzine, 6:37a; Oulmont, no. 11; Brunet, 2:1744).

*13. Lyons: Claude Nourry, 1518 (Tchémerzine, 6:36b).

*14. Lyons: Claude Nourry, 1526 (Tchémerzine, 6:36c; Brunet, 2:1744; Oulmont, no. 12).

*15. Lyons: Claude Nourry, 1529 (Tchémerzine, 6:36d).

16. Paris: Antoine Augereau for Galliot Du Pré, 16 May 152 (Paris, B.N., Rés. Ye 1332; Cat. Rothschild 493; Chantilly, Musée Condé, 850, IV.D.34).

*17. Rouen: Pierre Mulot, n.d. [ca. 1560] (Dresden, Sächsische Landesbibliothek, no. 50971; Tchémerzine, 6:37c; Brunet, 2:1744; Oulmont, no. 14).

18. Edinburgh: Roxburghe Club, 1905 (ed. Alfred W. Pollard).

Much of the information about the English editions can be found in the introduction by Alfred W. Pollard to the facsimile edition of Wynkyn de Worde's 1506 edition of the *Castell of Labour*. Although Pollard, p. lii, claims that the edition preserved in the British Library Huth 29 version and a leaf fragment from the Bodleian are identical, a close examination reveals a number of significant differences:

1. [Paris: for Antoine Vérard, ca. 1503, trans. Alexander Barclay], one-leaf fragment (London, B.L., C.59.ff.4).

2. London: Richarde Pynson, [ca. 1505] (London, B.L., Huth 29).

3. London: Wynkyn de Worde, 1506 (London, B.L., C.101. f. 16).

4. [1506], fragments (Oxford, Bodleian, Douce Frag. e.9; New York, Public Library, microfilm *XKC 67-1260).

5. London: Richarde Pynson, [ca. 1510], fragment (London, B.L., C.125.dd.15[5]).

6. London: Wynkyn de Worde, [ca. 1510] (London, B.L., C.21.C.21).

7. Edinburgh: Roxburghe Club, 1905 (ed. Alfred W. Pollard).

Extant editions of Pierre Gringore's *Chasteau d'amours*, with specific references to those copies examined (the edition preceded by an asterisk has not been located, but relevant references are indicated):

1. Paris: Philippe Pigouchet for Simon Vostre, n.d. [before 20 December 1500] (Paris, B.N., Rés. Ye 1322).

2. Paris: Michel Le Noir, 20 December 1500 (Paris, B.N., Rés. Ye 1019).

3. Paris: Michel Le Noir, 4 February 1501 N.S. (London, B.L., IA.40470).

4. Paris: Jean Trepperel, n.d. [ca. 1500]. Partial edition (Paris, B.N., Rés. Ye 270).

5. Lyons: Françoys Juste, 1533 (Lyons, Bibl. Mun., Rés. 811 483).

*6. Paris: Thomas Brumen, 1565 (Tchémerzine, 6:40c).

7. Paris: Silvestre, 1830. Partial edition (Paris, B.N., Rés. Vélins 2248).

Extant French editions of Pierre Gringore's *Complainte de Trop Tard Marié*, with specific references to those copies examined (editions preceded by an asterisk have not been located, but relevant references are provided):

1. Paris: for Pierre Gringore, 1 October 1505 (Paris, B.N., Rés. Ye 1333).

*2. Chartres: n.p., n.d. [ca. 1520] (Tchémerzine, 6:45; Oulmont, no. 2; Cat. Fairfax-Murray 211; Brunet, 2:1755).

*3. Paris: Guillaume Nyverd, ca. 1525 (Chantilly, Musée Condé, IV.D.133; Tchémerzine, 6:45; Oulmont, no. 4).

4. Paris: for Pierre Sergent, n.d. [ca. 1535] (Paris, B.N., Cat. Rothschild 497).

*5. [Bordeaux: Jehan Guyart, ca. 1535] (Brunet 2:1755–56; Oulmont, no. 6; Tchémerzine, 6:46).

6. Paris: [Alain Lotrian], n.d. (Paris, Bibl. de l'Ecole Nationale Supérieure des Beaux-Arts, Rés. Masson 468).

7. Paris: Firmin Didot, 1825, in *Le débat de deux demoyselles, l'une nommée la Noyre, et l'autre la Tannee, suivi de La vie de Saint Harenc, et d'autres poésies du XVᵉ siècle, avec des notes et un glossaire*, 109–27.

I have been able to locate only a two-page fragment of the Wynkyn de Worde edition of Roberte Copland's translation of Gringore's *Complainte de Trop Tard Marié* (London, B.L., C.20.b.32 [1]). However, a nineteenth-century edition provides the entire text of the so-called *Complaynte of Them That Ben to Late Maryed*; see *Illustrations of Early English Popular Literature*, ed. J. Payne Collier (London, 1863; repr. New York: Benjamin Blom, 1966), 1:1–19, no. 8.

Extant editions of Pierre Gringore's *Folles entreprises*, with specific references to those copies examined (editions preceded by an asterisk have not been located, but relevant references are provided):

*1. Paris: Pierre Le Dru for Pierre Gringore, 23 December 1505 (Cat. Fairfax-Murray 206; Tchémerzine, 6:48).

2. Paris: Pierre Le Dru for Pierre Gringore, 23 December 1505 (Paris, B.N., Rés. Ye 1323; B.N., Vélins 2244; B.N., Vélins 2245; New York, Pierpont Morgan Library, 66273/N/7/E).

3. Paris: Pierre Le Dru for Pierre Gringore, 23 December 1505 (Paris, B.N., Rés. Ye 1321; Chantilly, Musée Condé, XVII.B).

4. Paris: Pierre Le Dru for Pierre Gringore, 23 December 1505 (Paris, Bibl. de l'Ecole Nationale Supérieure des Beaux-Arts [ENSBA], Res. Masson 428[1]).

5. Paris: [Widow? Trepperel, ca. 1506] (Paris, B.N., Cat. Rothschild 495).

6. Paris: [Widow Trepperel, ca. 1506] (Aix-en-Provence, Bibl. Méjanes, Rés. D.107).

*7. Paris: [Jean or Geoffroy de Marnef], 19 March 1507 N.S. [Tchémerzine, 6:53a (Jean); Oulmont, no. 3 (Geoffroy)].

8. Lyons: n.p., 19 October 1507 (Paris, Bibl. Mazarine, Inc. 44251).

*9. Paris: Le Dru, 19 October 1507 (Tchémerzine, 6:62b; Oulmont, no. 6).

10. Paris: [Marnef or Le Dru], 6 January 1508 N.S. (London, B.L., 241.g.43).

*11. [Paris: Marnef], 30 January 1508 N.S. (Tchémerzine, 6:62; Oulmont, no. 5).

12. Paris: [Trepperel (Lotrian?), 1510] (Paris, B.N., Rés. Ye 292; Paris, Bibl. de l'Arsenal, 8 B 10907 Rés.).

13. Paris: n.p. [ca. 1510] (Paris, B.N., Rés. Ye 288).

14. Paris: Jannet, 1858, in *Œuvres complètes*, 1:1–144 (ed. Héricault and Montaiglon).

Certain alterations in two issues of the 1505 *Folles entreprises*, B.N. Rés. Ye 1321 and ENSBA Rés. Masson 428[1] (those copies presumably sold by Gringore himself, since they bear his Mère Sotte bookseller mark), suggest that a different, more learned public was targeted for these versions. Marginal notes in Latin providing sources for Gringore's comments appear in these two issues and in all subsequent editions of the *Folles entreprises*. Other textual additions and alterations appear as well. On folio 13^{v} (b^{v}) of both of these versions, the following rondeau is inserted under the section entitled "L'entreprise de tresoriers et payeurs de gendarmes":

> Par trop haÿr ou aymer ardamment
> On fait souvent de justice injustice,
> On abat droit et met l'en jus police,
> Affin d'avoir pecune en maniement.
>
> On profere maint cruel jugement,
> Dont equité ne peult avoir notice
> Par trop haÿr.
>
> Aucuns y a qui jugent justement
> Et exercent prudamment leur office;
> Mais les autres ne craignent faire vice
> Quant aux justes donnent empeschement
> Par trop haÿr.

On folio 25^{r} (d^{r}) of B.N. Rés. Ye 1321 (this folio happens to be missing in the ENSBA copy), the following rondeau attacking preachers is inserted under the section entitled "Des pasteurs ambicieux et symoniaques." This addition reappears in all subsequent editions:

> L'acteur
> Pasteurs, entrez desormais par la porte,
> Ne cerchez plus la voye ou sente oblique.
> Soyez humble[s] affin que Dieu supporte
> Vos simples ouailles quant le serpent les picque.
>
> Entretenez parolles evangelique,
> Gardez d'entrer par les murs a main forte,
> Ne cerchez plus la voye ou sente oblique,
> Pasteurs, entrez desormais par la porte.

Se ne observez nostr[e] foy catholique,
Dedens enfer vous et vostre cohorte
Trebucherez. Le renard baselique
De Lucifer par art dyabolique
Vous tirera a soy d'estrange sorte.
Ne cerchez plus la voye ou sente oblique,
Pasteurs, entrez desormais par la porte.

On folio 54^r (g vi^r) of B.N. Rés. Ye 1321, one stanza differs dramatically from the one appearing in the other 1505 issues examined (B.N. Rés. Ye 1323, fols. g v–g v^v, and ENSBA Rés. Masson 428^1, fol. g vi^r) and in many subsequent editions. It is placed in a section entitled "De l'erreur Jacobite et Nicolaïte":

Lors s'esmeurent aucuns Nicolaïtes,
Qui voullurent foy destruire et combattre;
Puis survindrent un tas de Jacobites,
Qui estoient prestz encontre elle debatre.
Bien tost aprés pour toute erreur abatre
Furent commis aucuns Freres Prescheurs,
Discretz docteurs, qui furent empescheurs.
Que on ne oultragast foy nostre sauvegarde,
Pour confondre erroniques erreurs:
La foy, la loy, leur fut baillee en garde.

The version in the other issues and editions reads:

Lors s'esmeurent ung tas de Jacobites
Que au temps present Jacobins appelons
Par eulx furent plusieurs erreurs escriptes.
La survindrent aucuns Nicolaïtes
Voulans brouiller la foy comme brouillons.
Mais se par eulx une foys nous reglons,
A leurs erreurs serons equipollez,
Pro secundo et huetz appelez,
Qui blasmerent saincte Eglise romaine
Et soustenoient preschans a haulte alaine
Que sacremens falloit faire autrement.
Telz gens erreurs regit, conduit et maine
Entreprises font souvent follement.

It is difficult to know which was the "original" version and which was a later, altered version. The first passage cited maintains a more correct chronology with the presentation of the Nicolaitans (first century) preceding that of the Jacobites (sixth century). It also features the example of the Frères Prêcheurs, disciples of Saint Dominique (twelfth century), which the other passage does not mention. For further explanations, see Héricault and Montaiglon, eds., *Œuvres*, 1:128.

BIBLIOGRAPHY OF WORKS CITED

PRIMARY SOURCES

Manuscripts (see also Appendices 1–5)

Aylesbury, Waddesdon Manor, James A. de Rothschild Collection, Ms. Delaissé 22.
London, British Library [B.L.], Cottonian [Cot.] ms. Vespasian B.II.
Nantes, Bibliothèque Municipale, ms. 204.
Nantes, Bibliothèque Municipale, ms. 1337.
New York, Pierpont Morgan Library, ms. 42.
Paris, Bibliothèque de l'Arsenal, ms. 2940.
Paris, Bibliothèque Nationale [B.N.], ms. f.fr. 1690.
Paris, B.N., ms. f.fr. 2200.
Paris, B.N., ms. f.fr. 2248.
Paris, B.N., ms. f.fr. 2274.
Paris, B.N., ms. f.fr. 2336.
Paris, B.N., ms. f.fr. 15215.
Paris, B.N., ms. f.fr. 17511.
Paris, B.N., ms. f.fr. 20055.
Paris, B.N., ms. f.fr. 24332.
Paris, B.N., ms. nouv. acq., f.fr. 794.
Paris, B.N., ms. nouv. acq., f.fr. 4061.
Poitiers, Bibliothèque Municipale, ms. 440.
Soissons, Bibliothèque Municipale, ms. 204.

Printed Matter

Amerval, Eloi d'. *Le liure de la deablerie*. Paris: Michel Le Noir, 1508.
——. *Le liure de la deablerie*. Ed. Charles F. Ward. Iowa City: University of Iowa Press, 1923.
Bouchet, Jean. *La déploration de l'Eglise*. Paris: Guillaume Eustace, 1512.

——. *Epistres morales et familieres du traverseur.* Ed. M. A. Screech. Yorkshire: S. R. Publishers, 1969.

——. *See also* Appendix 3.

Brereton, Georgine E., and Janet M. Ferrier, eds. *Le ménagier de Paris.* Oxford: Clarendon, 1981.

Bruyant, Jean. "Le chemin de povreté et de richesse." In *Le ménagier de Paris, Traité de morale et d'economie domestique composé vers 1393 par un bourgeois parisien.* Ed. Le Baron Jérôme Pichon. Vol. 2, 4–42. Paris, 1846; repr. Geneva: Slatkine, 1966.

——. *Le Livre du Chastel de Labour: A Description of An Illuminated Manuscript of the Fifteenth Century, Belonging to George C. Thomas, Philadelphia, with a Short Account and Synopsis of the Poem.* Philadelphia: Private Collection, 1909.

Chartier, Alain. *Le livre de l'Espérance.* Ed. F. Rouy. Paris: Champion, 1989.

——. *Les œuvres feu Maistre Alain Chartier.* Paris: Galliot du Pré, 1529.

——. *The Poetical Works of Alain Chartier.* Ed. James C. Laidlaw. Cambridge: Cambridge University Press, 1974.

——. *Le quadrilogue invectif.* Ed. A. Piaget. Paris: Droz, 1950.

Chastellain, Georges. *Œuvres.* Ed. Kervyn de Lettenhove. 8 vols. Brussels: Heussner, 1863–66.

Cretin, Guillaume. *Œuvres poétiques.* Ed. K. Chesney. Paris: Firmin-Didot, 1932.

Deschamps, Eustache. *Œuvres.* Ed. E. Hoepffner. 11 vols. Paris, 1891; repr. New York: Johnson, 1966.

Erasmus, Desiderius. *Praise of Folly.* London: Folio Society, 1974.

Froissart, Jean. *Espinette amoureuse.* Ed. A. Fourrier. Paris: Klincksieck, 1963.

——. *Œuvres.* Ed. K. Kervyn de Lettenhove. Vol. 15. Brussels: Devaux, 1871.

Gréban, Arnoul. *Le mystère de la Passion.* Ed. Gaston Paris and Gaston Raynaud. Paris: Vieweg, 1878.

Gringore, Pierre. *La chasse du cerf des cerfs.* Paris: [n.p., ca. 1510].

——. *La complainte de la cité crestienne.* [Paris]: Pierre Bige, [1525].

——. *La coqueluche.* Paris: Pierre Le Dru for Pierre Gringore, 1510.

——. *L'entreprise de Venise.* [Lyons: P. Maréchal & B. Chaussard, 1509].

——. *L'espoir de paix.* Paris: Thomas du Guernier for Pierre Gringore, 1511.

——. *Les fantasies de Mère Sote.* Ed. R. L. Frautschi. Chapel Hill: University of North Carolina Press, 1962.

——. *Le jeu du Prince des Sotz.* Paris: for Pierre Gringore, [1512].

——. *Les lettres nouvelles de Milan.* [Lyons: n.p., post 15 April 1500].

——. *Obstination des Suysses.* [N.p.: n.p., ca. 1513].

——. *Œuvres complètes.* Ed. Charles d'Héricault and Anatole de Montaiglon. 2 vols. Paris: Jannet, 1857–58.

——. *La piteuse complainte . . . de la Terre Sainte.* [Lyons: P. Mareschal & B. Chaussard, ca. 1500].

——. *La quenoulle spirituelle.* [N.p.: n.p., ca. 1525].

——. *L'union des princes.* [Paris: n.p., ca. 1509].

——. *La vie de Monseigneur Saint Louis par personnages.* Ed. Anatole de Montaiglon. Paris, 1877; repr. Geneva: Slatkine, 1970.

——. *See also* Appendix 5.

Hicks, Eric, ed. *Le débat sur le "Roman de la rose."* Paris: Champion, 1977.

La Sale, Antoine de. *Jehan de Saintré.* Ed. Jean Misrahi and Charles A. Knudson. Geneva: Droz, 1967.

——. *Œuvres complètes.* Ed. Fernand Desonay. 2 vols. Liège: Faculté de Philosophie et Lettres, 1935.

La Vigne, André de. *Les complaintes et épitaphes du roy de la Bazoche.* [Paris: Jean Trepperel, ca. 1501].

——. *Les epitaphes en rondeaux de la royne.* [Paris: n.p., ca. 1514].

——. *See also* Appendix 1.

Lemaire de Belges, Jean. *Les chansons de Namur.* Antwerp: Henri Heckert, October 1507.

——. *La concorde des deux langages.* Ed. Jean Frappier. Paris: Droz, 1947.

——. *La concorde du genre humain.* Brussels: Thomas de la Noot, January 1509 N.S.

——. *La concorde du genre humain.* Ed. Pierre Jodogne. Brussels: Palais des Académies, 1964.

——. *L'épitaphe de Chastellain et Molinet.* Antwerp: Guillaume Vosterman, 1508 N.S.

——. *Œuvres.* Ed. J. Stecher. 4 vols. Louvain: Lefevre, 1882–91.

——. *La pompe funeralle.* Antwerp: Guillaume Vosterman, 1508 N.S.

——. *See also* Appendix 2.

Machaut, Guillaume de *Œuvres.* Ed. Ernest Hoepffner. 3 vols. Paris: Firmin-Didot, 1908–21.

Marot, Clément. *Œuvres poétiques.* Ed. Gérard Defaux. Vol. 1. Paris: Bordas, 1990.

Marot, Jean. *Le voyage de gênes.* Ed. Giovanna Trisolini. Geneva: Droz, 1974.

Meschinot, Jean. *Les lunettes des princes.* Nantes: Larcher, 1493.

Meun, Jean de. *The Romance of the Rose.* Trans. Charles Dahlberg. Hanover: University Press of New England, 1983.

——. *Le roman de la rose.* Ed. Ernest Langlois. 5 vols. Paris: Firmin-Didot 1922; repr. New York: Johnson, 1965.

——. *Le roman de la rose.* Ed. Félix Lecoy. 2 vols. Paris: Champion, 1966.

——. *Le roman de la rose.* Ed. Daniel Poirion. Paris: Garnier-Flammarion, 1974.

——. *Le roman de la rose attribué à Clément Marot.* Ed. Silvio F. Baridon. Milan: Cisalpino, 1954.

Molinet, Jean. *Chroniques.* Ed. Georges Doutrepont and Omer Jodogne. 2 vols. Brussels: Palais de Académies, 1935–37.

——. *Les faictz et dictz.* Ed. Nöel Dupire, 3 vols. Paris: Société des Anciens Textes Français, 1936–39.

——. *See also* Appendix 4.

Montaiglon, Anatole de, and James de Rothschild, eds. *Recueil de poésies françoises des XVe et XVIe siècles.* 13 vols. Paris: Daffis, 1855–78.

Picot, Emile, ed. *Recueil général de soties.* 3 vols. Paris, 1902–4; repr. New York: Johnson, 1968.

Robertet, Jean. *Œuvres.* Ed. Margaret Zsuppan. Geneva: Droz, 1970.

Roesner, Edward, ed. *"Le Roman de Fauvel" in the Edition of Mesire Chaillou de Pess-*

tain. Introduction by François Avril, Nancy F. Regalado, and Edward Roesner. New York: Broude Brothers, 1990.

Rutebeuf. *Œuvres complètes*. Ed. E. Faral and J. Bastin. 2 vols. Paris: Picard, 1959–60.

Saint-Gelais, Octavien de. *Le séjour d'honneur*. Ed. Joseph A. James. Chapel Hill: University of North Carolina Press, 1977.

Seyssel, Claude de. *Victoire du roy contre les Veniciens*. Paris: for A. Vérard, 1510.

Tibaut. *Roman de la poire*. Ed. Christiane Marchello-Nizia. Paris: SATF, 1984.

Villon, François. *Œuvres*. Ed. Clément Marot. Paris: Galliot du Pré, 1533.

——. *Testament*. Ed. J. Rychner and A. Henry. Geneva: Droz, 1985.

SECONDARY SOURCES

Abelard, Jacques. *Les illustrations de Gaule et singularitez de Troye de Jean Lemaire de Belges: Etude des éditions, genèse de l'œuvre*. Geneva: Droz, 1976.

Adams, Ann Jensen. "Rembrandt f[ecit]: The Italic Signature and the Commodification of Artistic Identity." In *Künstlerischer Austausch / Artistic Exchange*, ed. Thomas W. Gaehtgens, 581–94. Akten des XXVIII. Internationalen Kongresses für Kunstgeschichte, Berlin, July 15–20, 1992.

Armstrong, Elizabeth. *Before Copyright: The French Book-Privilege System, 1498–1526*. Cambridge: Cambridge University Press, 1990.

Ascoli, A. "The Vowels of Authority (Dante's *Convivio* IV.vi.3–4)." In *Discourses of Authority*, ed. Brownlee and Stephens, 23–46.

Avril, François. "Les manuscrits enluminés de Guillaume de Machaut." In *Guillaume de Machaut, poète et compositeur*, 117–33. Actes et Colloques 23. Paris: Klincksieck, 1982.

Baudrier, H. *Bibliographie lyonnaise*. Paris: Réimpression Nobele, 1964.

Becker, Ph.-Aug. *Andry de la Vigne*. Leipzig: Hirzel, 1928.

——. *Jean Lemaire: Der erste humanistiche Dichter Frankreichs*. Strasbourg, 1893; repr. Geneva: Slatkine, 1970.

Blaise, Albert. *Lexicon Latinitatis Medii Aevi*. Turnholti: Typographi Brepols, 1975.

Bourdillon, F. W. *The Early Editions of the "Roman de la Rose."* London: Bibliographical Society, 1906.

Bridge, John S. C. *A History of France from the Death of Louis XI*. 5 vols. Oxford: Clarendon, 1921–36.

Britnell, Jennifer. *Jean Bouchet*. Edinburgh: Edinburgh University Press, 1986.

Brown, Cynthia J. "Author, Editor, and the Use of Illustrations in the Early Imprints of Villon's Works: 'Ung chacun n'est maistre du scien.'" In *Chaucer's French Contemporaries*, ed. R. Barton Palmer, 313–46. New York: AMS Press, 1995.

——. "The Confrontation between Printer and Author in Early Sixteenth-Century France: Another Example of Michel Le Noir's Unethical Printing Practices." *Bibliothèque d'Humanisme et Renaissance* 53 (1991):105–18.

——. "Du manuscrit à l'imprimé en France: Le cas des rhétoriqueurs." In *Les grands rhétoriqueurs*, vol. 1, 103–23. Actes du Ve Colloque International sur le

Moyen Français, Milan, May 6–8, 1985. Milan: Pubblicazioni della Università Cattolica del Sacro Cuore, 1985.

——. "L'eveil d'une nouvelle conscience littéraire en France à la grande époque de transition technique: Jean Molinet et son moulin poétique." *Le Moyen Français* 22 (1988): 15–35.

——. "The Evolution of André de la Vigne's *Le Ressource de la Chrestienté*: From the Manuscript Tradition to the *Vergier d'honneur* Editions." *Bibliothèque d'Humanisme et Renaissance* 45 (1982): 115–25.

——. "The Interaction between Author and Printer: Title Pages and Colophons of Early French Imprints." *Soundings: Collections of the University Library* (University of California, Santa Barbara) 23 (1992): 33–53.

——. "Poètes, mécènes et imprimeurs à la fin du moyen âge français: Une crise d'autorité." In *Pratiques de la culture écrite en France au XVᵉ siècle*, eds. M. Ornato and N. Pons, 423–40.

——. "Political Misrule and Popular Opinion: Double Talk and Folly in Pierre Gringore's *Jeu du Prince des Sotz*." *Le Moyen Français* 11 (1982): 82–111.

——. "The Rise of Literary Consciousness in Late Medieval France: Jean Lemaire de Belges and the Rhétoriqueur Tradition." *Journal of Medieval and Renaissance Studies* 13 (Spring 1983): 51–74.

——. *The Shaping of History and Poetry in Late Medieval France: Propaganda and Artistic Expression in the Works of the Rhétoriqueurs*. Birmingham: Summa, 1985.

——. "Text, Image, and Authorial Self-Consciousness in Late Medieval Paris." In *Printing the Written Word: The Social History of Books, c. 1450–1520*, ed. Sandra Hindman, 103–42. Ithaca: Cornell University Press, 1991.

Brownlee, Kevin. *Poetic Identity in Guillaume de Machaut*. Madison: University of Wisconsin Press, 1984.

——. "Transformations of the *Charrete*: Godefroi de Leigni Rewrites Chrétien de Troyes." *Stanford French Review (Boundary and Transgression in Medieval Culture)* 14 (Spring–Fall 1990): 161–78.

Brownlee, Kevin, and Walter Stephens, eds. *Discourses of Authority in Medieval and Renaissance Literature*. Hanover: University Press of New England, 1989.

Brunet, Jacques-Charles. *Manuel du libraire et de l'amateur de livres*. 5 vols. Paris: Dorbon-Aîné, 1865.

Buettner, Brigitte. "Profane Illuminations, Secular Illusions: Manuscripts in Late Medieval Courtly Society." *Art Bulletin* 74 (March 1992): 75–90.

Burns, E. Jane. *Arthurian Fictions: Rereading the Vulgate Cycle*. Columbus: Ohio State University Press, 1985.

Byvanck, W. G. C. *Spécimen d'un essai critique sur les œuvres de François Villon*. Leiden: de Breuk & Smits, 1882.

Campbell, Lorne. *Renaissance Portraits: European Portrait-Painting in the Fourteenth, Fifteenth and Sixteenth Centuries*. New Haven: Yale University Press, 1990.

Carruthers, Mary J. *The Book of Memory: A Study of Memory in Medieval Culture*. Cambridge: Cambridge University Press, 1990.

Cartier, Normand R. "Anagrams in Froissart's Poetry." *Mediaeval Studies* 25 (1963): 100–108.

Catalogue des incunables. 2 vols. Paris: Bibliothèque Nationale, 1981.

Catalogue des livres de la bibliothèque de M. le Baron James de Rothschild. 4 vols. Paris: Morgand, 1884.

Cerquiglini, Bernard. *Eloge de la variante: Histoire critique de la philologie.* Paris: Seuil, 1989.

Cerquiglini, Jacqueline. *"Un engin si soutil": Guillaume de Machaut et l'écriture au XIVᵉ siècle.* Geneva: Slatkine, 1985.

——. "Quand la voix s'est tue: La mise en recueil de la poésie lyrique aux XIVᵉ et XVᵉ siècles." In *La présentation du livre,* ed. E. Baumgartner and N. Boulestreau, 313–27. Actes du Colloque de Paris X–Nanterre, December 4–6, 1985. Paris: Centre de Recherches du Département de Français de Paris X–Nanterre, 1987.

Champion, Pierre. *Le manuscrit autographe des poésies de Charles d'Orléans.* Geneva: Slatkine, 1975.

Chartier, Roger, "Du livre au lire." In *Pratiques de la lecture,* ed. R. Chartier, 62–88.

——. *L'ordre des livres: Lecteurs, auteurs, bibliothèques en Europe entre XIVᵉ et XVIIIᵉ siècle.* Aix-en-Provence: Alinea, 1992.

——, ed. *Pratiques de la lecture.* Marseilles: Rivages, 1985.

Chastel, André. "Signature et signe." *Revue de l'Art* 26 (1974): 8–14.

Chaytor, H. J. *From Script to Print: An Introduction to Medieval Literature.* Cambridge: The University Press, 1945.

Chenu, M.-D. "Auctor, actor, autor." *Bulletin du Cange* 3 (1927): 81–86.

Clanchy, M. T. "Hearing and Seeing and Trusting Writing." In *Perspectives on Literacy,* ed. Kintgen, Kroll, and Rose, 135–58.

Claude d'Urfé et la bâtie: L'univers d'un gentilhomme de la Renaissance. Ed. Conseil Général de la Loire. Montbrison: CGL, 1990.

Claudin, A. *Histoire de l'imprimerie en France au XVᵉ et au XVIᵉ siècle.* 4 vols. Paris: Imprimerie Nationale, 1900–1915.

Collier, J. Payne, ed. *Illustrations of Early English Popular Literature.* Vol. 1. London, 1863; repr. New York: Benjamin Blom, 1966.

Copeland, Rita. *Rhetoric, Hermeneutics, and Translation in the Middle Ages: Academic Traditions and Vernacular Texts.* Cambridge: Cambridge University Press, 1991.

Coq, Dominique. "Les débuts de l'édition en langue vulgaire en France." *Gutenberg Jahrbuch* 62 (1987): 59–72.

Cornilliat, François. "Aspects du songe chez les derniers Rhétoriqueurs: Analyse du *Labyrinthe de Fortune* et du *Séjour d'Honneur.*" *Réforme, Humanisme, Renaissance* 25 (1988): 47–63.

——. *"Or ne mens"—Couleurs de l'Eloge et du Blâme chez les "Grands Rhétoriqueurs."* Paris: Champion, 1994.

Cotgrave, Randle. *A Dictionaire of the French and English Tongues.* London, 1611; repr. Columbia: University of South Carolina Press, 1950.

Dagenais, John. *The Ethics of Reading in Manuscript Culture: Glossing the Libro de buen amor.* Princeton: Princeton University Press, 1994.

Dahlberg, Charles. "First Person and Personification in the *Roman de la Rose*: Amant and Dangier." *Mediaevalia: A Journal of Medieval Studies* 3 (1977): 37–58.

Davies, Hugh W. *Catalogue of a Collection of Early French Books in the Library of C. Fairfax-Murray*. 2 vols. London: private printing, 1910.

Davis, Natalie Z. "Beyond the Market: Books as Gifts in Sixteenth-Century France." *Transactions of the Royal Historical Society* 33 (1983): 69–88.

———. "Gifts, Markets, and Historical Change in Sixteenth-Century France." Trans. into Russian, Irina Bessmerthy. In *Odysseus-92: Man in History, Historian and Time*. Moscow: Krug, 1994, 193–203.

Delisle, Léopold. *Mélanges de paléographie et de bibliographie*. Paris: Champion, 1880.

Dembowski, Peter. "Intertextualité et critique des textes." *Littérature* 41 (February 1981): 17–29.

———. "Learned Latin Treatises in French: Inspiration, Plagiarism, and Translation." *Viator* 17 (1986): 255–69.

Dragonetti, Roger. In *La vie de la lettre au moyen age: Le conte du Graal*. Paris: Seuil, 1980.

———. "Pygmalion ou les pièges de la fiction." In *Orbis mediaevalis: Mélanges de langue et de littérature médiévales offerts à Reto Raduolf Bezzola*, ed. George Guntert, Marc-René Jung, and Kurt Ringger, 89–111. Bern: Francke, 1978.

Du Cange, Charles du Fresne. *Glossarium Mediae et Infimae Latinitatis*. 10 vols. Graz: Akademische Druck-U. Verlagsanstalt, 1954.

Dupire, Noël. *Etude critique des manuscrits et éditions des poésies de Jean Molinet*. Paris: Droz, 1932.

———. *Jean Molinet: La vie, les œuvres*. Paris: Droz, 1932.

Eisenstein, Elizabeth. *The Printing Press as an Agent of Change: Communications and Cultural Transformations in Early-Modern Europe*. 2 vols. New York: Cambridge University Press, 1979.

Elsky, Martin. "Print and Manuscript: Bacon's Early Career and the Occasions of Writing." In *Authorizing Words: Speech, Writing, and Print in the English Renaissance*, 184–208. Ithaca: Cornell University Press, 1989.

Enders, Jody. *Rhetoric and the Origins of Medieval Drama*. Ithaca: Cornell University Press, 1992.

Faulhaber, Charles, and Jerry Craddock, eds. *Romance Philology* 45 (August 1991): 1–148.

Febvre, Lucien, and Henri-Jean Martin. *L'apparition du livre*. Paris: Albin Michel, 1971.

Ferrand, Françoise. "Les portraits de Guillaume de Machaut à l'entrée du prologue à ses œuvres, signes iconiques de la nouvelle fonction de l'artiste, en France, à la fin du XIVe siècle." *Publications de l'Université de Rouen* ("Le Portrait") 128 (1987): 11–20.

Foucault, Michel. *The Order of Things: An Archaeology of the Human Sciences*. New York: Random House, 1970.

———. "What Is an Author?" In *Textual Strategies: Perspectives in Post-Structuralist Criticism*, ed. Josué Harrari, 141–60. Ithaca: Cornell University Press, 1979.

Fraenkel, Béatrice. *La signature: Genèse d'un signe.* Paris: Gallimard, 1992.

Gellrich, Jesse M. *The Idea of the Book in the Middle Ages: Language Theory, Mythology, and Fiction.* Ithaca: Cornell University Press, 1985.

Genette, Gérard. *Palimpsestes: la littérature au second degré.* Paris: Seuil, 1982.

———. *Seuils.* Paris: Seuil, 1987.

Giard, René, and Henri Lemaître. "Les origines de l'imprimerie à Valenciennes: Jehan de Lièges." *Bulletin du Bibliophile et du Bibliothécaire* (1903): 349–62.

Godzich, Wlad, and Jeffrey Kittay. *The Emergence of Prose: An Essay in Prosaics.* Minneapolis: University of Minnesota Press, 1987.

Goldschmidt, E. Ph. *Medieval Texts and Their First Appearance in Print.* London: Oxford University Press, 1943.

Goody, Jack, and Ian Watt. "The Consequences of Literacy." In *Perspectives on Literacy,* ed. Kintgen, Kroll, and Rose, 5–27.

Green, Richard. *Poets and Princepleasers: Literature and the English Court in the Late Middle Ages.* Toronto: University of Toronto Press, 1980.

Greimas, A. J., and T. M. Keane, eds. *Dictionnaire du moyen français: La Renaissance.* Paris: Larousse, 1992.

Gros, Gérard. *Le poète marial et l'art graphique: Etude sur les jeux de lettres dans les poèmes pieux du Moyen Age.* Caen: Paradigme, 1993.

Guery, Alain. "Le roi dépensier: Le don, la contrainte et l'origine du système financier de la monarchie française d'Ancien Régime." *Annales* 39 (November–December 1984): 1241–69.

Gurevich, A. "Representations of Property during the High Middle Ages." *Economy and Society* 6 (February 1977): 1–30.

Havelock, Eric A. "The Coming of Literate Communication to Western Culture." In *Perspectives on Literacy,* ed. Kintgen, Kroll, and Rose, 127–34.

Hindman, Sandra. *Christine de Pizan's "Epistre Othéa": Painting and Politics at the Court of Charles VI.* Toronto: Pontifical Institute of Mediaeval Studies, 1986.

———, ed. *Printing the Written Word: The Social History of Books, circa 1450–1520.* Ithaca: Cornell University Press, 1991.

Hindman, Sandra, and James Farquhar. *Pen to Press: Illustrated Manuscripts in the First Century of Printing.* College Park: University of Maryland Art Department, 1977.

Hirsch, Rudolf. "Title Pages in French Incunables, 1486–1500." *Gutenberg Jahrbuch,* 53 (1978): 63–66.

Hoepffner, E. "Anagramme und Rätselgedichte bei Guillaume de Machaut." *Zeitschrift für romanische Philologie* 30 (1906): 401–13.

Hoffman, George. "The Making of Montaigne's *Essais*: Book-Selling Technology and Creation in the Late French Renaissance." Ph.D. diss., University of Virginia, 1990.

———. "The Montaigne Monopoly: Revising the *Essais* under the French Privilege System." *PMLA* 108 (1993): 308–19.

Huguet, Edmond. *Dictionnaire de la langue française du seizième siècle.* 7 vols. Paris: Champion, 1925–73.

Hult, David. "Author/Narrator/Speaker: The Voice of Authority in Chrétien's *Charrette*." In *Discourses of Authority*, ed. Brownlee and Stephens, 76–96.

——. "Lancelot's Two Steps: A Problem in Textual Criticism." *Speculum* 61 (October 1986): 836–58.

——. "Reading It Right: The Ideology of Text Editing." *Romanic Review* 79, 1 (1988): 74–88.

——. *Self-fulfilling Prophecies: Readership and Authority in the First "Roman de la Rose."* New York: Cambridge University Press, 1986.

——. "Steps Forward and Steps Backward: More on Chrétien's *Lancelot*." *Speculum* 64 (April 1989): 307–16.

Huot, Sylvia. *From Song to Book: The Poetics of Writing in Old French Lyric and Lyrical Narrative Poetry*. Ithaca: Cornell University Press, 1987.

——. *The "Romance of the Rose" and Its Medieval Readers: Interpretation, Reception, Manuscript Transmission*. New York. Cambridge University Press, 1993.

——. "The Scribe as Editor: Rubrication as Critical Apparatus in Two Manuscripts of the *Roman de la Rose*." *L'Esprit Créateur* 27 (Spring 1987): 67–78.

Imbs, Paul, ed. *Trésor de la langue française*. 14 vols. Paris: Editions du CNRS, 1971–92.

Jardine, Lisa. *Erasmus, Man of Letters: The Construction of Charisma in Print*. Princeton: Princeton University Press, 1993.

Jeanneret, Michel. "La lecture en question: Sur quelques prologues comiques du seizième siècle." *French Forum* 14, 3 (1989): 279–89.

Jeay, Madeleine. *Donner la parole: L'histoire-cadre dans les recueils de nouvelles des XVᵉ–XVIᵉ siècles*. Montreal: CERES, 1992.

——. "Une théorie du roman: Le manuscrit autographe de *Jehan de Saintre*." *Romance Philology* 47 (February 1994), 287–307.

Jodogne, Pierre. *Jean Lemaire de Belges, écrivain franco-bourguignon*. Brussels: Palais des Académies, 1972.

——. "Un recueil poétique de Jean Lemaire de Belges en 1498." In *Miscellanea di studi e ricerche sul Quattrocentro francese*, ed. F. Simone, 181–210. Turin: Giappichelli, 1967.

Johnson, Leonard. *Poets as Players: Theme and Variation in Late Medieval French Poetry*. Stanford: Stanford University Press, 1990.

Julleville, Petit de. *Histoire du théâtre en France*. 2 vols. Geneva: Slatkine, 1968.

Juren, Vladimir. "Pratique artisanale du Nord." *Revue de l'Art* 26 (1974): 21–23.

Kaestle, Carl F. "The History of Literacy and the History of Readers." In *Perspectives on Literacy*, ed. Kintgen, Kroll, and Rose, 95–126.

Kamuf, Peggy. *Signature Pieces: On the Institution of Authorship*. Ithaca: Cornell University Press, 1988.

Kane, George. *Piers Plowman: The Evidence for Authorship*. London: Athlone, 1965.

Kerdaniel, Edouard L. de. *Un rhétoriqueur: André de la Vigne*. Paris: Champion, 1919.

Kettering, Sharon. "Gift-Giving and Patronage in Early Modern France." *French History* 2 (June 1988): 131–51.

Kintgen, Eugene R., Barry Kroll, and Mike Rose, eds. *Perspectives on Literacy*. Carbondale: Southern Illinois University Press, 1988.

Kooper, Erik S. "Art and Signature and the Art of the Signature." In *Court and Poet, Selected Proceedings of the Third Congress of the International Courtly Literature Society*, ed. Glyn S. Burgess, 223–32. Liverpool: Cairns, 1981.

Labarre, Albert. "Les incunables: La présentation du livre." In *Le livre conquérant*, ed. Martin and Chartier, 195–215.

La Borde, L. de. *Le Parlement de Paris*. Paris: Plon, 1863.

Långfors, Arthur. "Jacques Bruyant et son poème *La voie de povreté et de richesse*." *Romania* 45 (1918–19): 49–83.

Langlois, Ernest, ed. *Recueil d'Arts de seconde rhétorique*. Paris: Imprimerie Nationale, 1902.

Laufer, Roger. "L'espace visuel du livre ancien." In *Le livre conquérant*, ed. Martin and Chartier, 479–97.

Lebensztejn, Jean-Claude. "Esquisse d'une typologie." *Revue de l'Art* 26 (1974): 46–54.

Lecoq, Anne Marie. "Cadre et rebord." *Revue de l'Art* 26 (1974): 15–20.

———. *François Ier imaginaire: Symbolique et politique à l'aube de la Renaissance française*. Paris: Macula, 1987.

Lemaire, Jacques. "Note sur la datation du *Séjour d'honneur* d'Octavien de Saint-Gelais." *Romania* 102 (1981): 129–49.

Lepage, Henry. *Pierre Gringore: Extrait d'études sur le théâtre en Lorraine*. Nancy: Raybois, 1849.

Looze, Laurence de. "Guillaume de Machaut and the Writerly Process." *French Forum* 9, 2 (1984): 145–61.

———. "'Mon nom trouveras': A New Look at the Anagrams of Guillaume de Machaut—The Enigmas, Responses, and Solutions." *Romanic Review* 79, 4 (1988): 537–57.

Macfarlane, John. *Antoine Vérard*. London, 1900; repr. Geneva: Slatkine, 1971.

Macherel, Claude. "Don et réciprocité en Europe." *Archives Européennes de Sociologie* 24, 1 (1983): 151–66.

Martin, Henri-Jean, and Roger Chartier, ed. *Le livre conquérant*. Vol. 1 of *L'histoire de l'édition française*. Paris: Promodis, 1982.

Martin, Henri-Jean, and Jean Vezin, eds. *Mise en page et mise en texte du livre manuscrit*. Paris: Promodis, 1990.

Mauss, Marcel. *The Gift: Forms and Functions of Exchange in Archaic Societies*. Trans. Ian Cunnison. London: Cohen & West, 1954.

Mayer, C. A. *Bibliographie des œuvres de Clément Marot*. Vol. 2: *Editions*. Geneva: Droz, 1954.

McLuhan, Marshall. *The Gutenberg Galaxy: The Making of Typographic Man*. Toronto: University of Toronto Press, 1962.

Meredith, P., and J. E. Tailby, eds. *The Staging of Religious Drama in Europe in the Later Middle Ages: Texts and Documents in English Translation*. Kalamazoo: Medieval Institute, 1983.

Minnis, Alastair J. "Late Medieval Discussions of *Compilatio*." *Beiträge zur Geschichte der deutschen Sprache und Literatur* 101 (1979): 385–421.

——. *Medieval Theory of Authorship: Scholastic Literary Attitudes in the Later Middle Ages*. London, 1984; 2d ed. Philadelphia: University of Pennsylvania Press, 1988.

Mortimer, Ruth, ed. *French Sixteenth Century Books*. Vol. 1 of *Harvard College Library Department of Printing and Graphic Arts: Catalogue of Books and Manuscripts*. Cambridge: Belknap Press of Harvard University Press, 1964.

——. "A Portrait of the Author in Sixteenth-Century France." In *On the Occasion of the Fiftieth Anniversary of the Hanes Foundation for the Study of the Origin and Development of the Book*, ed. R. Mortimer, 1–50. Chapel Hill: University of North Carolina Press, 1980.

Munn, Kathleen M. *A Contribution to the Study of Jean Lemaire de Belges*. Geneva: Slatkine, 1975.

Nelson, William. "From 'Listen, Lordings' to 'Dear Reader.'" *University of Toronto Quarterly* 46 (Winter 1976–77): 110–24.

Newton, Richard C. "Jonson and the (Re-)Invention of the Book." In *Classic and Cavalier: Essays on Jonson and the Sons of Ben*, ed. Claude J. Summers and Ted-Larry Pebworth, 31–55. Pittsburgh: University of Pittsburgh Press, 1982.

Nichols, Stephen G., Jr. "Introduction: Philology in a Manuscript Culture." *Speculum* 65 (January 1990): 1–10.

——. "The Rhetoric of Sincerity in the *Roman de la Rose*." In *Romance Studies in Memory of Edward Billings Ham*, ed. Urban Tigner Holmes, 115–29. Hayward: California State College Publications, 1967.

——, ed. "The New Philology." *Speculum* 65 (January 1990).

Olson, David R. "From Utterance to Text: The Bias of Language in Speech and Writing." In *Perspectives on Literacy*, ed. Kintgen, Kroll, and Rose, 175–89.

Ong, Walter J. *Interfaces of the Word: Studies in the Evolution of Consciousness and Culture*. Ithaca: Cornell University Press, 1977.

——. *Orality and Literacy: The Technologizing of the Word*. London: Methuen, 1982.

——. "Orality, Literacy, and Medieval Textualization." *New Literary History* 16 (Autumn 1984): 1–12.

——. *The Presence of the Word: Some Prolegomena for Cultural and Religious History*. New Haven: Yale University Press, 1967.

——. *Rhetoric, Romance, and Technology: Studies in the Interaction of Expression and Culture*. Ithaca: Cornell University Press, 1971.

Ornato, Ezio. "Les conditions de production et de diffusion du livre médiéval (XIIIᵉ–XIVᵉ siècles)." In *Culture et idéologie dans la genèse de l'état moderne*, 57–84. Actes de la Table Ronde Organisée par le CNRS et L'Ecole Française de Rome, October 15–17, 1984. Rome: Palais Farnèse, 1985.

Ornato, Monique, and Nicole Pons, eds. *Pratiques de la culture écrite en France au xvᵉ siècle*. Actes du Colloque International, Paris, CNRS, May 18–21, 1992. Louvain-la-Neuve: Fédération Internationale des Instituts d'Etudes Médiévales, 1995.

Oulmont, Charles. "Pierre Gringore et l'entrée de la Reine Anne en 1504." In *Mélanges offerts à Emile Picot par ses amis et ses élèves*, vol. 2, 385–92. Paris, 1913; repr. Geneva: Slatkine, 1969.

——. *Pierre Gringore: La poésie morale, politique et dramatique à la veille de la Renaissance.* Paris, 1911; repr. Geneva: Slatkine, 1976.

Ouy, Gilbert, and Christine M. Reno. "Identification des autographes de Christine de Pizan." *Scriptorium* 34 (1980): 221–38.

Oxford English Dictionary. 2d ed. Ed. J. A. Simpson and E. S. C. Weiner, Oxford: Clarendon, 1989.

Panofsky, Erwin. "Erasmus and the Visual Arts." *Journal of the Warburg and Courtauld Institutes* 32 (1969): 200–227.

Parent, Annie. *Les métiers du livre à Paris au XVIᵉ siècle (1535–1560).* Geneva: Droz, 1974.

Pellechet, M. *Une association d'imprimeurs parisiens au XVᵉ siècle.* Paris: Picard, 1897.

Piaget, A. "*La belle dame sans merci* et ses imitations." *Romania* 30 (1901): 22–48, 317–51; 31 (1902): 315–49; 33 (1904): 179–208; 34 (1905): 375–428, 559–602.

Pickens, Rupert T. "*Somnium* and Interpretation in Guillaume de Lorris." *Symposium* 28 (Summer 1974): 175–86.

Picot, Emile. *Les français italianisants.* Paris: Champion, 1906.

——. *Pierre Gringore et les comédiens italiens sous François Iᵉʳ.* Paris: Morgand & Fatout, 1878.

Picot, Emile, and A. Piaget. "Une supercherie d'Antoine Vérard: *Les Regnars traversans* de Jehan Bouchet." *Romania* 22 (1893): 244–60.

Picot, Emile, and Henri Stein. "Le Temple de Mars par Jehan Molinet, vers 1476." In *Recueil de pièces historiques imprimées sous le règne de Louis XI reproduites en facsimile avec des commentaires historiques et bibliographiques,* ed. Emile Picot and Henri Stein, 13–64. Paris: Lefrançois, 1923.

Pizarro, Joaquín Martínez. *A Rhetoric of the Scene: Dramatic Narrative in the Middle Ages.* Toronto: University of Toronto Press, 1989.

Poirion, Daniel. "Lecture de la *Belle dame sans mercy.*" In *Mélanges de langue et de littérature médiévales offerts à Pierre Le Gentil,* 691–705. Paris: SEDES, 1957.

——. *Le poète et le prince: L'évolution du lyrisme courtois de Guillaume de Machaut à Charles d'Orléans.* Paris: Presses Universitaires de France, 1965.

Quilligan, Maureen. *The Allegory of Female Authority: Christine de Pizan's "Cité des Dames."* Ithaca: Cornell University Press, 1991.

——. *The Language of Allegory: Defining the Genre.* Ithaca: Cornell University Press, 1979.

Raynouard, M. *Lexique roman ou dictionnaire de la langue des troubadours comparée avec les autres langues de l'Europe latine.* 6 vols. Edition of 1836–45; repr. Heidelberg: Carl Winters, 1928.

Regalado, Nancy. "'En ce saint livre:' mise en page et identité lyrique dans les poèmes autobiographiques de Villon dans l'album de Blois (Bibl. Nat. ms. fr. 25458)." In *L'Hostellerie de Pensee: Mélanges Daniel Poirion.* Paris: Presses de la Sorbonne, 1995.

——. "Gathering the Works: The 'Œuvres de Villon' and the Intergeneric Passage of the Medieval French Lyric into Single-Author Collections." *L'Esprit Créateur* 33 (Winter 1993): 87–100.

Renaudet, Augustin. *Préréforme et humanisme à Paris pendant les guerres d'Italie (1494–1517)*. Paris: Argences, 1953.

Rendall, Steven. "The Portrait of the Author." *French Forum* 13, 2 (1988): 143–51.

Reno, Christine. "The Cursive and Calligraphic Scripts of Christine de Pizan." *Ball State University Forum* 19 (Summer 1978): 3–20.

Renouard, Philippe. *Répertoire des imprimeurs parisiens*. Paris: Minard, 1965.

Revue de l'Art ("L'Art de la Signature") 26 (1974).

Rice, Eugene, Jr., ed. *The Prefatory Epistles of Jacques Lefèvre d'Etaples and Related Texts*. New York: Columbia University Press, 1972.

——. *Saint Jerome in the Renaissance*. Baltimore: Johns Hopkins University Press, 1985.

Rigolot, François. *Poétique et onomastique: L'exemple de la Renaissance*. Geneva: Droz, 1977.

——. *Le texte de la Renaissance: Des rhétoriqueurs à Montaigne*. Geneva: Droz, 1982.

Rose, Mark. "The Author as Proprietor: Donaldson v. Becket and the Genealogy of Modern Authorship." *Representations* 23 (Summer 1988): 51–85.

——. *Authors and Owners: The Invention of Copyright*. Cambridge: Harvard University Press, 1993.

Rouse, Mary A., and Richard H. Rouse. "The Book Trade at the University of Paris, ca. 1250–ca. 1350." In *Authentic Witnesses: Approaches to Medieval Texts and Manuscripts*, ed. Mary A. Rouse and Richard H. Rouse, 259–338. Notre Dame: University of Notre Dame Press, 1992.

——. "The Commercial Production of Manuscript Books in Late-Thirteenth-Century and Early-Fourteenth-Century Paris." In *Medieval Book Production: Assessing the Evidence*, ed. Linda L. Brownrigg, 103–15. Proceedings of the Second Conference of the Seminar in the History of the Book to 1500, Oxford, July 1988. Los Altos Hills: Red Gull Press, 1990.

Roy, Emile. "Les lettres de noblesse (1503) du poète Jean Molinet." *Revue de Philologie Française* 9 (1895): 19–22.

Russell, Daniel. *The Emblem and Device in France*. Lexington: French Forum, 1985.

Saenger, Paul. "Silent Reading: Its Impact on Late Medieval Script and Society." *Viator* 13 (1982): 367–414.

Sala, Charles. "La signature à la lettre et au figuré." *Poétique* 69 (February 1987): 118–27.

Scheidegger, Jean R. "La lettre du nom: L'anthroponymie de Jean Molinet." *Le Moyen Français* 8–9 (1981): 198–35.

Seguin, J. P. "L'information à la fin du XVe siècle en France: Pièces d'actualité imprimées sous le règne de Charles VIII." *Arts et Traditions Populaires* 4 (1956): 309–30; 1 (1959), 46–74.

——. *L'information en France de Louis XII à Henry II*. Geneva: Droz, 1961.

Smalley, Beryl. *English Friars and Antiquity in the Early Fourteenth Century*. New York: Barnes & Noble, 1960.

Solterer, Helen. *The Master and Minerva: Disputing Women in French Medieval Culture*. Berkeley: University of California Press, 1994.

Speer, Mary. "Editing Old French in the Eighties: Theories and Practices." *Romance Philology* 45 (August 1991): 7–43.

Spitzer, Leo. "Note on the Poetic and the Empirical 'I' in Medieval Authors." *Traditio* 4 (1946): 414–22.

Starobinski, Jean. *Les mots sous les mots.* Paris: Gallimard, 1971.

Stein, Henri. "Le sacre d'Anne de Bretagne et son entrée à Paris en 1504." *Mémoires de la Société de l'Histoire de Paris et de l'Ile de France* 29 (1902): 268–304.

Stock, Brian. *The Implications of Literacy: Written Language and Models of Interpretation in the Eleventh and Twelfth Centuries.* Princeton: Princeton University Press, 1983.

Strohm, Paul. "Guillaume as Narrator and Lover in the *Roman de la Rose.*" *Romanic Review* 59, 1 (1968): 3–9.

Sturges, Robert S. "Textual Scholarship: Ideologies of Literary Production." *Exemplaria* 3 (March 1991), 109–31.

Sutch, Susie. "Allegory and Praise in the Works of the Grands Rhétoriqueurs." Ph.d. diss., University of California, Berkeley, 1983.

Tchémerzine, Avenir. *Bibliographie d'éditions originales ou rares des auteurs français de XVe, XVIe XVIIe et XVIIIe siècles.* 10 vols. Paris: Plee, 1927–34.

Toubert, Hélène. "Formes et fonctions de l'enluminure." In *Le livre conquérant,* ed. Martin and Chartier, 87–129.

Trapp, D. "Augustinian Theology in the Fourteenth Century." *Augustiniana* 6 (1956): 269–72.

Tyson, Diana. "French Vernacular History Writers and Their Patrons in the Fourteenth Century." *Medievalia and Humanistica* 14 (1986): 103–24.

Uitti, Karl D. "From *Clerc* to *Poète*: The Relevance of the *Romance of the Rose* to Machaut's World." In *Machaut's World: Science and Art in the Fourteenth Century,* eds. M. P. Cosman and B. Chandler, 209–16. New York: New York Academy of Sciences, 1978.

——. "A Note on Villon's Poetics." *Romance Philology* 30 (August 1976): 187–92.

——, ed. "Poetics of Textual Criticism: The Old French Example." *L'Esprit Créateur* 27 (Spring 1987).

Uitti, Karl D., and Alfred Foulet. "On Editing Chrétien de Troyes: Lancelot's Two Steps and Their Context." *Speculum* 63 (April 1988): 271–92.

Van Praet, Joseph B. *Catalogue des livres imprimés sur vélin de la bibliothèque du roi.* 4 vols. Paris: De Bure, 1822–28.

Vezin, Jean. "La fabrication du manuscrit." In *Le livre conquérant,* ed. Martin and Chartier, 25–47.

Viala, Alain. *Naissance de l'écrivain.* Paris: Minuit, 1985.

Vitz, E. B. "The *I* of the *Roman de la Rose.*" *Genre* 6 (1973): 49–75.

Wadsworth, James B. *Lyons 1473–1503: The Beginnings of Cosmopolitanism.* Cambridge: Mediaeval Academy of America, 1962.

Walravens, C. J. H. *Alain Chartier.* Amsterdam: Meulenhoff-Didier, 1971.

Wartburg, Walther von. *Französisches etymologisches Wörterbuch.* 24 vols. Basel: Zbinden, 1969–83.

Willard, Charity Cannon. *Christine de Pizan: Her Life and Works, A Biography.* New York: Persea Books, 1984.

Williams, Sarah Jane. "An Author's Role in Fourteenth-Century Book Production: Guillaume de Machaut's 'livre ou je mets toutes mes choses.'" *Romania* 90 (1969): 433–54.

Wilson, Elizabeth R. "Name Games in Rutebeuf and Villon." *L'Esprit Créateur* 18 (Spring 1978): 47–59.

Winn, Mary Beth. "Publisher vs. Author: Anthoine Vérard, Jean Bouchet, and L'Amoureux Transy." *Bibliothèque d'Humanisme et Renaissance* 50 (1988): 39–55.

Zink, Michel. *La subjectivité littéraire autour du siècle de Saint Louis*. Paris: Presses Universitaires de France, 1985.

Zumthor, Paul. *Essai de poétique médiévale*. Paris: Seuil, 1972.

———. "Intertextualité et mouvance." *Littérature* 41 (1981): 8–16.

———. *Le masque et la lumière: La poétique des grands rhétoriqueurs*. Paris: Seuil, 1978.

———. "Le texte-fragment." *Langue Française* 40 (1978): 75–82.

INDEX

Acteur, as term, 197–8, 202–6, 213–14, 246; in Chartier's works, 207–11; in Gringore's works, 147, 183–84, 188, 192, 228–31, 233–36, 230–40, 244; in La Vigne's works, 228; in Lemaire's works, 204; in Meschinot's works, 236; in Molinet's works, 56, 214, 216–17, 223. *See also Actor; Aucteur; Auctor; Auteur;* Narrator

Actor, 198–200, 202–3, 205

Adam de la Halle, 101

Allegory, 53, 241; in Chartier's works, 208; in Gringore's works, 228, 230, 234–35, 238–39; in La Vigne's works, 114, 228; in Lemaire's works, 41, 46, 56; in Molinet's works, 215–16, 218–19. *See also* Personifications

Anne de Beaujeu, 42

Anne of Brittany: arms, 91–93; entry into Paris (1504), 18, 180–82, 206; and La Vigne, 18, 88, 90–91, 116–17, 166, 180–82, 228; and Lemaire, 53–54, 56, 146, 151; and Jean Marot, 43–44

Armstrong, Elizabeth, 53, 59

Aucteur, 198, 200–204, 206, 214. *See also Acteur; Actor; Auctor; Auteur*

Auctor, 198–203, 205, 213. *See also Actor; Aucteur; Auteur*

Auctoritas, 199, 202, 204. *See also Actor; Aucteur; Auctor*

Audience. *See* Readership

Auteur, autheur, 198, 204. *See also Acteur; Actor; Aucteur; Auctor*

Authors: advertisement of names, 15, 33, 40, 62, 90, 94, 97, 99–102, 153–54, 156–57, 194, 249; author-images, 7–8, 14–16, 58, 62, 82, 85, 91, 97, 99–151, 153, 194; changing relationship with their works, 2, 5–6, 14, 21, 28, 33–35, 38, 57, 157, 208, 215, 220, 227; defensive posture, 6–7, 62, 79, 154, 157, 194, 197–98, 207–8, 213–14, 245–46, 248; efforts to protect works, 3, 10–11, 14, 16–17, 20, 34, 58, 198, 248–49; enhancement of status, 38, 40, 62, 79, 91, 97, 102–3, 157, 195, 212–13; as first owners of their works, 14, 17, 19–21, 51, 58, 116, 246; involvement in theater, 198, 205–6; as originators of their works, 19, 21, 28, 32, 58, 153, 246; publication rights, 3, 32–33, 38, 58–59, 254; redefinition of role, 2–3, 5, 7–8, 11, 13, 30, 32, 38, 58, 40, 100, 103, 107, 116, 151, 195, 198, 203, 207; self-promotional strategies, 6–7, 11, 14, 17, 58, 62, 95, 151, 154, 157; signatures, 7, 15, 40, 151, 153–95, 194, 197. *See also* Compilers; Patronage; Printers; Publishers; Scribes; *entries for individual authors*

Authorship, concept of, 2–3, 7, 9–10, 19, 70, 102, 112, 163, 197–206, 213, 218, 245, 248. *See also* Bouchet,

Authorship (*cont.*)
Jean: on authorship; *Roman de la rose*

Badius, Josse, 47
Balsarin, Guillaume, 78
Beauvais, Vincent de. *See* Vincent de Beauvais
Bérault, Nicolas, 248
Béroul, 154
Bestiaire d'amour rimé, 155
Boccaccio, 167, 199, 204
Boethius, 199
Book: as commodity, 2, 5, 8, 14–15, 57–58, 106–7, 109–10, 133, 219; as cultural artifact, 8–10; in its hybrid (manuscript and printed) form, 99, 103, 107, 114, 116, 119–29, 134–36; as theme, 207–8, 212, 214–15, 221, 226
Booksellers: advertisement of, 33, 82, 95; and authors, 12, 76, 81, 96; marks, 100; role, 7, 10, 31, 85, 89–90, 213; success in Parisian market, 12, 91. *See also* Bouchet, Jean: attack against Parisian printers and booksellers; Gringore, Pierre: as bookseller
Bonaventure, Saint. *See* Saint Bonaventure
Bouchet, Jean, 21–33, 47, 58, 246–47; acrostic signature, 21, 23–24, 156, 259–60; attack against Le Noir, 23, 25, 31–32; attack against Parisian printers and booksellers, 23, 25, 27–28, 213; on authorship, 26–28, 30, 32–33, 38; and La Vigne's lawsuit, 1, 4, 25; lawsuit and attack against Vérard, 4, 17, 25–27, 30–32, 35, 40, 48–49, 252, 254; patronage, search for, 14, 20–21; in Poitiers, 4, 21, 25, 27; and theater, 198; works: *L'amoureux transi sans espoir*, 23; *Déploration de l'église*, 4; *Regnars traversant*, 160, 252, 259–60, (bogus authorship) 15, 21–23, (indebtedness to Brant) 30, (indebtedness to Chartier) 30–31, (La Vigne's authorized control of) 4, 25, (revision of) 28, 30, (title pages) 21, 23, 26–27,

30–31. *See also* Le Noir, Michel; Le Noir, Philippe; Vérard
Boulle, Guillaume, 251
Bourbon, duke of. *See* Jean II of Bourbon; Pierre II of Bourbon
Bourbon, Nicolas, 248
Brant, Sebastian, 4, 21–22, 25–27, 30–31
Bruyant, Jacques, 34, 229–36
Burgundy, court of, 63, 70, 108, 216

Capitalism, in book industry, 5, 61, 81, 85, 106, 254
Cerquiglini, Bernard, 8
Champier, Symphorien, 47
Charles VII, king of France, 206, 210
Charles VIII, king of France: acrostic, 111, 119, 161–62, 166–69; and Bouchet, 21; entry into Lyons (1495), 179, 181; image, 68–70, 103–6, 110–12; and La Vigne, 1, 18, 103–6, 166, 179–81, 207
Charles d'Orléans, 13, 17, 74, 212
Charles of Austria (Charles V), 224–25
Charles the Bold, duke of Burgundy, 63, 216, 218–19
Chartier, Alain, 64, 198–99, 206, 214, 236; Bouchet's indebtedness to, 30–31; signature, 210; works: *Belle dame sans merci*, 207–11; *Excusacion aux dames*, 207–12; *Quadrilogue invectif*, 220. *See also* Acteur; Allegory; Dream visions; Narrator; Personifications
Chartier, Roger, 6–7, 9–10
Chastellain, Georges, 14, 64, 108, 110, 207, 220
Chaytor, H. J., 12
Chenu, M. D., 203
Chrétien de Troyes, 154
Christine de Pizan, 10–11, 17, 74, 197, 212, 236
Clèves, Philippe de, 124, 164
Codicology, New, 8–9
Colophons, 7–8, 15, 49, 61–62, 79, 83–84, 99, 123, 153, 194; in Bouchet's works, 23; in *Castell of Labour*, 185; in Gringore's works: 62, 81, 83, 91, 94, 186, 188; (*Folles*

Colophons (*cont.*)
entreprises), 15, 35, 37–39, 95–97, 134, 204; in La Vigne's works, 62, 86, 88–91; in Lemaire's works, 41; in Molinet's works, 62, 70–72, 76, 126, 129
Compilers, compilation, 29, 31–32, 64, 198–201, 203, 205, 212–13
Copland, Roberte, 185–86, 266
Copeland, Rita, 213
Copyists. *See* Scribes
Copyright, 3, 19, 58
Court. *See* France, house of
Cretin, Guillaume, 42, 44, 47–48, 158, 204
Croy, Henry de, 78, 119, 121, 123, 160–62
Culture écrite du moyen âge tardif, 9

Dante, 204
Darnton, Robert, 9
Davis, Natalie Zemon, 109
Dedications, dedicatory material, 8, 15, 41–43. *See also entries for individual authors*
Devices, 7, 15, 99, 145–47. *See also* Gringore, Pierre: device; Lemaire de Belges, Jean: device
Dolet, Etienne, 246–49, 250–51, 253
Dream visions, 198, 245; in Chartier's works, 206, 208; in Gringore's works, 235–36, 241; in Lemaire's works, 41, 56; in Meschinot's works, 229; in Molinet's works, 215–19
Dupire, Noël, 263

Eisenstein, Elizabeth, 6
Enders, Jody, 205
Enfants sans Souci, 95, 144, 239
Erasmus, Desiderius, 145

Ferrières, Pierre of, 142–44, 239
Foucault, Michel, 6–7, 139
Fraenkel, Béatrice, 154
France, house of/French court, 2, 11, 47, 52, 54, 70, 144; La Vigne's association with, 39–40, 110; Lemaire's association with, 40, 44, 46, 52–54, 56–57, 146; political policies, 68–

69, 90, 111, 180. *See also* Readership: courtly
Francis I, king of France, 59, 223, 246, 249
Froissart, Jean, 101, 154, 212

Genette, Gérard, 7, 10, 61–62
Gift economy, 100, 106–10, 119, 133, 140, 145
Gorrevod, Louis de, 53–54
Gower, John, 199
Green, Richard, 11, 215
Gringore, Pierre, 34–38, 58, 79–85, 103, 110, 198, 228–47, 246–47; acrostic signature, 15, 34, 81–83, 94–95, 137, 142, 150, 183–93, 230, 233, 240, 244; as actor and director, 95, 134, 139, 144, 146–47, 198, 229; advertisement of name, 15, 83, 90–91, 94–97, 183, 186, 189, 192, 230, 240–41; author-image, 91, 133–40, 143, 145–51, 155, 192–93, 229, 245, 265; author privileges, 21, 34–38, 91, 97, 134, 144, 151, 193, 240, 245; as author-publisher, 85, 94–97, 134, 137, 144, 146–47, 150–51, 155, 193, 239, 245; as bookseller, 35, 38, 95, 97, 134, 136–37, 139–40, 144, 146, 150–51, 155, 245, 265–66; collaboration with publishers, 83, 85, 96, 188, 229; dedication illustrations, 38, 134–35, 140–45; device, 145–50; as *héraut d'armes* of the duke of Lorraine, 96–97, 147, 150; involvement in and control of publication, 10, 15, 35, 47, 79, 81–83, 85, 90–91, 94, 96–97, 133, 137, 183, 204, 236, 244–45; Mère Sotte/ Mother Folly, 95, 134, 139, 144, 146–47, 239; patronage, search for, 14, 20, 38, 110, 140–45, 150, 193, 241–43; use of rubrics, 134, 139, 142, 147, 183–84, 187–89, 192–93, 233, 235, 239–41, 244–45; works, 144, 192–93; *Abus du Monde*, 96, 144; *Castell of Labour*, 184–85, 265; *Chasse du Cerf des Cerfs*, 91, 144, 193, 241–44; *Chasteau d'amours*, 15, 37, 79, 82–85, 95, 133, 146, 187–92, 234, 265; *Chasteau de labour*, 34, 79–

Gringore, Pierre (*cont.*) 82, 85, 95, 133, 146, 186, 228–38, 242, 264–65; *Complainte de la cité crestienne*, 193; *Complainte de Trop Tard Marié*, 37, 85, 91, 94, 137, 186, 265–66; *Complaynte of Them . . . To Late Maryed*, 185–87; *Coqueluche*, 96, 144; *Entreprise de Venise*, 144; *Espoir de paix*, 96, 144; *Fantasies de Mere Sotte*, 96, 146–50; *Folles entreprises*, 94–97, 146, 192, 235–42, 266–68, (colophon alterations) 35, 37–39, 204, (first vernacular author privilege) 5, 35–38, 51–52, 94, 97, 134, 137, 144, 183, 194, 204, 229, (illustrations) 133–37, (title pages) 133–39; *Lettres nouvelles de Milan*, 37, 133; *Menus propos*, 147, 150; *Notables enseignemens*, 192; *Quenoulle*, 192; *Piteuse complainte de la Terre Sainte*, 37, 133; *Union des princes*, 144. See also *Acteur*; Allegory; Dream visions; Narrator; Personifications; Prefatory material

Guillaume de Lorris, 123, 154, 202. See also *Roman de la rose*

Guillaume de Machaut, 10, 17, 74, 101, 154, 212, 236

Henry II, king of France, 59, 153
Henry VII, king of England, 121
Henry de Croy. See Croy, Henry de
Hult, David, 13
Huot, Sylvia, 13, 101, 203, 212

Illustrations, 8, 62; coexistence of manuscript miniatures and woodcuts, 114, 121, 140; presentation miniatures, 8, 100–101, 103, 112; woodcuts, 99–103, 105–6. See also entries for individual authors and works
Isidore of Seville, 199

Jean II of Bourbon, 223
Jean de Meun, 123, 154, 198–201, 204, 213. See also *Roman de la rose*
Jerome, Saint. See Saint Jerome
Johnson, Leonard, 205, 235
Julius II, pope, 241–44
Juste, François, 251

Kettering, Sharon, 109

Lannoy, Bauduin de, 221–23
La Sale, Antoine de, 212
La Vigne, André de, 58, 85–93, 246–47, 254; advertisement of name, 20, 86, 88–91, 116, 172, 182; authorized control of Bouchet's *Regnars traversant*, 4, 25; involvement in and control of publication, 2, 4, 10, 18–19, 47, 85–86, 91, 94, 116, 151, 174, 181, 204; lawsuit against Le Noir, 1–4, 17, 19–20, 25, 27, 30, 33, 35, 37–38, 48–49, 70, 83, 116, 183, 194, 212–13, 228, 248–50, 254–56; privileges, 2–3, 20–21; relationship with Charles VIII, 1, 18, 103–6, 166, 179–81, 207; patronage, search for, 11, 14, 18, 20, 88, 110–11; secretary to Anne of Brittany, 18, 88, 90–91, 116–17, 166, 180–82, 228; signature, 86, 111, 158, 166–84; and theater, 198, 206; works, 182; *Atollite portas de Gennes*, 182, 228; *Ballades de Bruyt Commun*, 92, 182, 228; *Chascun*, 180, 184; *Couronnement d'Anne de Bretagne*, 180–82, 206; *Libelle des cinq villes d'Ytallye*, 92, 182–83, 228; *Louanges du roy*, 179–80; *Ressource de la Chrestienté*, 8–9, 29–30, 85–86, 111–12, 175, 182, 227, 256–57, (also known as the *Entreprise de Naples*) 86–88, 174, (Angoulême edition) 170–71, 174, (Charles VIII acrostics) 166–73, 184, 188, (dedication miniature of ms. 1687) 8, 103–6, 110–17, 119, 140, 170, 182, 207, 227–28, 245, 256–57, (derivative manuscripts) 29–30; *Temps de l'année moralizé*, 180, 184; *Vergier d'honneur* editions, 4, 8, 14–16, 18, 85–90, 94–95, 151, 174, 213, 256–57, (acrostics) 174–77, (author-images) 103–6, 112–17, 133, 151, 245, (first edition) 17–19, 89, (relationship with the *Ressource de la Chrestienté*) 29–30, 86, 110, 112, (second edition) 8, 18, 89, (title pages) 17–18, 20, 86–89, 112–13, 245; *Voyage de Naples*, 86–88, 175, 178–79, 181, 184, 188. See

La Vigne, André de (*cont.*)
also Acteur; Allegory; Narrator; Personifications
Le Dru, Pierre, 140, 256, 266; printer of Gringore's *Folles Entreprises*, 37–38, 95–96, 133–34, 136–37; printer of *Vergier d'honneur*, 18–19, 89
Lemaire de Belges, Jean, 38–59, 63, 193–95, 203–4, 246–47; advertisement of authorship, 40, 90, 182; and Anne of Brittany, 53–54, 56, 146, 151; awareness of the importance of print, 43–44, 46–48, 51, 57, 79; coat of arms, 54–56, 129, 137, 146–47, 151, 245; collaboration with Vérard, 41, 43, 48–49; consciousness of public, 41–44, 47, 54, 57; and Guillaume Cretin, 42, 44, 48; device, 41, 54, 145, 194; involvement in and control of publication, 3–5, 10, 17, 38, 40, 44, 46–47, 49, 51–52, 56–57, 90, 194; and Margaret of Austria, 44, 46, 53, 57; and Jean Molinet, 40, 42; patronage, search for, 14, 40–44, 46, 53–54; privileges, 5, 13, 21, 49–54, 57, 194; as publisher, 52, 58, 213; self-promotional strategies, 40–42, 46, 54, 56–57, 103, 245; and theater, 198; works, 44, 46, 54, 194, 204; *Concorde des deux langages*, 204; *Concorde du genre humain*, 56–57, 194; *Couronne margaritique*, 46; *Différence des schismes*, 48,194; *Epîtres de l'amant vert*, 194; *Epistre du roy a Hector*, 54; *Illustrations de Gaule*, 48, 54, 194; *Légende des Vénitiens*, 5, 38, 48, 49–58, 189, 194, 258, (title pages) 13, 49, 52–54, 146, 151, 245; *Singularitez de Troye*, 44; *Temple d'honneur et de vertus*, 5, 38, 40–44, 46–49, 54, 56–58, 63, 66,194, 220, 258, (introductory dedications) 41–43, 54, 194, (Le Noir's edition) 5, 40, 48–49, (Vérard's edition) 5, 40, 48–49, (title pages) 40–41, 43, 48. *See also Acteur*; Allegory; Dream visions; Narrator; Personifications; Prefatory material
Le Noir, Michel, 10, 31, 58, 85; attacked by Bouchet, 23, 25, 31–32;

and Bouchet's *Regnars traversant*, 4, 21, 23, 189, 259; and Gringore's *Chasteau d'amours*, 37, 83, 156, 183, 187–91, 193, 265; and Lemaire's *Temple d'honneur et de vertus*, 5, 40, 48–49, 189, 258; and Molinet's *Temple de Mars*, 66, 71, 261; and *Vergier d'honneur* and La Vigne's lawsuit, 1–3,17–19, 25, 189, 248, 255–56
Le Noir, Philippe, 27, 89–90, 257–59
Le Petit Laurens, 66, 70–71, 261
Liège, Jean de, 129, 224, 262
Ligny, Louis, count of, 41–42
Literary proprietorship, 2–3, 5–7, 17, 19, 20–21, 35, 38, 156–57, 194–95, 213, 254
London, publication of the *Castell of Labour*, 184–85
Looze, Laurent de, 157
Lorraine, Antoine, duke of, 96–97, 147, 193
Lorris, Guillaume de. *See* Guillaume de Lorris
Louis XI, king of France, 63
Louis XII, king of France, 47, 52–53, 68–69, 90; political policies, 57, 144, 243; royal privilege and Letters Patent for Lemaire's *Légende des Vénitiens*, 5, 52–54, 56
Lyon couronné, 220
Lyons: humanist printers, 47, 49, 181; and Lemaire's works, 5, 44, 46, 48, 52, 56–57; and Clément Marot's works, 247, 251; and Molinet's works, 71, 78, 131, 133; royal entries, 52, 179

Machaut, Guillaume de. *See* Guillaume de Machaut
McLuhan, Marshall, 6
Manuscript culture: coexistence with print culture, 37, 62, 76, 114; and *mouvance*, 28–29; compared with print culture, 2, 31, 33, 37, 42, 74, 99, 101, 107, 112, 185, 215
Margaret of Austria, governess of the Netherlands, 44, 46, 53, 57, 165
Marie de France, 154
Margival, Nicole de, 154
Marnef, Geoffroy de, 54, 258, 262, 266

Marot, Clément, 16, 223; attack on printers and publishers, 16, 33, 251–53; and Dolet, 246–48, 250–51, 253; as editor, 204, 212, 249, 254; *épître* form, 248, 253; indebtedness to the *rhétoriqueurs*, 33, 59, 246–49; involvement in publication, 247–50; privileges, 248, 250–52; works: *Adolescence clémentine*, 195, 204, 246, 248, 251–52, 254; 1538 edition of *Oeuvres*, 247–54. *See also* Prefatory material; Privileges
Marot, Jean, 21, 43–44, 47, 248, 254
Martin, Henri-Jean, 6, 9
Mary of Burgundy, 162
Maximilian of Austria, 70, 109
Mère Sotte/Mother Folly. *See* Gringore, Pierre: Mère Sotte
Meschinot, Jean, 229, 235–36
Meun, Jean de. *See* Jean de Meun
Molinet, Jean, 14, 246; advertisement of name, 70, 74–78, 124, 126–27, 129–31, 153, 156, 163; as compiler-editor of manuscript anthology of his works, 74, 79, 213; coat of arms, 129, 131, 146–47, 151, 224, 227, 245; financial situation, 6, 20, 108–10, 117, 130, 215, 220–24, 227; and houses of Burgundy and Austria, 20, 63, 70, 107–10, 117, 131, 162, 216–20, 222, 224–27; and Lemaire, 40, 42; manuscript reproduction of his works, 13, 63, 74,78, 117, 131, 214–15; metaphoric image of the mill (*molinet*), 70, 124, 127, 131, 145–46, 158, 164–65, 217–18, 220–23; as publisher, 6, 74, 79, 117, 129–31, 151, 164, 215, 224, 227; reproduction of works in print, 6, 13, 20, 63, 78, 117, 129, 164, 213; signature, 6, 64, 70, 79, 124, 127, 157–67, 184, 215, 217, 220, 227; works, 165; *Art de Rhétorique*, 78, 117, 127, 130, 158, 164, 262, (Charles VIII acrostic) 119, 161–62, 166, (dedication images) 117–23; *Chappellet des dames*, 162–63; *Faictz et dictz*, 76, 224, 261–62; *Gaiges retrenchiés*, 165, 215, 220–24, 226–27, 263; *Naissance de Charles*

d'Autriche, 78, 109–10, 117, 151, 165, 213, 215, 224–27, 245, 262-63, (author-image) 78–79, 117, 129–33, 137; *Roman de la rose moralisé*, 78, 163, 186, 262, (presentation scenes) 117, 123–29; *Temple de Mars*, 62–79, 81, 130, 156, 160, 261–62, (manuscript form) 62–64, 73–74, 76, (print form) 62–73, 76, (title pages) 64, 66, 69-72, 74, 76, (title-page woodcuts) 66–72; *Trosne d'honneur*, 162, 215–21, 224, 226–27, 229, 245, 263; *Voyage de Naples*, 165. *See also Acteur*; Allegory; Dream visions; Narrator; Personifications; Prefatory material
Montaigne, Michel de, 103, 145
Mouvance, 17, 28–32, 70, 140
Muset, Colin, 220

Narrator, narrative voice, 7, 197, 201–46; in Chartier's works, 206–7; in Gringore's works, 81, 228, 230–41, 244; in La Vigne's works, 228, 245; in Lemaire's works, 43, 56, 197, 203–4; in Molinet's works, 63, 215–23, 227, 245; in *Roman de la rose*, 200–203, 213
Nichols, Stephen, 8

Ong, Walter, 6, 9
Orator, 205, 207
Ovid, 199

Paratext, 7, 10, 14, 61–62, 139, 154, 157, 172, 182, 194, 198, 214, 249; and text, 10, 13, 15, 58, 197, 214–15, 254; development of features, 14, 86, 97, 116; exploitation of, 44, 47, 54, 81, 89; in Chartier's works, 210; in Gringore's works, 228, 244; in La Vigne's works, 8–9; in Lemaire's works, 43, 49, 56, 58; in Clément Marot's works, 247–48, 251, 254; in Molinet's works, 68; printers' control of, 70–72, 78; publicity, 15, 82, 95; sheds light on: author, 13, 15–16, 33, 245; dynamics of book production, 10, 13, 33, 41, 58, 78–79, 85, 123, 219, 229–30;

Paratext (*cont.*)
Gringore, 34, 81, 133, 137, 236, 240; La Vigne, 38, 88–89, 91, 228; Lemaire, 43, 49, 52, 56; Molinet, 66, 71, 76. *See also* Colophons; Title pages; *entries for individual authors and works*

Paris: Anne of Brittany's entry, 18, 181–82; and Gringore's works, 95–97, 184, 234; La Vigne's lawsuit (Parlement), 1, 4, 8, 19; and La Vigne's works, 86, 89, 180; and Lemaire's works, 40, 48, 54, 193; and Clément Marot's works, 251; and Molinet's works, 66, 68, 70–71, 76, 130, 164

Patronage, patrons, 101, 134; authors' challenge to traditional system, 3, 227; authors in search of, 20, 34, 102, 111; changing role of, 6, 11–14, 33, 90–91, 107–8, 131, 143, 150–51, 156, 215; commercialization of, 38, 44, 47, 110; image of, 100, 131, 215; and manuscript culture, 21, 33, 131; relationship with author, 11, 58, 100–101, 140, 179, 245; in the Renaissance, 33, 59; traditional system, 3, 11–12, 106, 111, 215–17, 220. *See also entries for individual authors and patrons*

Perréal, Jean de, 57

Personifications, 198, 245; in Chartier's works, 206–7; in Gringore's works, 226–30, 236, 238–39, 241; in La Vigne's works, 114, 166–67; in Lemaire's works, 56; in Meschinot's works, 229, 235; in Molinet's works, 63, 216, 218

Petit, Jean, 89, 256–57

Petrarch, 204

Philip the Good, duke of Burgundy, 162, 216

Philip the Handsome, archduke of the house of Austria, 70, 109, 131, 222–24

Philippe de Clèves. *See* Clèves, Philippe de

Philology, 8–9

Picot, Emile, 262

Pierre II, duke of Bourbon, 40–43, 56

Pigouchet, Philippe, 15, 79–82, 95, 187–89, 229–31, 234, 264–65

Pizan, Christine de. *See* Christine de Pizan

Plagiarism, 28–29, 34

Poitiers. *See* Bouchet

Pollard, Alfred W., 265

Prefatory material, prologues, 123, 156, 254; in Gringore's works, 230–36; in Lemaire's works, 182, 194; in Clément Marot's works, 195, 248–49; in Molinet's works, 158–59, 161

Print culture, 3, 5; coexistence with manuscript culture, 37, 62, 76, 114; compared with manuscript culture, 2, 31, 33, 37, 42, 74, 99, 101, 107, 112, 185, 215

Printers, 85, 90, 185, 250–51; advertisement of name, 33, 39, 70, 78–79, 82–83, 85, 89–90, 95, 188; and authors, 34, 40, 49, 58, 134, 185, 213, 229; in Brussels, 56; in England, 7, 47, 184–85; humanist, 32, 47, 49, 59, 246, 248; in Lyons, 5, 44, 48, 71, 78, 131, 133, 247, 251; marks, 100, 129, (Le Dru's) 95, 133–34, 137,140, (Le Noir's) 83–84, (Le Petit Laurens's) 70, (Pigouchet's) 79–80, 82, 229, (Trepperel's) 70, 78, 89, (Vérard's) 78, 129; in Paris, 1, 23, 25, 27, 54; profits, 2, 5–6, 19, 31; role, 7, 10, 12, 90. *See also* Booksellers; Lyons; Paris; Publishers; *entries for individual printers*

Priscian, 199

Privileges: early French, 3, 7, 97; for La Vigne's works, 2–3, 20–21; for Lemaire's works, 5, 13, 21, 49–54, 57, 194; for Clément Marot's works, 2, 48, 250, 252; printers' and sellers', 4, 38, 58, 97; for Ronsard's works, 59; royal, 5, 52–53. *See also* Gringore, Pierre: author privileges, Gringore, Pierre: *Folles entreprises* (first vernacular author privilege)

Prologues. *See* Prefatory material

Publishers, 3, 12, 32, 61, 121, 126–27, 250–51, 253; aggressive behavior

Publishers (*cont.*)

against authors, 21–23, 48, 70, 66, 69, 82, 156, 165, 185, 247, 251; challenged by authors, 4, 62, 81, 97; collaboration with authors, 11, 13, 41, 43, 48, 62, 83, 97, 248–49, 251; function, 10, 12, 107, 160; growing visibility, 88, 188; marks, 107, 126, 129; in Paris, 20, 70–71, 97, 156, 165; relationship with authors, 2, 14, 61–62, 185, 195, 213, 246, 250; tension with authors, 5–6, 33, 90, 99, 194. *See also* Booksellers; Printers; *entries for individual booksellers, printers, and publishers*

Pynson, Richarde, 185, 265

Readership, 249–50, 253–54; and author, 6, 12, 16, 34, 38, 61, 106–7, 184, 188, 197, 234–44, 238; courtly, 11, 16, 154–55, 157, 174, 208–11, 215, 220, 226–27; educated, 237, 267; non-courtly, 2, 6, 11, 102, 107, (of Gringore's works) 143, 183, 231–33, 236, 238–39, 242, 244, (of La Vigne's works) 112, 174, (of Lemaire's works) 43, 54, (of Molinet's works) 69–70, 157, 159, 215, 226–27. *See also* Patronage; *entries for individual authors and works*

Regalado, Nancy Freeman, 13

Renaissance writers, French, 8, 14, 59, 114, 195, 246–47

Rendall, Steven, 139, 145

Rhétoriqueurs, 14, 40, 47, 56, 246

Roesner, Edward, 13

Roman de Fauvel, 13

Roman de la rose, 13, 154, 186, 200, 202–3, 213, 220, 254

Ronsard, Pierre de, 59, 103, 145

Rose, Mark, 7, 19, 21

Rubrication. *See* Gringore, Pierre: use of rubrics

Rutebeuf, 155, 158, 220

Saint Bonaventure, 199, 202

Saint-Gelais, Octavien de, 47, 88, 113, 236

Saint Jerome, 100

Sala, Charles, 156

Savoy, duke of, 18, 88

Scève, Maurice, 102

Scribes, 12, 28–29, 86, 100, 199–200, 202–3, 209; authors as, 212–13, 217; relationship with author, 73–74, 100, 114, 203, 212

Seville, Isidore of. *See* Isidore of Seville

Signatures. *See* Authors: signatures; *entries for individual authors*

Stein, Henri, 262

Text editing, 8–9

Thomas of Britain, 154

Thomassin, Claude, 54, 57

Tieullière, Catherine de, 175–77

Title pages, 7–8, 15, 33, 40, 61, 78, 83, 99, 153, 194, 249, 253–54; in Bouchet's works, 15, 21, 23, 26–27, 30–31; in Gringore's works, 15, 62, 81, 83, 91, 94–97, 134, 137, 140, 143, 229, 241; in La Vigne's works, 8, 17–18, 20, 62, 85–89, 93, 112–13, 116, 172, 182, 228, 245; in Lemaire's works, 13, 40–41, 43, 48, 49, 52–54, 146, 151, 245; in Clément Marot's works, 248, 251; in Molinet's works, 62, 64, 66, 69–72, 74, 76, 78–79, 123, 126, 131, 163, 224

Trepperel, Jean, printer of: Gringore's works, 83, 264, 266; Molinet's works, 66, 71, 78, 160–61, 261–62; *Vergier d'honneur*, 89, 113, 256

Troubadours, 4

Tyard, Pontus de, 103

Valenciennes, 66, 70, 94, 108–9, 129, 224

Vérard, Antoine, 10, 31, 58; and Bouchet's *Regnars traversant*, 4, 21, 23, 29–31, 68, 156, 160, 259; and *Castell of Labour*, 185, 265; and Lemaire's *Temple d'honneur et de vertus*, 5, 40–41, 43, 48–49, 258; and Molinet's *Art de rhétorique*, 78, 117, 119, 121, 123, 127, 129, 159–62, 165–66; and Molinet's *Roman de la rose moralisé*,

Vérard, Antoine (*cont.*)
123–24, 126–29, 163, 262. *See also* Bouchet, Jean: lawsuit and attack against Vérard
Villon, François, 13, 204, 212, 220, 223, 236, 254
Vincent de Beauvais, 199–201, 213
Vingle, Jean de, 5, 51, 66, 71, 258, 261

Virgil, 167, 199
Vostre, Simon, 15, 79–82, 187–89, 230, 234, 264–65

Williams, Sarah Jane, 13
Worde, Wynkyn de, 185, 265–66

Zumthor, Paul, 17, 28, 215